£10

DI436004

ACTION LEARNING AT WORK

Action Learning at Work

EDITED BY
ALAN MUMFORD

Gower

© Gower Publishing Limited 1997

All rights reserved. No part of this publication may be
reproduced, stored in a retrieval system, or transmitted in any
form or by any means, electronic, mechanical, photocopying,
recording or otherwise without the permission of the publisher.

Published by
Gower Publishing Limited
Gower House
Croft Road
Aldershot
Hampshire GU11 3HR
England

Gower
Old Post Road
Brookfield
Vermont 05036
USA

British Library Cataloguing in Publication Data
Action learning at work
  1. Active learning   2. Business education   3. Executives – Training of
I. Mumford, Alan, 1933–
658.4'07'1245
ISBN 0 566 07890 2

Library of Congress Cataloging-in-Publication Data
Action learning at work/edited by Alan Mumford.
    p. cm.
Includes bibliographical references and index.
ISBN 0–566–07890–2 (cloth)
  1. Executives – Training of. 2. Active learning. 3. Action
research. I. Mumford, Alan.
HD30.4.A29 1997
658.4'07124–DC21   96–46427
                                                                 CIP

Typeset in 10/13 pt Century Old Style
by Intype London Ltd
Printed in Great Britain by Hartnolls Ltd., Bodmin.

Contents

Part III   Helping Others to Learn

Part IV   Programmes in Action

Part V Does Action Learning Work?

List of Figures

List of Tables

Preface

In this book I have brought together articles and papers about the only business school which has dedicated its contribution to management development solely through Action Learning. Whereas other educators, trainers and consultants may use Action Learning for some purposes for some programmes, this book records the efforts of an institution which decided to stand, totter but not fall on the basis of Action Learning. It describes the public record, and does not delve into the intimacies of Academic Board discussions, the debates on our Academic and Philosophic Review Day about issues on Action Learning; nor does it review changes in the design of the MBA programme or the reallocation of credits for particular academic programmes. It is concerned instead with things that happened as a result with learners and organizations. This ought not to be surprising in a book about Action Learning, since implementation is at the heart of what Action Learning has to offer.

The book has one limitation which I regret, and expresses one prejudice for which I do not apologize. My regret is that I have not been able to include material from many valued colleagues at IMC, for example, Joanna Kozubska and Karen Jackson who did so much to provide guidance in our early days to set advisers and tutors. The other regrettable absence is of material from many of the countries around the world in which IMC operates. Sadly, my colleagues in Malaysia, South Africa and the Netherlands are better at running programmes than they are at writing about them or causing others to write.

The aspect on which I offer no regrets is the emphasis on how people learn. Some might see this as simply my own prejudice in terms of priorities. Rather than simple prejudice, the emphasis is drawn from IMC's original philosophy, from its practice and from what I believe helps to make IMC unique. Action Learning is a duality, yet other books on Action Learning contain very little about the learning process itself. Further, two of the articles are written by those who were primarily learners, as distinct from tutors who may have been learners as well (the chapters by Caiae and Mead).

One final point before summarizing the chapters. They represent the author's view of truths, as he or she perceived it at the time. In some cases IMC's approach changed after the article, sometimes because of the experience recorded there. As editor I thought it my task to provide an interesting picture of IMC's struggle to offer and then improve its Action Learning processes. The views expressed are those of the authors, not of IMC as an institution. I have made no substantive changes to the original texts. The time-bound nature of the chapters is confirmed by the fact that the literary references have been left as in the original, though in some cases there will be later editions of the books referred to.

An Introduction to the Text

PART I ACTION LEARNING: CAUSE, THEORY OR PROTEST?

Chapter 1, 'Action Learning as a Vehicle for Learning', sets out what I regard as the main features of Action Learning, and introduces some of the adjustments to the original Revans statements about Action Learning.

Chapter 2 reviews a distinction between two approaches, where overlap and confusion in the minds, at least of academics, have arisen.

In Chapter 3, Gordon Wills, the first Principal of International Management Centres and one of its five original founders, gives a characteristically forthright view of its origins, some of the problems it faced, and some of the issues arising in managing the institution.

Margaret Reid, in Chapter 4, adds some specifics on the design of IMC programmes.

The late David Sutton, 'In Search of P', gave us an interesting and valuable insight into an important issue. If Action Learning is identified with Q in Revans' equation, does this mean that P – Programmed Knowledge – is irrelevant, inappropriate or just unsuccessful in relation to Action Learning?

In Chapter 6, Cliff Bunning presents some insights on different kinds of learning, and shows how reflective professionals can move towards greater awareness, ethical behaviour and enlightened practice, and how they might overcome the blocks for doing this.

Gordon Wills, in Chapter 7, not only writes on the relatively unstudied issue of Networking, but deals with it in terms of the complications of IMC's networks.

PART II LEARNING TO LEARN

Cliff Bunning again in Chapter 8 examines some of the processes through which individuals and organizations learn, with a particular emphasis on the connections between the learner, the project and organizational culture.

Mike Mead, a learner and not a tutor, provides in Chapter 9 one of the few extant descriptions of how a set actually helps a 'colleague in adversity'.

In Chapter 10, Brian Caiae describes how his own preferred learning style helped or hindered the way in which he learned on an IMC MBA programme.

In the next four chapters, Mumford describes first two rather different ways of looking at Learning Styles, through personal development plans and then on a group director development programme. The next two chapters, on the evaluation and assessment of managerial learning and learning logs, describe two of the disciplines IMC uses to encourage more reflective and therefore more complete learning on its programmes. Finally, in 'The Five-year Continuing Review', he looks at a unique IMC effort to encourage its graduands to record and report on their continued learning after graduation.

Prideaux, in Chapter 15, discusses learning diaries and learning contracts in the context of a learning community.

PART III HELPING OTHERS TO LEARN

Although Reg Revans has sometimes suggested that managers should get on with their own Action Learning programmes, without the help of set advisers, IMC has never accepted that proposal as one which leads to fully effective Action Learning. However, IMC has taken another Reg dictum, 'the inveterate hankering of the tutor to be the centre of attention', as something to be guarded against. It is no accident (though again perhaps reflecting this editor's priorities) that in this part there is only one chapter which focuses on the set adviser, rather than on participants.

Chapter 16 is about the role of the set adviser, but interestingly was drawn from a meeting of set advisers and reflects their views rather than the single-minded propositions of an expert on set advising.

In Chapter 17, 'Action Learning Pan-setting', Gordon Wills examines one of the most interesting yet most difficult aspects of trying to encourage groups who have not spent time within a single programme to learn from each other.

In the following chapter Margaret Reid looks at things the other way round – how an original Action Learning set acquired an additional learning group.

In another wholly unresearched area Mumford, in his chapter 'Managers Developing Others through Action Learning', describes the kind of support which was provided to set members by their line managers and mentors, and proposes improvements.

Chapter 20 reviews one of the fascinating issues on the construction of any action learning set: to what extent does a group solely drawn from one organization learn more or less, and in what sense, than an alternative group drawn from a variety of organizations? The authors provide original research on this subject (sadly not complemented by research from other business schools) to show what the actuality has been on IMC's programmes.

PART IV PROGRAMMES IN ACTION

Chapter 21 reproduces what James Espey and Pauline Batchelor wrote about IMC's first MBA programme, with comment about why IMC was chosen and on some of the results.

The following chapter, by David Seekings and Brian Wilson, also reviews an early IMC programme, but in this case a non-qualification programme. Brian Wilson comments with interesting (but to those who know him unsurprising) honesty about the effective and less effective aspects of his own contribution to the programme as Chief Executive.

The short chapter by James Kable had two specially significant claims for inclusion. It is about a programme run in Australia, as a change from the UK perspective of most of the other chapters. Second, it is about Action Learning in a management education institution – and until the recent efforts sponsored by the technical and further education institutions in Australia, Action Learning in education institutions was apparently unknown as an internal development activity.

Alan Mumford and Peter Honey in Chapter 24, 'Developing Skills for Matrix Management', describe an experience which used an Action Learning philosophy without employing a project approach.

In Chapter 25, 'Developing the Top Team', Mumford is back on more traditional Action Learning territory in the sense of content, but less traditional in the sense that he reviews work at director level.

From a development point of view, of course, an interesting question is how people are developed on their way to becoming directors. In Chapter 26, 'Leading Courageous Managers On', Lesley Gore, Kathryn Toledano and Gordon Wills describe the efforts being made at MCB University Press.

IMC has been involved in integrating work on Quality with an Action Learning approach. Both the principles and the practices of Action Learning programmes with this emphasis are covered in Chapters 27 and 28, first by Abby Day and John Peters in 'Rediscovering Standards', and then by John Peters alone in 'Operationalizing Total Quality'.

Finally in this part, Cliff Bunning reflects on this experience supervising doctoral projects and dissertations in an Action Learning business school – a variation on the themes dealt with by David Sutton in Chapter 5.

PART V DOES ACTION LEARNING WORK?

Action Learning is by no means alone among management development methods in lacking large-scale or comparative evaluation. One of the reasons is that precisely because it deals with real issues with observable returns, the clients usually feel no great reason to spend their time, and perhaps their money, on evaluating what they already know to be a success.

However, in Chapter 30, 'Measuring the ROI from Management Action Learning', Gordon Wills and Carol Oliver offer precisely that bottom-line justification which is so often lacking in any formal management development.

Krystyna Weinstein in Chapter 31 assesses the benefits of a variety of Action Learning programmes which included a number of IMC activities. She found many supportive statements, but also identified some of the problems and difficulties not always properly resolved through Action Learning programmes.

In another novel piece of research, Carol Oliver, Sandra Pass, Jayne Taylor and Pam Taylor describe the effect of an Action Learning MBA programme on people differently occupied as intrapreneurs and entrepreneurs.

Faith Howell carried out research on IMC's Australian programmes, and is able to show in Chapter 33 substantial levels of satisfaction amongst participants.

In his 'Rogue Learning on the Company Reservation', Tom Reeves presents a 'warts and all' picture of the effect of Action Learning in two companies. One of the companies was MCB University Press, which must have carried out more Action Learning per employee than any other organization in the world. The implication, achievements and limitations of the Action Learning approach within MCB, and the connection to modern themes of organizational learning provide a conclusion for the book. Since Action Learning is about Questioning Insight, the questions raised by Action Learning in one institution form an appropriate end note.

THE EDITOR

I have already referred to the possible impact of my own sense of priorities on the construction of this book. I should also add that I was the first member of IMC faculty recruited by the five founders, was Professor of Management Development there from 1983–1992, and am still Visiting Professor.

Alan Mumford

Acknowledgements

I am grateful to International Management Centres for permission to reproduce papers and material originally produced for internal use:

- 'The Evaluative Assessment of Managerial Learning'
- 'The Five-year Continuing Review'
- 'Rogue Learning on the Company Reservation'.

MCB University Press gave permission for the reproduction of articles on which they hold copyright; details of original publications are included as appropriate.

AM

The Learning Equation

Reg Revans *

In this life, everyone must learn something. But what *fresh*? The word 'learning' may mean all things to all people; for one may learn to speak different languages, to play different instruments, to solve hard crossword puzzles, to write computer programs, and to set up in business; one may even learn to hold one's tongue when unfairly attacked in academic argument. A collection of sea-lions in Hamburg once learned to play Scottish airs on klaxon horns . . . Learning has the widest scope.

Whatsoever we pursue, some ways of saying or doing fresh things can be learned from others – whether we like it or not. One is told or shown, beginning with Mother's warning, 'No more sweets unless you say "Thank you" for the last lot!' and going on later to copy Einstein's mass–energy equation from the blackboard, after the professor had copied it there out of a book. Throughout life, one is told by endless authorities what to do next, and one learns to obey. Much so picked up has already long existed, so it is here to be called *programmed*, and denoted by *P.*

Yet much other learning also comes, neither from command nor example, but from one's own experience. Finding out for oneself may also be very mixed, like walking into a brick wall, making other mistakes, realizing something does not work as expected, dreaming up a new recipe after the Chinese take-away, altering the shape one was told to make it by the last architectural critic, or, occasionally, deliberately asking quite fresh questions – like Newton, enquiring whether the force keeping the moon close to the earth was also that pulling the apple to the ground. Knowledge, ideas, attitudes, skills, new perceptions of what goes on are always turning up; what is so discovered, moreover, generally tells one something new about the self. 'Well! I must say! You do live and learn!' is so often said after the shock of finding out from one's own experience that some hallowed belief was long untrue. Some call it a lucky guess, or 'intuition', or 'something crossing the mind'. Learning of this nature comes from *questioning* insight, and is denoted by *Q*. Since it cannot be brought about deliberately, nor by programmed drill, it is stochastic, a product of the random. Simplistically, we

*Previously published in *Journal of Management Development*, vol. 6, no. 2, 1987.

may say that fresh learning is the sum of programmed instruction and questioning insight; without pretending to invoke any algebraic calculus, we may write this as $L = P + Q$: the learning equation. We note that P is also the initial letter of Professor, Panjandrum, Past, Pandect, Platitude, Pantologist, Package, Poppycock and Piffle; while Q introduces us to Qualm, Quandary, Quiz, Query, Quixotic, Quarry, *Qui Vive* and *Quid Pro Quo*.

So brief an outline of learning afresh tempts further terms. We can put O before P and R behind Q: O for 'origins', parental gifts like physique to survive and genes to identify; R for 'responses', from 'rejoicing' to 'repentance', to lived experience. John Locke, best of English philosophers, holds this the source of all knowledge, so cardinal to learning. But, since O is constant throughout our life, it is not about *change* within our minds. And, although much experience cannot be the programmed instruction of some teacher, it is still the lesson of circumstance, or P imposed by the authority of Nature – stimulating, perhaps, its fair share of Q. Thus, of O we have no need, and R has already been taken care of. As we shall see, given range enough within themselves, P and Q are sufficient.

It is not necessary to invoke spurious mathematical propositions to suggest that our two terms from the righthand side of the equation may get out of balance. The Association of American Colleges, for example, in its essay, 'Integrity in the College Curriculum', has scathingly indicted the bulk of undergraduate courses for presenting so much P and inviting so little Q; it forecasts disaster for the national education system, schools no less than universities. This was reinforced by the publication, also in 1985, of an article in Britain's leading management magazine suggesting that Action Learning, founded on Q, is now displacing traditional courses in our business schools, founded on P . . . But the two terms are to be seen as the poles of many other contrasts; the Yin and Yang of the Celestial Empire, the sparring partners of Platonic dialectic, and choice between being wise and being clever are three among them.

Action Learning is about *social* learning. Some of the greatest ideas were the fruits of solitude – Moses up the mountain, Christ in the wilderness, Bunyan in Bedford Gaol, and many masterpieces of genius – but they are not here for our present attention. How best can we help *each other*?

Some relevant quotations:

- 'Two extravagances: to exclude Reason, to admit only Reason' – *Blaise Pascal*
- 'The chief wonder of education is that it does not ruin all concerned in it, teachers and taught' – Henry B. Adams, *The Education of Henry Adams* (p. 55)
- 'One learns what one has it in one to learn, not what one's teachers have it in them to teach' – R.G. Collingwood, *Speculum Mentis* (p. 12).

Part I
Action Learning: Cause, Theory or Protest?

1 Action Learning as a Vehicle for Learning

Alan Mumford

CHARACTERISTICS

Action Learning is generally associated (though not always in the United States) with Reg Revans. Although there are antecedents in his earlier work, particularly in the coal mines and the National Health Service after the war, the first published use of the phrase was in 1968. The first programme he ran with an explicit Action Learning title was for a consortium of companies and universities in Belgium, public knowledge about which first became available through conferences and then in 1971 through his book *Developing Effective Managers*.

This historical introduction is provided because no other management development method is so clearly associated with a single individual, whose clarity of thought in writing and even more strongly expressed in person led to first interest in and then implementation of his philosophy. The choice of the word 'philosophy' here instead of 'method' is deliberate. It is desirable to read some of Revans' original work (see 'Further Reading' p. 21), but you will find there powerful articulation of beliefs, values and potential, not detailed illustrations of technique.

There is no single neat statement by Revans in any paper or book which captures all of his prime ideas. Here are some of his statements about Action Learning:

- It is recognized ignorance not programmed knowledge that is the key to Action Learning: men start to learn with and from each other only when they discover that no one knows the answer but all are obliged to find it.
- Action Learning requires questions to be posed in conditions of ignorance, risk and confusion, when nobody knows what to do next; it is only marginally interested in finding the answers once those questions have been posed. [While most Action Learning advocates would agree with the first half of this sentence, few would accept the second half.]
- To search out the meaning of the unseen is the role of Action Learning; to

3

manipulate to advantage all that is discovered is the expression of programmed teaching.
- Action Learning is a means of development, intellectual, emotional or
  physical, that requires its subject, through responsible involvement in some
  real, complex and stressful problems, to achieve intended change sufficient
  to improve his observable behaviour henceforth in the problem field.

Revans' statements on the nature of the learning process (discussed in more
detail on pp. xxi–xxii) include:

- System Beta
- A five-stage model involving survey, hypothesis, action, inspection and incor-
  poration
- His learning equation $L = P + Q$, where L = Learning, P = Programmed
  Knowledge and Q = Questioning Insight
- Learning is best achieved by people with similar problems working together
  as 'comrades in adversity'.

Mike Pedler in his *Action Learning in Practice* (1991) offers this view of Action
Learning:

> Action Learning is an approach to the development of people in organisations which
> takes the task as the vehicle for learning. It is based on the premise that there is no
> learning without action and no sober and deliberate action without learning. The
> method has three main components – people, who accept the responsibility for taking
> action on a particular issue; problems, or the tasks that people set themselves; and a
> set of six or so colleagues who support and challenge each other to make progress
> on problems. Action Learning implies both self development and organisation develop-
> ment. Action on a problem changes both the problem and the person acting upon it.
> It proceeds particularly by questioning taken for granted knowledge.

Pedler, however, goes on to say that Revans challenged some aspects of this,
for example saying that Action Learning did not necessarily involve relatively
small 'sets' of six people.

My own summary (1984, 1991) of Action Learning brings out some aspects
which are important in deciding what is involved in Action Learning as a method
of development:

1. Learning for managers should mean learning to take effective action.
   Acquiring information, becoming more capable in diagnosis or analysis has
   been overvalued in management learning.
2. Learning to take effective action necessarily involves taking action, not recommending action or undertaking analysis of someone else's problems.
3. The best form of action for learning is work on a defined project of reality
   and significance to the managers themselves. The project should involve
   implementation as well as analysis and recommendation.
4. Whilst managers should have responsibility for their own achievements on

their own project, the learning process is a social one; managers learn best with and from each other.

5. The social process is achieved and managed through regular meetings of managers to discuss their individual projects; the group is usually called a 'set'. The managers are 'comrades in adversity'.

6. The role of people providing help for members of the set is entirely different from that of the normal management teacher. Their role is not to teach (whether through lecture, case or simulation) but to help managers learn from exposure to problems and to each other.

Some confusion, misinterpretations and misunderstandings exist about Action Learning. The confusions are compounded when various authorities do not necessarily agree on whether something is a necessary or merely desirable feature of an activity for it to be properly described as Action Learning. Some designers of programmes which are claimed to involve or to be Action Learning seem to think that any kind of action which might provide the opportunity for learning is a form of Action Learning. As an obsessional writer about the virtues of and the practices involved in learning from real work experience I do not believe that such an all-embracing view is helpful in identifying the particular virtues of Action Learning. One of the points not covered in the statements above is that, in my view, Action Learning is:

> A planned and organized process for doing and learning, not a reactive post-experience view that something could be learned from a particular activity (desirable though that latter process is in itself).

Other forms of structured learning through action experiences such as outdoor or adventure training, or simulations of managerial experience have their merits, but by definition represent or simulate the managerial experience. They provide a kind of reality, but they are not working on the actual problems of particular managers in real work situations.

While many of the serious authors and designers of programmes in Action Learning would probably agree with the above comments, they would not necessarily agree with the following:

- The most productive form of Action Learning, and therefore the objective most to be desired, is that those working on it have a significant responsibility for implementing the results. A participant may be working on a problem/ project where no one else is involved in deciding what to do. More often, participants need someone else's approval before implementing the results.

- Working on a project on which you eventually advise others perhaps managerially quite distant from yourself on what to do about it can be helpful to the organizational process and a useful development process for groups and individuals. It is, however, the responsibility for implementation that constitutes the final element of managerial learning.

- Projects/problems can be assessed on a continuum between those where participants have the task of preparing and giving good advice, in effect as consultants, and those where they will have a responsibility for implementing any actions agreed as a result of the project. (See Figure 1.1.)

| CONSULTING → | RECOMMENDATIONS →
PLUS IMPLEMENTATION | IMPLEMENTATION |
|---|---|---|
| Advising someone else on what should be done, with no subsequent responsibility for implementation. | Presenting proposals for resolution of a problem or meeting an opportunity, with subsequent responsibility for implementation. | Direct personal responsibility for implementing. Carrying it through. |

Figure 1.1 Continuum of reality

Action Learning is undoubtedly the Q part of Revans' equation. Some Action Learning programmes have existed without any P input. While there can be different provisions of P – how much, when, through which source – a total absence of P seems unlikely to provide the best integrated form of learning. IMC programmes combine Q with the relevant P – i.e. relevant to resolving Q.

THE 'DOUBLE VALUE' ARGUMENT

While Action Learning is not simply 'learning from doing', but is a planned and structured way of learning from a particular kind of 'doing', it has special resonance for managers. Most of them talk about learning from real work experiences as the predominant and sometimes most significant way in which they have learned. One of the characteristics of Action Learning is therefore the potential attraction it has to managers who see in it a direct attachment to a familiar kind of learning experience. The fact that doing real work brings observable and measurable managerial benefits, which has been argued above as being one of the most desirable features of this method, is an important part of the attractiveness. The idea that you are spending time on real work, time which perhaps you ought to spend anyway on significant problems or projects, with a clear managerial purpose and return while at the same time learning from the process is understood and desired by most line managers. Thus the phrase I have developed, that it is a 'double value' process.

TYPES OF ACTION LEARNING PROGRAMME

Figure 1.2 shows different combinations of task and setting. Managers could carry out a project in their unit on issues on which they are totally familiar or

SETTING		TASK	
		FAMILIAR	UNFAMILIAR
	FAMILIAR	1	3
	UNFAMILIAR	2	4

Figure 1.2 Combinations of task and setting

they could carry out a project in a totally unfamiliar environment – even outside their own organization on issues or functions with which they are not familiar. The point made earlier about the extra value to be acquired through personal responsibility for implementation is not necessarily contradicted by working on an unfamiliar task in an unfamiliar setting (Box 4) – the manager could still be given responsibility for implementation of the project; it is however clearly less likely than in the Familiar/Familiar (Box 1).

EXPLICIT AND/OR IMPLICIT PURPOSES

The double value argument offered above suggests that for many organizations the purpose of an Action Learning programme or set is the resolution of a business issue, problem or opportunity, with learning as a subsidiary though desirable associated product.

From a development perspective, the reasons for offering, promoting or initiating Action Learning as a development method may be to meet one or more of the following:

- To offer 'learning from task' as a desirable end in itself, but also as a transferable idea for other work situations
- To provide experience in and knowledge about effective resolution of problems, opportunities, issues (perhaps particularly through a defined project)
- To provide conscious experience of how people can learn in groups
- To provide conscious experience of some aspects of team objectives and behaviours
- To provide a process for the generation and acceptance of P needs
- To provide a vehicle accepted as relevant and valid for working on P as a contribution to Q
- To provide a strongly bottom-line oriented development method as part of a development strategy
- To give variety of method, for example at the end of a management development programme containing a variety of other methods
- To develop skills of learning to learn.

OTHER PEOPLE, OTHER PURPOSES

The purposes recognized or articulated by management developers may be different in part or in priority from those of other people in the organization.

The driving force in the organization, as suggested above, may be to take up a development process the prime virtue of which is that it provides specific answers to particular organizational problems, i.e. it provides bottom-line value. Line managers may also feel that a general exposition of the virtues of management development is better supported by a process which looks fairly credible

---

Most suitable for

- Action Learning uses real organizational issues as the main medium for learning.

- It is based on learning, not on being taught.

- It is based on the manager's predominant view of learning – learning from experience.

- It provides a model for effective individual and group learning at work.

- It makes explicit (*talked about and thought through*) what is often implicit.

- It admits that organizational ignorance (*I've never done this before*) is an opportunity to move forward and to learn.

- It challenges the status quo.

- It encourages 'double loop', 'generative' learning.

- It allows people to share similar organizational issues even if they are technically different.

- It makes managers take action in a controlled way to see what happens.

- It encourages managers to plan experiences to learn from and to understand their own preferences for learning.

- It allows a variety of approaches including solving problems, undertaking enquiries, personal mentoring and coaching.

- It is well adapted to learning about change.

- It taps into and uses all the experiences of a wide variety of people.

- Because Action Learning addresses real organizational issues, evaluation of the effectiveness of that learning is relatively straightforward.

- It offers *dual value* – value to the learner and value to the 'host' organization.

- Reality is effective.

Figure 1.3 Suitability of Action Learning

to them in comparison with knowledge-centred development programmes, or programmes which require a great deal of transfer of understanding (e.g. case studies of quite different organizations).

Any apparent presumption that the organization does want to have real work done on issues, problems, opportunities, strategies must be tested out before engaging on such a programme. Figure 1.3 sets out the circumstances in which Action Learning is most, and least, suitable.

Further, individual participants may in general or in particular have different purposes for participation in such a programme. They may be more inspired by the prospect of individual development, or the possibility of personal identification with a successful project, than with the kind of issues identified above either for management developers or for the organization as an entity.

Least suitable for

- Action Learning is not the best device when you can follow an appropriate programmed course (e.g. accounting).

- People have to be prepared to share experiences including bad ones (mistakes).

- It is often counter-cultural to people whose experience in learning is mainly from attending traditional courses – they wonder when the 'course' will actually start.

- Results don't happen overnight.

- It needs careful help, advice and management which may be expensive.

- It may prove to be disruptive.

- It may lead to action which is not regarded as 'OK'.

- It may lead to mistakes.

- It may pose unwanted questions.

- It may be regarded as unglamorous if it takes place in the workplace as opposed to a business school.

- Action learning will not work if:

  - the boss has decided what will happen regardless of anything you do.

  - managers from different parts of the organization are not allowed to share experiences and discuss problems openly.

- People or organizations who are unable to accept that reality is dangerous.

Jonathan Coates/Alan Mumford

Figure 1.3 concluded

LEARNING THEORY

Revans' views on learning are expressed through a variety of statements, and clearly operate from the view that managers learn best from working on real problems, by working together on those problems. The most 'theoretical' elements of his philosophy are:

1. System Beta

Derives from his view that learning is the same as the scientific process. It is a five-stage model, involving in a circular sequence:

> Survey
> Hypothesis
> Action
> Inspection
> Incorporation

There are of course great similarities between this model and that of Kurt Lewin and David Kolb. (Suggestions that Kolb developed his cycle from Revans are inaccurate.)

2. The Learning Equation

Revans' equation is:

$$L \quad = \quad P \quad + \quad Q$$

| Learning | Programmed Knowledge | Questioning Insight |

Revans' view of P has varied over the years. He has sometimes seemed to deny its value entirely, but his more balanced view is that he does not reject P but wishes to put it in its appropriate place in the learning spectrum. He sees P as traditional instruction which prepares for the treatment of puzzles or difficulties for which knowledge is already available to provide a solution, in contrast to asking questions about the unknown.

This neat equation and the words describing it have been readily adopted by many Action Learning practitioners. Experience in IMC with Action Learning and discussion with my colleagues caused me to offer a different formulation:

$$Q1 + P + Q2 = L$$

The case for this is that since the most effective learning is driven by the need to resolve a managerial problem, then the equation should start with the process of asking about the problem, issue or opportunity ($Q1$).

There will probably be relevant knowledge available for the resolution of that problem. So the second stage of the equation should deal with the acquisition of that knowledge (*P*), with the emphasis that it should be relevant knowledge, i.e. is directly associated with the problems or issues that have been revealed.

The combination of looking at and working on the issues (*Q1*) and the acquisition of relevant knowledge (*P*) leads to a redefinition of the issue, a reinterpretation of experience and the raising of issues of a different kind or at a different depth (*Q2*). The learning group (set) facilitates this.

This revised equation is a better representation of the Action Learning process because:

- It provides immediately the visual image necessary to encourage developers to move away from the idea that *P* comes first. 'They must be introduced to marketing theories and methods before they try and tackle a marketing project.'
- It encourages the idea that learning is an iterative process not a single or simple-minded association of one type of learning called *P* and another type of learning called *Q*.

Arguably, the equation is still misleading, since it may still imply a finite period of learning, rather than a series of *P* and *Q* interactions.

Adult Learning

The common experience that managers learn by doing, and Malcolm Knowles' theory of adult learning, have sometimes been combined too readily to explain or justify simply asking managers 'to do things' as part of a development programme. As we have seen, the learning theory contained within Action Learning certainly emphasizes the 'doing' element. However in its best form it also displays an often disregarded element in Knowles' theory, i.e. that people like working on problems and issues of direct relevance. (But the extent to which *all* managers are primarily driven by issues of practicality and relevance is examined below.)

The Learning Cycle

The Honey and Mumford version of the Learning Cycle (based of course on Kolb and Lewin) differs from System Beta in being a four-stage model (see Figure 1.4).

The case made above for revising the equation to show that it starts with *Q* can be considered in relation to where Action Learning can be seen to start on the Learning Cycle. In the revised equation, *Q* is clearly most strongly associated initially with the Reviewing stage. Individuals and learning sets generate, consider, discuss, argue about the nature of the issues and problems.

They then reach some conclusions ('decisions') about what to do to tackle the issue. How much time? With whom? Who is the client?

Individuals then plan the action they are going to take as a result of the Reviewing and Concluding stages.

Finally they experience implementing their plan.

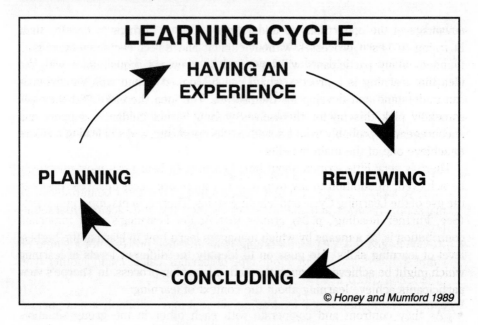

Figure 1.4 The learning cycle

Throughout this process, of course, a series of mini Learning Cycles is going on. Participants are experiencing working with others in Reviewing, Concluding and Planning. They are experiencing defining the problem or project and acquiring the contribution of fellow set members on their definition. They experience receiving the commitment of a client to the carrying out of the project and to the likely implementation involved in it.

So the Action Learning process is potentially extremely rich because it provides scope for consistently going round the Learning Cycle and discovering more about yourself, more about the process, more about how to transfer particular experience to other situations.

LEARNING TO LEARN

Action Learning provides, as indicated above, not just a single opportunity to go round the Learning Cycle, but also a chance to engage in mini Learning Cycles at different times in various set meetings. If explicitly presented as a process to Action Learning participants, and if opportunities are created to review learning against the Learning Cycle, then individuals and groups can learn how to learn more effectively. An important word here however is 'explicit'. Some authors have claimed that Action Learning is a particularly effective process for facilitating Learning to Learn, but give no indication of how participants are supposed to achieve its potential. To suppose that individuals will either recognize or take advantage of the opportunity to understand and then perhaps to develop their Learning to Learn processes without explicit and direct encouragement is ill founded. Many participants will have had no previous acquaintance with the idea that learning is a process which can be looked at and which individuals can understand and develop for themselves. The idea therefore that they will somehow pick this up for themselves without direct guidance, support and encouragement probably from a set adviser is optimistic, and will lead to a failure to achieve one of the main benefits.

There is very little written about how Learning to Learn can most effectively be achieved. In addition to my own material there are occasional references to the use of the Learning Cycle and learning styles. Thorpe, in his important article (See 'Further Reading', p. 24) argues that Action Learning's most important contribution is 'as a means by which managers learn how to learn at the highest level of learning skills'. He goes on to identify the different levels of learning which might be achieved through the Action Learning process. In Thorpe's view participants achieve learning about the context of learning:

- As they confront and co-operate with each other in the group situation, providing a basis for comparisons, contrast and challenge which can unfreeze previous learning.
- In dealing with real problems they are engaging in the application of relevant knowledge and analysis as the result of that knowledge to more appropriate managerial action. The group provides a basis for building solutions on each other's experience and managers are encouraged to reflect and perhaps change their attitudes and beliefs.
- The important part played by Reflection is achieved in two ways. They reflect on the results of practical problem solving, but also on their learning processes and personal development. They become more conscious of their conceptions of the world in general, how these were formed and how they are changed.

Facilitation of Learning to Learn whether at relatively basic levels of under-standing of learning processes through the Learning Cycle, or in the more complex form identified by Thorpe, can be stimulated by explicit discussion of theories, frameworks and practices. These must, however, be supported by aids such as Learning Logs, and explicitly created Learning Review sessions for full benefit to be obtained. International Management Centres provides as part of its MBA programme a requirement that participants complete an Evaluative Assessment of Managerial Learning as part of the formal submission for which they earn credits on the MBA. This covers the whole period of the MBA, and is drawn from the individual's Learning Logs. (See Chapters 12 and 13.)

LEARNING STYLE

Whereas with some management development methods there is a clear association between a strongly preferred learning style and the content of the method, this is much less likely with Action Learning. As has been shown earlier, there is provision for participants to go round each stage of the Learning Cycle. However, individuals with strong learning style preferences will give more or less attention to particular stages of the Learning Cycle related to their learning styles. Well designed Action Learning programmes will provide exactly that balance which will ensure that there is no undue emphasis on any particular stage of the cycle, and therefore no need for any participant to be significantly discouraged for any length of time during the Action Learning process. The proviso 'a well designed Action Learning programme' is very important. A programme which emphasizes the task and resolving problems, but does not provide sufficient opportunities to reflect on what is going on, or which does not encourage the process of drawing conclusions from particular experiences, will disappoint and perhaps frustrate those whose learning styles favour that kind of activity. The predicted responses are set out below.

Activists

A sense of participating in something relatively new would be attractive to Activists, as would the emphasis on attacking real problems, however they might be uncomfortable if the project or problem they were tackling extended over a long period of time. They are not likely to enjoy being reminded to clarify terms of reference, by attempts to provide structure, by encouragement to do detailed planning. Most of all they are not likely to favour what they would regard as too frequent or too lengthy attempts to review what has been done and what has been learned. They are quite likely to enjoy doing the project work. They would probably enjoy their own presentations in set discussion. They may well pick up ideas from other people. They are not likely to enjoy profound discussions about the meaning of what they or anyone else has done.

Reflectors

Reflectors would appreciate some main features of the Action Learning process, obviously in contrast with those of the Activists. They will, for example, relish the opportunity to produce carefully considered analyses, to collect data, to compare and contrast data, but may find it difficult to start a project. They will bring additional information to the group and help the group to generate its own data. They will want their role in this respect to be recognized.

They will be particularly pleased to engage in the process of reviewing what has occurred within their own project and that of other people. They will appreciate the advantages of doing learning reviews and learning logs and discussing what has been learned within the group. They enjoy the process of thinking things over and the opportunity to give and receive feedback. They are perhaps unlikely to volunteer any of these initially, and therefore will be pleased to be supported by a process which encourages sharing of air time. They are less likely to enjoy time limits in relation to a project.

Theorists

Theorists will be attracted to some elements of Action Learning and repelled by others. They will like the opportunity of being stretched by a complex problem. They will probably appreciate, without necessarily agreeing with, the theory behind Action Learning. They may be uneasy about the concentration on a particular project. 'Is it right to spend so much time on a single managerial experience?' They may feel there are insufficient opportunities to generalize beyond the particular project. They will bring strong views (which they will not necessarily regard as theories) about the nature of a project, and what is involved in their own or other people's project.

Whatever the care with which the initial structure of the exercise is set up, it is likely to move into conditions of ambiguity and uncertainty; these conditions are especially difficult for Theorists.

They are the most likely of the four styles to want to have input – P.

Pragmatists

The high-face validity of tackling real problems and the requirement to produce Action Plans, make an attractive process for Pragmatists. This is especially true where people work on problems for which they are accountable in their own organizations. Consultancy projects in a different organization may be less attractive, because of the potential difficulty of transferring learning from that situation to their own.

They may ask for P input, not dealing with theories and models as Theorists might, but dealing with practical skills involved in the project, such as interviewing, planning or presenting.

Where sets can be created in which there is a balance of different learning style preferences, the result can be enhanced learning for individuals and the group.

PARTICIPANT CONCERNS

The exposure and exchange which is an important potential benefit of Action Learning can also raise concerns at both an individual and an organizational level. 'Do I really want to share this information about myself with my colleagues?' 'Is this organization prepared to be challenged on its strategy, values, policies?' 'If

I engage in either of these forms of challenge is the organization or the group or the individuals really going to support me?'

The simplicity of Action Learning may cause participants initially to see it as 'a good thing', because it deals with real managerial issues. However, even those who are not strong on the Theorist learning style may develop some concerns about the very specific nature of projects, how much transfer of learning there is going to be, and if P is not provided, whether there is sufficient testing content and opportunity in terms of knowledge built around the programme.

A prime concern can be whether a client for a project, in those cases where participants are not fully autonomous in terms of carrying out action, will actually take action. There can be fears about projects being put on the shelf or being treated simply as interesting development exercises.

GROUP LEARNING

Revans has talked about 'comrades in adversity' or 'fellows in adversity'. My colleague Joanna Kozubska produced the interesting insight that this sounded perhaps unduly negative. I agree with her that a more appropriate term is 'fellows in opportunity'.

The processes by which individuals learn in groups (as distinct from general group behaviour) has been very little studied. One of the potential contributions, especially in meeting the Learning to Learn objective, is that groups can consider, reflect on and improve their behaviour as a group. Some ideas on this, based on experience rather than research, are shown in Figure 1.5.

SUPPORT MECHANISMS

Most Action Learning literature follows the Revans line of talking about fellows in adversity (or opportunity). Clearly this is a fundamental feature of the inter-action of people within the set discussion.

Unfortunately there has been insufficient recognition of the work context, i.e. the sense in which the participant's environment encourages effective work on the project or problem, and encourages learning from that. It is important to clarify the nature of the help that might be offered by a boss or a mentor or colleague, how and when it will be provided. (See Chapter 19 'Managers Developing Others Through Action Learning'.)

For those projects (almost certainly the majority) where the participant has no autonomous right to carry through the resolution of the problem or the implementation of the project, the identification of a client is crucial. Is there someone who is interested not only in having the project carried out, but in accepting responsibility for taking decisions on it?

- Enabling fellows to share air time appropriately

- Non-defensive about own actions and learning

- Supportive about issues/concerns of others

- Open in initiating and responding to issues

- Analytical

- Questioning in style, eliciting information – not defensiveness

- Listening effectively

- Accepting help

- Creative in response to problems

- Innovative in recognizing learning from task

- Risk taking

- Using Task and Learning Cycle

- Understanding and using learning styles

- Using strengths of others as learners

- Helping to motivate others as learners

Figure 1.5 Individual behaviours in effective learning groups

In all these cases, there is a learning opportunity for those acting as supports for the participant on the Action Learning programme – one of the main benefits substantially understated so far in the Action Learning literature. The choice of Action Learning as a method might be significantly enhanced if this benefit was understood, and help was offered for 'supporters' to use the opportunity.

ROLE OF ADVISERS

Advisers as support people are different in kind and relationship from people in the above section. The set adviser may have a number of different roles. There is a considerable amount of literature about this (see Chapter 16 by Bennett, and 'Further reading' at the end of this chapter). Perhaps the most important distinction can be made between:

- Set adviser as organizer and even administrator for the set, helping with decisions about location, timing, frequency, logistics.

- Set adviser as facilitator, sitting in on set meetings and providing the guidance which can assist the set to achieve maximum learning.

As my experience and the literature both attest, the latter role is not always fully understood or appreciated by the set adviser. Line managers, or people used to a more direct tutorial role, often have to adjust their style to suit the requirement of facilitation rather than direct teaching. As so often Revans has an appropriate phrase for this: 'Inveterate hankering of the tutor to be the centre of attention'.

ASSOCIATION WITH OTHER MANAGEMENT DEVELOPMENT METHODS

In most circumstances an appropriate integration of P and Q will be the best way of securing effective learning. A sensible combination of appropriate, relevant and timely inputs of knowledge and skills is likely to provide optimum learning. The integration should be consistent and genuine. Stand-alone sessions which are seen by participants as being quite different from and not properly integrated with the requirements of the Action Learning elements do little for either P or Q. It is partly a matter of relevance, i.e. choosing skills and knowledge which are appropriate to the Action Learning process itself, and to the projects tackled by individuals. It is also a matter of choosing to deliver knowledge of P elements in a way which is as close as possible to the process used in Action Learning, i.e. the use of questions, and emphasis on the specifics of the context and needs of the individual.

It is quite unnecessary nowadays for anyone to see P and Q as Cain and Abel.

ORGANIZATION CULTURE

It is quite clear that some organizations, while initially favouring the idea of a double value learning from doing approach, become worried and unable to accept the more challenging features of Action Learning. While the possibilities of Action Learning facilitating the creation of a learning organization, of enabling people to engage in double-loop learning or generative learning may be present, not all organizations are able to accept these more ambitious elements.

NATIONAL CULTURE

For many years the literature after the initial Belgian experience was generated through the derivatives of Revans' work in the UK, initially with the General Electric Company. The process has now been extended to a number of other countries, not all of whom have yet contributed to the literature. There have been significant uses of Action Learning in Australia, Scandinavia and (not always in line with the Revans philosophy) the United States.

I have no references, other than a very early experience in Egypt, to Action Learning in Africa. There are a few articles on Action Learning in China but none that I am aware of in Japan. It seems probable that there are national characteristics which might inhibit the introduction and successful implementation of Action Learning. Most particularly the need for a genuine exposure of views within the group, and a willingness to challenge the ideas of others in authority may not fit some national cultures.

Our experience in IMC is that some countries, especially in Asia, favour additional P input.

EVALUATION

There is a magisterial chapter on evaluation in Pedler's *Action Learning in Practice*. There is also a principal article by Wieland (see *MBR*, vol. 20, no. 6, 1994) which suggests that there were eventually significant results from projects done by Revans and the National Health Service. Otherwise evaluation seems to be much of a desert, but that is a comment which can apply to most management development work. A few oases in the desert are collected in Part V of this book.

One reason for the lack of evaluation is precisely the issue of 'double value' proposed earlier – that is, the results of projects, the identification and tackling of opportunities or problems can be so clear to participants and to their organization that the idea of a formal evaluation process has no attraction because it has no perceived benefit to them. As one managing director said to me: 'Since I can see a saving of X million pounds from that project already, I see no reason to let you in to do an evaluation which will take the time of my managers to prove what I already know, that the programme was worthwhile'.

As again is true for most other management development methods, the lack of evaluation makes a scientific choice about Action Learning in preference to other methods, or indeed even in association with them, more difficult. Is Action Learning more effective, and in what sense, than alternative ways of developing managers?

What one can try to do, however, as indicated by the content of this chapter, is to ensure that Action Learning is adopted in order to meet particular objectives, and that the learning processes are identified and managed so that they are more likely to meet those objectives.

ANOTHER ASPECT OF REALITY

It was argued earlier that the responsibility for implementation could be one of the defining features of how stretching an Action Learning experience is. It seems logical that since line management is primarily concerned with carrying out projects (though of course preceded by data collection and planning), the most advantageous variety of Action Learning for line managers involves them in implementing the results of the problem discussion or project proposal. If someone argues that implementation cannot be involved because 'I am not senior enough to carry this through', then questions arise as to the suitability of a project at that level for the participant.

However, it may be that not all participants in Action Learning are line managers, or indeed are managers at all – they may be senior professionals who manage no one else. In such cases it could reasonably be argued that they are in the business of advising and influencing rather than implementing, which underplays the significance of the implementation issue. For those who think that implementation is such an important feature of the most productive Action Learning, the choice of problem or project will then centre on those activities where the functional specialist or professional does have the responsibility for implementation.

All this underlines the importance of using reality as the basis for Action Learning. Of course there are legitimate and useful projects which may only involve advising someone else, and which may be the only kind of available project. It may represent a good choice in terms of investing time and money in the participant. In my view it is desirable to encourage, indeed to urge, people to progress as far as possible along the continuum of reality.

FURTHER READING

The growing popularity of Action Learning is attested by an increasing number of articles and books.

Literature Reviews

Two leading literature reviews have been published in the UK:

Alan Mumford, 'A Review of Action Learning' in *Management Bibliographies and Reviews*, MCB University Press, vol. 11, no. 2, 1985.
Alan Mumford, 'A Review of Action Learning Literature' in *Management Bibliographies and Reviews*, MCB University Press, vol. 20, nos 6 and 7, 1994.

In Australia:

> 'Action Learning in Vocational Education and Training', vol. 4, *Annotated Bibliography*, published by National Staff Development Committee, P.O. Box 42, Chadstone, Vic. 3148, Australia.

Books

Reg Revans has written several books, of which:

> R.W. Revans, *The Origins and Growth of Action Learning*, Chartwell-Bratt Ltd, 1982

is interesting as a demonstration of how Revans arrived at his ideas on Action Learning and also contains the best material on the learning process.

His best general book is:

> R.W. Revans, *Action Learning*, Blond and Briggs, 1980.
> Mike Pedler (ed.), *Action Learning in Practice*, 3rd ed., Gower, 1997

contains a great variety of chapters, many with specific case studies. Of particular relevance here are chapters by David Casey on 'The Role of Set Adviser' and 'The Shell of Your Understanding'; and John Morris, 'Minding our *Ps* and *Qs*'.

At the time of writing there are three other books:

> Ian McGill and Liz Beaty, *Action Learning*, 2nd ed., Kogan Page, 1995.
> Scott Inglis, *Making the Most of Action Learning*, Gower, 1994.
> Krystyna Weinstein, *Action Learning*, HarperCollins, 1995.

Again from the perspective of this chapter, the books by Inglis and Weinstein offer most about the learner and the learning processes.

Mumford's two literature surveys provide guidance on the many topics which it is possible to pursue on Action Learning. Here the focus is on those issues which are most fundamental to the review of the learning process.

Learning Processes

> M. Knowles, *Andragogy in Action*, Jossey-Bass, 1985.
> J. Coates, 'How People Learn on Management Courses' in *Industrial and Commercial Training*, vol. 21, no. 2, 1989.
> V. Marsick, L. Cederholm, E. Turner and T. Pearson, 'Action Reflection Learning' in *Training and Development USA*, 1992.
> G. Prideaux, 'Making Action Learning More Effective' in *Training and Management Development Methods*, vol. 6, 1992.

Coates shows how he builds the Learning Cycle and learning styles into one of his programmes. Marsick et al. emphasize the requirement for effective reflection, and is particularly interesting because they cite experiences in Sweden and the United States. Prideaux offers fascinating ideas about creating a learning community, and the use of learning diaries, and the association of learning contracts with Action Learning. Three main ideas in one article make this a 'must read' – thus its inclusion in this book (as Chapter 15).

The specific issues about individual learners are covered in:

D. Kolb, *Experiential Learning*, Prentice Hall, 1983.

P. Honey and A. Mumford, *The Manual of Learning Styles*, 3rd ed., Honey, 1992.

Learners

The scarcity of articles by learners themselves is a serious weakness in the literature. It is partly remedied by Weinstein's book, which centres on discussion with a large number of learners. Otherwise two relevant articles are:

B. Caiae, 'Learning in Style' in *Journal of Management Development*, vol. 6, no. 2, 1987 (which appears in this book as Chapter 10).

J.R. Mercer, 'Action Learning: A Student's Perspective' in *Industrial and Commercial Training*, vol. 22, no. 2, 1990.

Learning in the Set

A fascinating contribution here is:

M. Mead, 'From Colleagues in Adversity to the Synergy of the Set' in *Industrial and Commercial Training*, vol. 22, no. 1, 1990 (which appears in this book as Chapter 9).

A. Mumford, 'Effective Learning in Action Learning Sets', *Employee Counselling Today*, vol. 8, no. 6, 1996.

Though not specific to Action Learning, a very useful statement about team learning is:

K. Deschant, V. Marsick and E. Kasl, 'Towards a Model of Team Learning' in *Studies in Continuing Learning*, vol. 15, no. 1, 1993.

K. Deschant and V. Marsick, 'Team Learning Survey', published by Organization Design and Development, USA (a diagnostic tool).

Set Advisers

The absence of material by participants has been commented on. There is far more on what set advisers should do. Chapter 16 by Roger Bennett gives an IMC experience-based view. Two articles by David Casey have already been noted. Other chapters making additionally valuable points (though with some duplication) are available in:

Mike Pedler (ed.), *Action Learning in Practice*, 3rd ed., Gower, 1997.

People Who Help

Alan Mumford, 'Managers Developing Others Through Action Learning' in *Industrial and Commercial Training*, vol. 7, no. 2, 1995.

Evaluation

The little material that is available on evaluation is commented on earlier, and much of it referenced in *Management Bibliographies and Reviews*, vol. 20, no. 6, 1994.

Connections

There are no comparative studies, establishing for example whether Action Learning is a more effective process for group learning or for leadership or for team work than an outdoor or adventure experience.

From a rather different perspective, the potential association of Action Learning with organizational learning is interesting, although there are very few direct references. Relevant material here includes:

K. Watkins and V. Marsick, *Sculpting the Learning Organization*, Jossey Bass, 1994.

Nancy Dixon, *The Organizational Learning Cycle*, McGraw-Hill, 1994.

A. Mumford, *Learning at the Top*, McGraw-Hill, 1995.

All of these refer specifically to the association of Action Learning and organizational learning. Less direct associations which nonetheless provide interesting insights are to be found in:

Peter Senge, *The Fifth Discipline*, Doubleday, 1990.

Mike Pedler, John Burgoyne, Tom Boydell, *The Learning Company*, McGraw-Hill, 1991.

A. Mayo and E. Lank, *The Power of Learning*, IPD, 1994.

Peter Honey and Alan Mumford, *Managing Your Learning Environment*, Honey, 1996.

P & Q

The extent to which *P* is necessary, either to make a fully integrated learning programme or even in a more restricted use to make sense of Action Learning itself, is debated in:

P. Smith, 'Second Thoughts on Action Learning' in *Journal of European Industrial Training*, vol. 12, no. 6, 1988.

D. Sutton, 'Further Thoughts on Action Learning' in *Journal of European Industrial Training*, vol. 13, no. 3, 1989.

D. Sutton, 'Action Learning in Search of *P*' in *Industrial and Commercial Training*, vol. 22, no. 1, 1990 (which appears in this book as Chapter 5).

J. Peters (ed.), 'Customer First: The Independent Answer' in *Business Education*, vol. 9, no. 3, 1988.

R. Thorpe, 'An MSc by Action Learning: The Management Development Initiative' in *Management Education and Development*, vol. 19, no. 1, 1988.

Video

A professionally produced video of Reg Revans setting out his main ideas is available from MCB University Press, 62 Toller Lane, Bradford, West Yorks. BD8 9BY.

2 Placing Action Learning and Action Research in Context

Cliff Bunning

Action Learning and Action Research, which each arose separately more than forty years ago, are even now still at the stage of struggling for understanding and acceptance within the education and research communities. This slow rate of diffusion is attributable to the fact that each of these innovations represents a paradigm shift, challenging assumptions and traditional approaches which go back to the eighteenth century at least.

In order to proceed with clarification, definitions of both Action and Research, in terms of their purpose will be offered, together with definitions for the two interlopers, showing how they relate to the established approaches.

Action

The purpose of Action is to make improvements in the world.

Action Learning

The purpose of Action Learning is to make improvements in the world, and so contribute to private learning (i.e. the learning of the Action Taker and those associated with the Action Taker, particularly other set members).

Action Research

The purpose of Action Research is to make improvements in the world and so contribute to public learning (i.e. publication is an intrinsic aspect of Action Research).

Research

The purpose of Research is to gain a better understanding of some aspect of the world and so contribute to learning (via public action, of course).

The similarities and differences between these four practices, considered as pure types, can be portrayed graphically (See Figure 2.1).

There are both similarities and differences between Action Learning and

25

ACTION	ACTION LEARNING	ACTION RESEARCH	RESEARCH
Improve the world	Improvement and private learning	Improvement and public learning	Understand the world and public learning

Figure 2.1 A comparison of purposes

Action Research, as regards the deficiencies in current practice that they seek to address.

ACTION LEARNING

Action Learning addresses two problems manifest in traditional educational and staff development approaches:

- The conventional, expert-driven, didactic approach of lectures and the general view of knowledge as a valuable, pre-produced, easily transferable product is not very effective in terms of learning, especially with adults with experience in the topic area, i.e. much is taught but rather less is learned.
- To the extent that learning does occur, there is a significant problem in achieving the transfer of learning and skills from the place of learning to the place of application, typically the work place.

Action Learning avoids these difficulties by insisting that action be taken in the real world (the learner's or someone else's) and that learning be achieved primarily via reflection upon action and by interaction with colleagues. There is a place for previously distilled or programmed knowledge, but it is accessed at the discretion of the learner, when the need exists, rather than at the discretion of the expert, often before a need is experienced by the learner.

ACTION RESEARCH

Action Research addresses two problems manifest in traditional scientific research approaches when they are applied to situations involving human beings:

- The difficulty of making people not part of the research effort accept the findings as relevant to their situation and so to adopt them.
- The impossibility of maintaining that the researcher is a disengaged neutral party whose presence and activities have no effect upon the research results. The desire for results which can be replicated also leads to attempts to ignore or screen out the effects of other variables (particularly human

behaviour) which are naturally present in real-life situations, consequently making the research situation and the findings therefrom non-representative.

Action Research is based upon at least three central tenets:

- The natural functioning of systems are more clearly evident under conditions of intentional change than when the system is at rest or functioning routinely.
- 'Contamination' of the situation by the observer/researcher is inevitable and so involvement of the researcher as an active facilitator of change is not only permissible but advantageous from the point of view of both action and learning.
- It is important that social systems not be exploited in the research process and that preferably they be empowered (i.e. have more control over their future than before the research contact). This point is developed at greater length below.

Nature of Research Effects

An *exploitative* approach to research regards the people in the social system as subjects whose role is to conform to the research requirements. The purposes, design, conduct and learnings from the research are all under the exclusive control of the researcher and any benefits to the participants are incidental and somewhat unintended.

A *collaborative* approach to research seeks to find a mutuality of interest, initiated essentially by the researcher. Although discussions are bilateral and some attention is paid to the interests of the co-operating subjects, the parameters of the research project are set by the researcher and it is within that framework that co-operation is sought.

Emancipatory action research has as its goal that the people in the social system to be researched will, as a result of the research project, have more awareness, information, skills and control over their future than they had before the project. To this end, the researcher is more a facilitator/observer and has as a goal that participants:

- set the research parameters (decide the agenda)
- do the analysis and draw the conclusions
- plan and implement the improvements to their situation
- evaluate progress and respond to the results of such evaluations.

    . . . in the process of critical action research, there is room only for participants. In genuinely critical and self-critical action research, all participants must take on genuinely collaborative roles, as members of, not outsiders to, the research work, even if roles within the group are differentiated. The projects should be collaborative projects governed by open decision making in a group committed to examining its own values, understandings, practices, forms of organisation and situation.

                                                                    S. Kemmis[1]

Because of the participant-driven nature of emancipatory Action Research, the researcher does not have the presumption to establish beforehand the hypothesis for testing, but rather has a central question about which information is sought. As understanding of the situation, its issues and dynamics grows, the central question of the research activity might evolve into something different from what it was at the start.

COMMON ASPECTS OF ACTION LEARNING AND ACTION RESEARCH

There are a number of aspects common to Action Learning and Action Research, as indicated by Figure 2.1. One commonality not mentioned so far is that both involve the creation of a social forum for learning. Whilst action and research can be solitary activities, this is not possible with the framework of the two emerging methodologies.

The learning set, a group of individuals who are each carrying out some Action Learning project and who meet regularly to challenge and support each other, is the crucible for learning within the Action Learning paradigm. Individual reflection, challenging questions from other set members and synergic creativity of the group members are the mechanisms for learning. Learning can also take place, of course, from interaction with the people who are members of the system which is the subject of the Action Learning project but this is not the main mechanism for learning.

By contrast, whilst the action researcher might be part of a learning set, this is not essential.

The main forum for learning in Action Research is the discussions the researcher has with the members of the system which has decided to initiate an Action Research project.

In fact, within a fully emancipatory Action Research paradigm, the researcher's writings need the agreement of the people involved in the system before they can be regarded as valid, because they would otherwise be incongruent with the social reality experienced by the people being described.

CONCLUSION

Both Action Learning and Action Research have emerged because of the limitations of existing educational and research paradigms. Naturally these new methodologies bring their own problems and limitations, but they represent a moving forward in the relentless quest for greater understanding of, and capacity to influence, the world we live in.

REFERENCE

1 S. Kemmis in O. Zuber-Skerritt (ed.), *Action Research for Change and Development*, Gower, 1991.

3 The Origins and Philosophy of International Management Centres

Gordon Wills

A great many papers and conference presentations have been written on this issue since 1982, and the author devoted his Revans' Professorial Year in 1992 to writing *Your Enterprise School of Management*, MCB University Press, 1993. However, perhaps the most robust and enthusiastic rationale is provided by three graffiti taken from Gordon Wills *Creating Wealth Through Management Development*, MCB University Press, 1988.

'REG TOLD US SO'

From the very outset of British business schools in the 1960s, Reg Revans told us we had got it wrong. He quit Manchester when that business school was established, to go and work in Belgium. We who stayed behind all began creating schools modelled on North American practices.

Reg Revans argued then, as he does today, for a quite different approach which he calls Action Learning. Managers will learn best when they ask questions on the issues that confront them in running their enterprise more successfully. Only when those issues have been identified, and made the curriculum for study, can the academic make any really worthwhile contribution. The knowledge of which the academic is guardian, programmed from the past, must not be permitted to overwhelm the true purpose of management education which is to make managers more effective.

Action Learning not only has the power of instant appeal to the manager who is to be educated. It also has the power to offer reinforcement for what is learnt by action based on the conclusions reached. Finally, Action Learning creates an educational proposition which can be directly treated as an investment. It creates discernible wealth. Expenditure on a programme of such development can be compared against medium-term gains to the enterprise from the issues worked on, which contrasts strongly with the traditional soft view that 'education is a good thing, isn't it?'.

Why then did Reg Revans fail to influence us all in the mid-sixties? Were we not listening? Or was he unconvincing? Or is he wrong?

I concluded by the late seventies, on the basis of marketing research at Cranfield which was showing managers as gravely discontented with the products and services of business schools, that he was not wrong! He was simply not convincing us adequately. He showed scant regard for personal influencing skills. He preferred to denounce all professors and experts, although paradoxically holding on to the title of professor himself. A holier than thou stance was incidentally often adopted by the great majority of his disciples over the years as a defence mechanism for the equally unsympathetic reactions of those denounced.

The reality was that the Industrial Training Act of 1964 in Britain created a seller's market lacking in much sophistication for a decade. During that time, university scholarship of necessity took a firm hold as the fledgling discipline of management sought to win spurs within the academy where Lord Franks and others had ordained it should be located.

By the time a customer or market orientation emerged, it was too late. The institutionalization of our schools in the academy was a fait accompli. The lexicon of management knowledge per se had been constructed. Contrary views were ubiquitously derided as lacking in rigour or depth.

And so the market left the university business schools to languish with little or no growth. All the energy that emerged when vital questions were posed about the future of real enterprises was in the purview of management consultants rather than business school teachers. In management terminology, the schools became product-oriented rather than customer-oriented.

Action Learning's fatal weakness in seeking to overcome the institutionalized lexicon, however, was its lack of structure. As a movement in society it could not innovate effectively and then challenge the conventional product-oriented models of the academy. What was needed was not a controlling structure but a facilitating one. Despite all its potential dangers, the church of Action Learning had to come into existence. This was a challenge Reg Revans did not relish, was not skilled to lead, and always publicly decried. Rather, he prophesied that on hearing the word about Action Learning, spontaneous combustion should occur. Even the use of advisers in Action Learning groups (normally called sets) was frowned on in favour of a natural flowering of learning in the face of adversity.

In 1982, a group of colleagues with whom I had worked since 1965 both at Bradford University Management Centre and MCB University Press, resolved to address the challenge of creating just such a structure for an Action Learning business school. The school would be committed totally to the process. It would offer the resources and advice appropriate to Action Learning for mid-career managers, both on an open basis and at master's and doctoral levels (MBA and DBA). We called it the International Management Centre from Buckingham

(IMCB) and Reg Revans was eventually persuaded to become our President from 1983 to 1985 (and remains associated with us as Emeritus President).

Our conclusions by now are that Action Learning suits well some 80 per cent of managers. The balance have a more theoretical learning style. It also suits some but not all cultures internationally where we have worked. The Far and the Middle East, in particular, find the open and frank discussion of financial and human aspects of managerial situations more difficult than North Americans, Europeans and Australians. The difficulties in the Far and Middle East are not simply interpersonal. They are reflected in many employers' reluctance to permit the real issues from their enterprise to be focused on for Action Learning from fear of disloyalty by those who come into such knowledge – although this must also be seen as a reflection of a much greater preponderance of small/medium-sized enterprises in such cultures at least so far as participation on Action Learning programmes is concerned.

However, the case for Action Learning today is overwhelming in all western and also in many developing cultures where such sharing remains a dominant style. The product-oriented approach of the traditional academy is largely counter-productive both for the society from which it draws its resources to continue and for its own good. The traditional role of the university is not under threat for pure scholarship, but the charade that drags the development of more effective managers into a scholarship contest with examiners has overstayed its welcome.

The irony is that in so many academic disciplines, the processes of Action Learning are readily accepted. It constitutes no more than applied research on the enterprise and its unknown future. What we did at IMCB for curriculum design in Action Learning at qualification level differs little, if at all, from a master's or doctoral research programme in many university disciplines. As the research topic crystallizes, so the tutors can discern what previous knowledge will be of value in showing the way forward, and which research design and method can most usefully be employed to create acceptable ways forward.

While forever indebted to Reg Revans for his Old Testament contribution to our work at IMCB, we are now accordingly post-Revans in two key respects. First, Action Learning does not work as well in all cultural contexts or with all managerial learning styles. We therefore use it judiciously. Some prefer and work better with the more theoretical modes. Second, and I only briefly alluded to this earlier, we have increasingly found it necessary to focus on the politics of executive action and implementation as well as Action Learning per se. No matter how real the issues may be for Action Learning, managers must also learn how to act effectively when they have learnt what to do for the best. Here executive competences and skills must be honed whatever the answers that asking the right questions about the future might provide; and deployed to make those answers come true. Action learners must not in the future show the same arrogance that the academy has towards team working and presentation skills, to time management, delegation and negotiation skills.

Perhaps a more winning statement of the alternative to the quest for scholarship in the academy from Action Learning's advocates can be offered. Learning should address the future challenges of the enterprise for which the manager works. Once they are discerned, the appropriate knowledge from the past can be deployed to illuminate those challenges and the gap to be filled clearly seen. The motivation to fill such gaps will be powerful, and the outcomes beneficial for the enterprise and the individual alike. Provided the skills are present to find the necessary answers and carry the action forward, wealth will be created.

Action Learning permits a great many more managers to share in the intellectual equity of the business they work for. The potential this unleashes has only to be seen to be believed. Since 1982, I have observed so very many hard-nosed academics see, and believe. And even more senior executives.

'CUSTOMER ORIENTATION IN MANAGEMENT EDUCATION'

Most customers do not know what they want until they see it, and customers for management education – in the main – are no exception. As such, the proposition so frequently advanced by marketers that enterprise should simply give the customers what they want is specious. The process of knowing what customers want is relative to what they understand can be made available. Goethe observed long ago, 'We see what we know'. So how did business schools go about the dialogue of finding out what their customers wanted?

The answer during the seventies and early eighties is that in the main they did not. They simply observed what sold in the North American educational marketplace and what their academic peers in the existing universities found acceptable and called that 'education for management'. It was what we call a seller's market.

I am not for one minute suggesting I can quote chapter and verse that such education for management did any manager any real harm. After all, to study basic statistics or accountancy or micro-economics can hardly be called harmful. But I am suggesting that the marketplace in the UK has by and large gone unimproved. Of the million or more individuals who hold managerial, administrative and supervisory roles in the country, only a small fraction have any proper training that they can use in the conduct of those roles. That is a tragedy in an age when no one is allowed to be a school teacher without proper training, or a doctor or a dentist or even an auditor of the accounts of enterprises.

The errors we have made so consistently arise, it seems to me, from the unteachability of managerial skills and knowledge in the educational institution as such. The medical profession long since resolved to tutor in hospitals with real patients, diseases and the rest. We must learn that lesson in management if the effectiveness of our educational services is to be improved.

I do not, by such remarks, intend to suggest that all that is required is to transfer the academy to the training department of an enterprise. That makes matters worse quite often because such trainers are prophets in their own countries.

The only way to achieve customer orientation at practising manager level is to move in on the line managers, their patients and their diseases. Then not only can the tutor share in the immediacy of the challenges addressed but also live with the participating managers. He can dutifully assist as they work out what best to do, and then how best to live with the consequences. If the body of knowledge is as well honed as we believe it to be, the need for most if not all of it will occur in the heat of such debate, discussion and action.

Since so few managers have ever been or are currently offered such a revolutionary way to educate themselves, they have perforce either purchased the best product available or simply not bought at all. In most cases, it was the stay-away decision that was made.

All manner of alibis have been advanced by us manufacturers of management education, most of which involve taking a dim view of our customers. One celebrated study dubbed British managers 'scruffy' and hopelessly incapable of appreciating the fine products the university schools offered.

What bunkum. If customers don't avail themselves of our services, it is not because they are stupid. It is because we are magnificently failing to convince them that it is a worthy marginal application of their resources of time and money. The derision heaped on British managers for failing to spend more than the Germans or the French or the Japanese or the Americans on training is embarrassing and pathetic to behold.

As for a recent proposal that companies should pledge themselves to ensuring all managers spend at least four days a year on management development – that smacks of the Tudor fish-days or the fines payable under Canon Law for not going to church on Sundays.

What precisely do the progenitors of the notion of four days a year on management development propose should happen during those four days? What theory of managerial learning to improve effectiveness underlies the propositions? Are they on outside courses and, if so, of what merit? Should they be academically worthy and/or practically useful and, if so, over what time-scale?

Frankly, it is not difficult to make the case for all four days being far more fruitfully spent on the job at work, with one's own workplace team, addressing the real challenges through which managers can be developed. The transfer of learning dilemma never arises when the whole workplace team shares a common experience on themes not taken from the programmed knowledge of the past but from today's and tomorrow's key issues.

The most profound but unanswerable criticism of business school teaching programmes is that they offer basic courses in all the main areas of professional expertise but do not assist in proper managerial participation. Managers do not need to learn the basics of bookkeeping or theoretical frameworks of micro-economics. They need to understand how accountants and economists think, not to outwit them or to attempt to develop an amateur knowledge of the tricks of their trade. It is like suggesting that British industry would improve the balance of trade if we all learnt how to drive roll on/roll off trucks or to be masters of oceangoing container ships.

The courage to throw away the teaching obsession with the accumulated body of knowledge, the lexicon from A–Z, and to focus on what the process of management is known to be all about, is indispensable for any further advance in the sale of management education to its customers.

Not only, however, is the product offered defective as it currently stands and the customer ill-served thereby. The distribution system is almost wholly unre-lated to the realities of the lives of customers. To take one of the more idiotic examples, many if not all major schools require two academic years for their full-time programmes at master's level and target these at managers between 28 and 35 years of age. At that age, such managers have a wife and a family to support as often as not and a mortgage to pay. The university then proceeds to teach 3 × 10-week terms (perhaps 11 weeks) and to invite individuals to enjoy long vacations, just like Oxford and Cambridge have enjoyed since the days when harvest had to be gathered. What family wants to take two years without salary when 12 months' unremitting work or at most 15 months' could suffice? Well, none, but that is not how the university academics intend to organize their affairs or seek to make their decisions. The customer doesn't even play a role in such thinking in such institutions.

It has been established again and again beyond reasonable doubt that the wish for self-improvement as a manager, and the career satisfaction and rewards that go with that, are strong with all high-rising managers. Yet they cannot fit what the suppliers offer into their workstyle and lifestyle and as such cannot consume the products.

Everything we teach in our classrooms, and that successful industry practises, indicates we must make such services more attractive to managers and their customers. Why are we so reluctant? Sales of management books have soared since they have been offered on bookstalls where managers are travellers and through the post. That was a transformation of a channel of distribution from the high street bookshop that few managers frequent.

British railway stations today are increasingly a clear example as to how interception of target audiences can increase sales – whether it be of socks, ties, flowers, newspapers or snacks. Petrol filling stations have increased the consumption of sweets by adults astronomically even if we wish they had not.

What must management education do? The service we offer must be made obviously applicable to the world in which managers work and the distribution systems must be transformed to make the service available where it can be readily consumed. One of the most interesting factors I have unearthed in the last ten years is that hoteliers are by far the largest providers of management education facilities in the world, and at a standard that satisfies their customers much if not all the time. All those who have wailed long and often that without government aid no proper facilities can be made available, are self-seekers. Their attitude towards the state is simply an extension of their attitude towards their customers.

British managers are great. Just see how well they have performed in the past ten years in industry – at a time when little or no advance was made in the level of formal management education in Britain. If we as educators want to improve on how well they are doing without our help, we had better examine most carefully how far they have reached. We would do well also to ponder just how few scholars there are among our top industrialists. They must have found a secret way of learning that is alien to us in the academy that helps them proceed and succeed the way they have.

As research has frequently pointed out of late, academics like theorizing and recataloguing the past. That is one of their important roles and they are very good at it. Managers on the other hand are pragmatic and action-oriented. If the former is to help the latter (as his customer) to be better still as a manager, it is indispensable that the services offered reflect the values and preferences of management, not the academy. It can only be achieved with intellectual humility, something academics are noticeably short of. Our cultural esteem for the academy must be retained for that which it is superbly well equipped to accomplish, but the academy must know how to respect the providers of real wealth in society that fund the academy in its continuing work.

I began by observing that few customers know what they want until they see it. What the past ten years has done, however, is to increase the diversity of what is on offer. Major shifts in market share are accordingly to be expected together with most substantial market growth as the dialogue intensifies along the lines set out by Reg Revans and outlined in 'Reg Told Us So'.

'PILE 'EM LOW AND SELL ON HIGH'

The further development of effective management education is dependent on focusing on issues that will make the future happen. This transforms the process into an investment concern rather than languishing as a cost centre. The habit of cutting training costs, as one does the advertising budget, as a short-term tactic to improve profitability, is exposed as myopic in the extreme.

Yet to gain such recognition, it is inescapable that management education must be sold on high. The topmost executive levels of the enterprise must be marketed to and sold on the proposition. Management education is nothing more nor anything less than that thinking and learning time so regularly squeezed out in the rush of events but inescapably vital to the well-being of any enterprise.

Continual shooting from the hip as a substitute for careful thought is a ridiculous way to run any enterprise. It must be exposed as such, which is not to belittle the skills of the sharpshooter who is quick on the draw. In a fight, I would be with none other. But to win the war, never. Few successful generals are sharpshooters; indeed many of the very best are quite the reverse. They spend so much time on preparation that the battle is almost won before the first shot is fired.

There are some chief executives with whom I have sought to have a serious discussion on the role of management education as an investment in thinking time for the enterprise, who see little or no point in it. Their view is often that assets especially properties, and financial management, are the two supreme issues; people come, at best, third. Alternatively, the correlation of the individual's track record with commercial success is so great that he believes he walks on water and as such, his intuitive judgement on any issue is all that is required.

Third, I may be told that the analysis offered is correct but the matter is already well covered in the enterprise. Sometimes, of course, it is, but seldom to the satisfaction of the middle management that constitute the very resource on whom the future depends.

Virtually every enterprise I have worked with has its middle management corralled within a specialist function, unable to see over or far beyond its fence. When called upon to relate with other foreign functions, it does so on the basis of confrontation and/or barter. I well remember the struggle we all had within a leading US multinational company. It was competing for its life against the Japanese and fellow Americans in the European market, and we had to persuade the credit control and order handling activities of the finance department to commit to customer service and revenue generation. The situation is as old as the division of labour I suppose, but the bigger the enterprise becomes, the greater the management challenge to counteract the managerial diseconomies of scale.

Not that the fault all lay within the finance department. The marketing and sales departments showed deep ignorance of the role of finance within the total corporate process. There was little or no understanding of cash management principles that underlie the giving of credit. There was, until our involvement in thinking time management education, no attempt to develop a revenue-potential-based classification of customers or to drive forward customer account profitability analysis.

A focus on customer account profitability analysis was more than capable of bringing finance, marketing and selling managers together in the search for a corporate solution. It was then fed back into the selling and marketing strategies as well as into the financial management policies and procedures.

The point I seek to make, however, is that the thinking time management education process adopted here was sponsored by the line chief executive officer of the division concerned. He had the authority but also the perspective of the whole scene that his middle managers could only guess at. Thousands of sub-optimal decisions for the company were eventually avoided.

The training department had for many years sent managers away on programmes that encompassed customer account profitability analysis en passant. But no one had returned with enough energy or support internally to carry it through. The transfer of learning to a back-home environment, which had not experienced a similar learning process to the individual who had been away on the programme, is always a daunting task for us all. When the desk is piled high with today's issues, how can it be accomplished?

I have for years incidentally been seeking the manager, any manager world-wide, who when he gets back to his company from an away-from-it-all course of management education has been asked the following question: 'What have you learnt/what five key things have you identified, that I your boss should give you my absolute commitment to follow through in our organization over the next six months/year/two years?'

Attendance at some of the top schools, for an 8–12 week programme, including the opportunity cost of being away, can often reach as high as £30,000. Some programmes have a ladies' weekend in mid-stream, when great extra costs are added. The holiday atmosphere is enhanced. We often replay our student days with pranks and certainly teacher resumes the role of maestro.

Where is the considered attempt to obtain value for that money spent? A market research report costing £30,000 will be carefully considered, frequently acted on and its conclusions absorbed into the directional drive of any organization. More often than not, the report would be extensively and formally shared among a wide group. Very frequently, infinite care would have gone into the design of the study in the first instance and the framing of the precise questions to be answered and indeed the cross-tabulating of the data that might be most illuminating.

So at every stage management education needs to be sold at least one level higher, i.e. to the boss of the intended participant. Selling it to the training department is not the right way to go. If the boss insists 'training is done by the training department', then it's seldom worth continuing a discussion. The boss must be as closely involved with the design and outcomes of a management education experience for his staff as he is for market research or any other consultant's report involving a similar investment.

'Pile 'em low' may seem an inappropriate sentiment to link with the other phrase in this graffito's title but I will seek to demonstrate otherwise. Selling on high to the boss makes the management education decision a personal one for which the boss assumes complete responsibility in the same way as when he delegates any other part of the total task to a colleague. Indeed, that is what management education when sold on high becomes – allocation of some of the department's scarce resources to a project of management education for one of the team's members. It is not a selfish thing, nor a placebo, nor a reward. Keeping up to date, indeed ahead professionally, is for every management team and for each player in it vital.

Involving the boss accordingly makes management education into an organizational corporate matter as well as a relationship between tutor and tutored. Most of our life we have been told otherwise. Education, we have been led to believe, is the way we as individuals can achieve our personal fulfilment. Management education, when invested in by the enterprise, is not intended to do anything less than make the company more successful. The fact that it makes individuals more mobile and often more discontented with their lot is a defect of the process in the eyes of many senior executives. It leads some of them to refuse to countenance it.

Certainly, a long spell away from the realities of the enterprise, in an academy devoted to rational and theoretical models of how things ought to be done in a tidy world, frequently has disastrous effects. The MBA graduate is legendary for his job hopping and condescending attitude towards the shortcomings of management wheresoever he deigns to alight for a modest while. It is not the individual manager who is to blame normally but the tutorial environment that conditions him thus. Far away from the rough and tumble world where staff have to be motivated and jobs frequently delegated out of sight, the clear, cold analysis of a business school classroom is not always as valid as rationalists believe it should be. It is but a short step to overlook the skill of achieving objectives as opposed to being an individualist, i.e. martyr.

I do not allude here to compromise rather to appropriate behavioural theory of the enterprise, to the laws of successive approximation, satisficing and the art and science of muddling through. All of these are far more appropriate statements of the realities of management than most classroom rationality.

And so my concern to 'pile 'em low' may perhaps become clearer. The challenge is how we can hold on to the vision and at the same time keep shop. Think low. Think small groups and low numbers. Graciunas advised us nearly a century ago that we all have a very modest span of control and ability to sustain relationships. Whether the number is 5, 6, 9 or 10 does not matter. The point is that it is not 30 or 50. Classroom teaching, theatre style, for 50 or 60 or even 100 managers, is nothing more nor less than theatre. Tutors must be actors to win acclaim. But since managers are foregathered to become more effective, the question must be posed 'How much more effective do they become in groups of 50, 60 or 100 as compared with 5, 6, 8 or 10 – and what are the associated investment costs?'.

The evidence I have seen over the past decade indicates that small is beautiful, small is overwhelmingly more effective than large in the management education process. Small groups permit each individual to contribute, and demand as a social imperative that he be involved and make the best possible contribution. In the larger setting, it is not antisocial not to contribute. Subgroups, that are themselves small enough, spring up by their own natural process and ignore the non-contributors.

My conclusion therefore is that the most suitable learning groups are small ones, i.e. management education should be piled low. It is in small groups that we relate best and it is in small groups that we naturally work unless another seeks to force us to do otherwise. Perchance another does so wish, we seek to minimize the wastage by our own informal reactions in the bar or wheresoever. Hence the phrase: 'I learnt more in the bar than the classroom'.

Perhaps this is best illustrated by my own involvement over the past four years with two colleagues in selling a team management system they have developed, known as the Team Management Resource. It has two clearly identified markets now but it took us some while to delineate them carefully. The first is the training department manager who uses it as a simulated exercise on courses he offers to show participants what principles underlie team management. It is fascinating exercise, particularly for behavioural scientists, and it is nice to read your own horoscope.

The second market, the real market, is for real teams led by real captains against real opponents in the face of real challenges. The difference in the energy levels generated here is quite remarkable. The first is predominantly an intellectual exercise and the conclusion is conceptually intriguing. The second is an unstoppable flood of understanding of past interpersonal behaviours, successes and failures, allied to team role allocation strategies for the future. The first may well involve 20 or 30 managers, the latter 6 or 8. The return on the latter investment well outstrips the former.

INSTEAD OF THE LEXICON OF MANAGEMENT

When I assert that the teaching of the lexicon of management is often inefficient and frequently ineffective as a way of improving managerial performance, I am seldom asked why. The question is normally: how else?

I have a theory of generalship in management that can hardly be unique to me, but it does not require an elementary knowledge of all the specialisms deployed in an enterprise. Rather, it requires an understanding of what each can contribute to the overall performance. This accordingly leads me to propose that effective programmes for improving management must:

1. Ensure that the managers understand how other departments conceptualize their contribution to the whole.
2. Create a trust amongst all management team members in one another to do their specialist job professionally.

3. Involve working together on real issues and trusting one another as the process develops.
4. Have a significant requirement for follow-through action as a result that will reinforce what has been learned and make the whole programme worth while personally and for the enterprise.

On this basis a different curriculum emerges. It is not the lexicon. It is the future challenges for the enterprise, for the manager concerned and his colleagues appropriately involved with him. And it is the skill necessary to carry the enterprise forward. Ideally, managers teach one another.

Their first tutorials for their colleagues must be on what their specialization can contribute and does contribute to the enterprise; for example, the finance director teaches finance for the non-financial managers. The need is a conceptual understanding and it is readily accomplished by answering the questions that most frequently puzzle colleagues. It has little or nothing to do with technique.

Next, friction between professional approaches in departments at their inter-faces can be examined from both sides. What causes them? How can they be reduced?

Thirdly, how does the senior manager or the chief executive officer pull all the different contributions together, set priorities and allocate scarce resources? The pattern of corporate integration adopted determines the success of all enterprises.

Finally, all management can best learn to be more effective in real-life applications. A strategically important project addressing an issue fundamental to success over the next two to five years can be worked at and acted upon.

I summarize this alternative lexicon in the following way. Understand the core concepts; analyse the interfaces and the corporate integration within the enterprise; identify and practise the necessary skills; and work hard on an action project that must be followed through. This is the new curriculum. It is superior for the development of managers beyond a doubt and I have the evidence to prove that assertion.

4 The IMC Experience*

Margaret Reid

Action Learning was first developed by Professor Reg Revans, who has demonstrated its effectiveness in a wide range of organizations from coal mines to hospitals, factories and schools. The process evolved organically as he progressed with his work and as others launched programmes for themselves and wrote about their findings.

It is impossible to write about Action Learning without drawing heavily on the work of Professor Revans, and this indebtedness I wish to acknowledge to the full. On the other hand, it is also important to clarify that as others have worked and experimented in different ways with Action Learning, including its use as a basis for academic programmes, not all the views expressed here are necessarily those held by Professor Revans. Neither are they intended to be prescriptive; they should be seen rather as representing an eclectic overview of thinking and practices. In this respect I should like to acknowledge my indebtedness also to my colleagues at the International Management Centres (IMC).

WHAT IS THE UNDERLYING PHILOSOPHY?

Although it is a fresh and stimulating way of learning by doing, the theory behind Action Learning is not novel. A basic assumption is that we can best find a means of overcoming significant new problems and challenges by working with a group of people who have similar motivation to find solutions. The outcome of the group endeavour is not merely the answer to the problems, but invaluable learning and development for those who have been involved. As Professor Revans expresses it, 'Action Learning is cradled in the very task itself'. There is thus no problem of transfer of learning.

An important principle is that 'comrades in adversity can help each other', they do so by asking questions from many differing perspectives. Discussing problems with other people who have similar problems and want to help is a very powerful way of finding solutions and of improving performance; the

*Originally published in *Training and Management Development Methods*, vol. 4, no. 1, 1990.

process involves learning for all, including those who are asking questions and trying to assist others.

Professor Revans maintains that learning involves what he terms P and Q^1. P stands for Programmed Knowledge; this already exists and is to be found in textbooks, lectures and, increasingly, in computer programs. Q stands for Questioning Insights; the ability to ask the salient questions which will help to elucidate the problem and find a solution (see Figure 4.1). P is important; there would be no merit in devoting a lifetime to re-inventing the wheel. It is, however, concerned with events which have already occurred. If the environment were completely static and problems were therefore similar in all respects to those which had gone before, P would be able to provide solutions. In a context of rapid change, whilst knowledge of past solutions may be helpful, and it may be possible to build on them, historic information may be dysfunctional in channelling the mind in certain directions, thus creating entirely the wrong mental set. To solve problems to which no one knows the answers, the ability to ask penetrating questions is essential.

An important first step in Action Learning is to clarify and identify the relevant areas of ignorance, but one needs not only to ask the questions, but to find answers to them. It therefore requires the skills of 'finding out'. This can involve searching in the realms of P, but also obtaining information from colleagues, subordinates, superiors and relevant sources outside the organization, as well as analysing what the situation means (see Figure 4.2).

$$L = P + Q$$

Key
Recognized IGNORANCE not
programmed knowledge

Action Learning requires questions
to be posed in conditions of IGNORANCE
when nobody knows what to do next

Action Learning
– builds on *P*
– attacks problems to which answer unknown

Action Learning
– clarifies problems
– identifies courses of action
– implements action

Figure 4.1 $L = P + Q$

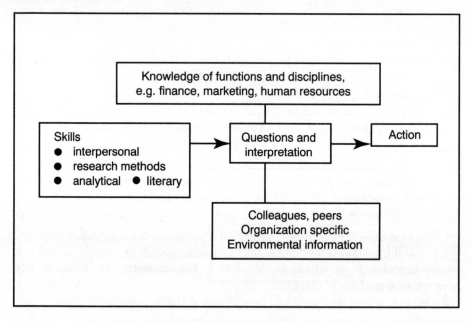

Figure 4.2 The formula in practice

HOW DOES ACTION LEARNING WORK?

Professor Revans' method was to arrange groups of people in what he termed 'sets' to discuss problems. There are four possible designs (see Figure 4.3).

Familiar problem or project in an area the learner knows well	A	Familiar problem or project applied to a new situation	B
Unfamiliar problem or project in a familiar work situation	C	Unfamiliar problem or project in unfamiliar situation	D

Figure 4.3 The four problem sets

MANAGERIAL LEVELS

It is suggested that the option of a familiar task in an area the learner knows well (Box A) is suitable for plant supervisors and foremen or junior managers. It is necessarily part-time as all will be continuing with their work. They meet on equal terms to discuss each other's problems.

The situation in Box B is suitable for functional managers – people who already possess the knowledge and skills to run their own departments, but who are likely to have to cope with imminent change. It is also a suitable

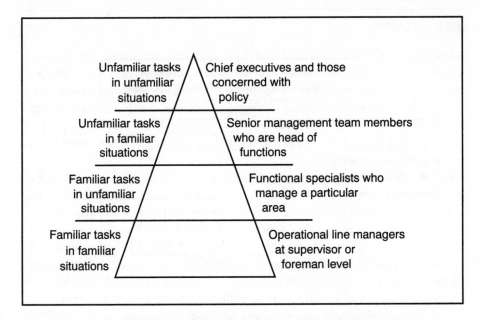

Figure 4.4 Managerial levels and Action Learning

situation for managers of different units which are under the direction of the same higher authority. Option C is recommended for experienced senior managers running a large department, charged with significant responsibility to carry out organization policy. The final level of unfamiliar tasks in unfamiliar surroundings is an appropriate learning experience for those concerned with policy formulation and critical decision making (see Figure 4.4).

The members of the sets help each other by asking questions from many different perspectives. People who are familiar with a problem and a situation are often channelled into particular trains of thought by past experience. Decision makers are likely to be influenced by their own value systems and must be prepared for these to be challenged during the course of discussion.

By asking questions and bringing to light assumptions previously unexposed, those who are 'outside the problem' can often initiate a completely new approach. The set can be a comforting support group and an invaluable sounding board.

The development of the set into a team is not usually a smooth progression. It is common practice to organize an induction course to help the members understand the process. Most sets undergo the familiar stages of 'forming, norming, storming' before reaching the final goal of performing. The length and pattern of this process will depend to a considerable extent on characteristics of the individuals and their particular mix.

THE SET ADVISER

Many forms of Action Learning therefore include a set adviser, or facilitator, whose duty is to help the members develop into a working team. This assistance can assume a number of forms, ranging from direct intervention, taking part in the set's discussions, counselling, advising, and acting as guide, philosopher and friend. The skill lies in appreciating what kind of help is needed; when to intervene and, if so, how or when to maintain a passive role and allow the set to learn its own lessons.

A theoretical knowledge of group interaction as well as an awareness of their own preferred team roles helps the set members to understand what is happening and to interpret events in terms of theory and processes rather than on personal prejudices and value judgements. A good set adviser can help to make these matters explicit. An invaluable by-product of Action Learning is that the participants develop the skills of team membership, as well as other managerial competences, such as presenting a case, counselling, and listening and considering the viewpoint of others; these skills transfer to the working situation.

The set adviser's role becomes less and less prominent as the members become able to control their own affairs. The role is crucially different from that of the normal management teacher. The objective is to help others to learn, not to teach them. The set members take charge of the detailed planning of their meetings and attendance must be regular. In fact, group pressure will make this mandatory. The set is a compelling force which drives individuals to keep up the pace and to attempt activities which they might otherwise have evaded. Wherever possible, decisions are left to the set. The members can be asked to review and reconsider judgements which may appear to have been hasty, but ultimately, must be allowed to manage their own learning. On very rare occasions this can involve extreme steps such as demanding a new set adviser, or expelling a set member! (See Chapter 16 for more on the set adviser.)

HOW QUESTIONS ARISE

Action Learning is very versatile; sets can be organized internally, as part of an organization's management development programme or they can be conducted by external consultants. IMC runs programmes within organizations, based on critical strategic issues, examples being that of a bank which urgently needed to improve its marketing, or an industry within the public sector which, because of government policy, has to learn to generate an income by tendering specialized services commercially.

The kind of questions sets will pose are shown in Figure 4.5. The set members, assisted if necessary by the set adviser or tutor, will help each other to define the problem and determine what knowledge they will need; where to obtain that knowledge, and how to seek help from other people such as colleagues, peers,

- What are we trying to do?

- What is stopping us from doing it?

- What might we be able to do about it?

- Who knows about the problem?

- Who cares about it?

- Who can do anything about it?

Figure 4.5 Action Learning questions

bosses, subordinates, or managers with experience in other organizations. They will report regularly and truthfully to their 'comrades in adversity' the outcome of the actions they have agreed to take.

The way in which set members' questions can be valuable is illustrated by the example of a company which urgently needed to increase turnover. To find answers to all the questions posed by the set it was decided to survey all customers; a set member then asked about 'those who are not your customers'. Accordingly, a wide range of organizations were surveyed, including many which had never dealt with the company. A considerable number of the latter were so impressed with the content of the questionnaire that they asked for further details and became new customers, resulting in a considerable increase in turnover. This was as a result of the process of the investigation. The ultimate findings brought about changes which ensured a better service and brought in even more customers.

The management of another company which was trying to increase its market share realized, as a result of an Action Learning programme, that the whole structure was product oriented and undertook organization development to become customer oriented. This necessitated great structural, cultural and attitudinal change, most of which was set in train by the activities of a set composed of all the managers concerned. Each learned to think strategically about the whole organization, rather than from the narrower functional specialism of his/her own department.

This attitude change can be compared with the slogan adopted by a set from yet another organization, 'No one wins unless we all win'.

The problems under discussion must be real and significant. The participant must own the problem, be totally involved and in high profile, and therefore open to an element of risk, otherwise personal development will not take place (see Figure 4.6).

Real management: Task
Problem
Issue

Piece of demanding work

At least one significant person must want results from the work

Participant must be in a position to ACTION his/her solution

Figure 4.6 Projects

The following examples give an idea of the type of projects undertaken:

- The implementation of EU legislation in a company producing and marketing fire safety equipment.
- A strategy for launching a small organization onto the unlisted securities market.
- A revised pricing strategy for a company producing and marketing photographic processing equipment.

SPONSORS AND CLIENTS

Every set member must have a nominated sponsor, a member of top management, who can act on behalf of the organization should the need arise, and each project must have a 'client' who has an overlying interest in seeing the matter actioned, and who wants to know the answers to questions. If necessary, the client should prepare the way for the investigation of the problem, and facilitate a fair and reasonable hearing for the findings. The support of top management is vital, both to put the set member in a position of high profile with much at stake, and to help to ensure that action is possible as a result of the project. Action is the goal; remove it and you take away the real life pressures which are essential ingredients in the learning process.

Action Learning is different from the case study method where the contributors are not permanently and personally involved in the solutions they propose. They may not have fully worked out the practical realities or political implications. In short they do not have to 'live with' their recommendations and implement them. Learning to take effective action necessarily involves taking action, not recommending it or analysing someone else's problem.

Neither is it the same as the organization of a normal 'working party' or 'task force'. It differs in that each member has his/her own similar problems and is meeting others for the purpose of mutual assistance. The concern is with process as well as task and politics and departmental interests and rivalries must not be allowed to interfere.

WHAT ARE THE RESULTS OF ACTION LEARNING?

Reports from those who have undertaken programmes using this method indicate results far further-reaching than the solving of the problems. Professor Revans refers to the process as 'system gamma' which involves 'the symbiosis of a person changing a situation (action) and of the person being changed by this action (learning)'. Participants say:

I have increased confidence.
I realize that I am only right 99 per cent of the time instead of all the time.
I have become more skilled at helping other people to alter their attitude and I realize that sometimes I need to alter my attitude.
It has completely altered my life.
The disciplined approach to problem solving has transferred to all other aspects of my life.

HOW ARE THE RESULTS EVALUATED?

Action Learning is concerned with outcomes and results. Projects are evaluated by the success of their implementation. The more the outcomes can be quantified, the easier it is to measure the success. Some projects have saved many thousands of pounds for the organization. One participant on an in-company programme found a means of saving more money than the total cost of the whole 18-month programme.

There is, however, a double return on investment in this form of learning because of the 'symbiosis' described above, significant management development takes place, as well as the valuable work which is carried out for the organization. The former is of course more difficult to evaluate. Indications are that many people are promoted during and after Action Learning programmes. Self-report questionnaires indicate that participants see changes in themselves. An illustration can be drawn from a set consisting of participants from a variety of organizations. One member was starting his own business, each stage of the development being discussed by the set. As a result of questioning and assisting, another set member gained the confidence and expertise to start a similar business of his own in a different part of the country; a step he would never have taken prior to his experience with the Action Learning set. Furthermore, there is sometimes a 'cascade effect' when those who have taken part in these programmes start Action Learning sets of their own subordinates. Companies which have had Action Learning programmes come back and ask for more. The method is now in operation worldwide, from Australia, the Far East, to Africa and the United States as well as Europe.

ACTION LEARNING AND LEARNING TO LEARN

Sets are encouraged to take responsibility for their own learning. They can be asked to record their learning experiences in log books. The questioning method is closely related to the learning cycle developed by Honey and Mumford[2] (after Kolb[3]).

HOW IS AN ACTION LEARNING PROGRAMME STRUCTURED?

Obviously there can be many variations depending on the needs of the set. Action Learning can form the basis of a complete MBA programme spread over a full 18 months, as at the International Management Centres (IMC); or it can be used on much shorter programmes focused on specific issues of strategic importance to an organization. Figure 4.7 represents the structure of a short Action Learning programme conducted by Joanna Kozubska on behalf of IMC.

The main thrust of the start-up period was towards the definition of projects, the aim being to assist managers to determine what topics (knowledge, information, skills), should be included in the subsequent meetings to help them undertake their projects. They also discussed the problems they might encounter while working on their project over the following six months. Plans for the remainder of the programme, including any necessary tutor-led sessions during weekend 1 and weekend 2, were drawn up on the basis of these deliberations, although it was necessary to maintain sufficient flexibility to allow for adjustment should new needs arise.

The projects were all successfully completed in time for the final presentations and resulted in detailed marketing plans for two separate divisions of the company, as well as a revised organizational operating structure.

THE LEARNING CYCLE

The Action Learning method necessitates completing the learning cycle many times (see Figure 4.8). It starts with the action or experience and works outwards to identify what needs to be learned (the answers to the questions, What? Why? and How?), rather than putting learning first. Questions are raised and information is gathered to answer them. This process usually generates more questions. The findings are discussed and analysed, possible options are generated and recommendations implemented. The member reports to the set the outcomes (experience) of implementing the recommendations agreed at the last meeting and thus starts off another round of the cycle. The set manage and monitor their own learning and thus they are studying processes as well as outcomes. This constitutes learning to learn which transfers to all aspects of life.

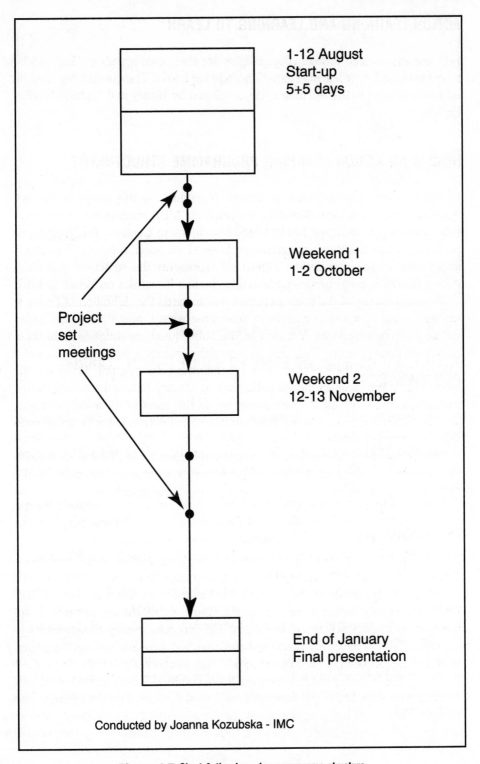

1-12 August
Start-up
5+5 days

Weekend 1
1-2 October

Project
set
meetings

Weekend 2
12-13 November

End of January
Final presentation

Conducted by Joanna Kozubska - IMC

Figure 4.7 Short Action Learning programme structure

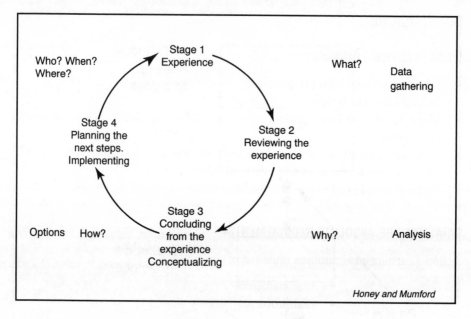

Figure 4.8 The learning cycle

WHAT LESSONS HAVE WE LEARNED ABOUT ACTION LEARNING PROGRAMMES?

Action Learning works. It is exciting, stimulating and makes a lasting impression. It is not an easy option. Sets go through phases of depression as well as of exhilaration. During their low periods, sets sometimes 'blame' the administration, the organizer, or the set adviser, who must be prepared and understand the cause.

Sets are at their most vulnerable at the beginning of the programme until the members have gained confidence in themselves. A good induction, smooth administration and a helpful set adviser are invaluable at this stage.

It is not easy to impart the philosophy of Action Learning in a *P* manner; a practical exercise is more effective.

Any change in the composition of the set represents potential disruption. New members have to be added with great care and only with the 'permission' of the set. In the infrequent event of a member leaving, the balance of the group is disturbed and the members feel uneasy.

Sponsors of programmes must be prepared to give support, a fair hearing to proposals and take action on the projects, otherwise the whole process will be demotivating. Sets often carry on their 'life' long after their initial purpose has been served.

CONCLUSIONS

WHAT IS ACTION LEARNING?

- Learning to take effective action.
- Taking effective action.
- Working on a defined project of reality and significance to the individual concerned.
- Learning through a social process with and from each other in a set.
- Working and learning in a set of 'comrades in adversity'.
- Helping people to learn – not teaching them – set adviser, tutors.

WHAT ARE THE ABSOLUTE REQUIREMENTS?

Action Learning programmes must have:

1. Sets	• real managers • real problems • real time • freedom to criticize, support and advise each other • appropriate help from external specialists/experts.
2. Projects	• a real problem in a real time frame. This becomes the project.
3. Client	• owns the problem • wants a solution • must be committed to Action Learning.
4. Set adviser	• an individual whose task is to facilitate the learning process.
5. Top management	• support.

USE ACTION LEARNING WHEN:

- No one knows the solution to the problem.
- No one knows the way out of the complex situation.

FORGET ACTION LEARNING WHEN:

- Answers are already known.
- The learning is programmable.
- It can be done more cheaply by other means.
- Systematic analysis can give the solution.
- The top person, top group of people are determined to go their own way regardless of outcome.

It is not possible to give a short neat definition of Action Learning. As Pedler so rightly points out, it is 'not really susceptible to the three line encapsulation'.[4] At first sight it appears a simple theory, but the more one becomes engrossed in it, the more one discovers about it. I leave you with a statement by Alan Mumford: 'Action Learning is a phenomenon, a cause, a movement, a theory and a protest'.[5] I commend it to you.

REFERENCES

1 R.W. Revans, *The ABC of Action Learning*, Chartwell-Bratt, 1983.
2 P. Honey and A. Mumford, *Using your Learning Styles*, Honey, Maidenhead, 1983.
3 D. Kolb, I.M. Rubin and J.M. McIntyre, *Organisational Psychology, an Experiential Approach*, Prentice Hall, Englewood Cliffs, NJ, 1974.
4 M. Pedler, *Action Learning in Practice*, Gower, 1983.
5 A. Mumford, 'A Review of Action Learning' in *Management Bibliographies and Reviews*, vol. 11, no. 2, 1985.

5   In Search of *P**

David Sutton

Action Learning's emphasis on *Q* type learning has obscured the need for continual growth in *P* material, both as knowledge in its own right and also as the base from which future *Q* learning can develop. Paradoxically, the rate of change which is the starting point of many of Reg Revans' lectures[1], is the reason why there must be continually increasing quantities of *P* material to use in investigating each problem or opportunity tackled by Action Learning. Increases in the rate of change are fuelled by increases in the knowledge base and every change and every increase in the sum of knowledge opens up further challenges, opportunities and problems.

In the earliest days of my acquaintance with Reg Revans I was irritated by his insistence that each programme should be fully written-up – preferably by the participants. There was I, self-employed with no company or institutional income to back me, completely committed to the value of Action Learning, but painfully aware that it needed five times the selling per unit of income compared with a short course in written or oral communications, in leadership skills or in the skills of negotiation. On top of which the man who was busy whipping the academic establishment with scorpions was insisting on the most academic of exercises – writing up your experiments: a task which had been anathema to me ever since the fourth form when I had difficulty in accounting for the peculiar actions of iron filings when a magnet was passed over them. Admittedly the writing was to be done by the participants but the whipping in, the editing, the proof-reading and all the messy jobs fell to the programme director/set adviser/facilitator who, apart from a two-line acknowledgement, would not even feature in the credits, although he may have written 50 per cent of it himself and rewritten the remainder.

*Originally published in *Industrial and Commercial Training*, vol. 22, no. 1, 1990.

SOURCES OF *P*

As usual, Reg was right – for two reasons. The immediate reason was that you have not truly learned anything until you have written it down and/or presented it in such a way that what you have learned is understood, and, desirably, learned from, by someone else. The second, long-term reason is that anything worthwhile which has been discovered adds to the store of knowledge available for *P* learning. One feature of the rate of change is that *P* learning is no longer enshrined in dusty tomes in libraries. The *Encyclopedie des Arts, Sciences et Métiers* may have included most of the known facts available to civilized eighteenth-century man but modern *P* material, to be of any value and not out of date, is more frequently found in journal articles, conference papers, operational manuals or even papers written as internal working documents and hence unpublished. For example, a recent IMC Action Learning MBA dissertation on computer integrated manufacturing quoted 107 references, only 11 of which came from published books: 87 were from journal articles, conference papers or consultants' handbooks and 9 from internal company papers.

WHAT IS *P*?

What, then, is this *P* material? Where can it be found? How much of it is relevant? How should it be drawn upon? How should it be incorporated into a learning programme? The answer to all these questions must be – it all depends! Depends on the objectives of the programme, the type of participant, the nature of the problem being tackled and the *P* material already available.

It is sometimes forgotten that the archetypal Action Learning programme for management development (*The Fondation Industrie – Université* programme for Advanced Management in Brussels) began with an eight-week academic input[2] and Action Learning Projects International Ltd's (ALP's) later GEC programme in the UK had a two-week formal start-up. These start-ups included an examination of core subjects which, whilst bearing traditional business school titles (e.g. operations, marketing, finance, personnel) were introduced by saying, 'Here is the *P* information – how does it apply in your company?', a significant variation on the theme of, 'Here is the *P* information – take it and use it: it is the Gospel. If needs be, bend real life to fit the *P* model'.

P learning may be part of an Action Learning programme as:

- the background necessary before work can begin on the project
- existing material which can be drawn on when tackling the project
- knowledge and theory to help the Action Learning 'set' to understand the group process working inside the set.[3]

These statements raise another problem: What constitutes appropriate *P* material?

It can range from what is little less than Holy Writ – some would say that the formula defining the coefficient of correlation has more authority than Holy Writ – to a partially substantiated expression of opinion which has no more authority than the intelligent, if sometimes uninformed, expressions of opinion exchanged inside the set.

WHAT MATERIAL TO USE?

The *P* material appropriate to any programme can be in two areas: that which can, and has to be, predicated by the programme designer and that which is called for by the project. The material chosen by the programme designer will depend on the nature of the programme; introductory material may not always be needed. One of the beauties of Action Learning, of which I have written in the past,[4] is the range of applications and the variety of learning situations to which it can be applied. These fall into certain broad categories:

- personal learning combined with problem solving
- individual management development
- management, team or organization development
- academic programmes
- problem solving incorporating personal development.

Any of these may need an introductory programme each of which will be different in content, design and method.

LEARNING TO LEARN

The one common factor will be an introduction to the method of learning. Participants on the programme will usually associate learning with a formal teacher-taught situation which has been cruelly defined as passing information from the textbook of the teacher to the notebook of the student without necessarily passing through the brains of either. This approach of receiving, analysing and interpreting information is deeply instilled in most of us from school, college and university and the breakout into the Revans' 'Alpha, Beta, Gamma' model of problem solving/learning[2] can be a cultural shock. Revans postulates three stages in the managerial learning process:

1. *System Alpha*: the definition of the complex system within which the problem is defined. The components of the definition are the:

- *value system* of the problem solver, usually defined by the culture of his organization
- *external system* surrounding the problem; customers, suppliers, demands of outside bodies etc.
- *internal system*: the resources available to the managers in tackling his problem.

2. *System Beta*: the strategy to be adopted in problem solving, comprising a cycle of:

   survey

   trial

   action

   inspection or audit

   control and follow-up

   corresponding to the stages of the traditional scientific method:

   observation

   hypothesis or theory

   experiment

   inspection

   consolidation.

3. *System Gamma*: the symbiotic relationship between the learning process of the manager and the change process of the organization.

The ideas of learning to learn and of needing to be consciously aware of the learning opportunities which emerge when taking or being involved in action is new to most people. Jerry Colonna (an American radio star of the 1950s) had a catch-phrase, 'You learn something new every day', which is, for most of us, more honoured in the breach than the observance. Some of the thinking of Revans, Kolb and Mumford/Honey is needed to concentrate the participant(s) on the importance of the principles of learning.

THE *P* OF ACTION LEARNING

All Action Learning programmes need an introduction to Action Learning, an explanation of the theory of learning, a model for personal learning and a key to understanding how people work together in groups.

Each programme has this material incorporated into it in its own way. Each tutor's approach demonstrates the way in which he works with the set. The participant is, therefore, subjected to an individual interpretation of what is only one man's theory of learning in the first place. International Management Centres has gone furthest towards codifying and formalizing the Action Learning, learning to learn and learning in the group into a *P* mould. This may be a means whereby important working meetings are prevented from being subjected to Disciple A's version of the truth according to Guru X, and thereby losing sight of the principles of Action Learning.

EACH PARTICIPANT WILL LEARN WITH AND FROM THE OTHERS

One of the fundamental beliefs of Action Learning is that, once in his/her set, each participant will learn with and from the others. They will learn a lot about the subject matter of their project. They will learn something of the skills of finding out, analysing, directing and presenting facts. They will learn the fundamental difference between doing something and talking about doing something. They will learn about working with, and against other people. Most valuable of all, unless they are completely insensitive, they will learn about themselves.[5] Much of this learning will owe more to the sense and the feelings than to the intellect and can only be arrived at by developing a sense of 'awareness' which owes little to *P* and a great deal to *Q*.

THE ROLE OF THE PROJECT

The foundation of all this learning is the project, and except for the rare cases when the problem is in uncharted strategic waters, a great deal of the information from which enquiry, debate and controversy arise will be of a *P* nature. In the earlier diagnostic stage the main sources of information will be *P* learning in all its degrees of certainty from a proven maxim to an inspired piece of conjecture which has found support from a few others. The nature and extent of this *P* learning which can lead the participant into the wonderful world of *Q* will depend on the subject matter of the project. When the project reaches the implementation stage, learning will be largely *Q* but predominantly from Revans' Beta model with its system of survey, trial, action, audit and control.

The desirable variation in *P* learning is demonstrated by two examples from the same programme in the writer's own experience. In one a 55-year-old charge-hand who had left school at 14 had been given as her project the re-design of the sewing room in which she worked. She was an expert in sewing techniques and operating sewing machines but with no supervisory training. Her first piece of *P* learning was four hours' elementary method study tuition. She then started to learn in *Q* style with great effectiveness. On the same programme the company's maintenance engineer embarked on a project in the then newly explored world of terotechnology. Having been put in touch with a university engineering department, he carried out a purely *Q* research project greatly to his own benefit and also to that of the lecturer whose research he helped along.

The strength of Action Learning and the ability of 'comrades in adversity'[1] to learn with and from each other was well demonstrated by this programme. Run for the production team of a medium-sized textile company it included (as well as the charge-hand, and the maintenance engineer) the works manager, a graduate chemist, the 26-year-old personnel manager, the charge-hand's boss and three other middle managers all of whom contributed to the debate and to each other's learning as well as completing projects much to the benefit of the firm.

$Q \rightarrow P$

It follows as night follows day that Q learning, when written up in a report, a dissertation or a thesis, will be available to make its contribution to P. The cautious use of 'available' is justified because the first unvalidated stage of a P contribution would not be academically acceptable as part of the body of P learning. It would merely be the fruits of one man's study of a complex situation and have no more claim to being part of the body of knowledge than other individual unverifiable propositions such as *The General Theory . . ., Das Kapital, Mein Kampf* or *The Theory of Evolution*.

This invalidates nothing. Much midnight oil was doubtless burned in the University of Syracuse and elsewhere before the Archimedean 'Eureka!' became page 27 of Bloggins and Snooks's geometry textbook, the epitome of P learning and the source of innumerable schoolboy jokes.

THE GROWTH OF P

In addition to its most obvious contributions in personal and organizational learning and problem solving, Action Learning can contribute to the world of P learning if:

- Programmes, of all types, are written up, preferably by the seekers and the learners and not by the ancillaries, be they tutors, programme designers, set advisers or academic hangers on.
- Information which can be a foundation for future learning is extracted and published.

Unlike material in the academic tradition, much of this information will only be transient in its usefulness; possibly only used by one or two other action learners in search of answers to practical problems. Compared with the satisfaction of seeing your life's work bound in morocco leather and displayed on the shelves of the Bodleian as *the* definitive work, these additions to the store of knowledge will bring little satisfaction to the writer in search of academic fame. They are, however, in keeping with the spirit of an age when change is so rapid that last year's PC is as old hat as the penny-farthing. Some P will endure, but it will be an infinitesimal fraction of the total information which has been painstakingly gleaned.

This is also in keeping with the times. The new wisdom is disproved on Monday, reproved on Tuesday, replaced on Wednesday, re-interpreted on Thursday, regenerated on Friday, re-assessed on Saturday and hailed as the new Eternal Truth on Sunday.

FOREVER *P*

Whilst acknowledging the value of *Q* in personal, team and organization development and in individual or group learning, the project work from which it arises will frequently start from an evaluation of the available *P* learning. Most projects produce *P* material or potential *P* material which, however ill-formed and ill-defined, could be the starting point for the next project. Any over-emphasis on *Q* which brushes *P* aside might have the effect of throwing out the baby with the bath water.

ACTION LEARNING AND THE FUTURE

One of Action Learning's most valuable contributions to the future may be the enlargement of useful *P* learning and the way in which its growth has been expedited because:

- participants on programmes have used the real, changing world as the source for their learning material
- the number and variety of 'seekers after truth' has been multiplied by using a learning process which is not only available to an academic élite but also draws on contributions from participants from many walks of life and, through them and their projects, on the contributions made by 'set' colleagues, clients, sponsors and, sometimes, their whole organizations.

REFERENCES

1 R.W. Revans, *The Origins and Growth of Action Learning*, Chartwell-Bratt, 1982.
2 R.W. Revans, *Developing Effective Managers*, Praeger, 1971.
3 D. Casey, 'The Role of the Set Adviser', in M. Pedler (ed.), *Action Learning in Practice*, Gower, 1983, ch. 17.
4 D. Sutton, 'A Range of Applications', in M. Pedler, (ed.), *Action Learning in Practice*, Gower, 1983, ch. 5.
5 A. Mumford, *Making Experience Pay*, McGraw-Hill, 1980.

6 Personal and Professional Development*

Cliff Bunning

The quality of the services provided in our community is dependent upon the personal functioning of the service providers. This is especially so with professional services such as education, law, psychology, medicine and accountancy. Although systems and equipment are involved, and do affect the quality of the outcome, professional services are a personal creation of the service provider.

Many services are created on the spot in conjunction with the users of the service, so that performance cannot be subject to quality control procedures of inspection and adjustment. Rather it is a spontaneous creation, reflecting both the personal and the professional functioning, at that point in time, of the person providing the service. Fully rounded professional development must address not only technical, but also personal functioning issues.

THREE TYPES OF LEARNING

There is a long respected model of human functioning that can be applied to human learning and development:

Knowing: Acquiring knowledge and information which can be recalled at will. (What I know)
Doing: Acquiring skills and the ability to do something practical in the real world. (What I do)
Being: Acquiring insight into self and developing desired qualities. (Who I am)

These three categories are relevant to the process of professional development (see Table 6.1).

*Originally published in *Tutor*, vol. 40, 1992.

Type of learning	Outcomes	What it affects	Impacts	Frequency of occurrence
Knowing	Propositions	Awareness	Superficial	Frequent
Doing	Practices	Role behaviour	Development	Periodic
Being	Praxis	Self	Fundamental	Infrequent

Table 6.1 Three types of learning

New information acquired concerning our professional work process is typically in propositional form. It expands our awareness, but is generally a fairly superficial experience, in terms of our overall life and functioning, and hopefully happens fairly frequently.

By contrast, learning involving ourselves is a more fundamental experience, affecting potentially our self-image, our views of the world and some aspects of our values, beliefs or assumptions. It is referred to as the domain of praxis, the functioning behaviour of the practitioner. Naturally it happens more rarely and, for some, not at all in their adult life.

Acquiring additional skills is an intermediate developmental experience which for most professionals occurs periodically and potentially leads to an enhancement of their role behaviour and professional practices.

ACHIEVING PERSONAL AND PROFESSIONAL DEVELOPMENT

Each type of learning has its part to play in our ongoing development as a professional and as a person. Some aspects of how each type of learning is achieved are summarized in Table 6.2.

Type of learning	Main development process	Main prerequisite	Your value to others
Knowing	Information transfer	Attention	Knowledgeable
Doing	Practice/feedback	Persistence	Useful
Being	Reflection/unfolding	Non-defensiveness/ Openness	Role model/Enriching

Table 6.2 Achieving personal and professional development

Learning something (in the sense of 'knowing about' something) typically involves an information transfer process requiring, on our part, attentive behaviours such as listening, watching, interacting or reading. We can also acquire a more fundamental and persuasive knowledge by reflection, a different process, dealt with later.

The result of expanding our *knowing* is that we become knowledgeable on some matter for the benefit of those we serve as a professional. By contrast, acquiring a skill (*doing*) requires practice and feedback. Persistence is the main prerequisite to acquiring a satisfactory proficiency. The effect is that we enhance our usefulness for our clients, because of the value-adding that our new skills provide.

The main development of self involves reflection and unfolding. Rather than something being added, as in acquiring knowledge or skills, the process of personal insight and growth is more one of taking away obstructions so that our essential pristine nature is more evident. These obstructions consist of defensive overlays and are caused by ignorance, fear, low self-esteem or some other effect of previous negative conditioning.

The main prerequisites for personal growth are openness and non-defensiveness, and the effect of such growth is that we provide an enhanced role model for our peers and potential enrichment for clients coming into contact with us, particularly if we work in the human service professions where the contact is of a fairly personal kind.

THE STRATEGIC IMPORTANCE OF BEING

We expect professionals to be knowledgeable and to have an up-to-date awareness of current research and best professional practice in their discipline. We also expect professionals to be skilful, and to be competent in practising their profession. Some professionals meet these expectations, and the more outstanding professionals surpass our expectations.

Because of variation between people, there are some individuals in every profession who do not develop, but rather stay frozen in time as regards their knowledge and skills, and so become increasingly out of date. It is to reduce the incidence of this happening that professional societies and most organizations provide and emphasize ongoing professional development opportunities for their members.

However, being a professional, or more clearly, being professional, involves more than just knowing appropriate propositions and doing appropriate procedures.

The foundation of professional performance is the personal functioning of the professional (praxis). Too often personal belief systems, personal characteristics and the inner world of the professional are left unattended and development avoided. Some professionals regrettably use their autonomy or professional discretion to deflect issues concerning their personal functioning. Yet it is their personal functioning that determines the quality of their relationship with their clients and, ultimately, how they deploy their knowledge and skills.

So learning in the *being* domain is both the most fundamental and also the most strategic for professionals, especially those concerned with human service delivery, such as teachers, doctors, nurses, trainers, psychologists, social workers and consultants. Moreover, it is only when development is taking place in all three domains that the whole person is involved and the development is balanced.

BLOCKS TO LEARNING IN THE *KNOWING* DOMAIN

The immediate blocks to professional learning in the *knowing* domain are many. The more common include:

- complacency and self-satisfaction about one's current functioning
- personal isolation, either physically or psychologically, from the mainstream of professional innovation
- workload pressure, which creates a factory production approach, or
- work occupying a low priority in one's overall life.

Each one of these blockages can be overcome and has been by other professionals. Although it would be possible to list some frequently used resolutions of these difficulties, the best approach if you are experiencing that particular difficulty is to talk the issue through with colleagues. (Misery likes company, so avoid those who have the same problem as you, because they are likely to agree that the problem is insurmountable.)

There are other blocks to getting to know more that arise from the *being* domain and are dealt with later.

BLOCKS TO LEARNING IN THE DOING DOMAIN

The blocks to skill acquisition, or *doing*, often involve some of the following:

- lack of a good role model or mentor
- lack of access to training, because of a perceived shortage of time, money or opportunity
- little organizational commitment to excellence, but rather an organizational acceptance of fairly basic standards of skill, or
- organizational disincentive to experimentation and innovation in professional practice.

These issues are best addressed by networking with those inside or outside your organization who have a development orientation. What is needed is encouragement of your inner-directed search for increased professional competence and innovation, and the development of strategies to address the particular situation. This is best done in a group situation with like-minded people.

As will be indicated in a following section, the belief that skill enhancement can only occur with the support of one's organization is a fallacy and perhaps the biggest block of all to learning. Just as with *knowing*, some of the blocks to innovative *doing* arise from the *being* domain.

BLOCKS TO LEARNING IN THE *BEING* DOMAIN

The blocks to learning in regard to personal functioning, or *being*, can include:

- defensiveness and fear of personal change
- an absence of external pressure to take the plunge
- a lack of clarity about what you should change to and/or how to effect such change, or
- lack of support at work and/or at home for personal change.

Defensiveness in particular not only blocks learning about self, but also makes it much less likely that the professional will make the most of learning opportunities in the *knowing* and *doing* domains as well. The reason is that low or conditional self-esteem has pervasive negative effects through all aspects of our functioning.

The pathways to personal growth are many and varied. They can be triggered by reading from the enormous range of literature available, attending personal growth workshops, spiritual unfolding or acquiring counselling. We can also acquire a mentor or seek feedback.

Personal growth is a direction we travel, more than a destination we arrive at, and so it is enough that we are moving in the right direction. Expecting that all problems can be solved in the short term is not realistic, but many have found that even some improvement at the *being* level has a beneficial effect, because it diffuses through all levels of one's behaviour, personal and professional.

THE SOURCE OF LEARNING

For as long as we associate learning with formally organized educational experiences such as workshops, conferences and higher degrees, our development will be a relatively rare occurrence in our professional life, dependent on finance, time and the availability of experts to create our learning for us.

Professionals who have a vision of whole-of-life learning have broken out of that mould and recognize that it is life itself that is the richest source of potential learning, including one's professional work experiences. However, a life not reflected on is not a rich source of learning. In such a case only the grosser and more traumatic events invade our consciousness and demand a change in our assumptions or future strategy.

And so the prerequisite for whole-of-life professional learning is to be committed to a whole-of-life developmental praxis. This is achieved by becoming a reflective practitioner,[1] because it is via the reflection and generalization process that insight and internalization takes place and future practice benefits. In this sense, it is true that you can learn very little from others in life, you must learn things for yourself.

Although this is fundamentally a personal and inner process, it can be helped greatly if our colleagues and the norms of the organizational culture in which we practise are supportive of openness, self-critiquing, challenge, reflection and experimentation. So what is the most desirable is that not only you as an individual professional, but also the collective of professionals around you and the organization from which you operate, are committed to learning, so creating a learning organization, or at least, a learning enclave.[2]

Development is ultimately a personal matter and is a path that we can tread in the company of the few, if not the many. The desirable situation is when your development as a person and your development as a professional are experienced as two sides of the one coin, with both taking place as a natural result of your conducting your professional life in a reflective and self-appraising manner.

CONGRUENCY, ALIGNMENT AND INTEGRATION

As we approach deeper levels of personal and professional development we find that the relationship between the *knowing*, *doing* and *being* elements in our life changes. In the early stages they are separate, and so are often not very well aligned. We may *know* (and believe) that smoking is bad for our health yet still smoke (*doing*). Or we may have mastered a sophisticated range of interpersonal skills for our professional *doing* role and yet, in our personal life when we are out of role (*being* ourselves), we may function in a much more basic way. We may behave with our family in ways that we would never dream of behaving with clients.

So an important stage of personal and professional development is when the *knowing*, *doing* and *being* aspects of your life begin to merge into one congruent whole – what you know and what you do is a deep reflection of who you are. If you have experienced this, you will possibly agree with me that when all elements of your functioning begin to be aligned, you experience a sense of inner coherence and seemingly endless amounts of energy. This is the energy that was previously used up in doubts, self-criticism and internal 'wars' between parts of self.

THE NEXT STAGE OF PROFESSIONAL DEVELOPMENT

The concepts of *knowing*, *doing* and *being* can be taken at face value as referring to our knowledge, skills and personal functioning, in the way that they have been so far in this chapter.

However, each of these concepts is really a signpost to more fundamental issues which have an even greater significance for the quality of our personal and professional functioning. This deeper stage tends to emerge naturally if we are making progress in our development and achieving a degree of congruence and integration between what we know, what we do and what we are as people and professionals.

KNOWING

Knowing is a state beyond mere possession and marshalling of facts and information. At a deeper level, it involves an intuitive, non-verbal awareness and increased understanding of ourselves, others and the situations that occur in life. It occurs unconsciously as we function and is best described as intuitive insight or wisdom.

Flawless perception (another term for the same process) emerges progressively as we reduce the distortions we ourselves create when seeing the intrinsic nature of the people and events around us. These distortions come from the mental maps we have and from attachment, ego-driven desires and an over-developed tendency to be judgemental. We all have the capacity to be wise, and increasingly become so, as we progressively remove the impediments to our own natural insight.

DOING

Doing is likewise more than the technical application of previously acquired skills. It raises, at a more fundamental level, the impact and worth of all that we do (personally and professionally). Issues such as ethics, clients' interests and social contribution inevitably become emergent in our awareness as we become more developed as people. The basic question raised is 'What is the meaning and significance of what I do?'

We all have the capacity to be ethical and concerned for the welfare of others and our surroundings. As the meeting of our own needs become less problematic, self-interest recedes as a high priority item in our awareness. We become more sensitive to the importance of our behaviour and our work for others and increasingly get our satisfaction from a sense of service and contribution.

BEING

Rather than only relating to the effectiveness of our personal functioning, *being* has, as its underlying issue, how appropriate and enlightened the values are that we are acting out. Who am I? and What is the message to be derived from my life? When we become more alive to the issues of *being*, reasons and logic drawn from past events or desired future goals lose their grip on our thinking. We realize that the past and the future are just concepts – there is only the eternal present in which to act, and that it is my actions now that create my past and my future.

When we reach this level of development we still think of the past occasionally with affection, but we do not harbour grudges from past events or relive painful experiences. Of course we plan for the future (short term and longer term), but our planning is, in fact, acting in the present. What we do not do is fantasize about the future in a way that leads us to avoiding dealing with issues in the present or terrorize ourselves about possible future problems, whilst doing nothing in the present to avoid those situations occurring in the future.

Another characteristic of development at this level is that we do not let *doing* issues overwhelm *being* issues. In other words, we are not so driven by goal achievement needs that we miss the significance of what someone is saying or feeling, or do not have time to notice the flowers in the park. The quality of our lives, rather than the quantity of our achievements, becomes of increasing importance.

THE OVERALL PROCESS OF DEVELOPMENT

The process of ongoing personal and professional development, as outlined here, can be summarized by Figure 6.1.

Work is never completed at any of the levels, and so the process of personal and professional development typically involves repeated incremental cycling through the various aspects, even for a person of many years of experience. The sign of development is that there is some progress at all three levels, as many professionals function only at the operational level, and any development that does take place for them is limited to information acquisition and occasional skill development.

The vision of a fully developed professional that emerges from these considerations is of people who are integrated and congruent within themselves and who act with discrimination so that their actions benefit not only the people they serve but also contribute to their ongoing personal unfolding, including their ongoing growth in knowledge and skills and progressively greater amounts of congruency and integration. Inevitably by their presence and behaviour such people also trigger similar opportunities for those they come in contact with.

69

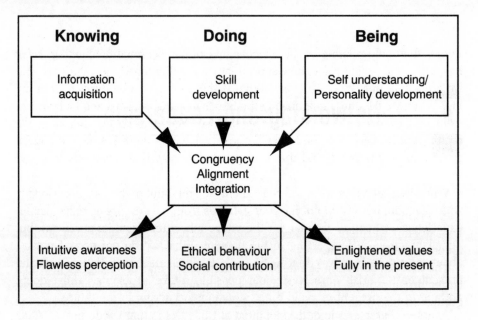

Figure 6.1 The overall process of development

The personal unfolding is the ultimate and deepest purpose of professional development. How to achieve it is something we must find for ourselves, but the important thing is that pathways exist for those who seek them.

REFERENCES

1 D.A. Schon, *The Reflective Practitioner. How Professionals Think in Action*, Basic Books Inc., New York, 1983.
2 C.R. Bunning, 'Turning experience into learning: the strategic challenge for individuals and organizations' in *Training and Development in Australia*, vol. 18, no. 4, 1991, pp. 5–9 (see Chapter 8).

7 Networking and Leadership*

Gordon Wills

'Networking' is a term now widely used to describe two contemporary organizational empowerment phenomena, both superficially the same but, in fact, fundamentally divergent.

The first phenomenon is a deliberate extension of matrix management within larger organizations, that gives increased importance to cross-functional work groups focusing on corporate outputs.[1,2] Such networks are empowered to energize the sclerotic enterprise and, in many cases, have achieved the seemingly impossible. They are the sociological equivalent of the intrapreneurship movement launched by Pinchot.[3] Huey calls it the 'age of post-heroic leadership'.

The second phenomenon does not originate within large organizations at all. It is a coalition of separate individuals voluntarily working together to achieve a common purpose or goal and who, in order to achieve that, are prepared to empower some among themselves to act as leaders and catalysts in the best interests of the network.[4]

The similarity between the two phenomena lies in their rejection of hierarchical and functional models of organization, based on authority and specialist expertise respectively. In place of these models 'networking' places the market as the engine of organizational purpose.[5,6] The marketplace and the customers within it who have transactions with the network determine who shall be involved for any particular purpose and how the relationship shall be focused to be conducted effectively.

The fundamental difference between the two phenomena is that socio-intrapreneurship seeks to make the large organization work better to help it to regenerate itself, while the socio-entrepreneur has no wish to live or work in a large enterprise at all. The networked socio-entrepreneurs are combined to achieve a democratically shared purpose. They also accept that it is their own responsibility to disengage from the network whenever its purpose can no longer be personally shared either temporarily or permanently.

The difference can be clarified using Pinchot's most memorable Law of Intrapreneurship – 'Come to work every day willing to be fired'. It implies that you

*Originally published in *Leadership and Organization Development Journal*, vol. 15, no. 7, 1994.

have an employer who has your fate in his hands. The networked individual reserves the right to hire and fire to himself alone.

This chapter will review what has been learned and published lately about the realities of networking both amongst socio-intrapreneurs and socio-entrepreneurs. But, most importantly, it will review the processes of leadership involved – be they delegated downwards by fits of empowerment in the large organization or serendipitously created in the democratic framework of the network of socio-entrepreneurs.

Such purposes are strictly selfish to the faculty and graduate members of International Management Centres, a network of socio-entrepreneurs. They must currently exercise their responsibilities as electors of their second generation of leaders. And it is ironic but not perhaps paradoxical that the task of undertaking this review should have fallen to myself as a first-generation leader. My first generation has refused to find its successors. We have challenged the network to decide for itself who might best lead them within a framework of their shared goals. But I have personally accepted their return challenge to draft a job specification and an induction guide for our successors. They assert that the first generation's insights linked to an evaluation of published literature is potentially highly valuable not only for their own purposes but also for networks more widely. The literature is replete with success stories, often journalistically presented. There is a dearth of insider critical analysis of the downside problems, or balanced advice on the issues.

THE CURRENT NATURE OF IMC AS A NETWORK

The origins and evolutionary growth of International Management Centres (IMC) as a network have been described in detail already.[7] Since 1992 we have progressed from a coerced network, through co-ordination to a nascent co-operative.[8]

IMC is now a socio-entrepreneurial network with the shared goal of helping managers to learn how to be more effective and to act on that learning. Below is the statement widely communicated within the network.

IMC'S PHILOSOPHY OF MANAGEMENT ACTION LEARNING

IMC aims to assist in the development of effective managers by designing a learning process which is both intellectually stretching and founded on the real problems and opportunities facing managers in their own environment. We call it Action Learning.

The key conceptual and practical framework for this is provided through:

- a diagnosis of the issues on which managers have to be effective in their work environment and the necessary competences
- a learning partnership between IMC and the client organization
- channelling developmental processes through taking action on real problems
- positive help to individuals on their personal learning processes to aid current and continued development.

The main outcomes of IMC's approach are:

- improved effectiveness of managers in their current and future jobs and thereby in their personal careers
- learning benefits to individual organizations and eventually to national economies through productive work on organizational objectives, opportunities and problems
- a continuous contribution to the body of knowledge and the identification of desirable actions on the effective combination of real work and managerial learning.

To achieve that shared goal IMC has evolved design, marketing, delivery and evaluation programmes that are based on an educational philosophy known as Action Learning. In line with the market and customer focus of networks IMC requires its students (known as associates) to specify their curriculum issues that shall be the vehicles for learning. Once these are manifest, the appropriate individuals within the network to achieve the goal are brought together as the tutorial team.

Such an approach is well distanced from the traditional hierarchical or functional models of management education and development which assert that the faculty know best as experts, and as ones in authority. Students are there to learn what the academy believes should be learnt.

Without the creation of a network approach, Action Learning programmes cannot be delivered, market focus cannot be the goal. The concept is perhaps closest to relationship marketing.[9]

Any network member making the sale of an Action Learning programme knows he can call on other members to assist in its delivery and evaluation. To make the sale in the first instance, he will have relied on network members to assist in the design and marketing activities. This neatly, but oversimplistically, dichotomizes the leadership processes in IMC. The programmes have first to be sold, and second, tutored. The oversimplification arises because a sale can take place only if the customer has very reasonable expectations of effective delivery, and the tutorial can be efficiently accomplished only if the right programme has been designed and marketed in the first place. As such, goal achievement for the network depends greatly on how the two elements support and strengthen one another rather than pull apart, notwithstanding the clear truth that those who most powerfully deliver and evaluate programmes are seldom those with the skills or understanding to design or market them to the same high level, and vice versa.

Such potential for misunderstanding and failure to appreciate disparate skills and their vital contribution to effective functioning of the network is exacerbated when IMC delivers programmes for awards at Bachelor, Master and Doctoral levels. Evaluation in those particular circumstances is, of necessity, outside the formalized network in the hands of 'external' examiners. 'Standards' that are all too frequently of the functional, not market-focused, variety are applied.

IMC has one further dimension, which is the inescapable outcome of its adoption of Action Learning as its educational philosophy. It designs, markets, delivers and evaluates its programmes wherever the market might wish. And over the past 12 years that has meant 31 different countries from Finland to New Zealand, Hong Kong to Argentina – in four different languages.

Any suitably committed entrepreneur is readily welcomed into IMC's socio-entrepreneurial network, provided that he is willing to be appropriately inducted and to abide by the network's rule book as it exists from time to time. This network discipline, obviously of vital significance to the cohesion of the network, is not intended to be oppressive. As soon as a new member has been inducted he becomes a fully participating member in the formulation of all future policies and practices, which are incorporated in IMC's rule book, known as the Conspectus. All network officers are specifically elected by one or other of the governing bodies – the Council or the Common Multinational Academic Board.

WHY NETWORKING NOW?

There seems to be considerable unanimity in the literature on networking that it is the next or coming pattern of organization for most if not all of us at work.[10] It is argued that economies of scale can no longer outweigh the fleetness of foot that a network affords. The network is a hypersensitive ecosystem, responding by shedding or taking on resources on an almost daily basis without the baggage of employment contracts, or politicization of decision making. New skills can be accrued almost overnight to tackle whatever challenges might arise.

Not only does the speed of change in the competitive and technological environments of any enterprise make flexible responses an imperative for success, however. The human resource movement argues most convincingly that the better and better-educated individuals seeking employment are unwilling to subordinate themselves to anything less than a work activity that engages their intellect. After all, most non-intellectual activities can be and are being automated in our current era.

However, writing from the inside of a socio-entrepreneurial network that has evolved a very long way since its original coerced launch in 1982, the downside issues are very tough indeed. All networks have to hold their members together by vision and shared purpose – a familiar enough observation in an hierarchical or traditional enterprise. The greater significance of the challenge of vision and shared purpose in a network is that, unless it is very strongly projected, members simply melt away. They do not continue to come to an office every day. To get the vision and shared purpose up and running in the first place, and to sustain it in a coherent fashion, is as improbable a goal as it has been discerned to be for Peters and Waterman's original 'excellent' companies.

Continuous renewal is the inescapable requirement in a network.[6] This requires, as elsewhere, a willingness to let good ideas occur anywhere at any level. The network leader must see his role as facilitating any and every one to be able to work their ideas into the network; searching for kindred spirits who want to share their pursuit.

Charan[11] describes this restlessness as the necessary social architecture of a network. A robust network does not imply harmony among members. More frequently it will be characterized by heated debate and legitimate disagreements. Network leaders must see their responsibilities as to encourage such ferment, and they must have the strength to get the network through it and out the far side to a renewed understanding of shared purpose.

Enthusiasm for the network at any time will be a measure of the extent to which its members feel an intense benefit from belonging and value the quality of interaction they achieve when they come together. This does not mean that networks need to reach agreement on every aspect of their vision or goals. But it does mean that they need the highest professional alignment on specific tasks.

At IMC the intensity of the debate and argument is clearly noticeable, particularly during the first working sessions together of each main get-together. It all gushes out – the new ideas, the criticisms, the injustices. Only when these have been addressed, if not resolved, can the network settle down to mature debate and find its common ground for the next phase of its activities.

We have learnt from ancient times that democratic institutions are well lubricated by bread and circuses. For us the bread takes the form of a shared understanding of how each can be a more effective tutor or salesman of Action Learning programmes. The circuses are our annual multinational congregations and local admissions ceremonies, the latter accompanied by robes and formal certificates.

While our multinational spread of activities has made regular, sustained communication almost impossible until recently, we have used the circus magnetism of our twelve annual ceremonial congregations and, for six years now, mid-year annual professional congresses to encourage, even structure, a plethora of fringe meetings.

FACILITATING MULTINATIONAL COMMUNICATIONS

I say 'until recently' because, as a result of upward pressure from Australian and Dutch members, IMC has pioneered the first multinational two-level Bulletin Board System (BBS) in any academic institution. Our electronic Atherton Intelligence System (AIS) (see Figure 7.1) enables any member of the network to access any other member, anywhere in the world. It has transformed the up-to-dateness of all resources offered to faculty, graduates or associates worldwide, and gives the opportunity for effective upward suggestions for network development for the first time.

Such seemingly trivial matters as up-to-date address and telephone/fax numbers, which are an eternal problem for any multinational organization, cease to be problems. Data's integrity improves as well as its quality and timeliness. But most importantly of all, the centre loses all perceived need to coerce. Our electronic BBS truly makes our network multinational in substance as well as name and its leaders have the wherewithal to listen and learn. From that learning they can discern how to orchestrate regeneration and with whom, or in what coalition.

If addresses and telephone/fax data can be mistakenly construed as trivial, the quality and relevance of intellectual support provided to managers cannot. For many years faculty and associates worldwide have, in the best traditions of any growing multinational organization, claimed that all guidance was skewed towards the culture of those who were concerned, albeit on the entire network's behalf, to create it. Using the AIS we are all now able, at no greater interval than one month (and less if it is of major urgency), to comprehend, respond if necessary or simply observe the divergent situations making their own decisions on these matters. Those officers charged with assessing the quality of learning programmes within the network are indeed more able so to do by monitoring divergence and cultural adaptation than they were in the days when we all really pretended that everyone was doing the same thing.

And of course the great strength of understood diversity is that it triggers lateral thoughts in our own contexts. The Singaporean members of IMC evolved, along US lines for example, our pattern of adult bachelor studies that was eventually taken up in Hong Kong, Macau and Finland, then South Africa and finally the UK. Each application was different but the confidence of success elsewhere encouraged change which, in each case, led the market concerned. What was true for the Bachelor programmes has been equally true for doctoral studies and Masters both of Business Administration and of Philosophy in Training and Development. It has even been true for the reorientation of banking cultures from transaction focus to customer focus starting in England, spreading to Australia, then back to Ireland and thence to Malaysia.[12] Each and every application was different but the network contribution was most substantial. In

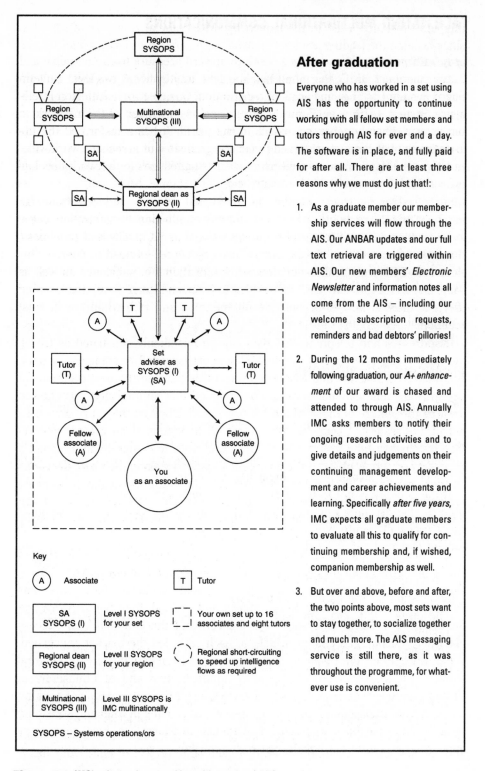

After graduation

Everyone who has worked in a set using AIS has the opportunity to continue working with all fellow set members and tutors through AIS for ever and a day. The software is in place, and fully paid for after all. There are at least three reasons why we must do just that!:

1. As a graduate member our membership services will flow through the AIS. Our ANBAR updates and our full text retrieval are triggered within AIS. Our new members' *Electronic Newsletter* and information notes all come from the AIS – including our welcome subscription requests, reminders and bad debtors' pillories!

2. During the 12 months immediately following graduation, our *A+ enhancement* of our award is chased and attended to through AIS. Annually IMC asks members to notify their ongoing research activities and to give details and judgements on their continuing management development and career achievements and learning. Specifically *after five years*, IMC expects all graduate members to evaluate all this to qualify for continuing membership and, if wished, companion membership as well.

3. But over and above, before and after, the two points above, most sets want to stay together, to socialize together and much more. The AIS messaging service is still there, as it was throughout the programme, for whatever use is convenient.

Figure 7.1 IMC's electronic networking with two-level BBS

this latter instance it led to the launch by IMC's official publisher of what has since become the leading academic journal in the area, the *International Journal of Bank Marketing*.

Perhaps most fascinating of all has been the way in which the IMC network has responded to the challenge of 'educational quality assurance'. It certainly also spawned another very successful journal, *Educational Quality Assurance*, but it has brilliantly demonstrated the quality definition 'fitness for purpose'. In a traditional academic world, using peer-group review to arrive at a consensus of purpose, IMC's far-flung multinationalism shouted boldly that 'purpose' had no end of definitions! MBA Associates can, for example, be seeking to become more effective managers in the South African context of black economic empowerment; in a South Pacific island seeking offshore investors and World Bank finance; or in a first-world economy struggling for marginal market share improvements or at the leading edge of technology. As a network we are united in insisting that the questions are the same: how to be more effective managers? Yet our answers will be very different depending on the context in which we must be effective. The measure of quality will be how well they suit their contextual management purpose.

FINANCING THE NETWORK

Throughout its history IMC's network has addressed its funding challenges with enthusiasm and some ingenuity! More than £30 million of sales have been generated, and the overall risks of the network have been broadly shared. Nonetheless, the overwhelming conclusion must be that networking still constitutes an almost insolubly great financing challenge.

If the network is not to be coercive each member must be self-financing and able to exercise independent judgement about participation. The challenge is most especially acute when any long-term investment issues arise. How can patient finance be mobilized without transforming the patterns of relationships within the network? How, in other words, can the benefits of equity finance be achieved in what is not perceived as a permanent enterprise? This constitutes a vital question for the future of all networks.

The answers that have emerged thus far[13] indicate that, while project financing is readily available and/or factoring of debtors, these do not assist long-term development. Major customers have sometimes helped here with long-term contracts to use as collateral for debt financing from banks, with settlements direct to the lending institution. Additionally, a number of instances of minority equity stakes have been reported, held by a few key clients. It is suggested that these can amount to sufficient funding in the effective network for all its needs, because networks expand or contract by definition to meet such changes as they confront. It does inescapably mean, however, that each large project or endeavour has to be financed *de nouveau* rather than by a board of management having share-holders' funds available to finance a portfolio of projects. It returns much of the top management function back to the marketplace. Such an outcome can be either a huge drag on development or a fillip depending on the competence and skill the network has at marshalling its case for project funding and delivering the targeted returns. Networking is, accordingly, an extremely harsh financial environment, and a high rate of failure must be envisaged. But networks are designed to be able to accommodate such problems, regrouping, reassembling, wiser than before about what can be achieved and how. Kensinger and Martin draw a close comparison between networking today and the medieval Hanseatic League.

IMC addressed these issues by establishing a not-for-profit central hub, with service contracts to three substantial network members who together had a wide spread of equity, i.e. we created a fluctuating equity-based partnership structure. These broad-ranging service companies took the risk out of the fluctuating fortunes of a wide spread of members right across the world. They were also able to act as a source of medium/long-term finance for the develop-ment of network assets. The official publisher, MCB University Press, which for a long while coerced the network, did so by providing the finance to create the Action Learning course materials and access to the body of knowledge on an up-to-date basis via the 130 journals which it publishes globally. Its offices worldwide also offered shared space, and it invested in a dedicated property in the UK. Five network members owned the publishing house between them.

The other two major sources of investment are geographically based – IMC (Europe and Africa) and IMC (Asia Pacific). They search for and encourage the development of locally based network members, earning a percentage share of sales for their efforts. Share ownership is open to any network member, and upwards of 40 participate currently. Most network members, however, are not highly capitalized and deploy what they do have available for the development of their own local network interests in a single country or even for a discrete product level within that country. Each finds the locus of investment with which he is most comfortable, and much debate takes place about the relative fairness of the margins and returns in the network.

At all levels there have been feast years and famine years, so none claims that the allocations are unfair in any substantial way in the medium term. The balance of advantage, as in all channel structures, really lies in ensuring that the cake to be shared is first maximized. Much thought and a great deal of subsequent discipline has gone into seeking to ensure that this is the focus. The centre (SYSOPS as it is now called) is very lean indeed, and able to invest in the medium- and long-term development of the network only if sales are achieved among the grassroots members. SYSOPS income is volume related and must, accordingly, do all it can to facilitate volume sales, and repeat sales arising from quality services delivered.

On the half-dozen occasions when one or other network member collapsed leaving liabilities (now largely avoided through insistence on the bonding of programme fees), the best interests of the other network members one way or another have caused them to act to ensure that customers received full value as contracted.

NETWORK ROLES AND CULTURAL EVOLUTION

Snow et al.[4] characterize the managerial or leadership roles in networks as 'brokering'. Any individual's leadership has two clear components – the role structure and the effectiveness with which a given individual plays the allocated role. While the Atherton Intelligence System (AIS) developed in IMC certainly reinforces roles and facilitates communications between network members (see Figure 7.1), it can do no more than that.

Snow et al. perceive three broking activities. The first, and in many ways the most influential in the accomplishments of the network, is its architect. It is the true socio-entrepreneurial role described at the outset of this chapter and, like all entrepreneurial processes must be concerned for the success of absolutely every element within the network. The total architecture must of itself be a pleasure to behold, but the design must also be wholly functional for the purposes of those who live with it.

The architect coaxes others into the network, at all levels and in all manner of roles and relationship. They join wholeheartedly only if the vision is one with which they can identify and, if needs be, amend. Furthermore, because the environment in which the network grows and flourishes is necessarily so dynamic and so flexible, the role of architect is a continuous one, or certainly seems that way. Remember, the network has none of the accustomed financial stabilities of the equity-financed enterprise, with its patient investors. The network is only as successful as its last match! So architects must be restless, always and forever seeking to adapt to the emerging situation while at the same time giving a vital semblance of order for those seeking at any moment to lead in operational and caretaking roles in the network. These are the two other critical roles which Snow et al. identify. Their analysis of how all interact bears very close resemblance to contemporary analytical work on successful teams.[14]

The invisible architect for any network will always be its marketplace, its customers.[15] But it is on the interpretation of what those phenomena require in product and service terms that Snow et al. are focusing. For IMC such architecture is encouraged out in the markets in discussion with customers. The seemingly apparent architects at dean and principal levels cannot really be said to hold that role. It is their role rather to unleash the network, not control it.[16] Any and every network member in contact with the marketplace and with customers must, within appropriate yet flexible and adaptive bounds, have the skill and the discretion to commit the network to a design. He must know that important new designs can and will be evaluated, evolved and supported by colleagues to a guaranteed service response level. He must know what constitutes a 'substantive' and a 'non-substantive' variation because, in the latter case, the network has the capability for virtually immediate response, with discretion at the customer interface. No network member sitting away from that interface may second guess what the customer needs or wants.

The challenge for the dean and principal is to make sense of the myriad market- and customer-derived communications inwards and to accommodate them as speedily as possible within the vision. Ironically the extent to which new ideas are readily accommodated within the vision depends on how clearly the vision is understood throughout the network at any node, at any moment in time.

The main misunderstandings and most heated debates arise between network members who have joined with extant institutional and cultural baggage that gets in the way of their embracing the network. It is the well-known phenomenon of culture clash which, for networks to survive, must be expeditiously and healthily resolved.[17] Two network cultures cannot be sustained albeit that a new synthesized culture must often result when we are able to learn well from our arriving members. There are few more revealing critiques of any institutional framework available than those proffered by an incoming intelligentsia as they seek to understand why and how the structure they have joined actually works. They bring to their critique insights born of different cultures. The sentient network watches, listens and learns. So far as possible it accommodates as well, seeking the win–win synthesis.

This was well learned indeed in IMC when first the Canadian School of Management (CSM) then Business School Nederland (BSN) acceded to IMC's common multinational academic board. The CSM showed us how to provide Action Learning adult Bachelor programmes based on experiential learning already gained. The BSN proposed and spurred our development of the AIS worldwide and with it the concept of 'action distance learning'. Sets held fewer face-to-face meetings, overcoming the very real problems of regular attendances for busy managers, but we were nevertheless strongly sustaining the peer-group support process of Action Learning electronically.

The need to synthesize as you watch, listen and learn has been overwhelmingly driven home to us in South Africa. IMC's mandate there is to empower black faculty and black managers despite their lack of normally anticipated prior experience or education in all too many cases. The nation's history simply has not afforded a traditional preparation and its future is not prepared to, indeed could not, wait.

Such learning opportunities will forever appear at all network nodes, of course, provided that the network members have constructively joined the network rather than devoted their time to fighting a rearguard action. The greater the discretion accorded to the network nodes within a framework of trust, the more opportunities to learn will arise.

The formal functioning of the network is not of course, the regular concern of its architects. The main functional roles are perceived as lead operator and caretaker. The first, the lead operator, certainly is a leader within the framework created by the architects, assembling the members to deliver and quality assure programmes. The caretakers are those individuals with especial concern to uphold and maintain the dignity and integrity of the network. They will be followers of the lead operators in the specific delivery of programmes but will have a unique role in developing and maintaining systems and sharing information, e.g. the AIS and IMC's registry databases, facilitating the ceremonial congregations and annual professional congresses, ensuring faculty training, induction, and five-year continuing professional renewal all take place. Ultimately the caretaker's emotions will be aroused most when disloyalty is perceived – when network members exploit the network for their own short-term gain at the expense of other actual or potential members.[18] The caretaker here will point out the dysfunctionality present and seek disciplinary measures to protect its reputation. They are those who believe that a network can function effectively only on the basis of trust.[19]

Sucessful lead operators are those who are visibly even-handed in their role play. Successful and acceptable caretakers do not overplay their hand. But IMC's 12-year history has been replete with examples of great successes and failures in both roles. Mature networks, and mature network members, can and do discuss and review how to overcome such dysfunctionality – on a regular basis – because the problem never goes away. It is endemic to networking no matter how many rules the mature network adopts.

MAJOR CAUSES OF NETWORK FAILURES

There can be little doubt that liberation management[20] has powerful appeal in many countries across the world – and networking is what the liberated manager (or democrat) engages in. Nevertheless, there are great downsides to the construct. Miles and Snow[21] who have been closely concerned as scholars with tracking the emergence and rise of networks, believe the most likely forecast is that their effectiveness will decline over time. Much of their reasoning has been trailed already in this chapter, but the value of their contribution is that they codify the main causes of failure:

1. First and foremost, any network has a life-cycle for any given vision or set of visionaries. To continue it must change, either by evolution or with a discontinuity. Its maturing architects must know how to facilitate the quest for their successors.

2. As networks become mature, the lead operator and caretaker roles, while vital to carry forward the projects concerned, will seek to institutionalize the network and constrain its market and customer responsiveness and flexibility. This, in its turn, will lead to disaggregation and loose coupling within the network unless the network is in a stable environment – which it seldom will be. Amidst calls for discipline the inspired networkers will frequently be heard either sounding the retreat or encouraging greater nodal autonomy to dissipate frustrations and release functional energies.
3. Networkers who do not fully understand the nature of the processes involved will make two kinds of subtle mistake: first, the extension of networking beyond the limits of its capability and, second, the modification of its form in such a way as to modify its operating logic. IMC has many examples of these subtle mistakes.
4. Dominant and coercive members are a necessary evil within any network. Successful networks only allow transitory coercion based on functional contribution to the network's purposes. They are quick to ensure heated debate when dysfunctionality occurs. Paradoxically, therefore, network architects need to be strong personalities but also extensive plagiarists of other members' ideas throughout the network. They must use situational role power to allow members close to the market and customers to flourish.
5. Sub-networks, or 'bow-ties', may develop within a network, engaging in secretive behaviours and excessive legalism, particularly where competition for markets and customers occurs. Successful networks must develop and uphold processes that avoid such dangers and respond speedily to whatever circumstances give rise to them in the first instance. Fairness, openness and trust, what Limerick[22] has described as the *amicitia* of the network, must be upheld and be seen to be upheld.

CONCLUSION

Socio-entrepreneurial networks may well be an intangible asset so far as accounting convention goes, but their relevance as an organizational form for citizens of the twenty-first century seems inescapable. Not only do they promise a liberated if tough workplace, but they have the ability to regenerate themselves without anything like the trauma associated with the downsizing or collapse of the traditional equity-based corporation of the twentieth century. In an age of rapidly changing environments based on superior intelligence more rapidly diffused, this alone is enough to ensure a real future.

Nevertheless, there are many managerial challenges involved, many of which have been familiar in the literature and to practitioners for decades – networks simply aggregate them differently.

The human resource movement has championed the individual's self-development and contribution in the workplace for many decades. Outsourcing, subcontracting, value-added channel management and procurement are all well-researched and understood issues. It is not in these areas, therefore, that the balance is most disturbed. It is in the fields of strategic purpose and funding that it is most considerably altered, where the discontinuities are greatest.

They are deeply interactive. The challenges of network financing are derived from the transitoriness of projects and tasks within the network vision. And strategic purpose is normally quite limited in its scope.

Sanity in the exciting chaos of networking will surely come to those architects who can best envision processes of rolling strategies and vision regeneration, with rolling funding to support them. The likelihood that a network can evolve into anything as stable as the traditional equity-based corporation is a contradiction in terms. If such stability is possible, the distinctive competences of networks will not command a premium. The architects must, without doubt, facilitate network funding if their visions are to be realized, either personally or in tandem with fellow networkers who clearly know how. The 'hollow corporation', as the network has been called, needs the sap to rise just like all other human endeavour, or its leaves and branches will fall.

My own network, IMC, has chosen to confront its challenge of vision succession by rearranging its marketplace position. It resolved first and as it transpired inappropriately, to link with a leading managerial consultancy enterprise. This incident has been described already.[7] Not deterred, it has now again sought out a large, potentially dominating partnership from the university sector to reflect the aspirations and expectations of the market and its customers. The wisdom gained from the previous failure has been deployed to seek a win–win relationship with the university sector. IMC's multinational network and its AIS electronic communications can greatly extend the work of any university; and IMC's work can at the same time be most considerably enhanced.

Only time can tell how well such strategic and financial envisaging will be. What is clear is that networks must use their ability to change shape to meet their market and customers' needs as the primary tool for securing their own futures.

REFERENCES

1 S. Feneuille, 'A Network Organisation to meet the Challenges of Complexity' in *European Management Journal*, vol. 8, no. 3, 1990, pp. 296–301.

2 J. Huey, 'The New Post-heroic Leadership' in *Fortune*, 21 February 1994, pp. 42–50.

3 G. Pinchot, *Intrapreneuring*, Harper & Row, New York, NY, 1985.

4 C.C. Snow, R.E. Miles and H.J. Coleman, 'Managing 21st Century Network Organisations' in *Organisational Dynamics*, vol. 20, no. 3, 1992, pp. 5–20.

5 S. Ghoshal and C.A. Bartlett, 'The Multinational Corporation as an Interorganisational Network' in *Academy of Management Review*, vol. 15, no. 4, 1990, pp. 603–25.

6 T. Theuerkauf, 'Reshaping the Global Organisation' in *McKinsey Quarterly*, no. 3, 1991, pp. 102–19.

7 G. Wills, 'Managing Networking' in *Scandinavian International Business Review*, vol. 1, no. 3, 1992, pp. 52–70.

8 B. Johannisson, 'Beyond Process and Social Structure: Social Exchange Networks' in *International Studies of Management and Organisation*, vol. XVII, no. 1, 1987, pp. 3–23.

9 D. Blankenburg and J. Johannson, 'Managing Network Connections in International Business' in *Scandinavian International Business Review*, vol. 1, no. 1, 1992, pp. 5–19.

10 M. Watson, 'The Networked Organisation' in *RSA Journal*, June 1990, pp. 480–90.

11 R. Charan, 'How Networks Reshape Organisations – for Results' in *Harvard Business Review*, September–October, 1991, pp. 104–15.

12 G. Wills, 'Enabling Customers to Drive Your Enterprise' in *European Journal of Marketing*, vol. 25, no. 4, 1991, pp. 199–216.

13 J.W. Kensinger and J.D. Martin, 'Financing Network Organisations' in *Journal of Applied Corporate Finance*, 1991, pp. 66–76.

14 C.J. Margerison and D. McCann, *How to Lead a Winning Team*, Team Management Systems, York, 1991.

15 G. Wills, *The Enterprise School of Management*, MCB University Press, Bradford, 1993.

16 J.B. Bush and A.L. Frohman, 'Communication in a Network Organisation' in *Organisational Dynamics*, vol. 20, no. 2, 1991, pp. 23–36.

17 C. Barnatt and P. Wong, 'Acquisition Activity and Organisational Structure' in *Journal of General Management*, vol. 17, no. 3, 1992, pp. 1–15.

18 D.P. Schmidt, 'Integrating Ethics into Organisational Networks' in *Journal of Management Development*, vol. 11, no. 4, 1992, pp. 34–43.

19 D. Krackhardt and J.R. Hanson, 'Informal Networks: The Company behind the Chart', *Harvard Business Review*, July–August 1993, pp. 104–11.

20 T. Peters, 'Rethinking Scale' in *California Management Review*, Fall 1992, pp. 7–29.

21 R.E. Miles and C.C. Snow, 'Causes of Failure in Network Organisations' in *California Management Review*, Summer 1992, pp. 53–72.

22 D. Limerick, 'The Shape of the New Organisation' in *Asia Pacific Journal of Human Resources*, vol. 30, no. 1, 1992, pp. 38–52.

Part II
Learning to Learn

8 Turning Experience into Learning*

Cliff Bunning

... can the pearls of wisdom that have been gathered by the old people be given to the young, or must the young always gather their own?[1]

Why do some organizations which employ so many intelligent people continue with strategies which are obviously not working, or fail to take actions which are clearly called for or repeat their mistakes, over and over? Why do some organizations put so much time and energy into not changing – into defending the past and avoiding the future? Why is it that large organizations, particularly, have a tendency to bring out the worst in human nature, so that instead of behaving with the collective wisdom of a thousand, management, at various levels, can display a profound commitment to defensiveness and short-term self-interest?

The purpose of this chapter is not to lampoon organizational life, although it does often lend itself to that, but rather to:

- advance the view that learning is the strategic variable in individual and organizational effectiveness
- discuss the processes involved in individual and organizational learning; and
- propose ways by which the organizational culture can be made more supportive of learning.

THE SIGNIFICANCE OF LEARNING

Learning can be defined as changes in behaviour resulting from experience. Unlike other animals, almost all of our behaviour is learned, rather than instinctive, which explains why the human infant takes much longer to attain self-sufficiency than the infant bird or animal. Taking a lot longer to acquire necessary life skills is a small price to pay for our enormous strategic advantage over other forms of life, namely, that we can learn to do things within a single

*Originally published in *Training & Development in Australia*, vol. 18, no. 4, 1991.

generation that could not have been imagined when our genetic blueprint was laid down.

So *what* we learn, *how* efficiently we learn and indeed, *whether* we learn anything at all from particular experiences are strategic variables, the effect of which leads to us being who we are at a point in time.

Formal educational institutions naturally make an important contribution to the learning of those who use their services. However, the period of time you spend in formal schooling (ten to twelve years) and post-secondary formal learning (three to six years, if at all) represent *only a small fraction* of the average life span. Moreover, most of these learning experiences occur in the first twenty-five years of life. For many, formal learning is completely over before their organizational life even begins.

So from an organizational point of view, the amount and type of learning that takes place during the person's working life is of critical importance and *most of this will be as a result of experience and informal reflection*, rather than arising from the occasional formally organized learning experience such as a conference, training course or higher degree.

If we 'learn' things which are unhelpful or untrue from an experience or fail to learn anything at all, then our effectiveness is diminished and our potential not achieved.

In the same way, at the collective level, the process by which the organization allows itself to learn from its experiences or avoids such learning is an important determinant of its capacity to adapt and grow or stagnate and atrophy.

So the crucial questions are 'What form of organizational culture and values is supportive of organizational learning?' and 'What mechanisms are needed for the learning to take place?'

LEARNING FROM EXPERIENCE

Experience, as a source of learning, has some clear advantages over formally organized training courses. These include:

- experience is not a scarce commodity – it occurs naturally on an everyday basis for all organizational members;
- it is not artificial or isolated from the real work situation. By definition, it is the consequence of the activity which occurs when staff carry out their normal work role; and
- its relevance is unquestionable. Any learning which is triggered by experience is highly likely to be applicable to the work situation from which it arose.

However, as indicated at the beginning of this chapter, many people (and organizations) do not seem to learn much from experience, especially if there is defensiveness or complacency present. So although unmanaged experience has been and will continue to be an important source of learning for all of us, *something more organized is needed, if we are to deliberately increase the amount and quality of the learning that takes place in organizations.*

One compromise has been to insert carefully designed short experiences into training courses or academic programmes. These activities include simulations, role plays, attention to here-and-now process and are referred to generically as experiential learning. Whilst these have improved the immediacy and impact of the learning process, there is still the problem of transferring the learning, which takes place outside the work context, back to the work situation.

ACTION LEARNING

Action Learning is an approach, pioneered by Professor Reg Revans.[2] It can be defined as a strategy by which people learn with and from each other as they attempt to identify and then implement solutions to their problems or developmental issues. There are three essential features which must be present for an activity to be legitimately an Action Learning programme.

These are:

1. There must be action in the real world rather than in some simulation.
2. The activity must be conducted in a way which involves others, especially other participants who are working on the same or quite different projects.
3. The emphasis must be upon learning, not just the taking of action and this is what distinguishes Action Learning from project team membership.

Although the meetings of the group, called a set, are typically assisted by a trained facilitator, this is not essential. In any event, the emphasis is upon individuals *learning*, rather than experts *teaching*. The more effective the set members are, the less the set facilitator will need to contribute, not only in content (the problems dealt with) but also in process (how effective the problem solving and learning processes are in the set).

AN OVERALL MODEL

An overall model of the Action Learning process includes three elements (see Figure 8.1):

- The action taker (the learner)
- The focus of action (the project)
- The action context (the organizational culture).

The effective functioning of each of these three elements is described in brief in the following sections.

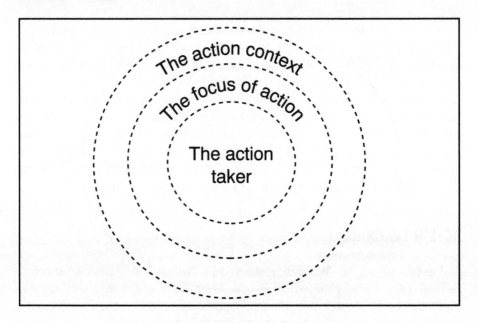

Figure 8.1 The elements of Action Learning

THE ACTION TAKER

What are the characteristics of the effective action taker – that is, one who maximizes their own and others' learning in the process of taking action? Figure 8.2 shows the main attitudes and skills which are fostered in an effective learning set.

Desired outcome: increased insight and skill.

Non-defensive/Growth-oriented

Learning can be painful because it can involve admitting you are wrong, have made a mistake, are confused or that someone else has a better understanding of a situation than you have. So if you have protection of your own self-esteem as a high-priority goal, you will instinctively turn away from or distort potential learning situations so that you don't feel bad in the short term. When protecting your own self-esteem ceases to be such an issue, you become free to grow – to open yourself to new and perhaps scary ways of looking at things.

Open/Curious

Just because you are non-defensive doesn't mean that you are necessarily open-minded and curious to learn. The older and more experienced you are, the more likely it is that learning will involve departing from some firm beliefs that have served you well in the past. So for optimal learning to take place, you need to be actively seeking new insights and ways of operating with the curiosity and openness of the young.

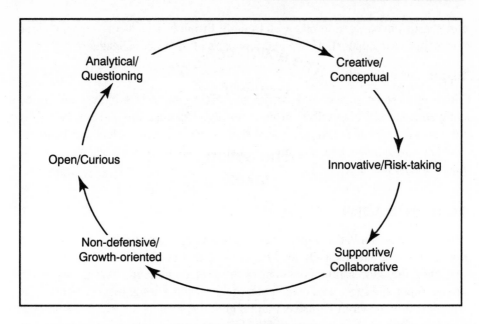

Figure 8.2 The action taker

Analytical/Questioning

At the heart of Action Learning is the skill to know what questions to ask. Learning from experience (both in the immediate past and the here-and-now) comes from being sufficiently detached to analyse and question what is, what has been or what is intended. We are all learners in life, but only to the extent that we are analytical, questioning and reflective.

Professor Revans proposed that learning (L) was a function of programmed knowledge (P) and questioning insight (Q). Although the equation is simplistic, it indicates the centrality of questioning skills to the process of Action Learning.

Creative/Conceptual

Moving from what is currently known to a new insight inevitably involves a creative leap. How do you obtain an insight? What is the creative process of idea generation? Whatever it is, it is fostered by providing a supportive but stimulating group environment. That is the climate that is typically achieved in the learning set.

Innovative/Risk-taking

Taking action involves a risk. Learning involves a risk. Passive, conservative people don't learn much because they don't take many risks. (The irony is they inadvertently take the biggest risk of all – not to learn.) So a willingness to have a go, to take a chance, to try something out is central to the ethos of Action Learning. The learning set is very helpful in this domain because set members

93

feel greatly encouraged to take well thought through risks as they are not alone – they have the support, advice and feedback of their set colleagues.

Supportive/Collaborative

Much of western society and formal schooling emphasizes individualism and competitiveness. This ethic is brought to organizational life and reinforced by the reward system. Yet we are social beings and most of us function best and learn best in a supportive, collaborative climate which creates a synergy impossible when acting alone.

THE FOCUS OF ACTION

The focus of action is the project, because learning comes from doing. However, doing does not automatically lead to learning and so the focus of action is not just upon the successful completion of the project, although that is important, but also upon the successful completion of the learning assignment. The principal elements are shown in Figure 8.3 and should be seen as a cycle that one goes through again and again, even within the space of a single meeting, as well as during the project generally.

The Project

Desired outcome: achievement of the goals of the project.

The project has to be real. It has to be something that needs fixing or

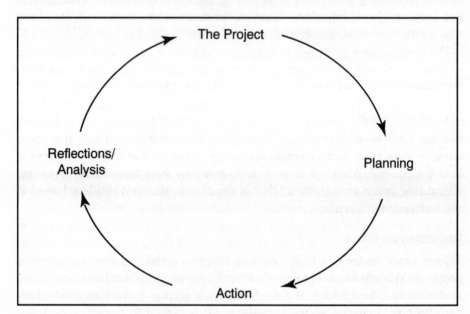

Figure 8.3 The focus of action

94

developing. Somebody with the power to influence it needs to care. Learning comes from challenge and so the situation has to present some difficulty and be something which the action taker can identify with and care about.

The project may be in a different part of the organization from where the action taker normally operates – it may even be in a different organization altogether. It may be so large a project that several individuals will work together on it or it might be of a size suitable for a single individual. Action Learning processes can be used for personal development programmes where the project is to improve one's own personal or managerial functioning, rather than address some organizational issue.

To ensure that the Action Learning project is fully integrated with organizational power and politics, all projects need a more senior person in the organization to act as the sponsor of that project. This person meets regularly with the action taker throughout the life of the project and may well be linked up with other sponsors to form an Action Learning set about how to be an effective sponsor of organizational change.

Planning

Planning takes place throughout the life of the project in three arenas – individual work and analysis by the action taker, in meetings with the sponsor and in meetings of the set where each person talks about his or her project.

The experience of many people who have done Action Learning programmes is that their project was much better planned than others they have previously done in the organization. This is because planning is done more collaboratively and more thoroughly than is normally the case, due to the involvement of the sponsor, the set colleagues, the set facilitator and the level of reflection and self-awareness engendered by the process.

Action

Whilst the first part of an Action Learning programme is normally concerned with diagnosis and planning of action, it is essential that some action beyond just data collection is carried out during the life of the programme. It is often the case that the project continues after the formal close of the programme (which may only have a duration of three to six months), but what is important is that at least a start is made while the situation is managed in a way intended to develop its full learning potential.

Sometimes projects develop in unexpected ways and dramatically change their nature, scale or orientation. Some projects will fail or at least fall well short of original expectations. But it is important to recognize the learning potential of unexpected events and of failure itself. Regardless of the substantive outcome, an Action Learning project is only a failure when the parties involved didn't learn from the experience.

Reflection/Analysis

Reflection/Analysis is at the heart of the Action Learning process. A model of the process by Boud et al.[3] is shown in Figure 8.4.

The role of the set facilitator is very important in the early meetings of the set because it is at this stage that the norms of reflective analysis and the skills involved in carrying it out are modelled, reinforced and progressively adopted by all the set members.

There is much in our organizational cultures which initially works against the reflection/analysis mode. Some examples are:

- A belief that content is more important than process, i.e. that what is to be done in the projects is more important than discussion about how the group is functioning or what can be learned from particular events.
- A norm of politeness which says don't criticize others and how they have handled their project because either (a) you will offend them or (b) they will criticize your handling of your project.
- An innate fear that talking about the personal behaviour of the members of the group in the here-and-now is dangerous and can lead to embarrassment or conflict which will make matters worse.
- A general impatience and anxiety to avoid a lot of vague, conceptual talk and get down to specific issues in the 'real world'.

What is being modelled in the set is, in most cases, counter-cultural to the everyday organizational life of the participants and so it takes a while for its nature to become clear and its value to be appreciated.

THE ACTION CONTEXT

The ultimate goal of Action Learning is not to have successful change projects or even to be successful in helping the participants acquire some valuable learnings and skills, although both these outcomes are valued in their own right. The strategic objective of Action Learning is to demonstrate a mode of functioning which maximizes learning during the process of taking action in the everyday world and which can become more widely practised in organizational life generally.

The context in which Action Learning takes place is typically an organizational culture quite contrary to the precepts and values of Action Learning. So the ultimate outcome desired from Action Learning is the generalization of the learning methods to the overall organizational culture, so that the organization's capacity to learn and therefore improve its responses to its changing environment is enhanced. Otherwise Action Learning is just a better way to run the organization's formal learning programme, rather than a prototype of an alternative and more effective way for organizations to function.

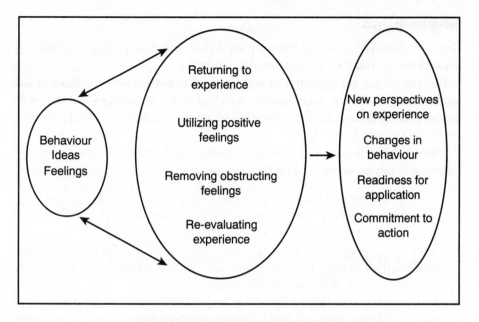

Figure 8.4 The reflective process in context

Figure 8.5 shows some of the main features of a desirable action context. Desired outcome: enhanced organizational capacity to learn and change.

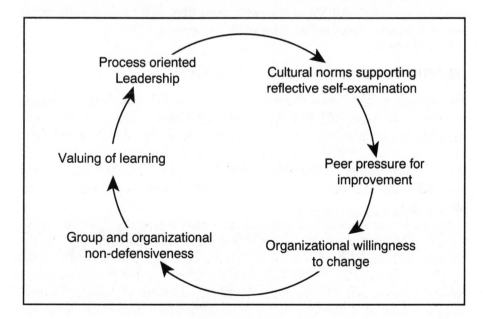

Figure 8.5 The action context

97

Group and Organizational Non-defensiveness

Just as individual defensiveness is destructive of individual learning, so too, when a work group or a number of senior managers collectively behave in a defensive manner, the opportunities for organizational learning are diminished. Helping a group or a committee be less defensive is a delicate task but is prerequisite to the organization learning from its actions.

Valuing of Learning

Learning is not universally valued in our society and its main competitor, ironically, is action. For those who by nature are impetuous or action-oriented, self-examination or reflection seems self-indulgent and narcissistic. There is also the fear that the truth, in some cases, will be unpleasant and painful to face.

The reality is that the danger for organizations lies, not in confronting the truth, but in *avoiding the truth*. It is only by maximizing learning that the organization can face a changing future with a degree of confidence.

Process-oriented Leadership

It is an unusual manager who gives an emphasis to process. Managers are so often chosen for their technical skills (content) that it is not surprising that attention to process comes a bad second. Yet the irony is that process is, in some respects, more strategic than content, because it is the process (*how* a person, group or organization functions) that determines the quality of the content (*what* they achieve). Managers who have been through an Action Learning programme typically become much more sensitive to and skilful at managing process.

Cultural Norms Supporting Reflective Self-examination

How many committees do you know that have a strict rule of devoting the last ten minutes or so of their meeting time to reviewing the degree of satisfaction with the meeting and how it might have been improved? Very few groups have a norm about self-examination, even though it is conducive to learning and improved functioning. Developing such norms is one of the desired outcomes of Action Learning.

Peer Pressure for Improvement

Peers exercise great pressure on organizational members, typically having more influence than the boss. Unfortunately this influence is often exercised to support conformity and conservatism, rather than learning and constant improvement. Clearly, if colleagues actively encourage experimentation, innovation and operational review, much more of it will happen than otherwise.

Organizational Willingness to Change

There is not a lot of point in learning, if you are blocked in putting the learning into use. So an organizational culture which is supportive of change is an important goal. Organizations will never be perfect and there will always be some degree of inertia, complacency and conservatism in large organizations. But a low level of innate resistance to change is a sign of organizational health and something worth working towards achieving.

FOSTERING ORGANIZATIONAL LEARNING

If you believe that the extent to which the people in your area of responsibility learn from their on-going experience is a strategic variable which strongly influences their future performance and if you would like to do something to foster organizational learning, what strategies should you consider? Set out below are some general possibilities. These need to be considered in the light of the particular needs of your work group or organization:

- Instead of using one-shot training courses for staff development, make more use of Action Learning programmes, which aim to foster learning from real projects conducted over a period of time.
- Encourage staff meetings and committees to pay attention to their process, rather than just to content issues. End all meetings with a review period aimed at evaluating the group's performance, with the intention of learning how to function better in future.
- Encourage all staff to engage in regular reflection and initial self-appraisal with the explicit intention of increasing insight and future effectiveness. Model these behaviours yourself.
- Encourage the giving and receiving of constructive feedback aimed at performance improvement and ensure that you encourage feedback about your own strategies and functioning. Actively listen to feedback when you receive it.
- Seek to develop an organizational climate which is supportive of people taking risks such as being constructively self-critical or innovating.
- If you have projects in your area, encourage project members to present their proposed approach to a meeting of colleagues early, in order to receive constructive reactions, to present progress reports for reflection and learning as the project proceeds and to do project debriefs with a wide audience for the same reason. In this way, the many can learn from the experience of the few and the few can learn from the experience of the many.
- Encourage your staff to network with others in similar or related roles in other parts of the organization and in other organizations, so as to exchange ideas and experiences.

The above are offered more as examples than as prescriptions. The heart of the matter is creating an organizational culture in your area of responsibility that holds the following two values as pre-eminent:

- Whole-of-life learning, not as an empty platitude, but as a day-by-day challenge and opportunity.
- Constant professional and personal improvement, so that knowing that you are good only means you can undoubtedly be even better.

People who work together and have these two values can form a powerful learning community, to the benefit of themselves, their clients and the larger organization.

CONCLUSION

The opening paragraph asked: '. . . can the pearls of wisdom that have been gathered by the old people be given to the young (*P*) or must the young always gather their own (*Q*)?'

Action Learning would answer that both are important and neither is sufficient by itself.

The answer to the second query, 'And if this be so, what then is a teacher?' could well be 'someone who helps others to learn how to learn'. Action Learning programmes show managers and others how they can learn using the experiences of organizational projects. The challenge is to incorporate those insights more broadly into everyday organizational life and operations.

REFERENCES

1 G.R. Lefrançois *Psychology for Teaching*, Wadsworth Publishing Co. Inc. Belmont, California, 1979.
2 R.W. Revans, *The Origins and Growth of Action Learning*. Chartwell-Bratt Ltd, Bromley, 1982.
3 D. Boud, R. Keogh and D. Walken (eds) *Reflection: Turning experience into learning*, Kogan Page, London, 1985.

9 From Colleagues in Adversity to the Synergy of the Set*

Mike Mead

THE BEGINNING

This is the story of a DMS to MBA conversion set that started much like any other and completed the programme not so much as 'Colleagues in Adversity', as Reg Revans labelled us, but as friends, and as people who can add to each other's strengths and in turn created the 'Synergy of the Set'. The set members were Roger Davis, Cliff Ferguson, Joti Ghali, John Hickey, Hussein Mirza and myself, Mike Mead.

Our story began in March 1988 when the DMS/MBAS programme started. The story is not over yet and the six members of the set who completed the programme expect it to continue for many years to come. The high point may have been when the set graduated in June 1989, but it was not the end. As a set we began like any other – as individuals that had come together through circumstance – but by the time we had finished we were a real team.

This chapter is based on my own recollections of the events leading up to the award of the MBAs and also as a result of the replies I received from my 'colleagues' to a questionnaire I sent them.

THE BEGINNING

When eight people assembled for a start-up week in Buckingham they knew little of what was in front of them; it was the start of a journey into the unknown. For some it was a quick return to learning, for others the gap between the DMS and the MBA programme had been in excess of ten years. After some brief administration we stood up in turn to present ourselves and our companies to the rest of the set as we were now collectively called. Much to our surprise one of the set members declined to stay beyond the morning session of the first

*Originally published in *Industrial and Commercial Training*, vol. 22, no. 1, 1990.

day. We understand that he anticipated problems of an ethical or business nature as a result of one or more of our backgrounds.

Our first week was a strange and sometimes uncomfortable affair. The reaction of set members varied from feelings of inadequacy that others had greater management skills, to questioning what possible contribution this motley collection of would-be academics who comprised the set could make towards an individual's project. Some of us searched for somebody we could team up with whilst others believed that only 'formal' set co-operation would come about. On reflection we believe the week did nothing to bind us together. If there was anything approaching a common feeling it was that the others would not/could not help us with our own projects. We were a group of people with the common thread that we had all completed the DMS and wanted to complete an MBA with IMC. The set comprised two engineers, two people with sales backgrounds, a college lecturer who was also an accountant, a banker, a small businessman and myself with a background of computing, human resource and administration.

THE NEXT STAGE

Having agreed a schedule for set meetings and weekends covering the next 12 months, we left Buckingham and went our different ways, back to our home locations which were as far as 170 miles apart.

Some set members had their project proposal questioned or pulled apart by their colleagues in adversity who either had a genuine interest in the project(s), or were intent on scoring points. Some went away to rework their proposal, others already had the EAML in their sights.

For those who had long completed their DMS, having to submit a 3,000 word Evaluative Assessment on own Management Learning (EAML) was in itself a struggle. The EAML was to have particular focus on the period since completing the DMS. Some of the set found this task to be a simple one – I did not. However, I found it to be a useful exercise that focused the mind on just what had been learned by experience or, to put it another way, by 'doing things' and I began to understand more clearly what Action Learning meant. The EAML was a struggle to produce and the thought at that stage of attempting a 20,000 to 30,000 word dissertation seemed the equivalent of swimming the Atlantic whilst towing the QE2.

By the time the EAML was marked we still seemed to be a collection of six individuals who met now and again. (One of our set members had dropped out of the course in July 1988 due to ill health.) However, confidence was increasing and some form of respect, albeit reluctant, for other members was also emerging.

The less assertive set members were now starting to question and probe their colleagues who were emerging as the dynamic, unofficial leaders of the set. Respect was also growing for the more methodical, precise set members who at first seemed to be the ones who would hold us all back. There was an increasing awareness of what their skills could contribute to us all.

Much of the early credit towards shaping our team goes to our set adviser, David Sutton, who in his role as facilitator mixed the skills up during group exercises or discussions. We all feel that we were fortunate with the allocation of our adviser. He was the initial catalyst and gently coaxed us along. Once we had begun to work together he skilfully withdrew from active participation at meetings to a role where his advice and counsel could be sought if needed. Once the process of working well together had begun, the increasing realization of the strengths (or weaknesses) of others continued.

But something else was happening. There appeared to be genuine concern when a set member was struggling. Two instances of this are very clear to me.

THROUGH SICKNESS AND IN HEALTH

There was a period approximately half way through our programme where one of us was struggling to get to grips with what appeared to be a real problem within his organization.

Over the course of two or three set meetings/weekends his colleagues pointed out, sometimes with increasing frustration, the issues they felt he must tackle head on if he were to make any progress.

One by one we came to realize that there was a danger of appearing negative whilst trying to be of assistance and as a result, our individual approach changed so that it was more encouraging and caring. It is to his credit that our colleague had the tenacity and strength of character to work through this difficult period and produce an excellent project.

The other occasion was when a set member sustained an injury which caused him to take a considerable time off work, although he could have used this time to make progress on his project.

He was sufficiently demotivated as a result of frustration at not being able to return to full health or work quickly that his project was in danger of being dropped or suspended to the extent that he would have missed deadlines regarding submission. Without exception his colleagues saw his contribution as essential to their own progress as he injected pace and enthusiasm when set meetings were lagging and gave encouragement to others. We were all so concerned that he was written to and telephoned at home, he was encouraged to attend set meetings and make his submissions on time. We are all pleased that he made a full recovery and completed his project with a distinction.

CARDS ON THE TABLE TIME

A process had begun. Nobody had deliberately gone out to start it; some set members did not realize what was happening, or how we had begun to change, but a change was taking place and it was to be for the benefit of all. All of the set members are now clear where the turning point in the set's progress occurred and how it happened.

After approximately six months on the programme in October 1988 something strange happened. During one of our set weekends two members were discussing their project and the attributes of other set members as related to their progress. This was overheard by another set member and they were encouraged to continue the discussions in the hotel's watering hole.

Having assembled we then agreed to let each other know our true feelings about them in the interests of greater understanding and encouraging further progress where possible. This session, which lasted until the early hours, became known as 'The Honesty Session'. It was spontaneous, conducted without any official chairing and was not attended by our set adviser nor any members of the IMC faculty.

The observations that were made included: 'You could make a greater contribution to the set if you did not keep apologizing for interrupting'; 'We need you to encourage us all and inject some sense of humour'; 'Your strength lies in your analytical ability which many of us do not possess'.

Following this session we all agreed to review what others had said. As a result we wrote what we believed were the main benefits and the observations of our colleagues and these were duly circulated. This process also served to focus individual attention on the suggested areas of improvement and/or strengths.

PURSUING REALITY

The successful completion of the MBA programme depended on achieving adequate grades on two submissions in addition to the master's dissertation. The EAML focused our minds on what had been learned since the completion of our DMS, but the process of completing the next submission – the WAIRCI – really brought some surprises to me.

The WAIRCI was a Written Analysis of Interface Relations and of Corporate Integration (at our own company). Having spent four years working in a fairly small company I thought I understood how things happened. How wrong I was, and what a voyage of discovery I had to embark on. I wanted to find out how information spread through our company: who said what to whom, who needed information and who received it. Putting assumptions aside a small questionnaire was developed concerning structures and communication flows.

I was startled to find out that processes did not happen the way I thought, or assumed they did. I had to check the results with my manager and at times he was equally surprised at the findings. This was a time of many meetings: meetings to restructure other meetings; meetings to ensure that information did flow or cascade from meeting to meeting; meetings to discuss improvements in communication, how to unite our people with a common vision, structures, strategies, objectives and goals – all were discussed. This time was the dawning of a new era of realization that we had to improve if we were to continue growing, and we intended growing and becoming more successful in the process.

Since receiving the information that the WAIRCI provided, we have approached many tasks differently. We have clearly defined policies covering such important matters as communication. We have had strategy and planning workshops and weekends. We are more aware of the need to plan for improvement in a much more detailed way.

THE PROJECT

I submitted the WAIRCI and suddenly it was out of the way, and the project was beginning to loom large on the horizon like a black towering peak, waiting to be conquered or to hurl me off its face for daring to scale the heights. Something very important that I learned whilst completing the WAIRCI is that I had to stand back from my own position, 'step out of the ring'. Only when I could look at my company as a management consultant might have done without the filters of a working manager, was I able to make any real progress. I suspect that this approach would be essential for any manager who wants to understand what, why and how things are happening in his own company.

By this stage in the programme, individually we were concerned about our own projects but collectively we were concerned with the progress that others were making.

Telephone conversations had long taken place outside of set meetings but the frequency of these calls increased as the deadline for submission moved ever nearer. Projects were submitted, the viva came and went, results were known and six new MBAs were launched on the unsuspecting world.

DID ACTION LEARNING TAKE PLACE?

To answer the above question we must consider if any new learning at all took place. Perhaps there is an obvious answer, considering that we all completed the programme. Of course we have all acquired new skills and honed existing skills at the same time. But what else?

Some of us have learned a great deal about our organizations. Through the questioning and probing of the set members we have been forced to re-examine our assumptions of the environments we worked in. For some this proved to be a sobering and, to some extent, an uncomfortable experience.

We have seen ourselves as others see us. Whilst this was a valuable experience it was not necessarily a pleasant one. We have learned that we can overcome difficulties and deficiencies by pulling together and that by doing so objectives can be accomplished.

Each of us has learned the true value of an Action Learning, work-centred project. We have had to talk to the people we work with in new ways and with a new purpose to obtain the information we needed. We had to tell some people what we saw within the organization even though it may have been unpalatable to them. The set members had to explain to peers and senior managers what the impact of the project would be, and in the process met with pockets of opposition which had to be overcome.

We are all richer for the experience of having spent 15 months together, learning from each other and our lecturers. We were also learning from ourselves just what we were prepared to give and were capable of. Most of all, we learned from the set as a whole. We knitted together and after six months we truly were six people whose sum was greater than the total of the constituent parts. The set worked well enough together that we were able to keep all members on the correct path towards the individual goal and on schedule. We listened, we cared, we counselled, we sought the advice of each other, we became more knowledgeable as individuals and we have become more knowledgeable as a team.

We believe that we have become a formidable force capable of achieving a great deal together and we are resolved to use the combined strengths in the future.

We did not set out to make sure that Action Learning took place; all we wanted to do was to complete the programme. But it did happen. The IMC programme provided the pattern, the framework.

The set members were the raw material or, as one of the team so eloquently put it, 'IMC was the cornflakes, the set was the milk and sugar and together we found the nutritional value'.

REFLECTIONS

There was no doubt in any of the set members' minds that a change took place in all of us and the pivot for the change seems to be the Honesty Session that was mentioned above. We were functioning like a team and yet we did not have a common objective, a common goal to reach that would drive us on as a team. This aspect of our work as a set fascinated me and led me to consider the 'team' further.

The Team Management Resource (Margerison and McCann) weekend illustrated that we had imbalance as a team. TMR showed us very quickly what contribution each member can make to a team and why a team should have balance. Team positions were identified with such titles as Concluder – Producer, Thruster – Organizer, Assessor – Developer, Explorer – Promoter, Controller – Inspector, Upholder–Maintainer, Reporter–Adviser and Creator–Innovator. The TMR illustrated a team as a wheel divided into segments with a hub at the centre. As a team we (the set members) tended to occupy the upper and lower right quadrants. As such the wheel was not in balance and we should have needed to import additional skills to succeed (*as a team*).

Dr R.M. Belbin has carried out much work on team role composition and, like the TMR, he suggests that a balance of skills is needed to ensure a chance of success. Team role positions according to Belbin include titles such as Chairman, Monitor Evaluator, Team Builder, Resource Investigator, Company Worker, Completer Finisher, Shaper and Plant. If the TMR did not indicate that we had a team, I wondered if Belbin would.

Through personal interest, I asked the other members of the team to complete a personality test. I was using the test to assist with recruitment by providing information which is unlikely to have been obtained through interviews. In addition to plotting scores on seven dimensions of personality the test also constructs team role preferences according to Belbin.

As the results from my colleagues came in I thought I may have found the key as to why our team worked so well. With five of the six replies in we had the important team role positions covered, either by first or second preference and if the last reply indicated a preference for company worker or team builder position, I thought I may have found the answer. But this was not to be. Once the results from the last questionnaire were processed another completer finisher was identified. I puzzled over this problem for a while and began to ask myself the question, 'As the team did not have a common goal, was it essential that the main team roles were covered?'

It was only on the eve of our vivas at Bradford, when we met again with our set adviser, that I discovered what could have been the missing link. I had not asked David Sutton to complete a questionnaire as he was not an official member of our set. I discussed the results of the test and the identified team roles and remarked that I was expecting a company worker or team builder but did not identify one. David remarked that I should have sent him a questionnaire after all he was a *company worker*! David was not a member of our team ... or was he?

I then turned my attention towards the personality profiles of our team or set and discovered the following:

- five of the six members were very assertive
- five of the six members were very imaginative (different mix)
- four of the six were very persuasive.

The other dimensions that were examined included:

- tense
- driven/relaxed
- genuine/persuasive
- anxious/stable
- reserved/sociable
- independent/conforming.

They revealed such a spread of scores that the only conclusion to draw was that no two members were alike.

CONCLUSIONS

Each of the members of the set believes that we worked well together. We have discussed on more than one occasion that we would make the ideal board of a company as there is no competition between us. There is respect for each team member's skills and ability, and a genuine desire to contribute the maximum we can to achieve the best results possible from any situation.

We have discussed how our success could be repeated and offer the following advice to future set members, set advisers and administrators within IMC.

- The commonality was that we had a reasonable level of intelligence to begin with – this, of course, can be determined by the results of the entry exam and/or previous qualifications.
- We all wanted to complete the programme for different reasons.
- Age did not appear to be a relevant factor as approximately 20 years separated the youngest and the oldest set member. What was important was maturity.
- At all times everybody approached the tasks, whether personal or collective, in a responsible, mature way.
- We believe that the mixture of backgrounds was important and would go so far as to suggest that this may have been a critical factor.
- The engineers amongst us operated as the brakes to the racehorses who were our representatives from the world of sales. They in turn injected pace when everything was going a little too slowly.
- In turn we took responsibility for organizing and chairing set meetings and without threat or embarrassment any of us were prepared to pick up the reins and move the set along if needs dictated.
- More care should be taken with possible team construction. If people are expected to work together over a 12- to 18-month period, sharing anxiety,

doubt, pressure and each other's problems, they need to have complementary skills and some empathy for their fellow set members.

We know we were fortunate in our allocation of set adviser. He coaxed and sometimes goaded us along in the early part of the programme, organized us into small units when group exercises or discussions were necessary and left us alone when we were able to manage ourselves. But he was always available for advice and counselling if required.

Our set adviser suited us and in many ways became one of our colleagues by not interfering or posing any threat/hindrance to our progress.

We understand that commercial considerations may not allow the opportunity to mix skills and ability to the extent that they were mixed in our set. However, if we could only make two recommendations this would be one of them: a test as part of the entry process could assist in identifying possible team role positions or preferences. In my opinion it does not matter whether this is TMR or any other tried and tested method, as long as it is done and the results used to construct sets which *must* function as a team for the 12 or 18 months they are together if all are to have the opportunity of benefiting equally.

The other important recommendation is much more difficult to put in place. Having achieved the right set mix and mixture of abilities, our set are all agreed that the Honesty Session was the single most important and beneficial event of our programme that was not organized.

I believe it can only take place after the set has been together for a sufficiently long period so that each team member knows the other and the contribution that everybody makes or can make. That may take three months or six months; in our set it was approximately six months after we first came together that the event took place. In some ways it almost has to be a natural process for there to be full benefit. I do not believe that maximum benefit will be gained if one set member stands up to suggest that everybody starts talking about everybody else.

If the set adviser has an HR background then we would suggest that he/she gives some encouragement to this process. We believe that although we could have reached our own goals individually, the synergy of the set contributed to our success.

Individually we believe that as a result of the Honesty Session we were forced to evaluate ourselves to a greater level than we had previously done. Our perspective and thinking were broadened and unknown strengths and weaknesses were identified. Self-confidence and career ambitions were increased and genuine friendship and support was a great benefit.

Further benefits were not immediately obvious. By coming together so frequently during the course of the programme we became colleagues outside of the 'work arena' that the programme created.

The group demonstrated true team-work when there was a problem to be overcome, and we shared a belief that if we were to lose any of the set members throughout the programme, we would all be the poorer for it. This of course had the effect of making us work to ensure that we did not lose a set member.

We also believe that the shared responsibility of chairing and organizing meetings proved far more beneficial than if one member had taken the chair throughout.

10 Learning in Style: Reflections on an Action Learning MBA Programme*

Brian Caiae

Much is written in the literature on the theory and principles of Action Learning but comparatively little is available to describe the process from the viewpoint of a set member. This chapter attempts to breach that gap by describing my own experiences as a member of the first London set to complete the Action Learning MBA programme with the International Management Centre from Buckingham (IMCB). The chapter is based on the concluding logbook summary submitted as part of the course requirements. It reviews the effectiveness of the learning experience throughout the 18-month course, looking particularly at the opportunities to use various styles of learning in different parts of the programme. It also attempts to provide some insights into the usefulness of Action Learning as an approach to an MBA degree programme.

THE IMCB PROGRAMME

It is probably useful at this stage to describe briefly the structure and philosophy of the IMCB degree course. The MBA programme consists of a residential start-up fortnight, followed by 30 weekly evening sessions of four hours each and six residential weekends. The first half of each evening session is a formal input on one of five core syllabi – Marketing, Finance, Operations Management, Human Resources and Strategic Management. The last two hours of each session are reserved for set discussions in the Action Learning mode, and are therefore left totally unstructured to be used in whatever way the set decides. Tutors and facilitators do not get involved in this session, although they do occasionally observe the proceedings.

The start-up fortnight is a general introduction to the programme. Here each core syllabus is introduced and the participants start to bond into the set which will be the main vehicle for learning. Each residential weekend covers a main

*Originally published in *Journal of Management Development*, vol. 16, no. 2, 1987.

topic such as Communication and Presentation Skills or Design and Management of an MBA Project. The weekend topics are generally designed to be useful for the final MBA project which is the centrepiece of the programme. However, considerable time is reserved during each residential weekend for set work through Action Learning.

Assessment is by submission of five written analyses of cases (WAC's), one for each core course, two comparative projects based on the member's job and company and a masters project centred on a real issue from the member's work environment. This project and the associated literature review account for just under half the total marks. The Masters project must be for a specific senior management client in the company, must be real and significant to the individual and must involve action on implementing whatever proposals are generated. It is therefore not sufficient to theorize and make recommendations; the project must involve action.

The London set consisted of eight individuals from seven very different companies in the private sector including publishing, oil, electronics and manufacturing. All the members involved were operating at managerial level and three were company directors. The mix of disciplines was ideal, with two marketers, two accountants, two personnel people and two members with production backgrounds. Almost the full range of management skills was therefore represented in the set. The only large drawback was the geographical spread of the members from Northampton to Orpington. This resulted in long travelling times and pre-empted the possibility of impromptu set meetings.

The set met for its start-up fortnight at the Simpact Centre near Portsmouth in October 1983. Evening set meetings then took place at the Reform Club in London each Tuesday night from November 1983 till July 1984. Masters projects were submitted in April 1985 and we all graduated that July. This chapter was written more than a year after the end of the programme, enabling my experiences to be placed in a wider context.

LEARNING STYLES

One important benefit of an Action Learning approach is that it provides a greater range of learning opportunities than a more traditional programme. For this reason, I have classified my own learning experiences into four learning styles rather than simply given a chronological account of the course. Since the programme itself utilized the learning styles questionnaire of Honey and Mumford,[1] I have used their classifications of Activist, Reflector, Pragmatist and Theorist for this analysis. Their learning styles model is, of course, a development of Kolb's earlier work where learning is seen as a circular process involving Concrete Experience followed by Reflection and Observation, the formulation of Abstract Concepts and Generalizations and finally the testing of their implications in new situations through Active Experimentation. My own Masters project was clearly seen to move several times through this cycle.

The learning styles questionnaire is administered as part of the selection process for the MBA programme. So at the start-up fortnight each participant was given the opportunity to identify his own learning style preferences with the help of the guidebook *Using your Learning Styles.*[2] The questionnaire results are most meaningfully presented using a four quadrant approach as shown in Figure 10.1. The activist and theorist scores are plotted on opposite ends of the vertical axis with pragmatist and reflector scores similarly portrayed on the horizontal axis. A detailed description of the four learning styles is available in Honey and Mumford.[1] In the course of this chapter the key characteristics of each style will be discussed briefly.

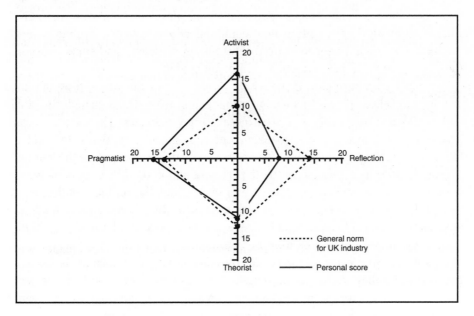

Figure 10.1 Learning styles

Figure 10.1 also shows my own score on the learning styles questionnaire compared with the norms identified for a wide cross-section of managerial and professional people working in UK industry. My own style preferences are seen to be activist/pragmatist with an average theorist preference but a low rating as a reflector. Throughout the London MBA set there was a wide distribution of LSQ scores representing the full spectrum of styles. So although my analysis of the course will inevitably reflect my own preferences, other members of the set would probably see each learning experience in a different light.

THE ACTIVIST

My own predominant learning style is activist. It is not therefore very surprising that much of my learning was achieved by taking advantage of new experiences, problems or opportunities. The activist likes to be thrown in at the deep end, to take the limelight, to deal with a crisis, to lead discussions and give presentations. The whole MBA programme, particularly the live project, provided ample opportunity to exercise this style.

My Masters project was entitled 'Face to Face Employee Communications'. It was concerned with identifying and implementing effective means of upward and downward communications in the company's head office. The main thrust of the project was the introduction of a variation on team briefing into the company. The key action stages were an internal survey on employee communications to justify implementing new communications systems, gaining senior management commitment to the project, training managers and supervisors in the principles of the new system and implementation.

The main learning point of the whole project, if not the whole programme, was how to sell proposals to a senior management team. Once gained, the skill and confidence to do this is a great asset to any manager. The long process involved in influencing senior management culminated in a 30-minute presentation on which the whole future of the project rested. It was therefore thoroughly prepared and rehearsed both in the department and in the MBA set until every conceivable angle had been covered and every potential problem anticipated. The presentation used positive feedback to present the opinion survey findings and win management commitment. This presentation was undoubtedly the highlight of the MBA programme from my viewpoint.

Action Learning projects rarely sail on calm seas – the learning is usually greatest when they almost run aground. There is always a risk in a live project that unforeseen circumstances, totally beyond one's control, will prevent implementation. This occurred in my project just as the main problems seemed to have been overcome. Management had become committed to a team briefing system, supervisors had been trained in its use and the first two briefs had gone out to the organization. Then in the space of a few months, my own boss (the project client), his boss and the company president were all transferred to new assignments overseas. At around the same time I became very involved in the personnel aspects of a company acquisition which became my main work objective. Overnight, the environment changed and the new key managers replacing those who had left, while very sympathetic to improving employee communications, felt uncomfortable with a new system in whose development they had played no part. The project therefore had to return to the drawing board for a relaunch the following year.

As it turned out this crisis provided the opportunity to review the system, reflect on its shortcomings and improve on the initial approach. The team briefing system ultimately put in place survives to the present day because of the care taken to implement it properly and the lessons learned in what became known as the pilot project. However, implementation was not achieved until a few months after my MBA was completed.

Because of my activist learning preference much of my learning from the core courses came through working on the written analyses of the cases (WACs) on which they were assessed. This was particularly true of the Marketing WAC – 'The Rise and Fall of the EMI Scanner' – and the Finance WAC – 'The Kendle Company'. In the latter case, the WAC provided the motivation to learn the basic principles of accounting which might otherwise never have been digested. Extensive discussion of the WACs in set meetings was an important source of learning in each core course. The residential weekends involving personal activity were also very useful, especially those concerned with communication and presentation skills.

THE REFLECTOR

Reflection is the learning style which I tend to use least and therefore required considerable application on my part. Reflectors are most comfortable when they can listen and observe, review what has happened, engage in painstaking research and produce detailed analyses of situations. My own foretaste to painstaking research took place during our introduction to information science at the start-up fortnight. To equip us for our forthcoming project literature review, we visited Portsmouth Polytechnic library to try out a manual literature search. This proved an interesting but frightening experience, confirming my dread of detailed research in libraries. I made an instant decision to use computer searches wherever possible in reviewing the literature on employee communications.

To encourage reflection throughout the course we were all asked to keep a logbook of our experiences over the 18 months, under 'threat' that this was a requirement for award of the degree. The activists among us found this very hard and I must confess that entries were made at fairly long intervals. However, since much of this chapter is based on that logbook, these entries have not been totally in vain.

My first entry in the logbook was made at the end of the start-up fortnight which compared the usefulness and enjoyability of each daily session. The most useful was probably the introduction to each set member's company through presentations of monographs. A 6,000-word monograph on the company's business and one's own role in it is a prerequisite for joining the course. The most enjoyable sessions were the Summertown case study, introducing the basic concepts of marketing, and the day spent practising communication skills. Overall, the start-up fortnight was excellently designed and executed and proved a superb experience both socially and academically. It provided a lucid introduction to all five core courses, enabled insights to be gained into each others' companies, and formed a cohesive group through which the Action Learning process could be developed. The evening courses could start on a high point.

By the Christmas respite at the end of 1984, two months into the programme, most of our logbooks were recording fairly different feelings. The common feeling in the set was that Action Learning equated with do-it-yourself. We were certainly beginning to appreciate the full meaning of Revans' phrase 'comrades in adversity'. Additionally, the importance of managing effectively the interfaces between family life, the work environment and the MBA programme had become a main preoccupation for almost everyone. My own logbook focused strongly on 'survival strategies', ranging from keep-fit programmes to detailed time management for every hour of the day. Even reading the morning paper on the commuter train had become a forgotten luxury as we submerged ourselves in a sea of textbooks, articles and essays. Another problem common to most of us was that we came to expect no recognition from our sponsoring companies of the added burdens posed by the course.

Other reflections were faithfully recorded in my logbook at regular intervals throughout the course. Many are reproduced elsewhere in this chapter. For example, the early demise of my pilot project forced me to reflect seriously on the basic principles of team briefing and to rethink many of my ideas. These reflections ultimately enabled the relaunch to succeed. Nevertheless, despite being fully aware of its benefits, I personally still feel uncomfortable with this learning style.

THE THEORIST

Theorists like systems, models and concepts, the opportunity to challenge assumptions and distinguish patterns. They enjoy stretching themselves intellectually by analysing complex situations and generalizing reasons for success or failure. Personally, I am quite well attuned to this style and discovered this early in the course when we examined our own learning styles questionnaires and Belbin's Team Roles Inventory. Initially the group was very sceptical about the results from both questionnaires, but within a few weeks they had been totally vindicated, forecasting with deadly accuracy the roles which each member would play in the set throughout the rest of the programme.

The theorist heading is probably a good one under which to consider the core courses, but I will discuss the Human Resources course under the pragmatist style since, in my case, so much of the material could be applied at work.

The Marketing core course ideally reflects the theorist learning preference. The four Ps of product, place, price and promotion provide a neat and logical structure for the theory. Though not myself a marketer, I found this to be the

116

most interesting of the five core subjects. The book on which the Marketing course is structured, *Maximising Marketing Effectiveness*,[3] is beautifully written, simple without being simplistic, concise without being confusing and relates marketing concepts to real-life situations. While the set reading for each marketing session was virtually unattainable, the advance preparation ensured that the evening sessions were lively, meaningful and participative.

The Strategic Management core course has also obvious appeal to theorists. My own view is that it is somewhat divorced from the realities of business life in the turbulent economic environment of the 1980s. Much of the theory makes assumptions based on the comparatively stable environment of the 1960s and early 1970s before the oil crisis. Nevertheless, I enjoyed the course, particularly the Kitchen Queen case study and the essay on the company's internal planning process which later formed a foundation for one of the comparative projects. My key learning point from this course was the strategy formulation process which is an invaluable tool in any planning situation.

I do not intend to describe the Finance and Operations Management core courses in any depth. With a tendency for glazed eyes at the very glimpse of accounts, I found finance an uphill struggle, but learned a lot along the way. My own weakness in this area made me much more sympathetic to the plight of others in subjects where I felt more comfortable. With mathematical inclinations, I found Operations Management relatively easy, although I doubt whether I will ever get the chance to use techniques such as exponential smoothing in my own working life.

My theorist preference surfaced early in my project with an idea on how the standard team briefing system applied by the Industrial Society might be simplified for use in a multi-layered organization. Although the idea had strong face validity, it did not work well in practice. Proving this empirically was a learning experience in itself, stressing the need to look before leaping. Interestingly, the Industrial Society team briefing rules were totally vindicated during the project, both in the literature and in practice. Theorists sometimes need to learn the hard way!

THE PRAGMATIST

Pragmatists learn best from activities where there is an obvious link between the subject matter and a problem or opportunity on the job. They like to try out techniques, focus on practical issues and be given immediate opportunities to implement what they have learned. The two comparative projects enabled me to exploit this learning style to the full. The first is an analysis of one's own job and how it relates to the rest of the company. My own proved invaluable in internal discussions on a wide range of policy issues and I reorganized my own work group as a result of insights gained from this project.

The second asks one to analyse the organization as if one were the chief executive and then propose solutions to the problems and opportunities identified. I was very fortunate in that the project coincided with an organizational improvement programme in which I was already involved. I analysed the company under the four headings of strategy, structure, systems and shared values and developed a number of recommendations for change. Some of these recommendations were in fact implemented by the company.

The Human Resources core course dealt with my own area of operation and provided almost weekly opportunities for on-the-job application. I was particularly pleased that IMCB chose to analyse employee relations from a human resources perspective, rather than the more traditional industrial relations/compensation viewpoint. This is a refreshing variation on the standard personnel theme. My own philosophy of employee relations has been considerably reshaped as a result of Alan Mumford's sessions and the key textbook, *Understanding Organisations* by Charles Handy.[4] The concepts of managing change, differentiating the organization and assessing organizational style exemplified by 'The Leisure Group' case study now find almost daily applications in my job. In moving to a new job in a different part of the company, I have found these materials very useful in establishing new approaches to human resources.

Of course, the most pragmatic element of the course was the MBA project, which involved identifying a pressing company issue forming theories on its solutions and testing these out in practice. Employee communications was highlighted as the key employee relations issue for the company in 1984, and this project was concerned with addressing it. The client for the project was my immediate boss, the employee relations manager, who was very keen to see this issue addressed. Employee communications is an ideal subject for an Action Learning project because it is so specific to the environment in which it is being applied. There is no immediate fund of knowledge on which to rely. It is therefore a rich source of what Revans calls 'Q' learning – that which can only be learned through experience. My pragmatist inclinations were exercised to the full as reflections on actions led to theories for experimentation several times around the learning cycle.

ACTION LEARNING

The foregoing summary shows that learning has been achieved to varying degrees in all four styles. Let us now look briefly at the contribution of the Action Learning set to this process.

The start-up fortnight enabled some enthralling group dynamics to be experienced. This included a complete reversal of leadership roles during the fortnight: the comfort of two small groups of four followed by the discomfort of switching their membership and the final bonding into one coherent group of eight.

However, no real Action Learning took place over the first few months of operation. Set meetings tended to be bogged down in process without achieving much productive work. The breakthrough came around mid-January when the set discussed various approaches to the literature search and the problems of margin drift in one member's company. The issue of the marketing WAC then pushed the set from the 'storming' into the 'performing' mode of operation. Therefore, discussions of WACs dominated the Action Learning sessions up to midsummer.

After the enthusiasm generated at the first residential weekend on the design and management of MBA projects, everyone assumed that project discussions would dominate the set activity. However, by mid-February almost everyone had abandoned their projects due to work overload. Accordingly, most of the Action Learning was achieved through discussions of WACs rather than MBA projects. Indeed, my own project was one of the few to receive detailed consideration at more than one evening session.

Since the MBA projects were mostly written and implemented after formal set meetings had ceased, they received insufficient consideration by the set. This was because the problems of geographical separation made set meetings difficult to organize, so they were very intermittent and often poorly attended. Much of the opportunity to learn from each other's project experiences was therefore lost. Nevertheless, even at a distance, the set provided psychological support for its members who were often under severe pressures at work and at home. One or two members experienced personal crises at work which I doubt they would have survived but for the set's support. As 'comrades in adversity' we often felt that other members of the group were the only ones who could understand the pressures we were under. Boddy's[5] three distinct functions for a set meeting – project resource, source of pressure and psychological support – were all experienced by our own set, but especially psychological support.

One conflict in the course design was that between assessment and development; I felt that often the pressure to produce academic results through the various projects combined with work overload led to too much individualism. The need to pass the degree tended to subjugate the fullest use of opportunities for learning. This said, we all learnt many times more from each other than participants on a traditional business programme. Often this learning involved insights into our own characters and how we performed in groups, rather than simply factual knowledge about each other's businesses and experiences. We have all learned a tremendous amount from each other's situations.

CONCLUSION

Overall the course has been stimulating with many insights into other set members' experiences and companies. The opportunity to use the real-work situation as a learning environment in the three main projects has proved invaluable. It is arguable whether this particular programme constituted Action Learning in its fullest sense, since much of the MBA project work was carried out with minimal set input. Nevertheless, this is a very effective way to educate managers since it is immediately relevant to their needs, provides a bridge between the work environment and the learning situation and focuses on application and implementation as well as theory. I thoroughly recommend it as a way to develop managers for tomorrow's needs.

REFERENCES

1 P. Honey and A. Mumford, *Manual of Learning Styles*, Peter Honey, Maidenhead, 1982.
2 P. Honey and A. Mumford, *Using Your Learning Styles*, Peter Honey, Maidenhead, 1983.
3 G. Wills, S.H. Kennedy, J. Cheese and A. Rushton, *Maximising Marketing Effectiveness*, IMCB, Bradford, 1983.
4 C.B. Handy, *Understanding Organisations*, Penguin Books, Harmondsworth, 1976.
5 D. Boddy, 'Some Lessons from an Action Learning Programme' in *Journal of European Industrial Training*, vol. 3, no. 3, 1979.

11 Putting Learning Styles to Work*

Alan Mumford

In 1982 Peter Honey and I published our *Manual of Learning Styles*, in which we moved beyond the original ground-breaking work of David Kolb. In the third edition in 1992[1] we added considerably to the advice on how to make use of the principles of the learning cycle and the learning styles questionnaire (LSQ). Two chapters were especially concerned with using the LSQ results for the creation of personal development plans and for course design. In our work with trainers and developers we find that there is a constant thirst for specific illustrations of particular circumstances in which these ideas have been put into effect. This chapter not only presents such a detailed illustration, but takes a particular case to a higher level of use. It shows how, in one organization, the LSQ was used in a way which integrated learning through a personal development plan and learning through an off-the-job programme.

Clearly the opportunity identified here is not available to all trainers and developers. The case does show, however, how an integrated approach provides additional benefits beyond those available through the more frequently encountered deployment of the LSQ separately on either personnel development plans or courses.

THE LEARNING CYCLE AND LEARNING STYLES

Some readers may not be familiar with the Honey and Mumford learning styles questionnaire and the following brief summary is necessary in order that they can understand the comments made later in this chapter.

THE LEARNING CYCLE

The Honey and Mumford version of the learning cycle is shown in Figure 11.1. In our view the learning cycle embraces the processes involved in all kinds of learning – solitary or shared, on the job or off the job. Particular methods

*Originally published in *Journal of European Industrial Training*, vol. 17, no. 10, 1993.

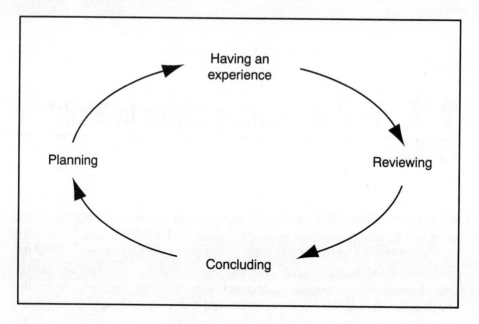

Figure 11.1 The learning cycle

of learning, however, are often more strongly associated with one stage than another. Business games or outdoor training are often most clearly geared to the 'having an experience' stage, whereas lectures and books seem often to be geared to delivering conclusions – concepts, structure, models.

The second proposition derived from the learning cycle is that many activities with learning potential fail to achieve their full potential because they concentrate too much on one stage of the learning cycle. To take an off-the-job example, business games or outdoor experiences sometimes concentrate too much on exciting activity, and provide too little time for thinking about what had happened, drawing conclusions and planning what to do as a result of your conclusions. Lectures or books, on the other hand, are often too concerned with delivering information at the expense of providing time to act practically on the information provided.

The conclusion we drew from these first two propositions, having, of course, gone through a learning cycle in relation to those experiences ourselves, is that even those specially designed off-the-job learning experiences are ineffective because they fail to balance the four stages of the learning cycle in a way which provides for a complete rather than a partial learning experience.

LEARNING STYLES

While the event can 'in principle' be designed as a more effective tool, another element then emerges. Individuals differ in the extent to which the learning methods deployed within each stage are attractive to them. The concept of learning styles preferences is based on the recognition that some individuals prefer learning in one way as compared with another. While it would be wonderful, both for the learner and for the designer of learning experiences, if we were all good all-round learners, in the sense of having equal interest in learning at all four stages of the cycle, the fact is there are substantial differences:

- 'I found that case study on quality assurance in the space programme really interesting.'
- 'The case study on quality assurance in the space programme had no relevance to our problems in insurance.'
- 'I like the role-plays best. Such a change from sitting about listening to other people talk about the principles of interviewing.'
- 'I did not like being forced into acting a part in the role-plays.'
- 'At the end of the day's sales visits my boss asked me what I had learned about the clients and about sales visits. It was very helpful to go through the points with him.'
- 'After the day's interviews my boss asked me what I had learned about the clients and about sales visits. I just wanted to concentrate on who we should appoint, not dig over a lot of personal stuff.'

The learning styles model proposes that these individual reactions to the same learning experience are strongly associated with the four stages of the learning cycle. Some individuals are attracted to or repelled by the kind of learning expressed in one or other stage of the cycle. Figure 11.2 shows the association between the learning cycle and learning styles preferences.

The likelihood of an individual learning well from a particular kind of experience is illustrated below. The illustrations are a much abbreviated version of the full lists given in the *Manual of Learning Styles*.[1]

Activists will learn best from activities where they can engross themselves in short here-and-now activities such as business games and competitive teamwork tasks.

They are thrown in at the deep end with a task they think is difficult.

They learn less from and may react against activities where learning involves a passive role, e.g. listening to lectures, reading. They are offered statements they see as theoretical, i.e. explanation of cause of background.

Reflectors learn best from activities where they are able to stand back from events and listen and observe.

They are asked to produce carefully considered analyses and reports.

They learn less well from activities where they are involved in situations which require action without planning.

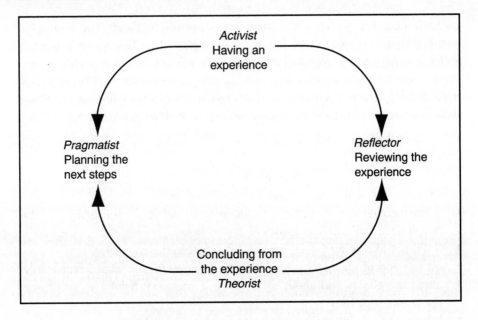

Figure 11.2 Learning styles and the learning cycle

They are worried by time pressures or being rushed from one activity to another.

Theorists learn best from activities where what is being offered is part of a system, model, concept or theory.

They are offered interesting ideas and concepts even though they are not immediately relevant.

They learn less well from activities where they are involved in unstructured activities where ambiguity and uncertainty are great.

They feel themselves out of tune with other participants, especially when of a lower intellectual calibre.

Pragmatists learn best from activities where there is an obvious link between the subject matter and the problem or opportunity on the job.

They are exposed to a model they can emulate, e.g. respected boss, a film showing how it is done.

They learn less well from activities where the learning event seems distant from reality or there is no practice or clear guidelines on how to do it.

COMBINING LEARNING CYCLE AND LEARNING STYLES

The design and implementation of learning experiences will be made more effective when the developer, trainer and, best of all, the line manager are equipped with the understanding offered above. The learning cycle offers the potential of a full learning experience not focused primarily on one stage. Learning styles material offers more complicated improvement. If you know what an individual's learning style preference is, two strategies are available. The first strategy is to provide experiences as close as possible to the preference of the individual. Off-the-job programmes, particularly, may have been designed without attention to balancing all stages of the cycle. If so, it is more immediately useful to give people experiences related to their preference, from which they may learn, rather than to provide them with experiences different from their preference from which they are less likely to learn.

The increased interest in the concepts and practices of 'learning to learn' encourages a second strategy. Here, instead of simply following the route of congruence between learning style preference and the activity, individuals are given the chance of expanding learning style preferences so that they can accommodate to, and therefore learn more effectively from, a wide range of experiences or from different stages within an experience. This is, of course, much the more desirable route, but one which may not be available where a programme cannot be designed or redesigned to provide for the time necessary to tackle this subject. There is unlikely to be a demand from line managers for 'learning to learn', so the issue here is whether trainers and developers will act on the beliefs many of them espouse about 'learning to learn'.

ESTABLISHING PREFERENCES

The extent to which an individual is attracted towards, or repelled by, particular kinds of learning activity, can be established through the LSQ. Constructed largely through questions about managerial behaviour, the LSQ establishes levels of attraction or repulsion through the scoring of answers. Details of the construction of the questionnaire, issues of reliability and validity, and the calculation of norms from answers to the LSQ are contained in the manual. The comments in the case reviewed are founded on the norms based on 3,500 results from the general managerial and professional population.

INTEGRATION: AN ORGANIZATIONAL CASE

An organization gave me the remit to assist a group of senior managers (all male) through identification first of personal development plans, and then through a general management programme shared by all of them. The case shows not only the potential use of the LSQ on each of these activities, but indicates how the LSQ helped to integrate useful work on learning between the two activities. The results for the eight individuals are shown in Table 11.1.

	Activist	Reflector	Theorist	Pragmatist
Green	Moderate	Strong	Very strong	Very strong
Brown	Moderate	Very strong	Strong	Very strong
Red	Moderate	Strong	Very strong	Very strong
Yellow	Strong	Strong	Moderate	Very strong
White	Strong	Very low	Low	Very strong
Black	Moderate	Moderate	Strong	Strong
Blue	Moderate	Moderate	Strong	Very strong
Pink	Low	Low	Very strong	Moderate

Table 11.1 Learning style preferences

ANALYSING LSQ RESULTS

Initial discussions, with the managers involved, focused on establishing through the same interview between myself and the manager a diagnosis of individual and group needs. The details of this approach are not the subject of this chapter, except to say that the benefits of getting the answer to two issues from one interview is very attractive to line managers! It is sufficient to say that each manager completed the LSQ, which was then used in assessing the desirability of particular solutions to identified development needs. The LSQ was used as both a stimulus and a constraint.

As a positive stimulus, the results were used initially to ask the question: 'Which of these possible activities best fits his learning style?' In some cases we were able to go further than this by turning the question another way: 'Given that he has this learning style preference, what kind of activities can we think of which might be attractive to him?' While this double-barrelled approach was not achieved in all cases, clearly the second tends to generate more possibilities.

The use of LSQ score results as a constraint was much more of a single barrel: 'Which of these possibilities is he likely to dislike as a potential learning experience?'

The relationship between identified development needs, possible solutions in terms of development processes, and the learning style preferences of the individual, are fundamental to the production of an effective personal development plan. In this chapter, focusing entirely on the use of learning styles, no details are given of the first two steps. We are concerned here solely with how learning styles information can be used to produce development solutions which are more likely to be good learning vehicles.

The illustrations given below are shorthand versions of the notes used to construct, and in some cases to explain, the proposed solutions in the plan. The statements of 'will learn from/will learn less well from', referred to earlier, were applied to the particular circumstances of the individual and his learning style results. The kind of diagnosis which can be made is illustrated through each learning style in turn. For convenience in this illustration, the strong and very

126

strong results are amalgamated as 'strong', and low and very low have been amalgamated as 'low'. The extremity of the case indicated by the designation 'very' is important in terms of giving emphasis for the need to select or avoid a particular kind of learning experience for an individual, but does not alter the basic nature of the preference and desired solution.

Strong Activist (white). He welcomes the additions to his job and is not disturbed by the uncertainties involved. He enjoys picking up the new tasks and responsibilities. He is sure he will pick up some new ideas, but does not think you can plan that sort of thing.

White's enthusiasm will take him into experiences from which he will learn, though he may not do so at the depth which would be ideal (very low reflector score).

Low Activist (pink). Pink says his worst experiences have been working for a previous boss who roared around stirring things up with no clear plan. He does not like to rush into things unless they have been spelled out, with some sort of structure (see his very strong Theorist score).

The low Activist score for pink is appropriate to the demands of his job. He will not be adventurous in pushing for new opportunities, or for taking risks.

Strong Reflector (brown). Brown says the collection of data has always been fundamental to his approach in his job. The need he expresses to assess the effectiveness of his relationships with his colleagues could be met in part by encouraging him to make notes after significant meetings.

Low Reflector (pink). Pink is unlikely to respond favourably to the idea that he could learn from his new activities, by keeping a log, or reviewing these experiences with his boss.

Strong Theorist (green). Green has attended two management courses at different business schools. He says he enjoyed the diversity of experience among faculty and other participants. He rated some of the faculty very high in terms of intellectual quality.

The ideas suggested on creating a more extensive network of local managerial contacts from other industries, and the suggested books (at the heavy end of the market) should suit him.

Low Theorist (white). White says he has less interest in concepts and theories on management than about whether something works (see also his very strong Pragmatist score result).

The need to ensure that his knowledge of manufacturing techniques and standards is up-to-date is unlikely to be met comfortably through a course or books – hence the suggestion of identifying two or three class manufacturers in similar industries who he might visit. He will need help in setting up and planning the visits, and strong encouragement to report to his boss on them afterwards (very low Reflector).

Strong Pragmatist (red). Red says he left a course on managing time half way through because he saw no way of being able to apply it in the reality of his job (see also his strong Activist and very low Reflector scores).

In terms of improving his own abilities the suggestions made here are for one or two short courses run specifically for the industry.

Low Pragmatist. Real life cases are rarely neat. There was no low Pragmatist in this group!

As a general proposition, a low Pragmatist would not have a strong concern that a development process should be clearly geared to the specific current needs of his job and the organization.

LEARNING STYLES ACROSS THE GROUP

It will be noted from the group scores that only one individual had only one strong or very strong learning style. This group was unusual in that sense, because about 35 per cent of managers have only one strong or very strong score.

At the other extreme, four had three strong or very strong preferences, whereas only 20 per cent of our general sample had three strong preferences. In terms of the actual personal development plans these results were helpful because they suggested that half of the group had the potential to be good all-round learners, as compared with those with fewer strong preferences or even low preferences where the potential for learning may be limited. In addition, it could be predicted that if an off-the-job programme was designed for them, on the basis of balanced attention to all stages of the learning cycle, half of them were likely to be well disposed during most of the cycle.

The group also contained an individual with a very unusual result – strong in both Activist and Reflector preferences. This is unusual because the Activist and Reflector questions are in many cases opposite in their meaning and therefore make it unlikely that a manager will assess himself as being both. As part of the subsequent programme, the manager concerned was asked to go through the various processes indicated in the *Manual of Learning Styles* which might legitimately have led to a changed result removing the apparent conflict. Again unusually, none of the approaches led to changed results. Interestingly, however, this aberration in the results became less important because of the discussion which occurred in the subsequent management programme. The conclusion of his boss, his colleagues on the programme, and my observation of his behaviour during the programme, all concurred that he was a strong Activist.

It will also be noted that there were only 3 low learning style preferences, in contrast with 19 strong preferences. A higher number of low preferences would more frequently be counted. It should be noted that what is being illustrated through this group is not typical in terms of the number of strong or low scores, but relationships in terms of learning styles and desirable learning solutions.

APPLYING THE CYCLE AND STYLES ON THE PROGRAMME

The subsequent programme was designed to meet the identified general needs of the group to improve their capacity to define and meet their managerial objectives. Those needs are not reviewed here and, in the subsequent comments, it should always be remembered that the prime purpose of the programme was not to show that it could be designed through the learning cycle. The cycle was a means to an end – though if you do not get the means right, you will not reach the desired end.

In fact, I planned to use the learning cycle and learning styles in three ways:

- as a means of controlling both the design in general of the programme, and in relation to the specific learning styles contained within the groups
- as a vehicle for developing 'learning to learn' concepts and techniques and thereby improving the capacity of participants as learners, and
- as a means of continuing discussion on, and perhaps increasing the implementation of, personal development plans.

DESIGN WITHIN THE PROGRAMME

The overall philosophy for the programme was Action Learning. Participants worked through a linked series of five workshops, addressing themes and issues identified in the first stage outlined above. The design structure involved them in working on their real issues and problems, around which knowledge or insights appropriate to those issues were built. Within that structure the learning cycle was used both as an objective and as a check.

The objective was that, during any day on the workshop, participants would experience all four stages of the cycle. While the greater emphasis was on the stages of reviewing, concluding and planning, the experiencing stage was covered, since the participants were working on real problems. The experiencing stage was also a substantial contributor to the reviewing stage, since they were often responding to variants of the question: 'What has been our experience on this issue so far?'.

In practice, the workshops constantly encountered a familiar problem even within a deliberately constructed attempt to balance the stages. The planning stage was always at risk of being underplayed or postponed until after the workshop 'because we need to work on the problem a bit more'.

The issue of individual learning styles, in terms of the general design of the programme, was less significant with this group because half of them had three strong or very strong preferences. In addition, the small number of low preferences meant that there was unlikely to be acute antagonism to any stage of the cycle. Other groups with whom I have worked have presented a different picture. Sometimes there are fewer 'all-round learners', which increases the chances of individuals being less attracted at particular stages of the cycle, i.e. by the learning process being emphasized at a particular time. In other groups there can be a strong clustering of strong preferences. For example, I have worked with groups dominated by strong theorist scores.

With this group there was no need to adjust the overall principles of learning cycle design in order better to accommodate the distribution of preferences, as was necessary in the theorist-dominated group mentioned above.

LEARNING TO LEARN

The programme was also designed explicitly to assist participants not only to understand better the nature of the learning process through which they were going, on the workshop, but also to assist them to develop their capacity to learn outside the workshop.

The two alternative strategies of working with the learning styles possessed by individuals, as compared with assisting individuals to develop beyond those styles, were mentioned earlier in this chapter. At the stage of producing personal development plans, the 'congruent' strategy was used; as was indicated in the cases quoted, development solutions were suggested that would be appropriate to strong or low preferences. On the workshop it was possible to give attention to the second strategy, which involved assisting participants to make better use of their existing strengths, and to take some steps to improve their ability in their moderate or low learning styles.

Understanding of the learning process, in which we were involved on the workshops, was achieved initially by a session in which the meaning of the learning cycle and learning styles and application throughout the programme was discussed. Not incidentally, the learning cycle was used to design this session! So individuals were asked to look at their past learning experiences, then at their experiences so far on the workshop. They reviewed their LSQ results and discussed the validity. Through the booklet, *Using Your Learning Styles*,[2] they were introduced to the idea of optimizing their existing strengths and building up those areas in which they had moderate or lower preferences.

In a second session, they were introduced to the idea of a learning review, supported by a learning log or learning diary. Learning reviews continued throughout the programme. They covered two different areas of ground. First, participants were asked in succeeding workshops to discuss what they had done with what they had learned from the previous workshop, and what they were doing to meet any learning objectives set for themselves as individuals, either in the previous workshop or through their personal development plan. A second version of the learning review was the introduction, usually around the middle of the afternoon, of a learning review responding to the question: 'What have we learned from the workshop so far?'.

The learning reviews were conducted mainly in pairs, sometimes in groups of four. The pairs were chosen, with the agreement of the participants, as far as possible on the basis of strong opposites. So white (strong activist, very low reflector) worked with green (moderate activist, strong reflector). Because of the number of people with four strong preferences, this allocation by differences might seem less significant in this group than in some others. In fact, however, in relation to the learning review process itself, there were significant differences which could be used as both illustration and development.

There were four strong or very strong reflectors who could be paired with two low and two moderate reflectors. The strong reflectors would be predicted to find more value in the learning review and even the learning log. This was indeed largely the case. Feedback from the pairs confirmed that the low and moderate reflectors got more out of the learning review process in pairs than they did when they undertook this as individuals at the beginning of the first workshop.

The results of the suggestions on keeping a learning log were less positive. Some of them did keep notes in between workshops, but at nothing like the level of review and reflection which a learning log is intended to encourage. The design in this area was too informal and relaxed – participants should have been asked to tackle both the learning log and the learning review sessions more seriously with, for example, an exchange of notes. This was also true of the plans they made through the *Using Your Learning Styles* booklet, where I erred in not suggesting that these plans were shared and discussed more formally.

PERSONAL DEVELOPMENT PLANS

It was my expectation that the workshops would provide an opportunity for individuals to review progress on the personal development plans they had agreed before the workshop started. This was in fact designed into and achieved on the first workshop but was not really successful. Participants had discussed the PDPs in brief with their boss and were not so willing to discuss the same issues with their peers. In addition, they felt that the PDPs had been a useful process, but not one which had high priority in terms of the group issues they were trying to tackle on the workshop. Their view, with which I concurred in designing the subsequent workshops, was that the PDPs could and should be discussed outside the workshop context. Another contributing factor here was that the sequence of workshops was chosen to reflect their managerial priorities which meant that a workshop on selection and development was the last in the sequence.

THE ACHIEVEMENT OF INTEGRATION

The process described here not only enabled dual use of the LSQ, but provided the opportunity to integrate understanding of and work on more effective learning processes for the individuals involved. Valuable as the LSQ would have been for either personal development plans, or the general programme, it became even more formidably useful when employed in these two linked development activities.

Two further benefits emerged from the level of integration that was achieved. First, there was explicit attention to 'learning to learn'. The approach illustrated through this programme, of helping individuals to understand their own learning on the programme by declaring and reviewing the learning processes in which they were involved, is still relatively unusual. It seems still to be one of the great lost opportunities of any formal programme that they do not take advantage of the opportunity to enable individuals to discuss how they learn, and how their improved knowledge about their learning might be employed away from the programme.

The second main benefit of explicit attention to learning issues, using the shared yardstick of the LSQ, is that this group of managers understood itself and the individual participants better. They saw each others' strengths and their relative weaknesses as individuals, and began to make use of those strengths in some of their group processes.

A third benefit emerged: participants also saw, and addressed on the final workshop, that the knowledge they had gained about how they learned could be valuable in their work as superiors of other managers. Since the great objective of any 'learning to learn' process must be not just to improve their capacity to learn on a course, but their capacity to learn outside a course, and in addition to help others to learn through real work experiences, a further kind of integration can happen. It is the recognition that it is important to know how a boss likes to learn and how one of his subordinates likes to learn – and the need to manage any differences. It is the link between the way in which a mentor will identify and offer learning opportunities, and the way in which potential learners will respond to the mentor. It is the link between someone who is trying to assist someone else to learn (formally called coaching) and the way in which the learner likes to respond. These latter issues can best be addressed, of course, by enabling manager-developers to see themselves as learners, before they try and help others to learn.[3]

REFERENCES

1 P. Honey and A. Mumford, *Manual of Learning Styles*, 3rd ed., Honey, Maidenhead, 1992.
2 P. Honey and A. Mumford, *Using Your Learning Styles*, Honey, Maidenhead, 1986.
3 A. Mumford, *How Managers Develop Managers*, Gower, Aldershot, 1993.

12 The Evaluative Assessment of Managerial Learning (EAML)

Alan Mumford

[*Note* This is the guidance given to participants on programmes requiring an EAML: 5 per cent of credits are assigned for this on MBA programmes.]

OBJECTIVES

This assignment gives expression to an important feature of our philosophy of management development. We believe in the effective combination and integration of experience and learning from experience. We believe the learning process is enhanced by explicit overt questioning and review by the individual undergoing the learning experience.

The objectives are:

- to provide a disciplined structure for the review of learning achieved during the period of the programme
- to provide a helpful process through which learning during the programme is made more conscious and evident
- to provide a link between the programme experience and future learning, especially in relation to continuing membership and the five-year review
- to provide an academic reward for undertaking this learning review successfully.

CONTENT

EXPERIENCES

- Learning during and around timetabled programme sessions.
- Learning from set discussion and in particular from assisting other set members with their project/dissertation.

- Learning at your place of employment from work associated with the programme.
- Learning from your normal work experiences.
- Learning outside work, for example, from involvement in professional institutions, personal life and other non-work centred activities.

THEMES

- Your understanding of the learning process, especially the learning cycle.
- Your understanding of how your activities on the programme relate to those processes.
- Your understanding of yourself as a learner, with comments on your learning styles preferences and other information you have secured about yourself as a learner.
- A review of the problems and opportunities associated with each of the 'experiences' indicated above and what you have learned from meeting them.
- Information derived from feedback on your performance at work and of your contribution during the programme as it relates to your learning processes.
- A review of the main learning opportunities you have perceived within and around the programme, and the extent to which you believe you have taken advantage of them. The dissertation represents a major part of the programme and it is therefore expected that what you have learned from the problems and issues arising from the problems of other set members will form an important part of the EAML.
- Comments on learning opportunities which you now recognize you may have missed, and what you may do in the future to make better use of them.
- Comments on what you have learned in relation to:
  - your job
  - your past and future career
  - yourself as a person rather than as a manager.
- Your plans for further action, in relation to how you will build on what you have learned already, how you will identify new opportunities, what your priorities are and how you will achieve enhanced learning.
- Comparison of your experience with the statements about managerial learning made in the materials you have read.
- You should choose structure, sequence and methodology for this assignment which:
  - best expresses your own view about the learning process
  - is also clear to your examiners.

You may, if you wish, change the sequence of items covered as compared with the list given above, and also select within them if you think that appropriate.

134

You may feel that some of your learning is highly personal, and not something which you want to reveal in an open document.

DATA AND OTHER RESOURCES

You are expected to make use of the following:

Learning styles questionnaire results.

Using Your Learning Styles by Honey and Mumford.[1]

Discussion at the start-up on learning, with the associated notes and exercises.

Guidance notes on learning log.

Learning log itself.

Feedback on your learning processes from students on the programme, and from other sources – a review of what you have learned from discussing the projects of other students.

Discussions at set meetings on your learning processes.

Information about learning processes, e.g. from *Making Experience Pay*[2] on learning opportunities.

A review of learning plans you may have made at various stages in the programme, for example through *Using Your Learning Styles* or in your learning log.

THE MARKING SCHEME

Your assignment will be assessed against your coverage of the content and themes indicated above. The distribution of credits is as follows:

Format:	Style/Structure/Presentation of final written document	20
Content:	Planned methodology	10
	Execution	10
	Analysis and the application of theory	40
	Future plans for learning	20
		100

Indicative length 3,000 words.

REFERENCES

1 P. Honey and A. Mumford, *Using Your Learning Styles*, Honey, Maidenhead, 1986.
2 A. Mumford, *Making Experience Pay*, McGraw-Hill, 1980.

13 Learning Logs*

Alan Mumford

THE IMPORTANCE OF THE LEARNING LOG

An associate on one of IMCB's programmes, during which the completion of a learning log is required, wrote the following:

> Although the Associate found the keeping of a log book a somewhat tedious chore, the benefits are now apparent. Reflection on the log book contents revealed to the Associate just how much he has learned during the MBA Programme, and it reminded him of important learning points that have become half forgotten.

The comment is significant for what it says about the likely reaction of many managers to a requirement to keep a log book. The suggestion that managers should keep a note of relevant experiences, what they have learned from them and what they might learn from them when engaged in activity, is one which very few of them will have encountered. At IMCB we are certainly unusual in taking the view that learning as a process is something which ought to be identified and worked on both by us as designers and, even more importantly, by individuals as learners. The idea that someone should attend an important programme on which the learning process is never discussed, and individuals are not helped to understand (let alone improve) their learning processes is one which we attack most vigorously, through the most stringent requirements on our MBA programme, and is a problem which we also address on shorter programmes.

It is entirely understandable that managers themselves will not have thought of the idea of keeping a learning log. Our own common experience in management and, for those of us prepared to read, the research on what managers actually do, show that reflective analytical processes are not widely valued or implemented across the range of management skills. It is not surprising they are not identified as a main learning skill. However when managers are exposed either to the requirement or the suggestion that they should keep a learning

*Originally published in *Training & Management Development Methods*, vol. 1, 1987.

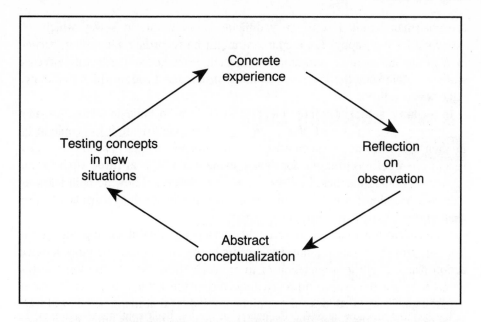

Figure 13.1 The experiential learning cycle (Kolb)

log, many experience it as what it is intended to be, a fundamental part of an effective learning process.

The experiential learning cycle first identified by David Kolb gives a graphic form to the reason why this is so (see Figure 13.1).[1]

The important point of this circular learning process is that many managers who claim to learn from experience, learn partially and badly because they do not engage carefully and with sufficient depth in reviewing what has actually happened and determining what they might wish to do at some future event. I emphasize that I am talking here both about structured off-the-job learning experiences and about the much more preponderant experiences which managers have on-the-job. A process which shows managers how to review their experiences more effectively is therefore likely to be central to improving their learning effectiveness.[2,3]

KEEPING A LEARNING LOG

IMCB make the following suggestions about keeping a learning log.

Managers should pick out the most significant experiences they have had on any particular day, and record what they have learned from the experiences. In normal managerial work it may have been something acquired from a meeting in terms of content knowledge: 'I did not previously understand why the customer was looking for that particular benefit'; or process knowledge: 'I saw how

137

the chairman handled some very difficult interventions in a way which left everyone feeling happy'. On a course it might be recording something learned in a group interaction, something significant learned from a lecture or case study, or again something learned from the processes through which the knowledge was acquired.

In a course setting it is possible, as IMCB does, to build in formal learning log review sessions as part of a timetable, rather than leaving it to people to fill in their log at some unspecified time after dinner, drinks and snooker. In a recent one-week programme for senior managers I built in three such formal review sessions. An article by Peter Honey has described how he built learning logs and learning review sessions even more frequently into a particular programme.[3]

On a course it is desirable to draw the threads together at some point (on the last day, probably) and to point participants in the direction of the more familiar action plans. It is the association of the material described in the log and the desire to take action which improves the nature of the action actually undertaken.

Our experience of successful completion of logs is that many people will want to be selective in the notes they make. The most effective logs often also include very specific statements, both about things experienced and about action plans. They will, for example, use the actual words or describe the specific behaviours, rather than generalizing: 'I tried to persuade the group that we should set out our objectives before we started. I was unsuccessful in this, partly because I proposed we should have both task and process objectives'.

An action plan would similarly have something like: 'I learned from the last meeting that the quieter members will never contribute unless I help them. I will draw them in more specifically early on, and find ways of showing how valuable their contribution is, for example by referring back later in the discussion'.

USING THE LEARNING LOG

As these examples show, a log book should both *record*, through the process of introspection and self-diagnosis, and should also *propose* in the sense of drawing up action. This is particularly important not only because there is a necessary learning association between these processes but because otherwise managers may see the process as being purely academic and theoretical, i.e. the purpose of filling in a learning log is to fill in a learning log, rather than the purpose being to enhance learning and to improve performance as a manager.

This last point takes me to an accompanying proposition. It is quite possible to introduce learning logs without any attention to the total process of learning, or to individual differences in how people approach the actuality of learning. However, the process is in practice made much more powerful when both issues are addressed. Our experience is that to fit them into a wider discussion both makes more sense of the proposition that a log should be completed, and enhances the attraction of the process. Completion of a learning log is itself a mini-version of the learning cycle. It requires managers, once they have had an experience, to review it, to draw conclusions about it, and to plan their next steps. The learning log is therefore both a central part of the reviewing process, in the sense of encouraging the reflector mode, but is also in total a demonstration of the sequence of the cycle.

Differences in learning styles can be used to point up previous discussions on (for example) blockages to learning or influences on it. The learning log can be used, as it is by IMCB, in association with an analysis of individual preferences and approaches to learning. This can be done either through David Kolb's own Learning Styles Inventory[1] or through the Honey and Mumford Learning Styles Questionnaire.[4,5] Both these diagnostic instruments can be used to help a learner understand his or her learning processes better in the first place, and then to understand better their reaction to learning experiences as they occur. The Honey and Mumford approach takes the process further by showing how an individual can prove his or her capacity to learn – and the completion of a learning log can be an important contribution.

REFERENCES

1 D. Kolb, *Experiential Learning*, Prentice Hall, 1984.
2 P. Honey, 'Styles of Learning' in A. Mumford (ed.), *Handbook of Management Development*, Gower, 1986.
3 P. Honey, 'Learning from Outdoor Activities: Getting the Balance Right' in *Industrial & Commercial Training*, November/December, 1986.
4 P. Honey and A. Mumford, *Manual of Learning Styles*, 2nd ed., Honey, 1986.
5 P. Honey and A. Mumford, *Using Your Learning Styles*, 2nd ed., Honey, 1986.

14 The Five-year Continuing Review

Alan Mumford

ORIGINS

The basic idea was set out from the beginning of IMC, in its Charter for Management Development and Articles of Association:

> The highest standards of postgraduation management as a profession require not only initial learning and understanding but continuing refreshment with new knowledge and frequent revision of the old. Our International Management Centre seeks to meet such requirements.
>
> The Articles of Association set out quite specifically the requirement (Article 16i) that any member shall *ipso facto* cease to be a member ... 'if he shall fail to submit every five years from the day of his admission to a degree of membership within IMCB written evidence in such manner as the Council on the advice and with the consent of the Academic Board may determine of his continued and enhanced development.'

Subsequently Ordinance no. 7 offered guidance on what was expected as follows:

1. The written evidence should not exceed 7000 words and should be written specifically for the purpose.
2. It shall be submitted to the Registrar's office in triplicate and typewritten but layout shall be wholly at the discretion of the member.
3. The onus for deciding what to include that will demonstrate 'continued and enhanced professional development' is upon the member entirely. Nonetheless, Council, on the advice and with the consent of the Academic Board, has resolved to indicate that it should normally include, *inter alia*:
   3.1 Reflective comments on the uses made of learning acquired during the original programme of study for membership (for those at their first five-year provision of evidence).
   3.2 Observations on the issues which have arisen over the five-year cycle which were unfamiliar and for which prior learning had offered no real preparation.
   3.3 A report on how, within the member's own experience and organization, action learning methods are being deployed.

3.4 A report on what exactly the member is seeking to do to develop his own subordinates.

3.5 An annotated list of courses, conferences and programmes attended during the five-year cycle and the learning and benefit derived from them.

3.6 The prospect as the member sees it at the time for future managerial learning for himself.

3.7 A description of achievements in relation to problems or projects tackled during the programme. For example, the implementation of recommendations made in original projects and the learning derived from such implementation.

3.8 A review of formally designed learning experiences engaged in during the five-year cycle. These may include special assignments, additional projects, a new job, or courses or other formal programmes. The report must cover the learning achieved and managerial benefits sustained.

3.9 Observations on issues which have arisen over the five-year cycle which have represented totally new experiences not covered through the original programme.

3.10 At second and subsequent renewal the experiences of the original programme will be remote. On these occasions achievements reported upon will be assessed against the managerial audit undertaken at the previous five-year submission.

4. All five-year written evidence submitted to the Registrar will receive formal written feedback from IMCB's Panel of Advisers, together with any recommendations felt useful for the member concerned.

5. An Evaluation Fee is payable on submission of a member's Written Evidence each five years which covers the formal written feedback and certification process.

6. The Registrar's office will alert all members at the time of their fourth, ninth, fourteenth etc. subscription renewal that the written submission requirement needs to be met twelve months hence giving a deadline for its submission.

7. Members failing to meet the requirement that they must submit written evidence of continued and enhanced professional development every five years shall *ipso facto* cease to be a member of IMCB thenceforward until such time as a satisfactory submission is made.

8. At no time shall the provisions of this Ordinance imply that IMCB shall remove from its records the fact that any individual did at a given date attain membership. However, it will no longer be legal for any who fail to meet the requirement for written evidence to describe themselves as current members of IMCB or to use the post nominal initials to which membership had previously entitled them.

The provision applied to both faculty and members. The first of the faculty submissions were made in 1989, followed by members in 1990.

CONTEXT

IMC's philosophy of Management Action Learning is set out in the conspectus:

IMC aims to assist in the development of effective managers by designing a learning process which is both intellectually stretching and founded on the real problems and opportunities facing managers in their own environment. We call it *action learning*.

The key conceptual and practical framework for this is provided through:

- a diagnosis of the issues on which managers have to be effective in their work environment and the necessary competences
- a learning partnership between IMC and the client organization
- channelling developmental processes through taking action on real problems
- positive help to individuals on their personal learning processes to aid current and continued development.

The main outcomes of IMC's approach are:

- improved effectiveness of managers in their current and future jobs and thereby in their personal careers
- learning benefits to individual organizations and eventually to national economies through productive work on organization objectives, opportunities and problems
- a continuous contribution to the body of knowledge and the identification of desirable actions on the effective combination of real work and managerial learning.

Two aspects of this statement can be highlighted in relation to the five-year continuing review:

- channelling developmental processes through taking action on real problems
- positive help to individuals on their personal learning processes to aid current and continued development.

IMC's encouragement of continued learning was based on the fact that during their qualification programme, IMC's members addressed the issue of how they learned. This was achieved through initial sessions designed to facilitate understanding, not only of the Action Learning process but also of individual reactions to different kinds of learning. So the concept of the learning cycle, in either the Kolb or Honey and Mumford versions, was explicitly delivered, as were the results and interpretations of individual learning style preferences (Honey and Mumford). Participants on IMC qualification programmes were at least encouraged, and on some programmes required, to keep a learning log, and to discuss in their Action Learning sets the results of keeping a learning log. One of the culminating features of the MBA programme is the Evaluative Assessment of Managerial Learning, through which MBA participants are required to submit an overall review of what they have learned during the course of their programme. The EAML provides 5 per cent of the credits through which their MBA qualification is achieved.

While structured attention to learning is achieved through these processes, the nature of IMC's Action Learning programmes constantly required that participants worked on, reviewed, analysed and wrote about the real problems and opportunities within their organizations. The idea that work and learning not only could be integrated, but actually had to be integrated because they were symbiotic was one which participants were constantly reminded about through the assignments they completed during the programme.

The idea expressed through the five-year continuing review therefore was not a sudden transformation from the processes with which associates were familiar. They were not faced, as they might have been on traditional MBA programmes, with a requirement that philosophically and practically was very different from the traditional knowledge-based, course-centred traditional academic approach. Instead, with both conceptual logic and practical experience behind it, the requirement was designed to be a continuation of a learning philosophy, rather than a sudden lurch into a different learning philosophy.

DEVELOPMENT OF GUIDELINES

Alan Mumford as Dean of the Faculty of Action Research and Continued Management Development had organizational responsibility for assisting faculty and members in meeting the requirements. In best experiential fashion he completed his own five-year review in 1988, and led the internal discussions which enabled the production of guidelines in 1989.

DEVELOPING THE PROCESS – FIRST EXPERIENCES

A document was produced and issued within IMC, 'Continuing Membership within IMCB', and given to members as part of their graduation package. As the first cohort of faculty and members approached their due date, it became clear that more substantial guidance was needed. Questions were already emerging from such people, indicating that the guidance given in Ordinance 7 was not sufficient to show them what should be done, and therefore was not sufficiently motivating for them to undertake the task. The Annual Professional Congress in December 1989 contained a session in which the forthcoming requirements were discussed, with a considerable focus on those who felt there

143

would be difficulty in meeting the requirements. While there was much support for the principle of the review, there were also suggestions that the existing provisions were:

- too academic
- too much geared to the reflector learning style preference with no attention to the activist learning style preference
- too demanding for busy managers and part-time faculty
- too much geared to literary skills.

It was agreed that these and other points that might arise in the next few months should be reviewed, in time for a further discussion at the Academic and Philosophic Review Day in June 1990. The Academic Board also decided to suspend the 'Do it or else' provision which meant that anyone not submitting a review in time would cease to be a member.

By June 1990, eight faculty and three graduands had presented their review, and the specifics of their submissions contributed to the discussion document presented by Alan Mumford on the Academic and Philosophic Review Day.

Whereas the congress discussion in December of 1989 had emphasized the reasons why some people felt they would not undertake the five-year review, the feedback from the people who had done so had universally been extremely positive. Interestingly, in terms of the worries of people in December, some had commented that the exercise had seemed daunting to begin with but when they got into it they found it very valuable.

The June 1990 discussion centred on a range of options on what should be done to encourage more participation. Ideas ranged from adding to the briefing note, particularly by including more statements of benefits. It was thought that offering the positive benefit of a certificate, and a negative in the sense of removing people from membership was insufficient. Discussion continued also on a theme raised in the previous December of trying to find a process which did not require people to submit what they saw as a main assignment. It was felt, for example, that the statement that the submission should 'not exceed 7000 words' seemed somehow to indicate that that was the target figure. It was therefore agreed to make this statement read '3000 to 7000 words is acceptable'. The more substantial problem was to try and find a way of meeting the interests of those who did not want to write a significant submission at all. The idea of oral presentations had been proposed as a replacement. It was thought this would be particularly attractive as an alternative to those with an activist learning style. However, further discussion brought out the fact that for an oral sub-mission to be anything like equivalent to even 3000 words it would be more than a casual unprepared five-minute chat. It was recognized that in addition to the administrative problems of setting up such an oral presentation, a serious piece of work would involve almost exactly the same time and preparation as would a written document. It was one thing to have an oral presentation, for example during an Action Learning Set, to a small group of colleagues. A discrete oral presentation, perhaps to a group with no other purpose than to listen to each other's presentation seemed less and less attractive.

DEVELOPING THE PROCESS – THE REVISED VERSION

It was agreed as a result of the review of progress to date, and the discussion in June 1990, that while it should be made easier for people to make an effort at some level, the idea of oral presentations simply would not work. In addition to the change already made to allow the submission to be clearly between 3000 and 7000 words, it was agreed to offer a significantly different level of required commitment. This would mean that there were two awards:

- A questionnaire-based review, considering all the learning opportunities with which an individual might have been faced (see Appendix to this chapter). It was thought that although modest in its demands on the individual in terms of thoughtfulness and preparation, it would at least represent a more considered review than the vast majority of managers would undertake of their learning over the previous five years. It was also thought that perhaps people who would undertake this audit level approach would, through it, be persuaded that it would be sensible to go on to what we decided to call the 'full' approach.

    People who had completed the process at the audit level would be given a certificate attesting to this.
- While no changes were made in the provisions already existing for what we were now calling the full version, it was decided to distinguish this level of achievement by conferring on such people the title 'Companion of International Management Centres'. It is interesting to note that the original idea of awarding certificates, and its latest additional distinction of being called a companion was seen as being a pleasant but secondary reward. It was not thought likely that most people would want to undertake the exercise in order to receive the certificate, or to be given a more elevated distinction as companion, since it was recognized that these carried no real significance outside the world of IMC. They were thought to be a pleasant additional reward, intrinsic to the process and to the person, rather than an extrinsic motivating factor.

DEVELOPING THE PROCESS – THE 1991 ANNUAL PROFESSIONAL CONGRESS

The congress in December 1991 which followed these decisions provided the next opportunity to consider with a group of faculty and members what had been achieved. While always anxious to create some more converts, Alan Mumford was worried about putting across the same message to many of the same people who had attended previous discussions on the five-year review. So he decided to take a different approach, and produced a quite different paper.

Painting the Forth Bridge: Do individuals really benefit from the five-year review?

SETTING THE SCENE

Gordon Wills to Alan Mumford: 'You will have your usual slot at the Annual Professional Congress to encourage people to do the five-year review.'

Alan Mumford to Gordon Wills: 'OK, I will have another go.'

Alan Mumford to himself: 'Oh God. I do my bright enthusiastic presentation on why learning is a good thing, and reviewing it is very important. I ask people who have done it to say how transformed their life has been as a result of doing it. The response varies from bewilderment to guilt. The ones who have done it can't understand why anyone can miss out on such a splendid opportunity. The ones who have not done it say how busy they are, that it's all too academic.

'But the ones who do it say how much they value it – and we have persuaded a few people at past congresses'.

Alan Mumford to Gordon Wills: 'Of course we've now got a couple of years' experience. I think I will reread all the submissions we've had and write a paper.'

Alan Mumford to himself: 'Surprise, surprise! I always think that people ought to be influenced by facts. The story has been the same for years – Alan is great on collecting facts and analysing them, and pretty good at presenting them. He is not so good when it comes to accepting other people's emotional feelings – in this case about the benefits of a review of the last five years.'

ACTION STAGE 1

The note appears in Alan Mumford's bring forward file: 'Write a paper on five-year review for congress'.

Alan knows what everyone will expect. A cool lucid analysis of the facts. How many people have done the full review, how many have done the audit level. Has the audit level helped to bring more people into the field – those who didn't want to write 3000 words? What seemed to have been the motivations of those who have undertaken the review? What benefits do they think they have received from it?

Alan structures a short plan on those lines, and then begins to read.

The first two submissions stimulate him to think of trying another route. One of the things the reviews bring out is that they have helped people to attempt to do things differently. Why not try and do this paper differently? Instead of sticking to the familiar style known and loved by thousands of readers round the world, try something different.

A devil then enters: 'Won't that be rather self indulgent – trying something new just for the sake of it?'

Alan to himself: 'But that comment is exactly the rational analytical approach that does not grip everyone. So try something different not just because it's exciting for yourself, but because it might touch other people who will be less interested in a neat analysis.'

The devil pops up again: 'That sounds to me like a rationalization rather than a reason.'

Alan: 'Rational devil, you can go to hell.'

Decision – just use quotations from the reviews.

ACTION STAGE 2: *Whatever turns you on, baby*

'It has been difficult to write this review but worth the effort, for it has focused my attention upon the development I have achieved in five years, and I am pleased with my progress. I proved to myself several times that I can achieve what I thought I could not.'

'You do not understand the reality of a local office when all you've done is visit from head office. You have to work there.'

'I come as strong reflector and theorist on the learning style questionnaire. It is interesting to see that despite my interest in concepts and theories, all my real-time learning has been driven first by Q in Revans' terms. So when we needed to develop a marketing strategy and a system of marketing planning, we did not start by reading the books. We looked at our own problems and opportunities first and then checked our answers against the standard text.'

'You do not have to create something called an Action Learning set. You can sit with a group of colleagues in adversity, and learn a lot from each other because of your different experiences, though you may be in a similar situation.'

'This review made me look more precisely at the satisfaction than dissatisfactions I had experienced in my work, and the extent to which I had consciously and unconsciously pursued the resolution of these.'

'Except for academic purposes, there is no real satisfaction in reviewing learning for its own sake. Reviewing what you have done and what you have learned from it in order to make decisions about what to do in future does make sense.'

'Familiar situations can also provide retrospective learning experiences. These often require a greater discipline to perform the review since you are attempting a fresh look at existing knowledge.'

'Retrospective learning is particularly strong after making an error of judgement.'

FURTHER ENTRIES IN THE DATA BANK

'Customers are in the market not to buy the cheapest product but to buy at a price which delivers more value for money than the cost incurred.'

'Whenever I am criticized my inclination is to spring to my own defence. Whenever I succumb to this tendency my defensiveness is an automatic barrier to learning. I do better when I ask questions rather than proffer explanations.'

'I have persuaded clients in the past to agree to do something they didn't particularly want to do, and it has always backfired on me.'

'Until writing this explication the extent of my (blank) activities hadn't truly registered.'

'It was quite a cathartic experience writing the review.'

'There is the management of that tension between the autonomy that people desire and the control that organizations need to exercise over them if objectives are to be achieved.'

'In our culture the response to difficulties is often to battle on without the pause for calm reflection or solace of supportive discussion.'

'At least these problems (strategy, time management) are recognized and the writing of this review has forced me to address them more cogently.'

'This review has shown me that I must maintain a steady emphasis on marketing services rather than let the activity slide during periods of intensive work.'

'I must admit to extreme reluctance in starting the review and to pain in working through it. However, I am sure you will be pleased to hear that I have been converted. The discomfort of recognizing and putting into perspective the recurring mistakes of the last six years had led me to several important career decisions.'

'Looking back over the last five years through this review I have been able to see a great contribution to my effectiveness. The Q aspect of the Action Learning approach

– the discriminating questioning which facilitated reaching the roots of problems at hand in order to tackle them effectively.'

'The most significant find is how I have developed and extended external opportunities to compensate for a poor work situation.'

'Dependency relationships inhibit learning because they inhibit truth.'

'One of the main reasons for failure among newly appointed executives is an imbalance between the need for speed of action and thoroughness of preparation. He or she is operating under a spotlight of glaring expectations with precious few guidelines to follow.'

'I decided to try and strengthen my activist style, but the way in which I have tried to do it has in practice been strongly influenced by my reflector style – as this review indicates.'

'Over 80 per cent of the learning experiences were considered to occur in good circumstances, i.e. those where the experience was enjoyable and the result satisfying. In all probability this arises from the ability of the mind to blot out negative experiences. These are frequently associated with failure.'

'So my action plan includes the need to scrutinize failures and familiar situations more closely for benefits.'

'YOU CANNOT BE SERIOUS'

The decline of John McEnroe is revealed not only in his failings as a tennis player but in his inability to add to his existing entries in the *Oxford Dictionary of Quotations*. (*Questioner*: 'Is he actually in the *Oxford Dictionary of Quotations*?' *Author*: 'Don't be pedantic'.)

Devil: 'You cannot be serious – are you really going to present a paper just consisting of a series of points made in reviews? Don't you remember the boss who criticized you for presenting him with what he said was purely anecdotal evidence?'

Author: 'Well of course he was an academic who had strayed into industry – a misfortune for both parties. My defence is that war stories (anecdotes to my boss) are powerfully evocative to some individuals.'

Devil: 'Evocative?'

Author: 'Evocative – tending to draw forth. *Oxford English Dictionary*.'

Devil in suave tones: 'So your case is that giving these anecdotes will cause people to recognize similarities in their own situation, and see that they might benefit themselves from undertaking the review?'

Author: 'I could not have put it better myself.'

Devil: 'But a collection of disconnected comments does not really prove anything.'

Author: 'I can see you, you devil, trying to persuade me to go back into my good old ways. Never mind whether this is serious, feel the meaning.'

Devil: 'Just one question before I do. How many anecdotes will you need in order to prove your case?'

Author: 'Kindly leave the stage.'

More comments

'For me the lesson of this European experience is that it is undoubtedly a mistake to imagine that "we" are somehow better than "they".'

'I ought to learn French.'

'One of the things that comes out most clearly is the need to recognize where real interests lie as opposed to stated interests.'

'I believe I have to:
  – take on only a few new challenges per year

- gear core action to each challenge, using the 80:20 rule
- use others to discuss issues.'

IS THAT IT?

Devil: 'I am back gain. Of course what you ought to do now is complete your learning cycle. You've collected a number of experiences, given people's explanations of them and gently inserted the sales proposition of the benefits they clearly have obtained. In terms of your own learning cycle you ought to set out some clear conclusions, before asking people to plan their own next step – by which you mean doing the five-year review.'

Alan Mumford: 'On this occasion, for this paper, I do not want to do that. I do not have to offer conclusions, because I am inviting people to draw their own.'

Reader giving appearance of being a sub-devil: 'You still haven't convinced me why I need to write it all down. I am quite capable of thinking these things through, but I am not turned on by the idea of writing it up.'

Lee Iacocca: 'The discipline of writing something down is the first step toward making it happen. In conversation you can get away with all kinds of vagueness and nonsense often without realizing it.'

New sub-devil: 'I know Iacocca once had a high reputation as a manager – but the figures for Chrysler suggest otherwise now. Does he really support your case?'

Someone else, in the human form of Alan Mumford: 'Any bright manager can produce reasons why not to do something. The most successful managers are the people who try a lot more, at the risk of failure.'

Academic: 'Where is the evidence for that statement?'

Alan Mumford: 'Never mind the evidence, look for the sense.'

Devil: 'You really have changed your tune.'

Alan Mumford: 'Not really. I have just given more emphasis to the sense people have made from their five-year review, without presenting a neat package of facts.'

Puzzled reader: 'Where does the Forth Bridge come into this?'

Alan Mumford: 'You never finish painting the Forth Bridge – when you reach the end you start again.'

AUTHOR'S NOTE

The comments attributed to the devil are the product of the author's imagination. They should not be taken to indicate direct contact with the devil.

MOVING ON FROM 1991

There was little direct feedback on 'Painting the Forth Bridge'. It was perhaps an example of an ingenious attempt at a different presentation which would largely be interesting only to those who already had some commitment to the five-year review. The most relevant feedback was from an individual who said that he found the metaphor of the devil rather overstretched, but he liked all the quotations from people's five-year reviews.

Perhaps this was confirmation of an already understood fact – certainly letters which went out in subsequent years advocating that individuals should undertake the five-year review included some of these quotations.

The 1992 annual professional congress introduced a further attempt to remove

149

the process from sole dependence on Alan Mumford's persuasive powers. On previous congresses first he and then later Peter Honey had talked from their own experience about the virtue and results of doing their own five-year reviews. On the one hand it was desirable to show that, as Chris Argyris would put it, their espoused theory (learning reviews are a good thing), was demonstrated to be the same as their theory in action (what they actually did). They were perhaps in another sense rather unpersuasive advocates. Precisely because they were known to be such strong advocates, while they would have been criticized for not doing it, the fact that they had completed their own reviews was probably taken for granted.

So in 1992 a new form of contribution was found. Two members, one an MBA (Charles Gurassa) and an MPhil (Dennis Towler), described to the congress why they had decided to do the review and the benefits they had gained from it. Charles Gurassa represented another development in the five-year review saga. IMC selected each year individuals who received additional recognition for their work. There is a special award, for example, to the most meritorious MBA graduand. In 1991 this kind of recognition was extended into the five-year process; the submission rated most highly led to the individual being awarded 'Companion of the Year'. Charles Gurassa was the 1992 Companion of the Year.

While there were no important new initiatives in terms of literary productions, the five-year review continued to be promoted each year to the relevant cohort. In August 1992 Alan Mumford was given the opportunity at events revolving around the congregation in Kuala Lumpur, of talking directly to a group of that year's graduands, and of giving direct feedback to the cohort from five years earlier, who had submitted their five-year reviews. Other peripatetic members of UK faculty, especially Gordon Wills as principal, have also taken opportunities to try and influence people outside the UK.

In 1994 a further aid was extended, with the intention of again making it easier for people to do a review. The new Atherton Intelligence System enabled individuals, if they wished, to communicate direct to Buckingham via the electronic internet. In fact in 1995 only two members chose to submit in this way, both from the Far East.

THE A-PLUS ENHANCEMENT

The connection of the five years to the advocacy on conscious introduction to, and work on, individual learning processes was the most significant part of the context in which the five-year review was introduced. A more recent and connected innovation has been the A-plus enhancement. This is a process through which members review, one year after completing a programme, what they have implemented from their Action Learning programme and what they have learned from that implementation.

While the prime thrust of this has been on the implementation issue, because of a concern that this aspect often occurred after the formal end of the programme, the 'What have you learned?' element is also significant. It may be that members who have completed the A-plus enhancement will develop eventually a stronger motivation to undertake the five-year review.

THE RESULTS – A QUALITATIVE VIEW

The 'Painting the Forth Bridge' paper of 1991 includes a number of quotations which show both what people had learned over a five-year period and, of especial importance for this review, why they thought the process had been worthwhile. A similar collection of comments could be taken from the subsequent four years. It is relevant to emphasize how frequently individuals volunteered to comment that they have found the process worthwhile, because there is no requirement or even suggestion that they should comment on the benefits of doing the review. On the grounds that 'a volunteer is worth twice a pressed man', these expressions of the value of the process are important.

Rather than repeat a general survey of interesting quotations, it is particularly interesting to look at a larger number of comments made by particular individuals, whose reviews achieved the designation 'Companion of the Year'.

REVIEWER A

'Corporate culture has undergone a transformation. Strategic business units are fashionable because they enable the performance of specific elements of the business to be monitored and called to account.'

'Synergy is out and the practice of suppressing true cost has been replaced by an unbundling of operations. This means that SBUs are now aware of, and responsible for, their real costs.'

'I believe Action Learning has greatest relevance to major issues involving significant investigation. Such issues possibly affecting strategic direction want more in depth consideration than secondary issues.'

'Our culture does not usually allow time for the luxury of extensive interface with colleagues and friends able to put forward alternative perspectives to the matter in hand.'

'The need to develop improved interpersonal relationships has been, in reality, only one leg of an ongoing self-analysis. In some ways it is a day-to-day thought process utilizing casual opportunities for personal development in addition to grasping more formal invitations, such as appraisals and subordinate's development programmes.'

An outplacement course

'Encouraged in-depth evaluation of a broad range of options, which effectively amounted to a SWOT analysis. This led to questions and eventual answers about what my future employment direction should be.'

'Self-analysis has helped to indicate the direction in which to develop in the future. Similarly this paper has been an additional contribution to the self-analysis process.'

REVIEWER B

'The learning acquired during the programme has been applied during a number of instances.'

'It enables me to stand up to financial professionals, both internally and externally, and fully debate the issues rather than being totally reliant on their interpretation.'

Market Research

'I have been involved in a study with a new organization looking at leisure travel in the Far East and the understanding gained from the thesis has proved a useful background to the study. The specific knowledge re different motivations that drive the Chinese consumer has been directly confirmed again by other research this new study has unearthed.'

Behavioural

'It has been interesting as part of this review to look again at some of the literature studied during the programme and the recommendations made there, i.e. Honey and Mumford on *Using Your Learning Styles*. Whilst I suspect that my personal management style will not strongly be identified with Reflector characteristics, nevertheless there has been improvement in this area over time, and the process of understanding behaviour initiated by the programme acted as a catalyst in this area.'

'It also became clearer to me that an improvement of listening skills in general was required.'

'Team management has been an important part of my job since the programme. The concept of teams being bound to different role types as well as different technical skills and experience was a useful tool. Understanding my own role within a team, the strengths and style that I contribute shape to some extent the way that I pull together management teams since.'

'I have taken a much greater interest in management literature since the programme, particularly in areas that have had a direct impact on my own role.'

'I have more frequently attended general business conferences where leading specialists in their field present their research and opinions.'

'It is difficult to claim that within my own organization Action Learning as a philosophy is systematically applied. There are, however, in real terms many of the elements of Action Learning employed.'

'Problems and strategies are developed within specific functional areas but are reviewed, amended and progressed by cross-functional teams. All major business projects require this interaction in my view.'

'My own experience is that increasingly no function can function in isolation and part of any business process needs to be the mutual education of involved areas through joint development and implementation of a programme.'

'I have also thought to develop subordinates by putting them in roles where the technical skills are not always directly relevant but their management and business skills are. This has considerably broadened the individual and enabled them to bring a more holistic perspective to the role in question. Examples in specific terms have been moving a senior sales executive into Operations and Human Resources, a Business analyst into Marketing and a product manager into Information Technology.'

'This particular business has embarked on a major programme of systems investment. A training programme will look at a case study of the impact of systems change on the workforce and the workplace, with myself and the management group affected, and then look to identify the lessons and actions that are required to avoid the pitfalls and maximize the effectiveness of the investment.'

On Future Learning

'Learning never stops but there are a number of areas over the coming period where I see particular emphasis.'

'Developing and implementing programmes for organizational development/culture change. These are real live issues in the companies I am responsible for and the need to successfully manage a holistic and sustainable strategy is paramount.'

'Planning and internal promotion of long-term business developments. The need to improve the process of reaching a conclusion for major new investments, developing a clear framework for implementation and achieving the buy-in of a diverse matrix organization.'

'On a more personal level a better capability to benefit from computer support and continued improvement of language capabilities.'

'Moving company after 11 years had a profound impact and has created a very clear awareness of organizational culture and how to work within it. To attempt to impose one's own style usually based on previous cultural baggage can be ineffectual in achieving the desired outcome.'

'The learning goes on.'

REVIEWER C

'The MBA project work I had undertaken (and the subsequent critique of it) helped me to develop and structure action-oriented reports.'

'I have used broadly Action Learning set ideas in working on quality improvement projects within my current job. My approach has been to bring together staff from different disciplines to work on cross-functional projects. This approach has provided solutions to several organizational problems and helped my staff and me to learn and develop.'

'From working with ICL and with X I knew that IT vendors were seeking to work with perceived industry leaders to develop computer software packages that could then be sold to others in the industry. During this assignment I proposed that the clients seek an IT vendor to work with in a joint venture.'

Consulting

'Tended to be either feast or famine. Intense periods of assignment work (requiring activism and pragmatism) were often followed by lulls when there was no fee-paying work available. I learned to use this time profitably, and took advantage of the opportunity to develop my reflection and theorizing skills. After each assignment I would consciously consider:

– what I had done on the assignment.
– what I would have done if I could have done the assignment again.
– what I could do to improve future assignments.

This led to development of a new product. For me this was a good illustration of the Kolb model of experiential learning. I had an experience. I had reflected upon the difficulties I had encountered during that experience. I had come up for ideas for improvement that were then tried out in practice.'

'Although time-consuming, I forced myself to write up detailed notes after every client meeting. The process of listening and recording helped to ensure key points were not overlooked. Developing my listening skills has proved invaluable since coming out to Asia.'

'I came to Asia with experience of dealing with western staff and western ways of management. I learnt quickly that western management styles are not always appropriate or understood in Asia. So issues that I would have tackled with little thought or with a standard approach like issuing an instruction, seeking a person's views or disciplining a member of staff are now tackled differently.'

For example:

'Throwing open a meeting for questions in Asia usually provokes a deafening silence, a marked contrast to my European experience. How then can I obtain feedback?'

'Attempting to involve people in problem solving is not easy, particularly as the "boss is expert" syndrome is still a prevalent attitude. So how can I persuade staff that it requires everyone's contribution if we are to succeed?'

'I have learnt to be more careful to distinguish between "real" and "imagined" language and cultural issues, particularly those issues that are conveniently put down to a cultural difference because inadequate thought or attention has been given to understanding or surfacing the real issues.'

I encourage my staff

'to review fully any project or discrete work activity once it is completed. Initially this request was not well received – the problem had been fixed, the person was too busy on other things to go back and look again at this problem. I point out that I am not interested in establishing blame. Once the problem is documented I ask them to reflect on what happened, and to consider options for preventing it happening again or doing it better the next time. I then want them to make recommendations on what should be done and to implement the changes.'

'A powerful learning experience for me over the past two years has been the birth and development of my daughter. I have observed and learnt about her needs for attention, for congratulation, for discipline and for constructive help.'

'I worked on a management course built around a very sophisticated computer simulation.'

'I was able to observe time and time again how different participants tackled the same problem. This was fascinating, I was able to observe groups working together on what was at the outset at least the same problem. I was able to observe how successful groups worked and how unsuccessful groups worked. I observed the many different ways there were of being successful and about the many right answers that were achieved. This was an excellent opportunity for me to learn.'

'On a more personal level I have undoubtedly not grasped or made opportunities to engage my boss or peers in my development.'

In his action plan he writes:

'Seek constructive help from boss, peers and staff on my own development needs and how I can improve my management capabilities.'

In his summary he says the Review

'had proved useful. It made me stop and think. It gave me the opportunity to reflect on issues from the perspective of what I have learnt and how I have used that learning. It has also pointed out some gaps where either I have not used the learning opportunity or where I have tried to use the opportunity but failed.'

'This exercise has stimulated again my interest, renewed my resolve to continue development and is a timely reminder that I need to not only experience but also to draw from that experience and use the knowledge gained.'

REVIEWER D

'Generally my personal learning and management development exceeded expectations against those planned five years ago. Much of this is attributed to the most valuable gift from the MBA, the faith to venture into new challenges and welcome what would have previously been presented as considered barriers as learning opportunities. This attitude combined with enhanced self-knowledge and skills enabled me to succeed in a completely unfamiliar environment.'

My personal learning includes:

'adopt a policy of complete honesty with clients and my organization, in exposing failure and risks even when these may bode against me.'

'focus on other people's strengths, ensuring that these are encouraged and fully acknowledged.'

'be totally receptive to other people's ideas, constantly using these to challenge my own.'

'My work, with different employers, has proceeded through a series of projects.'

Lessons learned include:

'Declaring equal ownership of achieving the benefits through delivery of the XYZ project, thus building a partnership of mutual trust and aims.'

'Direct, intense and honest interface with managers in deriving projected benefits.'

'Encouraging managers to set their own aims rather than pushing them to commit to anything for which they did not feel comfortable.'

'I have repeated the success of subsequent projects by adopting the same approach.'

He decided to look for another job.

'I was unhappy with my performance at the first two interviews. Again this reflected poor self-marketing skills, manifest in a lack of clarity and describing achievements to date and benefits offered to prospective employers. Consequently I adopted model answers to recurring questions.'

'Subsequently I had no difficulty in projecting concise confident answers and was able to concentrate on projecting self-image.'

'Another powerful tool was feedback from interviews. Whether successful or not I contacted the interviewer to seek advice on how to improve my CV, personal appearance and technique.'

'Some of the most important lessons were learned later in the project when major problems and delays made the going very tough.'

'I decided to adopt a completely honest approach. I also ensured that I was equally ruthless in declaring my own mistakes, even though this exposed me to criticism, and the successes by team members were reported.'

This strategy worked. Key people 'gave me the necessary support until the end of the contract.'

Amongst the specifics I learned from this project were:

'team organization and delegation.'

'the need for precise specifications.'

Key lessons from this project included:

'early planning is more important than late accuracy.'

'thorough start-up including agreement by all parties to plan and clear terms of reference is essential and should be linked to the plans.'

'controls such as reporting, risk and change management, and quality procedures are also essential, and must be defined simply and applied pragmatically to avoid excessive bureaucracy and cost.'

'The model was evolved using a combination of previous experience and innovative new ideas which I was able to incorporate. This assignment represented a major advance as it provided the opportunity to fully exercise the approach of model in a truly generic sense.'

REVIEWER E

This individual represents a particular demonstration of the value of the five-year review, because he has done it twice.

He has completed the learning style questionnaire three times, and reported that he had moved originally from Strong Reflector to only Moderate Reflector – a shift which seemed somewhat contradicted by both the fact of doing the review twice, and the detailed content of it. For example, at the end of his first review he had set a number of objectives, which were the basis for his second review. He had also used Mumford's model of learning from experience: 'The Four Approaches' – Intuitive, Incidental, Retrospective, Prospective.

He outlined his experiences in detail against the following criteria:

- Were they in familiar or unfamiliar circumstances?
- Were they perceived as good or bad?
- Is there a connection familiar/unfamiliar and good/bad?
- Did a particular management discipline predominate?
- Was there a dominant learning style exhibited?
- What was the perceived value of the experience of the individual?
- Did the experience lead to action or purely understanding?

Familiar or Unfamiliar

Of the experiences selected 68 per cent occurred in unfamiliar circumstances to the writer.

'However in selecting experiences to show a breadth of learning there is likely to be a bias'

toward the new or unfamiliar.

Good or Bad

Examples here were of the closure of an operation and a large damage to premises. The aim was to see if experiences in bad circumstances gave rise to more significant learning. The result is not conclusive, when measured against value to the individual.

Familiar/unfamiliar and Good/bad

Again, experiences in unfamiliar situations were evenly split to occur in good and bad circumstances, but he will seek out new experiences in unfamiliar surroundings to extend his knowledge.

Management Discipline

There were examples under all disciplines except marketing, not part of the individual's brief during this time. The context perhaps explains that more effort was expended in the finance area.

Learning Style

'As with the previous review a Reflector style was most common.'

This is of course in accord with reflecting on experiences through this review after the event.

Both Introspective, Incidental and Retrospective experiences gave Reflector style learning as expected. Intuitive and Prospective experiences were more allied to Pragmatist and Activist styles, where the individual is keen to try out new ideas or have new experiences. The Theorist style occurred the least frequently, suggesting more 'thinking on your feet' than time to approach an issue in a logical measured manner.

Perceived Value

'Perceived value of the learning experiences chosen is subjective. On a scale of one to three with three the maximum the experiences were rated in significance to the writer.'

With one exception the scores were fairly evenly spread.

Action or Understanding

The experiences were reviewed to assess whether they had led to action or understanding; more led to action.

'These findings conflict with the 1990 review and reflector bias towards the selection of action-oriented experiences.'

An explanation was given for this later.

Progress on Objectives

Detailed review of the nine objectives set in 1990 confirmed the earlier finding that bad experiences could not be shown to produce more significant learning.

'It is possible that when actively seeking learning experiences, those that are seen as good become more balanced with the often more memorable bad ones.'

One of the objectives had been

'to review progress annually. This had been done for the first three years of these five, but not for the latter two. The lesson has been learnt concerning the value of the reviews.'

Learning Styles

The LSQ results compared between 1983, 1990 and 1995 showed a stronger Activist and a lower Reflector score in 1995 than in 1983. Partly the Activist score was a deliberate attempt to be more adventurous, partly changes in working environment may have brought this about.

'Comparing my situation with five years ago today some progress has been made. However this would not have been appreciated without this review.'

SOME FACULTY REVIEWS

Faculty are in general no more inclined to do the five-year review than are the membership. The following two cases (neither from the writer himself) make points of particular relevance to the five-year review process.

REVIEWER F

'I keep a sketchy "Learning Log" on my Mac, in which I explore aspects of my learning about developing managers.'

'A group has to be built into a learning community from the beginning. If effective learning is to occur then this is the most important initial task to be done. I have come to believe that it is the most important factor in achieving the real development of managers.'

It is important therefore to develop collaborative norms.

'Start collaboratively – the norms have to be set from the beginning. For example at the commencement of a programme conduct a session in which participants develop some guidelines relating to norms which they would like to see operating in the group. This can provide some useful ideas for the effective working of the group, but it is also a collaborative action in itself.'

'Learning contracts provide a way of engaging participants more strongly in the learning process. Fundamentally they are a way for participants to set and pursue learning objectives. The process makes participants take stock of where they are in their development and turns them to focus on where they want to go.'

'I worked to make it an important part of the programme with the contract of each participant being made with a small group of others who will support, assist and monitor the activity. When this is set up appropriately it becomes a challenging process.'

'Some of the most useful management development sessions I have been involved in are those where managers have discussed aspects of the contents of their learning diaries. They have talked about the most critical management issues and dilemmas, confronting them, the management knowledge and confidences which these challenges call for, and the options for management action which can then develop.'

'Some participants readily adapt to keeping a diary while others find it a struggle and need assistance to develop their capacity to do this. To assist in its acceptance and use, I present it as a "management evaluation diary". In addition I found it important to assist participants to focus the content of their diary in a way that they would find useful. For example in one organization the management development programme was largely focused around the organization's need to find some creative solutions to problems. Through discussion with participants it was decided that the MEDs would be used largely to designate and map problem areas, to evolve alternative solutions, and to specific skill development requirements for themselves and others.'

'Some management educators that I have seen setting up Action Learning programmes have given the impression that what is involved is simply the provision of some additional management work experience. However, this may or may not be beneficial. What needs to be put in place is the set of processes which can maximize the possibility for a useful learning experience. These include:

- a contracting process
- a peer monitoring system such as that provided by teams
- a system of reflecting upon learning.'

REVIEWER G

'I am not given to retrospection or introspection (and my memory about past happenings quickly fades as I become engrossed in the "here and now"). Until I was forced to look backwards I hadn't realized how much I had packed into a five-year period.'

'A review of my most successful and least successful workshops has emphasized again the importance of top management support, clarifying with participants to ensure they arrive with appropriate expectations and "real tasks are fine, but keep them simple".'

I am a believer in learning logs, but as part of this five-year review I have looked at how consistent I have been in keeping them:

'I agree wholeheartedly with Iaccocca who wrote in his autobiography "the discipline of writing something down is the first step towards making it happen". In conversation you can get away with all kinds of vagueness and nonsense, often without realizing it. But there is something about putting your thoughts on paper that forces you to get down to specifics. That way it is harder to deceive yourself or anybody else.'

'I have come to the conclusion that keeping a learning log benefits from being a gregarious, rather than a solitary activity. Sharing the results and insights makes the whole thing mutually supportive and far more purposeful. For this reason I believe the focus should be on building learning reviews into the system with learning logs retained as essential preparation.'

The reasons why I sometimes fail to keep logs include:

Complacency

'I have found it more difficult to sustain my learning log routine when as does sometimes happen things are going well. This is despite the fact that I fully accept that potentially you can learn as much from successes as from failures.'

Tight Deadlines

'When I am under extreme pressure to produce something fast, I find that in these circumstances all my energy is devoted to producing whatever had to be produced and temporarily learning from experience goes by the board. This is analogous to managers rushing around in a short-term, high-pressure, go-go sort of environment.'

Exasperation

'Extreme feelings of frustration and the calm analytical process of keeping a learning log do not mix. I find I can return to my learning log routine after the strong feelings have abated but not while they are present.'

Concessions

'My review of longer-term projects has brought out some interesting features. I think I err on the side of being too compliant. When a client is in difficulties I tend too easily to see it from their point of view and make concessions.'

THE QUANTITATIVE RESULTS

Table 14.1 shows the number who might have done reviews and the number who actually did so. It includes people who completed IMC doctoral programmes, one part of which requires them to complete the equivalent of the five-year process.

Year for review	Members eligible	Members' full reviews	Members' audit reviews
1990	27	10	NA
1991	28	11	3
1992	35	20	8
1993	58	15	4
1994	48	17	6
1995	57	14	3

Table 14.1 Five-year reviews – quantitative results

FINAL COMMENTS

The problem with attempting to assess achievement on the five-year continuing review is that it is very difficult to define an appropriate standard. Clearly we would like everyone to do a five-year review, not just because we have pride in the process we have invented, but because we believe managers would benefit from clarifying what they have learned. In view of our commitment to the recognition and use of the learning cycle this is not a surprising view. On the face of it this is the reviewing stage of the cycle – but in fact the advice we give does urge people towards the concluding and planning next steps stage.

Feedback from those who have completed the full version of the review often includes the comment that the individual has benefited from doing it. Some have started reluctantly but become converts. Our problem is to convey the felt benefits of those who have completed it to those who are considering whether they want to spend the time on it. This has turned out to be an insoluble problem. As our retreat from proposing to cancel membership for anyone who does not do the five-year review shows, the process has to rely on intrinsic satisfaction rather than extrinsic rewards or punishment. It is wholly unlike the qualification process wherein if you do not submit your written assignment you fail to win credits for that particular part of the programme. (Contrast, for example, the awarding of five credits as an extrinsic reward for completing the evaluative assessment of managerial learning on the MBA programme.)

Nor have we found a solution to the problem of offering a wider range of options than the written submission. The lower level audit submission has some minor benefits, but it is clear from reading the results that in many cases there is inevitably a lack of depth in the analysis and conclusions reached. The audit approach is better than nothing, but not as good as is desirable. Other options for presenting the results of experience over five years have on examination not been found to be feasible.

In the writer's own discussions with colleagues and on formal IMC events, the point has very fairly been made that the whole process really best suits those who are, in learning style terms, Strong Reflectors – 'just like you, Alan'. I have not been able to analyse the learning style preferences of all those who have contributed. It is clear from those individuals of whose learning styles I am aware, that it is not the case that it is only Strong Reflectors who do their reviews, though I quite accept that they are more likely to undertake them. Although I have excluded myself from the cases mentioned earlier, it is appropriate to say that I have completed and benefited from the five-year review process myself. I have certainly made some discoveries about my own approach to my work which I had not made previously.

However, my advocacy of the process, and the guidance I give on effectively completing it, has not been the sole determinant on the process. We have had many discussions at both individual and group level of alternative ways of doing it – so Activists, Pragmatists or Theorists have had their chance to develop a range of alternatives, but none has been found to be workable.

PARTNERS, PROGRAMME DIRECTORS, SET ADVISERS

As with other aspects of IMC's attempt to provide structure and commitment to understanding and using the learning process, a great deal depends on those who are in direct personal contact with members. What we need, and probably do not have, is that every partner, programme director, set adviser is an enthusiast of the five-year review process, mentions it during programmes, provides personal encouragement to their participants five years later. Even better, they would show by personal example their belief in the five-year review. While this has not been present, it is clearly the case that for most of them who do not have continued contact with individuals after completion of the programme, it would be very difficult for them to provide this direct personal encouragement.

THE WIDER CONTEXT

The need for continuous learning has become a management developer's cliché. Even George Bain, Principal of the London Business School, advocates it (though he seems to mean more learning at the business school). IMC's five-year review is a real effort to encourage this. In the wider world it is equivalent to what many professional bodies now require – see the Engineering Council, and the Institute of Personnel and Development.

THE CURRENT GUIDANCE

The current briefing note includes an amendment to the original ordinance, clarifying that '3000 to 7000 words is acceptable'. It also shows that IMC adopted more formal recognition to go with the feedback mentioned in paragraph 4 of the ordinance. Those successfully meeting the requirements are recognized for the following five years as a Companion Member of IMC, and receive a Certificate of Continued Management Development at the next congregation.

The briefing note goes on to provide advice on how to create the review.

COLLECTING EVIDENCE

You will have been introduced to the idea and practice of a learning log at IMC and for graduate members a summary of it will have been part of your formal submission. Some of you will have kept up that process, and will therefore have access to the information which you require.

Some of you will not have kept a learning log. In your case, the evidence which you will need is probably scattered in a variety of documents, and in addition you have your memory. As far as written material is concerned you should look through old diaries, actions lists, priority statements, which may indicate the highlights of your managerial work. You will find other material probably in reports which you have written, the minutes of committees which you have attended, the letters or memorandums which you may have written on important topics.

Your memory will be useful, although probably fallible. It may be stimulated by looking for the written material mentioned above. Or you may go through a process indicated in the next paragraph.

STIMULATING YOUR MEMORY

The following little exercise, undertaken either before or during the collection of written evidence mentioned above, may be helpful to you:

- Review the highlights of your career over the last five years.
- What were the main events, problems, opportunities, successes and failures?
- What action plans did I set myself at the time I finished my programme?
- How far did I carry them out?
- What did I actually achieve?

- Who else can contribute to my memory of what has happened over the last five years – colleagues, bosses, subordinates, mentors, friends, spouse?

INTEGRATING WORK AND LEARNING

It will be clear from the way in which we have set out these suggestions that we expect a great deal of your evidence of continued development to derive from your work. It will be most helpful to you, and most likely to produce a well-rounded statement of evidence, if you ensure that the evidence which you produce about different kinds of learning experience is integrated. As an example, it will not be sufficient to say that a particular kind of managerial experience was productive of learning. It will be most valuable to you, and helpful to us, if you indicate why and how learning was achieved. In terms of the learning cycle, we are asking you to give emphasis to the 'concluding from experience' stage.

ACTION PLANS

Paragraph 3.6 of the ordinance asks you to write about the 'prospect' for future managerial learning for yourself. We suggest that you might like to sharpen this requirement somewhat by indicating any specific action plans which you have. Some of these may have been produced in the normal course of your involvement with your organization, and others we predict will emerge as a result of drawing up this submission to IMC. It is in keeping with our philosophy that we finish this note by suggesting that you think about future action, having reviewed the past.

RECOMMENDATIONS FOR ACTION

1. The five-year review process is valued by those who complete it. While the administrative effort involved in sending out encouraging letters and the briefing note is not to be discounted, this is an approach unique to IMC amongst business schools. It should be continued.
2. We should continue to highlight the opportunity not only through mailings but through the internet.
3. We should continue to highlight successes at congregation by making the awards, and by registering the distinction of 'Companion of the Year'.
4. We have used, perhaps not wholly consciously, two different titles for this process: 'Continuing Review', and 'Continuing Renewal'. Renewal probably crept into the vocabulary as a recognition of renewal of membership. But in fact it conveys perhaps better than the word 'review' the idea that this process is refreshing and enabling. Review perhaps conveys rather too much the

idea of dispassionate analysis and data collection. While it would be unlikely to make a great difference to the number of people who actually completed the process, it would be useful to settle on one of the two titles, and to choose 'Continuing Renewal'.

APPENDIX: MANAGEMENT DEVELOPMENT LEARNING OPPORTUNITIES AUDIT

Here is a list of opportunities which may have been available to you during the past five years. If so, you may have learned from them. It has been prepared by Drs Alan Mumford and Peter Honey and will act as a constructive basis for thumbing through your 'full' report for five-year continuing professional renewal. Review the list and decide how to respond to the four columns by placing a tick (√) as follows in Parts 1 and 2:

Column 1 An opportunity you have used and found to be a valuable learning experience.

Column 2 An opportunity you have used but not found to be valuable.

Column 3 An opportunity which you now see was available but which you have not used.

Column 4 An opportunity which is not available to you.

When you have completed this, move on to Part 3.

PART 1 INFORMAL OPPORTUNITIES

	Column 1 Used and valuable	Column 2 Used but not valuable	Column 3 Available but not used	Column 4 Not available
Job change within same function				
Job change to a new function				
Same job with additional responsibilities				
Boss				
Mentor				
Colleagues/Peers				
Subordinates				
Network contacts				
Projects				
Familiar tasks				
Unfamiliar tasks				
Task groups				
Problem solving with colleagues				
Domestic life				
Charitable work				
Professional groups				
Social committees				
Sporting clubs				
Reading				
Others . . .				

PART 2 FORMAL OPPORTUNITIES

	Column 1 Used and valuable	Column 2 Used but not valuable	Column 3 Available but not used	Column 4 Not available
Being coached				
Being counselled				
Having a mentor				
Job rotation				
Secondments				
Stretched boundaries				
Special projects				
Committees				
Task groups				
External activities				
Internal courses				
External courses				
Reading				
Others . . .				

PART 3 LEARNING OPPORTUNITIES REVIEW – ACTION POSSIBILITIES

Consider your answers to Parts 1 and 2 together.

Column 1

Is there any way in which you could extend the use of these opportunities? Could you use them more frequently? Could you use them more effectively?

Consider specifically how you might make better use of informal activities as learning opportunities.

Column 2

Why do you think these opportunities were not valuable to you? What could be done to make them more valuable in future? Who would need to do what to make them more valuable?

Column 3

Consider why you have not taken advantage of this particular kind of opportunity. Were you not aware of it as a learning opportunity? Is there some other reason why you have not used it? What would enable you to make use of it in the future?

[ ]

Column 4

Is there anything that could be done to make these opportunities available to you? Who would have to take what action to achieve this? Is there another way of providing a similar opportunity?

[ ]

If submitted, reluctantly, for 'audit' level five-year renewal, complete below:

Name: _____ Signed: _____ Date: _____

© Honey and Mumford 1989

15 Making Action Learning More Effective*

Geoffrey Prideaux

For a number of years I have been using Action Learning activities in a variety of management development programmes. These have included programmes for managers, in public and private settings, as well as for graduates at university level, such as the MBA. Often, in these programmes, Action Learning has been only one of the approaches used, and the precise way in which it has been applied has varied, depending on the demands or limitations of particular situations. However, such programmes have always had the key ingredient of Action Learning, i.e. that participants are engaged in learning which comes from real experience in work-based activities or projects.

As I look back on many of these Action Learning adventures, there are a number of emphases, approaches or activities which stand out as having been important in contributing to more effective learning outcomes. I now endeavour to incorporate all of them into all Action Learning activities in which I am engaged. None of them is particularly new; they have been around in some of the literature for some time. However, they are worth reiterating, since application in practice so often lags behind the literature.

They are:

1. Build a learning community.
2. Build strong learning sets.
3. Use learning contracts.
4. Use learning diaries.
5. Build challenge.

*Originally published in *Training & Management Development Methods*, vol. 6, 1992.

BUILD A LEARNING COMMUNITY

While working with various groups of managers in Action Learning programmes, and in management development generally, it is obvious that some groups appear to be working well and enthusiastically together and are eager to learn, whereas others seem to be characterized by low morale, a reserve about contributing positively, a lack of cohesion, and sometimes an inclination to bicker amongst themselves and with faculty.

The first type of situation is well described by the concept of the 'learning community'. This is basically a situation where managers work well together, learn from one another, and can explore, challenge, test the relevance of ideas, and find applications to their management situations. When it is well developed we find that participants take responsibility for identifying and working hard to meet their own development needs, and take a role in assisting others to do the same.

A group has to be built into a learning community from the beginning, and this requires particular facilitator skills and is a particular developmental process. If effective learning is to occur, then this is the most important initial task to be done. In addition, continuing attention needs to be given to the ongoing maintenance of a sense of community. Even though this may seem obvious, and is well established in the educational literature, it is easy to overlook, particularly in a desire to 'get on with the programme'.

In addition, it is not easy to do. The strategies, activities or interventions which might be used to achieve it are not easy to delineate, and relatively few people engaged in the role of management educator seem to have the required skills. Yet I have come to believe that building a learning community is one of the most important factors in achieving the real development of managers. It is, consequently, surprising to find that some faculties launch themselves into a programme and pay no attention to the fundamental issue of ensuring that participants have opportunities to become reasonably acquainted with one another, without which a sense of community cannot even begin to evolve.

In the following, I suggest a number of strategies that I have learned to pursue in establishing a learning community, and a number of activities which are associated with them.

DEVELOP COLLABORATIVE NORMS

Developing collaborative norms means that the management development activity needs to be seen not as something being done to the participants by the faculty, but as a collaborative enterprise. It is important that managers are assisted to act in independent, rather than dependent, ways and that they take responsibility for their own development. This cannot be achieved where teacher/student-type relationships are cultivated by faculty. There are a number of ways in which such norms might be established. Some examples are:

- Start collaboratively. The norms have to be set from the beginning. For example, at the commencement of the programme conduct a session in which participants develop some guidelines relating to norms which they would like to see operating in the group. This can provide some useful ideas for the effective working of the group, but it is also a collaborative action in itself.
- Act and speak in a way that values the contribution of participants who very often have considerable knowledge and skills.

Of course, such approaches often require reorientation by some faculties who prefer to operate in ways which emphasize their expertise, or a power role of teacher *vis-à-vis* students, trainer *vis-à-vis* learners.

PASS RESPONSIBILITY OVER

This is an extension of the previous strategy. In as many ways as possible, the participants need to be given responsibility for aspects of the programme. This could, for example, encompass matters related to the timing and location of meetings, aspects of the programme content, programme processes, and the choice of faculty. The more this can occur, the more the participants are likely to become engaged in the educational process and have a sense of ownership as regards its success.

Where possible, self-direction should also be extended to give participants choice, regarding the specific content of their own learning and how they undertake it. This can often be achieved most readily in programmes organized around the use of learning contracts as a tool to assist participants to set learning objectives and plan their learning activities. Providing maximum possible self-direction for the participant is not meant to be any different from real management life, where appropriate consultation, participation and delegation will occur between managers. The faculty will have a particular contribution in terms of their expertise, and participants will also have specific expertise and interests.

PUT THE PERSON INTO THE EQUATION

One of the most powerful ways to contribute to the development of a climate where participants are active in sharing learning is through activities where they have the opportunity to discuss issues about themselves, in addition to their activities as managers, relatively openly. Getting to know themselves, and one another personally, will lead frequently to participants being more interested and involved in the development and concerns of one another.

I am not referring necessarily to very personal or intimate matters, although there are occasions when it might become appropriate to raise some of these. I am referring to career aspirations, team management styles, learning styles, management development needs, balance of work and home, and many other issues which readily can be seen to be relevant to the life of a manager. Of course, such issues are discussed in many programmes in the normal course of events, but often with nothing of the climate change to which I refer. There are skills in doing this successfully – of developing appropriate levels of trust and of legitimizing appropriate levels of self-disclosure.

BUILD STRONG LEARNING SETS

The use of learning sets, or small teams of managers, is a central aspect of Action Learning activities. Members of sets provide support to one another, learn from one another, and learn from the process of working in a team. However, not all sets appear to work equally well.

SETS HAVE TO BE BUILT

Sets do not always evolve as effective vehicles for learning, simply by a group of people meeting together. Attention needs to be given to devising ways of assisting groups to develop into effective sets, for example, by using programme sessions to work on this issue, and by using faculty members to act as consultants to assist sets to develop.

SETS AS THE NORM

Participants need to know that the sets are an essential part of the programme and that they have the responsibility to make them work effectively. The set activity needs to be presented as an important part of the learning experience.

RESPONSIBILITY FOR THE SET

The responsibility for the effective operation of the set needs to rest, ultimately, with the set members themselves and not with trainers or faculty. Faculty may have a role in assisting the set in its initial development, but it needs to be clear that the members must keep it working well. This, in itself, can provide good management learning.

SELF-SELECTION INTO SETS

One approach which can often be used to reinforce the members' responsibility for the set is to have participants self-select into sets, rather than being allocated.

172

This seems obvious, but is sometimes not done. If participants do their own selection they know they need to act for themselves to ensure their set operates effectively; and cannot hide behind any idea that someone put them into a poorly chosen set.

RESPONSIBILITY FOR ONE ANOTHER

Sometimes it evolves that set members develop a sense of involvement and responsibility in relation to one another's activities. One way of developing and strengthening this dynamic is to use a system of learning contracts in which set members enter into written agreements with each other in relation to the activities each is going to undertake.

LEARNING FROM THE SET INTERACTION

The set is an arena in which interactive management skills are displayed. These skills include teamwork, negotiation, communication, group decision making, feedback, etc. The set members need to discuss their own set's performance regularly on these dimensions if performance as a set is to be maintained and improved.

USE LEARNING CONTRACTS

Learning contracts are basically a system for participants to identify and pursue learning objectives. Such contracts can take a number of forms, and may be an elaborate process or a relatively simple activity.

One approach is for participants to enter into a contract with their set members on the Action Learning activity they are going to undertake; and the expected outcomes in terms of project achievements and learnings. The other set members will support, assist and monitor the activity.

The important issue is that the process should make participants take stock of where they are in their development, and turn them to focus on where they want to go. Though some participants might already be accustomed to doing this, many find it an enormously important learning event. They make statements like: 'I now have a tool for my continuing development'.

However the activity is developed, the aim is that participants become much more closely connected to planning for their own development, more closely involved in the programme; and more deeply engaged in assisting the development activities of other set members.

USE LEARNING DIARIES

The learning diary involves the maintenance of an ongoing record of management experiences, activities and related management learning. They assist participants to reflect on their experiences, to confront questions and dilemmas, to analyse data and situations, and to discover meaning and applications.

Some of the most useful management development sessions in which I have been involved are those where managers have discussed aspects of the contents of their learning diaries. They have talked about the most critical management issues and dilemmas confronting them, the management knowledge and competences which these challenges call for, and the options for management action which they can develop.

There is no doubt that the effective use of learning diaries is a considerable source of learning for some participants. However, it seems that in some management development programmes where diaries have been introduced they have not been successful. This may relate, at least partially, to the way they have been used. My experience suggests that diaries are most useful when they are packaged as an integral part of the programme, and where part of the process involves discussion of diary entries amongst participants.

Some participants adapt readily to keeping a diary, while others find it a struggle and need assistance to develop their capacity to do this. One approach which seems to assist the diary's acceptance by some managers is to present it as a management tool rather than, as is sometimes done, a personal learning activity. For example, it can be introduced as a 'management evaluation diary' which is 'a tool effective managers might use to analyse and evaluate their management activities and develop ideas and proposals relevant to future action'.

Regular discussion of diaries needs to be built into the programme. Participants' learning develops through both the process of writing, and the activity of discussing the issues they have been writing about. One useful way of doing this is to have a session devoted to diary entries at the beginning of each meeting.

BUILD CHALLENGE

Managers learn most from situations where they are challenged and stretched, and this needs to be built into programmes deliberately. Challenge may take a number of different forms, and there will be differences between participants as to what they find challenging. The following are some practical ways to build challenge into Action Learning:

THE CHALLENGE OF THE TASK

The Action Learning activity must be a challenging one. If learning is to occur, it must raise questions for the participant. It may challenge the participant's knowledge, technical skills, organizational skills, or personal competence. Action Learning projects which take participants into unfamiliar territory achieve this best. Projects where a participant has to change something are usually preferable to those where something has only to be investigated or studied. It takes some effort for a participant to obtain a challenging project, and support and assistance from the set should be available.

THE CHALLENGE OF THE ORGANIZATION

Participants can be more strongly motivated to achieve and to learn if senior managers in the organization where the Action Learning activity is occurring have an interest in the outcome. There is an incentive to perform well when, for example, the chief executive wants a result.

One way of managing this is to require that each participant has a 'sponsor' at a senior level in the organization, who values the project and wants a result. Another is to have a steering committee of more senior managers who meet periodically with participants to review progress.

THE CHALLENGE OF PEERS

One of the roles of the set is to ask questions, provide support and to review the progress of set members. The set can, consequently, provide considerable challenge to achievement. This is enforced greatly when a learning contract system is in place and a strong norm of collegial monitoring of performance has developed.

THE CHALLENGE OF THE SELF

Participants must accept responsibility for their own level of involvement in a programme and their own development. This chapter has drawn attention to a number of ways in which this can be facilitated. For example, many participants appear to set higher achievement standards for themselves when a sense of a learning community has been developed; when learning sets are developed strongly, when a contracting process provides challenge in the identifying and attaining of objectives, and when the Action Learning activities are real and stretching.

Part III
Helping Others to Learn

16 Effective Set Advising*

Roger Bennett

The principles and processes of Action Learning are increasingly being used as the learning foundations for many training and education programmes, including those that lead to a qualification. Amongst the first institutions to adopt Action Learning as their central learning philosophy were the International Management Centres (IMC).

Like some other institutions, the IMC try to practise what they preach. A key – and sometimes problematic – element within the Action Learning process is the set adviser. In 1989, a group of IMC set advisers met for a day to share and reflect upon their experiences.

This brief chapter summarizes some of the key points to emerge from the discussion.

WHAT MAKES FOR AN EFFECTIVE SET ADVISER?

- Breadth of experience, i.e. a wide understanding of business in general, and being able to take a 'helicopter view' of the situation.
- Experience of the Action Learning process itself, or processes relevant to that approach: e.g. experiential learning. It was felt that whilst some people might intellectually accept Action Learning, they needed experience of it if they were going to feel deeply about it.
- Resourcing the set. This calls on experience or knowledge of resources of information etc. that the set can draw on as well as other resources in terms of well-experienced people in particular fields.
- Highly developed personal skills, which range across both those required for facilitating as well as those for directing. It was felt that whilst facilitating skills were of key importance, there were occasions when the need to direct the group a little would arise.
- Availability. It was felt that, even when the set adviser was not present at the

*Originally published in *Journal of European Industrial Training*, vol. 14, no. 7, 1990.

set meeting, he/she should be reasonably available on the location or by telephone if at all possible.

- Knowledge of the institution's bureaucratic systems. The set adviser needed to know and be able to explain the regulations that affected a particular programme, and also the network of activities.
- Expectations. The set adviser should be able to help the set develop their expectations of what they should gain from Action Learning programme, and be able to place these in the context of the cultural differences represented within the group.
- Being firm about outputs – applicable to both non-qualification and qualification programmes. The set adviser should be able to convey or establish the output dates and ensure that outputs are achieved.
- Contracting with the set – by setting up contracts at the end of, for example, one set meeting regarding what each individual associate would do between that time and the beginning of the next set meeting, and what he/she will bring to the next set meeting.
- Counselling – being able to take a non-judgemental approach to the issues and problems faced by the set and by individual associates.
- Being responsive to the set and being sensitive to its needs and requirements.
- Adopting a low profile. It was considered necessary at times for the set adviser to adopt a low profile, i.e. not to be too much the centre of stage or be involved too much in discussions.
- Checking on administration, by being the linker between the people on the programme and the faculty and support staff. If this goes wrong the entire development of the set activities and group processes can be put at risk.
- The 'log book enforcer'. Ensuring that associates are reminded from time to time that they should be completing a log book, and giving some guidance on how to do that.
- A credible tutor. A set adviser does from time to time need to give tutorial input. He/she must be seen to be effective in that role.
- Using the platonic questioning method – this probably speaks for itself!
- Problem-theory link – being able to establish (with or for) the set how problems can relate to particular theories or conceptual frameworks, or vice versa, without necessarily knowing in depth the theoretical foundations involved.
- Briefing tutors. Set advisers should know the requirements of a tutor and be able to brief him/her accordingly.
- Setting the environment. Establishing a secure environment in which associates can ask insightful and probing questions.
- Balancing the different roles. The set adviser has to adopt many roles, for example tutor/assessor/adviser, and these should be in balance.

This last point was developed further.

THE ROLE OF THE SET ADVISER

Set advisers need to adopt many roles. In discussion, and with input from the workshop leader, the following roles emerged as being potentially relevant to the set adviser.

THE PROCESS ROLES

Process here refers to the many things that have to be carried out so that the process of coming on a programme and the action learning process itself are seen to be effective. The following roles are appropriate here.

- *The bureaucrat* – dealing with the many rules, regulations and procedures of IMC and ensuring that these are communicated to, and understood by, both tutors and associates.
- *The initiator* – ensuring that associates start work on their appropriate assignments and that dates for hand-ins have been communicated.
- *The linker or liaiser* – making sure that information flows to and from the set and all appropriate people.

ACADEMIC ROLES

There are four possible roles that the set adviser may wish to adopt:

- *The expert* – particularly in relation to the action learning process, the development of group working, institutional procedures, and the specialist subject or subjects in which the set adviser has majored.
- *The mentor* – associates often require guidance on many aspects of their work. The set adviser must be able to guide and counsel across a wide range of issues, problems and requirements.
- *The innovator* – sometimes the set adviser may need to throw possible ideas into the set discussions, as well as suggested approaches and alternatives as to how they might tackle a particular piece of work or problem.
- *The tutor* – set advisers should have good tutoring skills which include presentational skills. All set advisers from time to time have to take on a tutorial role. They must have the requisite skills and experience for this to be done effectively and with credibility.

INTERPERSONAL ROLES

Because the Action Learning approach is very much a social process involving group interaction, the set adviser has roles to adopt here. The following were considered:

- *The friendly helper* – the set adviser has, from time to time, to deal with stress, frustration and depression that some associates and some sets experience on programmes. They may need someone to talk to, someone who can provide help, support and a smile. The set adviser's role is important here.
- *The motivator* – in addition to providing the 'cup of tea and sympathy', the set adviser must also help some associates to jerk themselves out of the despondency and despair into which they may have sunk and give them prods and probes to keep up their motivation.
- *The negotiator* – set advisers occasionally have to negotiate on behalf of associates with faculty, and vice versa. Skills in this area could be important.

VALIDATION ROLES

Set advisers may have to assess work submitted by associates and take part in the examining procedure. They need, therefore, to consider the following roles:

- *The stern critic* – all associates must be able not only to put forward ideas and arguments but also to defend them. The set adviser should develop a challenging environment in which this kind of response from associates can be developed.
- *The evaluator* – this covers many aspects of the work of a set. It may concern the realism and feasibility of proposals for a project, or the timetable and plan for the submission of a piece of work. Evaluation with the associate will enable him/her to establish the right level and quality of work.
- *The judge* – in terms of assessing pieces of work and taking part in the *viva voce* process, the set adviser has to make judgements about associates' performance levels. This can sometimes take the set adviser away from possibly preferred roles in the earlier parts of the process, e.g. the friendly helper or the motivator, and can be difficult for some set advisers to adopt.

Most of these roles will be necessary from time to time, but not all of them all of the time. Some will be required at the beginning of the programme and perhaps again at the end, others more during the middle of the process. Set advisers should be able to think through these roles and adopt or practise them effectively.

17 Action Learning Pan-setting*

Gordon Wills

Management development executives are always concerned to ensure, wherever feasible, a good level of cross-fertilization among senior managers on programmes of management development. It is perceived culturally as likely to be beneficial for a variety of reasons and programme participants invariably comment favourably on it. The deliberate design of events to ensure or enhance such benefits is rarely reported, however. There is also a total lack of definition of what cross-fertilization means, and how any substantive, as opposed to ephemeral, benefits flow from it.

The process described here was designed to overcome one of the most regular criticisms of Action Learning sets that is clearly closely related to the cross-fertilization issue. The lessons learnt and the methods used are more widely applicable, and have indeed been used on in-company programmes subsequently.

Ever since International Management Centres (IMC) commenced its qualification programmes for Action Learning, participating managers have expressed 'curiosity' about how other sets pursuing similar qualification programmes were working nationally and multinationally.

Until 1989, the only occasion when sets formally mixed together to share such information was at the pregraduation debriefing workshops. That is a multinational affair and, for a day, sets from all over the world share and compare how they succeeded in reaching their common qualification goal – normally an MBA or Bachelor of Management. In the euphoria of success, the process of mixing has been deemed fascinating/interesting. It helps greatly to create a sense of broad community among IMC's Action Learners that working in sets can never achieve. But it all takes place in a celebratory atmosphere. Critiques of the way IMC works with sets were, of course, derived and common issues highlighted for action by set advisers and others in the future. However, it could hardly be said that sets *learnt* from one another in any meaningful way.

*Originally published in *Training & Management Development Methods*, vol. 5, no. 2, 1991.

PAN-SETTING INTRODUCED

To celebrate IMC's 25th anniversary in 1988, we resolved *inter alia* to attempt what many saw as a contradiction of Action Learning. We targeted our sights on encouraging well-established sets to break out for two of their weekend workshops and mix with others at a broadly similar stage of learning development. The two themes chosen were international business and action for implementation. These themes had hitherto been considered by sets on their own.

Pan-setting was designed for six sets of approximately ten managers each, on the first occasion we attempted it. Two were exclusively single-company sets and the other four mixed-company or 'open' sets. Not surprisingly, as the outcome showed, the different sets had very diverse cultures which had evolved over their working lives. They had differing relationships with their set advisers. They had different patterns of self-discipline – timekeeping, dedication, supportiveness one to another.

To assist in coping with these issues, set advisers were encouraged to attend the pan-set workshops. They began and ended with normal set meetings to prepare and debrief among familiar faces.

Preparation required each set to have previously discussed, and provided to the tutorial team leading the pan-set workshop, details of the significant issues affecting each individual in the subject area to be covered. In order to overcome any feeling that the pan-set into which all managers were going to be placed (there were to be seven pan-sets) was a better configuration than any other one, a flipchart gallery and a key issues noticeboard were instituted for cross-checking of themes emerging.

THE FIRST ENCOUNTER

The first encounter was a nervous one. The venue was bristling with faculty members who were there either to help, to watch, or to take advantage of discussing this and that with so many set members in one place at one time. More than one or two Doubting Thomases were there as well.

It was an uncomfortable first weekend. Certainly the curiosity of set members to meet one another was satisfied. But there was little evidence of the seven specially convened pan-sets working well together. One set mutinied, by opting out of the pan-setting process to do the work in their familiar framework of members. Disparities between levels of set advising and tuition between one set and the other surfaced and blurred the landscape.

The focus was international business, but many were not appropriately aware of its implications in their enterprises – be it a government department or personnel function. They were emotionally disaffected from the theme and had not done the preparation in as rigorous a way as others had. The cultural analogy we drew between pan-setting and international business, though extremely elegant academically, missed the point with the vast majority of participating managers and faculty. So did the proposition that almost every enterprise makes very considerable use of international business on the input/supply side of its activities, even if it does not always export or have offices or ventures overseas.

With hindsight, such reactions should have been expected because they are frequently encountered throughout set processes. What was different, of course, was that pan-setting magnified them and less attention was available to deal with them on a pro-rata basis.

Yet we were convinced (and wanted to be convinced) that the notion of pan-setting had to be good. The challenge was how to make it work effectively. We confessed to all managers that we felt it had not gone too well, and asked for their advice on what to do better/differently next time.

TRYING TO DO BETTER NEXT TIME

The sets and their advisers all agreed that a stronger P (knowledge) input was required, including outside speakers on the topic under discussion. Secondly, it was not felt to be feasible to expect pan-sets (which remained favoured except with the dissident set) to replace the normal set mechanisms, so we should not try. However, the pan-sets should be formed on the basis of the pre-collected themes and issues. In this way, each pan-set would share a common adversity, making it an appropriate forum for sorting out how to proceed.

Thirdly, the key issues noticeboard and flipchart gallery should be more aggressively exploited. They provided an excellent basis for sharing important issues as they emerged.

In each of these recommendations, the managers involved were saying implicitly and intuitively: 'Don't get us together on the basis that it would be interesting, wouldn't it, to meet other managers on other sets. Get us together on a businesslike basis:

1. To give us some powerful P input up front.
2. To get us working in pan-sets on common adversity themes in relation to the P input.
3. To get us to work on a dynamic basis sharing and comparing what emerges.'

These recommendations were adopted as the basis for the second pan-set workshop on action for implementation. All attending were told beforehand that we had considered their ideas and were keen to persevere until we had pan-setting right.

Not surprisingly therefore the second workshop went better. The whinges of the first workshop did not recur. The feedback session voted the revised model worthwhile for the future because pan-setting:

1. Indeed created a broad sense of community for IMC set members who would otherwise meet only one another.
2. Permitted focused cross-fertilization, once the threshold was overcome, with others who shared goals to complete the qualification within the subject addressed.
3. Provided scope for mass grassroots lobbying on the centre of IMC which could be more effective in securing action on issues and problems.
4. Provided variety in the learning events which was good for motivation.

The pan-set approach was accordingly continued.

The feedback workshops' advice went further, however. The pan-sets recommended that future 'international business' workshops should be convened on the European mainland, provided the costs were managed wisely – with continental managers participating.

They also recommended that an additional pan-set, an unashamedly *P* leading edge conference (LEC) should be convened annually. This has now been taken up and the first LEC is scheduled for 1992.

They reminded IMC that it had to do an excellent 'selling' job on why pan-setting was undertaken in the first place for all sets at their start-ups, so that the first pan-set workshop would get off to a quicker start than had been achieved on this occasion. They felt that this point could not be over-emphasized. To spring pan-sets as a surprise, disrupting the regular pattern of work without a very coherent explanation, and the maximum support from set advisers and tutors, was never likely to be successful on any occasion. The structure and culture of the sets as evolved in any Action Learning programme was too powerful for it to work.

Finally, they recommended that IMC should bring their managerial helpers sponsors/mentors from their workplaces together annually at a 'pan-managerial helpers' workshop'. This has not yet been acted upon in that form, but is being addressed through a management development workshop series and with a workshop for helpers on in-company programmes.

EXHIBIT 1: THE EVOLVED PAN-SET GUIDELINES

Managers tend to learn best in groups. For those using an Action Learning approach to development and learning, the term 'set' is often used to describe such a learning group. A set is characterized by mutual support, shared problems or opportunities and a degree of self-management (among other things). The set then grows into a strong, motivated, more or less self-sufficient unit.

So far so good. But if the set has a weakness it may be, paradoxically, that the very things which give it such strength and effectiveness may cause it to be insular, introspective and convergent in its thinking.

The pan-set process seeks to introduce divergence and a greater degree of cross-fertilization, without losing the dynamics of the set. It involves a number of sets who will work together temporarily, in new groupings called 'pan-sets'. These groups come together most beneficially on a common issue of concern rather than being formed at random, or by team or learning styles.

The following notes aim to give tutors, trainers or programme directors a full picture of how they can design and run a pan-set workshop.

PREPARATION AND BRIEFING

The important priority is to prepare a synopsis of key issues facing learners in their organizations.

Almost every manager has something he or she is changing or would like to change. The briefing should ask for details of perceived barriers or problems, and desired outputs.

Each participant should submit one sheet of paper as a suggested maximum on which his or her key issue, problem and objective is outlined in about 300–500 words.

The purpose of this submission is twofold: to give tutors an outline of the key issues in the pan-set, and to give a focus to the closing, action planning session. It is very important that the submission is completed. A reminder should be sent four to six weeks prior to the date of the pan-set workshop.

CREATING THE NEW GROUPS OR PAN-SETS

The recommended option is identified by issue, as follows. As preparation, the tutorial team identifies, individually, the key issues emerging from the submissions. These might be changing markets, environmentalism, legislation, organizational culture changes, etc.

Immediately before the pan-set workshop begins, the tutorial team meets and compares key issue notes. A sensible number of issues should be identified (say 8–10 for a group of 40) and written as headings on flipcharts. Then the session starts with a general introduction and a brief synopsis of what each issue means in broad terms. Quotations from submissions should be used liberally, to demonstrate to the group that the submissions have been read and planning is obviously based on them.

Following the introduction, each member of the group is asked to note their name under the one issue which they feel is of most relevance or interest to them, before breaking for coffee, lunch, etc. Over this break period, tutors create pan-sets based on those identified under the headings. Some issues will be combined, some may have to be split. Pan-sets should have around six participants each.

IDENTIFYING OBJECTIVES

The tangible result of a pan-set workshop is an individual action plan to tackle those key issues which were identified at the outset. This should be clearly stated as an objective, and possibly posted on a permanently displayed flipchart.

The focus of the sessions moves from the general to the specific, so that by session five, managers, having wrestled with the subject area in general terms, are back on their own company issues. The dissection of a case example from their own company, such as 'pick an innovation which failed/was successful and identify the critical factors in that success/failure', provides one way to do that.

RUNNING THE SESSIONS

Each session should last around $1\frac{1}{2}$–2 hours, composed as follows:

- 5–15 minutes' tutorial introduction, outlining the objectives of the session and giving an overview or anecdotes/insights on the topic to be covered.
- 60–90 minutes' discussion in syndicates. Tutors attend each syndicate in turn (one tutor to each syndicate) or move between two to three per session. No more than one tutor should visit a syndicate in one session, to avoid unhelpful contradictions. Their role should normally be an advisory one, offering comment when asked or when appropriate, and keeping the group focused on the objective.
- 15 minutes' presentation. Each group has a presenter (in turns) who will summarize a few key discussion points, in two to three minutes only, to the group in plenary.

RED AND GREEN CARDS

Throughout the pan-set sessions, managers are encouraged to complete red and green cards and bring them back to the plenary session for discussion.

Red cards are for interesting problems which have remained unsolved in the syndicates but would provide interesting debating matter for the group in plenary.

Green cards are simply interesting statements or realizations which again serve as prompts for debate in plenary.

FLIPCHART GALLERY

Managers are encouraged to capture thoughts, discussions and conclusions on flipcharts and to bring them back to the plenary meeting room. These are displayed around the room to make, literally, a gallery for the other syndicates to inspect.

TIMETABLE FOR AN 'ACTION FOR CHANGE' PAN-SET WEEKEND

DAY 1

09.00–10.00	Tutorial team meeting to discuss submissions, key issues, tutorial strategy and pan-sets composition.
10.00–11.15	Participants assemble, own-set meetings; coffee.
11.15–12.30	*Session 1* Introduction (tutor-led); key issues, change overview, etc.
12.30–13.45	*Lunch.*
13.45–15.45	*Session 2* External change pressures (pan-set). Opportunities/threats analysis. 10 minutes' introduction, 10–15 minutes' presentation of key issues arising from discussions.
15.45–16.00	*Tea.*
16.00–18.00	*Session 3* Receptiveness to change (pan-set) (see Workbook pp. 14–15 and 31). 10 minutes' tutor-led introduction, 10–15 minutes' presentation of issues arising.
18.00	*Summary Day 1* 'Homework' as applicable in pan-sets.

DAY 2

09.00–10.00	*Session 4* Summary red and green card issues from Day 1 (tutor-led).
10.00–10.15	*Coffee.*
10.15–12.30	*Session 5* Human issues (pan-set). Focus on policies and people. Introduction and presentation as above.
12.30–13.45	*Lunch.*
13.45–15.45	*Session 6* Intrapreneurship and innovation (pan-set) (see the chapter on intrapreneurship in the book, *Action for Change: The Politics of Implementation*, and p. 69 of the Workbook). Introduction and presentations as above.
15.45–16.00	*Tea.*
16.00–18.00	*Session 7* Anatomy of an innovation; one success and one failure (pan-set). Introduction and presentations as above.
18.00	*Close Day 2* With excellent outside speaker at dinner.

DAY 3

08.45–09.45	*Session 8* Red and green card summary to date (tutor-led).
09.45–12.45	*Session 9* Action plan and presentation, as follows.
	09.45–10.00 Introduction (tutor-led)
	10.00–10.15 Coffee
	10.15–11.00 Pan-set discussion
	11.00–11.45 Individual action plan writing
	11.45–12.45 Presentations.
12.45–13.00	*Summary.*
13.00–14.00	*Lunch back with own set and end weekend.*

[*References throughout are to the PLIA Resource 'Action for Implementation', 1989, MCB University Press.*]

ACTION FOR CHANGE: NOTES ON THE TIMETABLE

DAY 1

09.00–11.15 Tutorial team meet. Agenda item: discuss key issues as submitted by participants.

Tutors reduce key issues to a sensible number. For example, these might include recruitment, environmentalism, devolution downwards, cultural change and conflict, internal communications, new product development, changes in markets and customers, acquisitions and mergers, channels of distribution, technology and management information systems, professionals as managers, restructuring, and market orientation.

Where possible, tutors should have had sight of the synopses in plenty of time to make their own listings and notes, but human nature being what it is, there will always be some late submissions. The morning is therefore devoted to tutors agreeing on the key issues and deciding sensibly how the pan-sets should be formed (see below.)

This synopsis should be one side of a sheet of A4 only, normally between 250 and 500 words. The briefing asks participants to outline very briefly the circumstances in which they are trying to achieve change, which barriers they would expect to encounter, the objectives they would be looking for and the environmental and external pressures which motivate this change.

Session 1 11.15–12.30: Introduction
The introduction is tutor-led, and gives an overview of the whole of the change area, calling on case studies as appropriate, and a summary of the key issues as outlined by the tutors and drawn from the submissions. It is good psychology at this point to use direct quotes wherever possible, to demonstrate that the synopses have indeed been carefully read and duly respected.

190

The lead or most experienced tutor should take the general introduction session and the whole of the tutorial team gives a short (up to five minutes) explanation of each key issue.

The remainder of this session is devoted to pan-set selection. The key issue headings are written on a flipchart and the group is invited to put their names under the main issue on which they wish to focus. Each participant will no doubt have two or three issues, but by indicating their main issue the groups will 'naturally' cover all which are relevant.

12.30–13.45: The group breaks for lunch.

Before the tutors join the participants for lunch, they spend a short time juggling the pan-sets around the key issues. The ideal number per pan-set is about six.

Session 2 13.45–15.45 approximately: Change pressures – External
After an introduction of approximately ten minutes, break the group into its pan-sets. The briefing here evaluates the external environmental pressures which necessitate change. The group might like to look at opportunities and threats corresponding to the Workbook Session 1, although there is little or nothing for participants to draw on in there.

15.45–16.00 would be an appropriate time to break for tea.

Session 3 16.00–18.00: Receptiveness to Change
Five or ten minutes' introduction on receptiveness to change. Participants again break into pan-sets and look at the most important things which make an organization, or their organization, receptive to change.

Some useful workbook exercises come into play here (see pp. 14–15 of the Workbook).

One or two groups chose to use the tables as outlined on p. 14, figures 6 and 7, and applied the parameters on p. 15, figure 8, to the intrapreneurial versus corporatist management style continuum. This gives an interesting picture of the various cultures in the group.

The other article to read for this session is the one beginning on p. 23, 'Innovations/A State of Mind', by Ian McDonald Wood. The innovation audit, on p. 31, again is a useful way for people to focus thinking.

Both Sessions 1 and 2 end ten to fifteen minutes early, when the participants reconvene in plenary. Each pan-set is asked to make a *very brief* presentation, of no more than three to five key issues, probably one or two minutes, on the most important outcomes of this discussion.

18.00: Any 'homework' is set.

Throughout the first two, and following, sessions the managers use the red and green card system, and the flipchart gallery. Here is a brief explanation again:

Red cards are for interesting problems, which have remained unsolved within the group, but would provide debating points for the whole group in plenary. Green cards are simply interesting statements or realizations which again serve as prompts for debate in plenary. Both are pinned to a noticeboard in the plenary room.

The flipchart gallery is exactly what it says. Flipcharts used within the groups are fixed to the walls, for all the pan-sets to wander round and inspect.

DAY 2

On a three-day programme, Day 2 would normally be a Saturday. The first session, between 09.00 and 10.00, would be red and green card feedback. In this session, the tutorial team leads discussions on the red and green cards which have been submitted to date. Focus initially on the red cards. Ask the person or group who have submitted a particular card for a brief explanation, and open the floor to debate. Be sure to prewarn the individuals concerned to achieve the best contribution. This hour-long session, as well as raising some interesting points, does justice to their contributions.

10.00–10.15: Coffee.

Session 4 10.15–12.30: Human issues
This session focuses on politics and people. Again there is an introduction, of ten to fifteen minutes, followed by a short presentation back to the plenary group by each pan-set, of approximately 15 minutes total. This means that the group would be in pan-sets between, say, 10.30 and 12.15.

12.30–13.45: Lunch.

Session 5 13.45: Intrapreneurship
Again a 10-minute introduction leads off the session, and a 15-minute close-down to finish off.

'The Intrapreneur's 10 Commandments' from the booklet, *Action for Change: The Politics of Implementation*, edited by J. Peters, can provoke much discussion. Another useful checklist and exercise is on p. 69 of the workbook, entitled 'Are You an Intrapreneur?'

15.45–16.00: Tea.

So far the programme has focused on general issues. Tutors should ensure that participants keep their eyes on the end of this programme, the individual action plan. As such the programme moves specifically to stories of success and failure within participants' own organizations.

The shock of moving from generalist, motherhood statements, into specific, action-oriented styles of thinking, can prove difficult for many participants. Therefore the timetable, with its very specific action plan output at the end, is written large somewhere in the room, and participants' attention is drawn to it frequently.

Session 6 16.00–18.00: A successful innovation and a failed innovation
Participants now move into a more specific mode, by focusing on particular case examples within their organizations. The reasons for success and failure should be outlined as clearly as possible.

Why did it fail/succeed?
Who is most responsible for its failure/success?
What could have been done better with hindsight?

This session closes Day 2. Dinner, with a focused outside speaker and pan-sets seated together, is a most valuable way to spend the evening.

DAY 3

On the morning of Day 3, which may well be a Sunday, the first session begins at approximately 08.45. Remind participants that a relatively early start is ahead of them and that this is the most important part of the whole programme – not that this will prevent some of the diehards from coming in late, or not at all, but tutors should do what they can.

Between 08.45–09.45, hold another red and green card debriefing session along the lines of the one on Day 2.

Between 09.45–10.00 an introduction to the action plan sets out exactly what we are looking for. A very useful focus for participants is to look at change as a product. This encourages them to take change in terms of market research, marketing planning, customer benefit statement, etc.

Another useful technique is to ask: 'What do I have to do to achieve this?' This, repeated, brings participants to immediate action: 'What do I do about this tomorrow morning?'

For example, a very general statement of 'changes of culture', may reduce to 'launch of training programme', 'outline objectives to the managing director', 'write a plan outlining the benefits to the managing director and to the organization', which may lead to, tomorrow morning, 'ring the managing director's secretary to fix an appointment for later in the week', and 'start work on putting the plan for change onto a single sheet of A4, outlining the benefits clearly'.

10.00–10.15: Coffee, followed by pan-set work as follows:

10.15–11.00: Discussion on the action plans.

11.00–11.45: Individual plans written.

Between 11.45–12.45 approximately, presentation is made to the plenary group. Depending on numbers, and let us say there are six pan-sets of six, this will allow ten minutes each, including questions. So the presentations must be relatively brief, around five minutes each.

It is probably most appropriate for the pan-sets to suggest their *own* nomination to make the presentation, and all of them join in on a question and answer session.

193

12.45–13.00: Closedown and summary session by the tutorial team.

13.00: Everyone breaks for lunch with their *own* set debriefing conducted during and afterwards as appropriate.

18 A Set within a Set*

Margaret Reid

The use of Action Learning with the first group of senior managers at MCB University Press has been documented elsewhere.[1] Because of its success, Action Learning has been an ongoing process within the company and a number of other sets, involving different members and levels of staff, have followed.

The latest set, the Senior Managers' Action Learning Programme (SEMAP III), had an interesting and useful structure which showed great promise for further development.

COMPANY BACKGROUND

A vision for 1994 had already been developed and published by the company's board, two main axioms being:

BUILD YE NO EMPIRES

'The first strategy must be to starve the top of the empire to let Operations operate.' There was already a precedent for 'passing the parcel' at the earliest opportunity and for building taskforces amongst operational staff. This philosophy both minimized interface problems and provided important learning opportunities for staff at all levels.

CONCENTRATE ON STRATEGIC ISSUES AND POLICIES

All areas – product/market, regional/country strategies, pricing strategies and tactics, agency relations and margin management, new launches, HRD/training, etc. – should be captured in the corporate plan, which will then directly trigger the organization from the bottom upwards, tasks being based on promotional and logistical operations, plans and budgets in accordance with determined schedules.

*Originally published in *Training & Management Development Methods*, vol. 8, 1994.

The emphasis, therefore, is to focus on projects and group taskforces to achieve the vision determined by the board.

SEMAP III

Against this background was born SEMAP III, an Action Learning set comprising ten members of the senior management team. Their brief was to consider the impact of 'Vision '94' on their own departments and roles, to complete a project (including a written report to management) on what the necessary changes would be, and to submit proposals for implementation. Where possible, projects were also to generate further projects for subordinates, thus effecting the philosophy of 'passing the parcel' and ensuring participation and involvement right down the line.

THE SET WITHIN THE SET

As well as the ten members of the SEMAP set, other managers were also involved in the change and some were undertaking projects of their own which might overlap or affect the SEMAP projects. It was therefore felt necessary to involve them also and, accordingly, a further list of eight managers was drawn up to attend some SEMAP meetings.

The problem was how to involve these other managers without disrupting the 'core set'. At the first meeting, attended only by the 'core' SEMAP members, it was decided to designate certain meetings when it would be useful to have other members present and to send the eight managers a specific invitation, well in advance, with definite times and dates. It was felt that, if this was not carefully planned, there would be a danger of upsetting the team spirit as, if the additional eight attended at their own convenience, it might be a different group of people who met every time, which would be bad for set motivation and morale. Previous experience of 'pan-setting'[2,3] had demonstrated the difficulties and the advantages of mixing sets.

The set adviser played a traditional role – it was felt that set members should be well informed and work from the 'leading edge' in each of their own areas. Accordingly, they required access to sufficient P (Revans' 'programmed knowledge'), but formal input should occur only as and when it was felt necessary by the set. One member of the parent set acted as information consultant and participants were able to make extensive use of the company's Anbar abstracting services. Two areas which were deemed by the set to merit special attention were total quality management and presentation skills, and these needs are reflected in the programme.

THE PROGRAMME

The programme was conducted during 1993 and took the following form:

- *March*: Meeting of 'core group' to determine objective and programme ($\frac{1}{2}$ day).
- *March*: Meeting of core group and parent group to determine project topics (full day).
- Informal meetings of sub-groups.
- *April*: Progress meeting of core group ($\frac{1}{2}$ day).
- *May*: Meeting of core group and parent group to evaluate project outlines (full day).
- *June*: Meeting of core group ($\frac{1}{2}$ day).
- *June*: Written submissions of project proposals to the board.
- *July*: Meeting at Bradford University library. Workshop on 'Effective use of information resources' (core set).
- *July*: Quality workshop (core set).
- *September*: Presentation skills (core set).
- *30 September*: Written submission of project reports to the board of directors.
- *October*: Oral presentations to the board.

Each set member gave a presentation to the board and to members of the parent group, and was given private feedback. On the following morning, four areas of strategic importance were defined and the set members, along with the parent set and the directors, were allocated to specific groups, each of which focused on one of the four areas, and a general discussion took place. This was to ensure concentration on strategic issues – the second axiom of 'Vision '94'.

PROJECTS

The projects undertaken were as follows:

- Launching a region-specific journal. A case study: Empowerment of black managers: the Southern African experience.
- A country-specific development model.
- Benchmarking for quality.
- Developing a qualitative framework for editorial excellence.
- What price quality in the role of customer service?
- An evaluation of MCB's current copyright procedures.
- Enhancing corporate/operational performance and developing middle managers within the production department.
- Literati and RPTS: the way forward.

- The development of a logistics strategy for the distribution, handling and stockholding of MCB's publications and promotional materials.
- Identifying and implementing the key training requirements within the new sales operations department.

EVALUATION

As yet, it is too early to evaluate the results of the projects. A number of projects were generated for subordinates and future sets, but again it is too soon to consider the merit of these. What can be said is that the arrangement of a parent group and a core group appears to be a promising development. In this case, the purpose was to keep everyone informed and participating. One of the problems which can be encountered by Action Learning is that of interesting and involving other employees. Sets I have encountered have felt that they were regarded by the rest of the organization as an 'élite', arousing suspicion and even jealousy. Bringing those concerned into the set as a parent group involves them directly and reduces the danger of a 'them and us' syndrome. In appropriate circumstances it could also be a useful way of bringing in mentors or clients. People from outside the core set can bring in new perspectives and ways of thinking. This structure might also help in the development of members of the parent set in giving an understanding of the problems of others.

REFERENCES

1 D. Sutton, 'The Problems of Developing Managers in the Small Firm' in *Training & Management Development Methods*, vol. 1, 1987, pp. 1.05–1.15.
2 G. Wills, 'Action Learning Pan-Setting' in *Training & Management Development Methods*, vol. 5, 1991.
3 G. Prideaux and B. Smith, 'Pan-Setting II: An Experience in Integrating Management Learning Sets' in *Training & Management Development Methods*, vol. 5, 1991.

19 Managers Developing Others through Action Learning*

Alan Mumford

A good deal is known about the design and delivery of Action Learning programmes. Philosophy, content and delivery have been discussed extensively. The role of set advisers has been described and a few participants have written about their experiences.[1,2] However, very little attention has been paid to the context at work within which the individual learner attempts to carry through the content and processes of the programme. Particularly, although reference has been made in the literature to the significant role of bosses, mentors and clients, very little is available on how the interaction between these individuals and the learner on an Action Learning programme should be managed most effectively. This chapter looks at the experiences of learners, bosses, mentors and clients in MBA and BMgt programmes based on Action Learning, run by International Management Centres in the UK.

DEFINITIONS

There has been confusion in the management development literature over the different roles of boss, mentor and client. Clutterbuck[3] gave the biggest push to the idea and practice of mentoring through his bestselling book; in the second edition he gave greater emphasis to the different roles of boss and mentor. I believe there are six different roles for people in a line management relationship with managerial learners at work – the six helpers:

1. Grandboss.
2. Boss.
3. Mentor.
4. Client.

*Originally published in *Industrial and Commercial Training*, vol. 27, no. 2, 1995.

5. Colleagues.
6. Subordinates.

This project focused on boss, mentor and client, although there were a few references from those interviewed about the other three roles.

- *Boss* The direct line manager of the programme participant.
- *Mentor* A manager within the programme participant's organization outside a direct line relationship, i.e. not a boss or grandboss.
- *Client* A manager within the programme participant's organization for whom the master's project is undertaken; other assignments may also have a client.
- *Programme participant* The individual who is undertaking the IMC programme.

METHODOLOGY

Because the project focused on the effectiveness of relationships between individuals, it was decided to gain the necessary information by personal interview. The alternative of a questionnaire was considered because it would provide a much larger quantity of information. However, the likelihood of a greater depth and therefore quality of information from personal interviews led to the choice of this (more expensive in time) approach. Twenty-six participants were seen – 16 male, 10 female. All four mentors and the one boss were male. Of the five mentors and bosses, all except one was commenting on a relationship about which the programme participant was also interviewed. Twenty-two participants were talking about experiences over the last two years; four were delving further back in their memory, perhaps as far as five years. Additional comments were gained from the business school faculty most involved, and from two sponsoring management development advisers.

VIEWS OF PARTICIPANTS

Participants were not asked to discuss the general effectiveness of the programme, what they had learned from it or what they had applied; nor did the discussion review the general effectiveness of Action Learning as a process, the skills of tutors or the nature of interaction in the Action Learning sets.

UNDERSTANDING THE PROGRAMME

The relationship between participant and boss or mentor is influenced by factors outside the immediacy of that particular working relationship, but particular to the programme the participant is attending. The participant may have arrived on the programme through an organization-sponsored process – but this may or may not have involved real support from their immediate boss. Several participants identified that their bosses were very supportive of the idea of the MBA programme and particularly an Action Learning MBA programme. In contrast, one participant reported his boss as saying 'The MBA is bullshit'.

Other participants had identified the programme for themselves and then sold it within their organization. However, in those cases where participants discussed this initiating element there seemed no difference between organization-sponsored and self-identified participants in terms of the attitude of bosses or mentors.

The shared characteristic was that more often than not bosses and mentors were reported to be not fully aware of what the MBA programme was about and, particularly, not really familiar with the philosophy and practices of Action Learning. A number of them, however, seemed to have grasped that because this is an in-post programme there was a great deal of emphasis not only on the demands that would be placed on participants in terms of time, but specifically that most participants were told not to expect any time to be given to them at work for their MBA requirements.

UNDERSTANDING THE ROLES OF BOSS, MENTOR AND CLIENT

Most participant interviewees were not very clear about what the IMC input had been on the issue of these different roles, and how they should be handled. Some quoted some discussion during the start-up process but none of them could identify particular points that were made. Some also mentioned discussion once the programme got under way as sets discussed problems and issues, especially as the various written assignments were given out and completed and participants discussed with colleagues help they were receiving or not receiving at work.

The universal feeling of participants was that they felt that bosses, mentors and clients seemed not to have a clear view of their role as required by the programme. None of them seemed to be aware that some bosses and mentors would have attended an IMC event designed to help them with the role. The one exception to this was where participants were fortunate enough to have as a boss or mentor someone who had himself completed the IMC MBA and was therefore more familiar with what was required, at least in general terms.

None of the participants had ever discussed with a boss, mentor or client what the participant's expectations of those role holders were.

The general conclusion was that IMC should do more to develop understanding by bosses, mentors and clients. In contrast, none of the participants seemed to think that they should have taken the initiative in bringing about a discussion themselves.

DESIRED BEHAVIOURS

In retrospect participants identified behaviours of these role holders which were seen as helpful:

- listening
- being accessible
- being interested
- opening doors
- providing information
- reviewing problems
- giving support
- reading my work
- helping me with implementing the projects
- being proactive and not solely reactive
- giving me some work time for the MBA.

Similarly, participants identified some things they did not want:

- I want to discuss my problems and the work given me on the MBA, not get answers to the problems.
- My boss took the first written assignment I gave him and went through it as if he were the academic marker. I never gave him another chance to do that.

Some, but not all, participants recognized the distinction between a boss and a mentor. The general comment was that whereas a boss would emphasize work, performance-related issues and the relevance of the assignments being undertaken, a mentor would be more likely to talk about wider issues.

The majority had not timetabled their discussions with either boss or mentor, and some now wished that they had done so. Equally, some preferred a situation where they could ask to see a boss or a mentor whenever they had a need. Similarly, some liked the process used by their bosses in which discussion about progress on the programme in general or on particular assignments was tacked on to a normal one-to-one management meeting. One participant highlighted the issues many had experienced: 'I found that dropping in on my boss did not really work satisfactorily for either of us, and eventually I arranged a series of dates with him'.

In a sense these were the mechanical aspects of expectation negotiation between the two parties. The issues of what kind of relationship the participants were looking for could be more subtle. Were they looking for a brain to help them, or a shoulder to lean on? In other words, were they looking primarily for managerial-type help or personal help? Participants' descriptions of the kind of thing they were looking for were essentially brain centred. Did they not want a more personal relationship – or did they not expect to receive it and therefore not ask for it or comment on its absence? 'Neither of us was much into soul searching' and 'I could not discuss my stress with my boss – I was not at all sure how he would use it' were typical comments.

EFFECTIVE RELATIONSHIPS AS DESCRIBED BY PARTICIPANTS

How far were the positive requirements expressed by participants met and the negative aspects avoided? In the previous section the general features were described; here is a more specific list of particular behaviours.

WORK-CENTRED BEHAVIOURS

The following comments were made:

- The main thing is he does not pressure me at work.
- He gives me time and suggests other people I should see.
- He shows interest.
- He made a special effort to see me when he came to my site.
- It is okay to spend work time provided I meet my work targets (on the MBA).
- My mentor *asks* and then talks to my boss about how things are going.
- My mentor tells me, 'If you have a problem and I don't know about it, you will be in trouble'.

QUESTIONS AND LISTENING

A number of favourable remarks were:

- He rarely told me what to do – he asked me questions.
- He was good at stretching discussions beyond the immediate problem.
- He saw academic points around the particular issues we were discussing.
- He could see things that would be relevant two or three months ahead in our work.
- Basically it was his ability to look at things from a different angle.
- His questions really made me think.
- He did not overwhelm me with his own views.
- Discussion helped clarify my ideas.
- My mentor listens to my frustrations.

INFORMATION AND OPENING DOORS

Some statements on this issue were:

- He provided information I wouldn't otherwise have had.
- He talked to people from whom I needed information or ideas – opened doors.
- My mentor suggested my project, who to see, and opened doors for me.

READING

Typical comments were:

- He was an avid reader of everything I wrote.
- My mentor gave me comments on my draft project report.
- My boss would not read my assignments but would always help if I had a particular problem.

OTHER CONTRIBUTIONS

Various other observations were made, such as:

- He ensured I was given help in the office.
- He commented on how much he was benefiting from what I was doing.
- He is different from me but we like the difference.
- My mentor was that before the MBA programme.
- I would choose the same mentor.

It was interesting to note that all these comments are about things that bosses or mentors did. There was only one exception where a participant described something he did: 'I go into the discussion with a list of questions'.

UNSATISFACTORY RELATIONSHIPS

There were many fewer comments about negative aspects of relationships, but this may be because expectations were low or unclear as indicated earlier in this chapter. The causes of unsatisfactory feelings by participants included:

- My boss was geographically distant.
- My mentor visited my site and would fail to see me.
- It is always work first – MBA a poor second.
- You feel guilty about asking someone who is so busy.
- He does not interfere, but he does not help either.
- More interest would have helped – it was hard work doing the MBA and tackling a new job at the same time.

- He just says in our normal management meeting, 'Is it going okay?' This is not really much encouragement.
- I think my boss felt threatened by my doing the MBA.
- I had four bosses during the programme – all of them inactive.
- I had two jobs and four bosses and never really got close to them in relation to the MBA.
- I had three bosses, all with different attitudes.
- I had three bosses at the same time.

Finally a comment that seems particularly important: 'I should have asked for more help'.

OTHER ISSUES

A variety of comments were made on a range of subjects affecting the effectiveness of the relationship:

- My boss was very keen because my work was so relevant to improvements he wanted.
- The senior managers do not have a stake in my longer-term development.
- My boss is scared if I see more senior people.
- My boss is rare in seeing both business and development benefits.
- I wish I had had both a boss and a mentor.
- We need both a boss and a mentor – different interests, knowledge, priorities.
- We ought to set out our mutual expectations and commit.
- We ought to have regular reviews of progress.
- I got less help from the set than I would have liked (on work relationships).
- This organization does not reward learning, or the work that boss or mentor puts in.

The female participants had all had male mentors and bosses; none of them indicated any problems arising from this.

There was very rarely any reference to involvement by a participant's grandboss.

There was very little specific reference to the client, other than the few points made earlier. This may be because boss and client were the same person, and participants during the interviews may not have distinguished between the roles.

The project did not direct attention towards colleagues of participants and the extent to which they might have helped. A few references were made, however, often to colleagues acting as a surrogate mentor.

VIEWS OF BOSSES AND MENTORS

Views were obtained from one boss and four mentors, compared with 26 participants. Within the constraints of the total number of people it was possible to interview, this disproportion was deliberate: 'help is defined by the person being helped'.[4]

SELECTION OF MENTORS

All four mentors interviewed were organizationally chosen (a few of the participants had actually found their own mentors). Those interviewed agreed on two main issues about selection:

1. The mentor must see the relationship as being one which is crucial for business reasons as well as development.
2. The chosen mentor must be able to give time. 'This is more important than mentoring skills, which he won't have time to exercise.'

TRAINING

Most of the mentors had received some training – a half-day or one-day workshop which generally included an introduction to Action Learning on the programme as a whole as well as specifics about mentoring relationships. Several of them commented, however, that other mentors in their organization had not participated and thought this was unfortunate.

BENEFITS TO MENTORS

Mentors were offered four reasons why they might have acted in this role:

1. Improving the performance of an individual would reflect favourably on your own management ability.
2. You would derive satisfaction from helping someone to grow.
3. You might develop your own skills, knowledge and insights as a result of discussion with the individual.
4. Your organization required you to be involved, through its formal management development system requesting you to act as a mentor.

The majority saw 'personal satisfaction' as being the main benefit, accompanied by the development of the mentor's own skills, knowledge and insights. One of the mentors talked about it being a reciprocal relationship: 'Every ten minutes I spend with him gives me six minutes' benefit as well'.

ARRANGING DISCUSSIONS

The majority of mentors talked about *ad hoc* discussions in offices and sometimes in the corridors. One deliberately arranged meetings outside the office in the evenings so that they could be longer and less subject to interruption. They all commented on the time required. Two of them said that although they had not understood how much time would be required of them they would still choose to be mentors; one said he would be discouraged by the time requirement in future. Two mentors said that on reflection they would now timetable the discussions better, partly to see the needs of the participants and partly to manage their own time more effectively.

RELATIONSHIP WITH BOSSES

Only one of the mentors had had a discussion with a participant's boss during the programme.

MEETING OF MENTORS

One mentor referred to attempts to arrange meetings with fellow mentors (sponsored by the management development adviser), but said this had not worked successfully. Several of them said that such a meeting would be a good idea 'if you could get everyone to go'.

HELPFUL BEHAVIOUR

Understandably mentors focused on the behaviours they saw as appropriate from bosses and mentors rather than the behaviours of the participants. Their comments included:

- I read his assignments.
- I offer hints, not instruction.
- I am oblique but X wanted more direct guidance.
- I opened some doors for him – and I tell the door what is involved.
- I point them to sources of information.
- If they come back to you, you can feel that you have been helpful.
- One of the benefits to me was learning what was going on in a different part of the organization and at a lower level of management.
- It is more difficult being a mentor than being a boss – you have to give guidance, not instruction.
- We were geographically distant, using the e-mail and the telephone as a poor substitute.
- We can get away with a casual relationship between boss and mentor in the UK – it would not work that way in France.

Some identified things they had not been comfortable with:

- I did too much off the cuff; I was too reactive.
- I should have met and discussed things with other mentors.
- His felt urgency was not always mine.

Finally, one mentor said there were three real issues involved:

1. How much help should be offered?
2. What kind of help?
3. When should it be offered?

Another mentor would have added a fourth point to the list:

4. Who should you talk to about what?

COMMENTS FROM IMC FACULTY

Faculty agreed that no single strategy for bosses and mentors will work everywhere. Personnel specialists and possibly even managers will welcome serious effort on the boss and mentor relationship in some organizations. How far can IMC press the case for serious attention to, for example, selection and training where there is not initially such a welcome? Currently the one-day training programme is offered to mentors and not necessarily to bosses. This was thought to be a mistake. This is true not least because there is still confusion over the different roles of boss, client and mentor.

SELECTION

There are problems when mentors are appointed from the centre – they may neither particularly welcome the appointment nor be welcomed by the participants. On the other hand, it is too much to ask of participants that they manage to find their own mentors. Some participants, already senior in their organization, will need less of a mentor, for example in opening doors. More junior managers require more effort.

The main requirement of mentors is that they should be accessible and should provide time.

THE LEARNING ORGANIZATION?

The ideal position would be that of an organization, the culture of which welcomed learning, and also a designed and managed boss and mentor relationship with the participant. IMC, fortunately, had the experience of working with one or two organizations which came close to the desirable model. If there is an existing good-quality management development process in being, which may well have involved some work with mentors, this provides a better environment.

The personnel function tends to see the mentoring role as one providing development for the mentor – does the mentor see it the same way?

PARTICIPANT EXPECTATIONS

The point that too much reliance can be placed on participants to negotiate the selection of mentors and of the relationship with bosses and mentors has already been made. In addition it was commented that the level of participant affects both what they have the confidence to do and the confidence to ask for in terms of the relationship.

COMMENTS FROM ORGANIZATION-BASED MANAGEMENT DEVELOPMENT ADVISERS

Two in-house advisers gave their perspective on a number of the issues raised earlier in this chapter. Some of their points follow, although not all the valuable insights they offered have been included here in order to protect the confidentiality of their comments.

SELECTION OF MENTORS

Both had originally selected the mentors. In one case now he asks the participant himself to suggest a mentor but then decides whether this choice is appropriate. In the other case the participant is told to find himself one. In both cases they have gone for mentors two levels up in the organization.

TRAINING OF MENTORS

Both had provided a one-day training programme for mentors.

MENTOR MEETINGS

Both had arranged mentor meetings, but there were big problems in bringing them all together in one place at the same time. The idea was to discuss progress and problems.

INITIATIVE FROM PARTICIPANTS

Both emphasized that participants must not just expect to have everything done properly, but must take the initiative and ask for what they want, when they want it and how they want it.

BOSSES AND MENTORS

One adviser had expected a clash between bosses and mentors but it had not happened so far.

GUIDANCE FOR MENTORS

In addition to the training day there should be a one-page 'A mentor should' list. There should be additional information about the programme and Action Learning but this should not overwhelm the mentor aspects.

CONCLUSIONS

HAS ENOUGH BEEN ACHIEVED?

At the highest level of generality it can be said that most participants gained something from most bosses and mentors. Some had gained great benefits. The overwhelming impression, however, is of participants who had undefined original expectations, and whose experiences led them later to define what would go into an effective relationship at a level well below that which might have been achieved.

This comment is supported by two observations. First, the issue of how and when discussions are arranged. On reflection the majority of the participants wished there had been more structure, more clarity and more determination about holding meetings. This was not to deny the value of having a boss or mentor who was available for immediate issues, but merely to say that that could then have been treated as an additional process rather than the basic provision. A more controversial observation is that if we look at the list of positive behaviours experienced and sought by participants it does not set very high targets in terms of a developmental relationship. Skills of listening and asking the right questions, for example, are absolutely necessary (particularly in an Action Learning programme). However, this does not really extend the relationship beyond a decent expectation about discussing managerial problems. The potential exists for a more in-depth relationship based on developmental processes.

This is after all a unique opportunity. To base a developmental relationship between, for example, a mentor and a participant on that potentially extraordinarily fruitful issue of the combination of task and learning is for most people novel. It is understandable that the interviewees in this project should not have expressed this as being absent. If you do not know what the possibilities are, you do not know what you have missed. Generally the impression here is of a number of bosses and mentors who made a decent attempt to be available to deal with problems, and a few who expressed much more profound involvement with the participant. To achieve fuller advantage from this unique relationship, however, they would need to understand more about the nature of learning and the nature of a helping relationship. Since Action Learning is based on the immense productivity involved in learning from undertaking real tasks, the relationship between participants, bosses, mentors and clients, itself a managerial task, ought also to be recognized by all parties as a developmental experience, not simply a problem-solving one. This could be achieved, for example, by enabling all those in these relationships to recognize the stages of the learning cycle they are going through – and indeed to make positive use of differences in learning style as was attempted in one organization early on in IMC's development of the mentor relationship. Another contribution would be to enable bosses, mentors and clients to understand better the nature of help.[4]

INHERENT CONFLICTS

The potentially marvellous productivity involved in creating learning from tasks which is at the crux of Action Learning is one which is constantly challenged by the nature and priorities of managerial tasks. Managers are relatively easily influenced to recognize the possibilities involved in learning from tasks as structured through IMC's MBA. The general attractiveness of this proposition is often challenged, however, and overwhelmed by the specific nature of an in-post programme where the challenges of tasks reassert themselves as the highest priority. Even within those tasks structured within the MBA there is an inclination to regress into treating successful achievement of the task as a target and benefit in its own right. More has to be done to bring about recognition that the fullest benefit is obtained when it is treated as a balanced task and learning process.

ROLES OF BOSSES, MENTORS AND CLIENTS

Although many have had worthwhile experiences at the level of expectation commented on above, many participants commented that bosses and mentors were insufficiently aware of what exactly they should be doing. Not surprisingly, there were differences of view about what, for example, a mentor should provide. Sometimes one participant expressed conflicting requirements. On the one hand, a participant does not want too much interference. On the other hand, they want help with a problem. Some like relatively unstructured *ad hoc* discussions of need, but also said that of course busy bosses were not always available when you needed them. Some in retrospect would have preferred much more structured discussion, structured partly around expectations, even perhaps a learning contract, and partly at the more immediate level of a timetabled set of meetings.

The need surely is not to provide a single template to which all mentors, bosses and participants must fit, but to ensure that all those involved are enabled to make conscious choices about what they want from each other, how they want it and when they want it. It is fine to say that managers who are thought of sufficiently well to be given an expensive MBA programme ought to be able to sort things out for themselves. The question is really exactly what it is that they are expected to sort out. The main requirement is surely that an agreement needs to be negotiated, that the participant can take the initiative in setting up a discussion about expectations, but that the discussion ought to be based on a set of suggestions about the range of expectations from which they can choose. An agreement of this kind is likely to be more powerfully influential than the inevitably short doses of coaching and mentoring skills provided in some organizations.

Compared with most other forms of management development (perhaps all other forms) Action Learning provides not only a greater opportunity for integrated learning in the interaction between bosses, mentors, clients and participants, but also places a greater requirement if the potential gains are to be achieved.

LEARNING FOR MENTORS

In at least some organizations represented in this survey, and no doubt in others, mentors are seen as being given a developmental experience. In the same way that the learning of participants from the relationship ought to be a matter of conscious review, so the nature of the development secured by the boss or mentor ought to be part of a formal review. At the basic level they should be encouraged again through a simple checklist to review their learning for themselves. In some organizations it would no doubt be more appropriate to suggest that this is shared more widely among other mentors, and could even form part of the structured personal development plans that many organizations now try to encourage managers to design for themselves.

SELECTION

It was interesting that the experience of at least two of IMC's leading clients has moved away from the somewhat authoritarian appointment of mentors to a process requiring more agreement at least between the mentor and the participant. Faculty members commented that, in some other organizations where participants had been left to find their own mentor, this had been found to be very unsatisfactory. Of those participants interviewed, a couple preferred to find their own after initial disappointments with the originally appointed mentor, but a couple of others described the difficulty involved in, as it were, taking themselves round and selling themselves to a potential mentor.

No doubt this again is something on which appropriate processes will vary according to the past history and nature of the organization. The extreme form of 'find your own' seems unlikely to produce the best result in most organizations. Some form of discussion between the participant and a management development adviser would seem more likely to be profitable. Equally, in organizations which take seriously the development of senior managers this is genuinely a development opportunity where the initiative might be taken by the management development function and suggested to the participant. In this latter case, however, if this is to be taken seriously, the kind of learning review process indicated above ought to be followed through.

As one of the participants commented, the differences between himself and his mentor were significant but helpful in developmental terms. Ideally a decision about pairing of mentor and associate would be taken with the two of them aware of, for example, their learning styles so that if a strong reflector is placed with a strong activist they are aware of the reason for differences of behaviour and agree how they will manage those differences. Even more idealistic might be the proposition that the same kind of analysis would go into pairing of boss and mentor so that what each provided to the participant was different. (Again, seek comments from participants on this.)

IS THIS TOO IDEALISTIC?

The general thrust of my comments has been that in a world of management development which has only just begun to recognize what has to go into the construction of effective developmental relationships, IMC has probably taken a lead in doing something to make the relationships effective. More could be achieved if more was attempted. I can hear the voices now, perhaps, of a few faculty and certainly of a few management development clients who might be saying that this was an idealistic view and they would like to agree but 'managers are too busy to pick up the points you are making'. The answer must be that all managers are interested in more effective ways of using their time. Thoughtful effort of the kind indicated here will increase productivity in the relationship.

IMPLEMENTATION

A project about Action Learning should desirably lead to action! The data conclusions and recommendations from this project were discussed by IMC's Academic Board. A number of the recommendations have been implemented, specifically 'Notes for guidance for participants, bosses and mentors'.

REFERENCES

1 A. Mumford, 'Review of action learning literature' in *Management Bibliographies & Reviews*, vol. 11, no. 2, 1985.
2 A. Mumford, 'A review of action learning literature' in *Management Bibliographies & Reviews*, vol. 19, no. 6, 1994.
3 D. Clutterbuck, *Everyone Needs a Mentor*, 2nd ed., Institute of Personnel Management, London, 1991.
4 A. Mumford, *How Managers Can Develop Managers*, Gower, Aldershot, 1993.

20 Who Cross-fertilizes Most on MBA Programmes?*

Carol Oliver, Sandra Pass, Jayne Taylor and Pam Taylor

The International Management Centres (IMC) organization was founded in 1964 to develop the effectiveness of managers in public and private enterprises worldwide. By 1990 it was Britain's leading independent multinational business school, dedicated to providing in-post management development programmes wholly based on the principles of Action Learning, pioneered by Professor Reg Revans.[1]

IMC offers the MBA on an in-company open and company consortium basis, as described elsewhere by Peters[2] and Wills.[3]

IMC's extensive MBA in-company client list comprises many blue chip enterprises, including Du Pont, Seagram, ICI, IDV, Jones Lang Wootton, Ernst and Young, CMB/Metal Box, Cummins, Pilkington, Dow Corning, Trafalgar House, Malaysian Airlines and Crown Berger. Over 600 enterprises have supported the Action Learning MBA work of IMC during the past eight years on an open set basis.

RESEARCH APPROACH

We identified a tightly defined purpose to explore and compare the relative benefits – to both associate and enterprise – on IMC's open, consortial and in-company (MBA) programmes, of cross-fertilization, including implementation, by set members. We were, it will be perceived, able to make a three-way comparison (thereby reading beyond the opinion of Baston[4]).

The term 'cross-fertilization' is certainly widely perceived as educational good news. But what is it? We resolved to define it as IMC's associates and faculty did, as:

> The absorption and implementation of ideas resulting from interaction with other members of one's own set.

*Originally published in *Industrial and Commercial Training*, vol. 23, no. 3, 1991.

We quickly learned that while cross-fertilization is thought by them to be an important criterion for improving managerial effectiveness, there were some differences as to how it took place, and how it worked. Nonetheless, we needed to clarify whether the achievement of cross-fertilization was in itself a measure of a successful management development programme and, if so, just how measurable was it?

The research instrument we favoured was a pre-agreed open-ended schedule which would enable us to conduct telephone interviews on a structured basis. We decided that by talking to people we could get the most reliable and thorough insight into their thoughts and experiences. Also, in this way we could overcome those problems of lack of response and lack of substantive data that are inherent in the structured questionnaire approach.

Indeed, our experience in attempting to pilot this research, by circulating structured questionnaires at a specific weekend workshop for immediate completion and return during the same weekend, showed just how readily such a piece of paper can be disregarded. Only a 20 per cent response was gained from 50 associates.

Because we intended to question only a relatively small sample, we were able to use a telephone interview and could more easily enlist their co-operation, guide them through the questions (whilst taking care not to influence their responses) and obtain richer information on which to base analysis. No method is ever complete plain sailing – a few associates were constantly unavailable, while one or two gave terse responses. However, the overwhelming majority were extremely helpful and willing to share their opinions and experiences.

Thirty-one MBA associates were chosen randomly from a population of 130 to participate in this study. They came from the three main types of MBA sets: open, 10; consortial, 7; in-company, 14.

The associates confirmed that cross-fertilization has occurred in their sets both at a personal level and for the benefit of others to their certain knowledge. The immediacy of an associate's awareness was limited, however. Most typically they perceived a lagged effect, sometimes not discerned until reflected upon after completion of the programme.

It has always been apparent to IMC faculty members conducting in-company, open and consortial sets that their Action Learning dynamics potentially differ. They have constantly taken a contingent approach.[5] Whether the dynamics differ in a manner which specifically affects the improvement of managerial effectiveness will be contingent on a wide range of factors that go well beyond the obvious observation of the company origins and mix of associates.

However, the simplistic view has been reported by Baston,[4] albeit on no basis of relevant published evidence, that there is a 'strong body of opinion which suggests that consortial programmes are preferable to solely in-company programmes because of the lack of opportunity for cross-fertilization of ideas between managers from different companies on the latter type of programme'.

He similarly asserts that: 'The opportunity for participants to mix with managers of different cultures and the resulting cross-fertilization of ideas and viewpoints is regarded by many as an essential element of the MBA experience'. Baston's report of the opinion of others has been echoed by Anderson,[6] Devine[7] and Rogers,[8] yet still without any evidence presented.

Most of the individuals whose opinions were being reported are unlikely to have been involved in any depth in the reality of the range of MBA programmes under comparison. The explanation for their opinions must, accordingly, lie in their own theory of the intrinsic nature of the reality of all MBA programmes and the processes of cross-fertilization therein.

Although IMC has pioneered the growth worldwide of the in-company MBA programme, for several established reasons of customer motivation, these have not encompassed cross-fertilization as a distinctive benefit. IMC has, along with those listed above, always espoused a belief that cross-fertilization is intrinsic to all such activities. Nevertheless, the fact that readily offered opinion seems to hold the view that less will occur in the form IMC uses most frequently, makes it a significant area for seeking to understand reality better. Our first exploration reported below can readily be seen as modest, but we firmly believe a start needed to be made if the unsubstantiated basis of increasingly voiced opinion was not to be consolidated through sheer repetition.

The only serious analyses of in-company MBA programmes, which do not specifically address cross-fertilization, have been by Boot[9] and Espey.[10] They discussed Lancaster University's Management School work with British Airways, and IMC's with IDV (UK).

LANGUAGE OF REALITY FROM THE SETS

Table 20.1 tells us what associates said when asked what cross-fertilization they experienced. The language is their own.

It is evident that the benefits acquired from cross-fertilization were varied. One must surely be struck, however, by how relatively few instances were cited overall. Prima facie evidence seems to emerge to suggest the opinions reported by Baston,[4] that consortial sets create more cross-fertilization than in-company sets – with open sets outperforming both by a wide margin.

What is perhaps most intriguing is that by far the most dominant factor was given as the improvement in human resource skills. This was felt by several participants to have led to a substantive reappraisal of their management styles which, in its turn, had led to increased visibility within the organization.

Whilst all respondents referred to human resource skills as examples of cross-fertilization, it is interesting to note that only open set members (almost all of them, in fact) mentioned exchange of information. This would lead us to believe that they appeared to have received more stimulus from interaction with a

	Consortium (n = 7)	Open (n = 10)	In-company (n = 14)
Team-building techniques	4	4	–
Learning style techniques	2	–	–
Presentation skills	3	2	2
Improved listening skills	2	4	1
Camaraderie within set	1	–	1
Advice/problem solving	1	1	1
Understanding of different company functions	–	2	4
Report-writing skills	1	–	1
Human resource skills generally	1	3	2
Interviewing skills	–	–	1
Negotiation skills	–	–	1
Networking	–	–	3
Empathy	–	–	1
Time-management techniques	–	–	3
Learning how to apply processes (e.g. forming, storming, norming, performing)	–	–	3
Learning from other set members' methods	–	3	–
Communications skills	–	3	–
Exchange of information	–	8	–
Increased self-confidence	–	2	–
Increased self-perception	–	2	–
Openness	–	1	–
Total mentions	15	35	24
Average per associate	(2.1)	(3.5)	(1.7)

Table 20.1 Cross-fertilization personally experienced

greater variety of people from different backgrounds and organizational cultures. It begs the question, like all other comments, as to what they might do with the information gained to fertilize their managerial performance.

Finally, it was interesting to note that team-building skills were cited by open and consortial associates but not mentioned as an example of cross-fertilization at all by in-company associates. Perhaps this indicates that our in-company respondents had already developed these skills prior to joining the formal structure of a set; or have we identified a characteristic of the nominated as opposed to the self-driven associate that is frequently encountered on open programmes?

REALITY OF ACTION

Table 20.2 indicates that cross-fertilization, personally experienced, resulted in less action than might be supposed if cross-fertilization means what we defined it as meaning, i.e. absorbing and acting upon ideas gained from other set members. Even allowing for a time lag in eventual action, evidence of a halo effect, an intention to believe one has acted when one has not, seems to surround the concept of cross-fertilization. An echo perhaps of the theory of the intrinsic nature of reality of an MBA programme.

	Consortium (n = 7)	Open (n = 10)	In-company (n = 14)
Improved team building	5	5	–
Time-management skills	1	3	–
Learned value of literature search	–	1	–
Report-writing skills	1	–	–
Improved negotiation skills	–	–	1
Networking	1	–	6
Improved interpersonal skills	–	2	8
Improved listening skills	–	–	1
Use of learning styles	–	–	1
Improved marketing techniques	–	–	1
Questioning techniques	–	1	–
Decision-making skills	–	1	–
Assertiveness	–	2	–
Openness	–	1	–
Total actions	8	16	18
Average per associate	(1.1)	(1.6)	(1.3)

Table 20.2 Actions resulting from cross-fertilization

We were surprised at the lack of tangible actions that were perceived as resulting from cross-fertilization. Again the main theme was human resource skills, with a percentage of those questioned claiming to have emerged from the experience of cross-fertilization as a 'better employee' (whatever that might mean). There appeared to be some confusion in the minds of associates between what resulted from their understanding of cross-fertilization and the learning that arose from being part of an Action Learning MBA set in any event, i.e. their own self-learning from the intellectual challenges in their own reality at work.

Networking emerged as significant amongst associates from in-company sets; they appear to have built up/improved upon relationships with their workplace colleagues.[11] This compared well with the improved team-building techniques that were recognized by participants on consortial and open sets, and is perhaps a similar phenomenon in the development of managerial effectiveness.

BENEFITS OF CROSS-FERTILIZATION

There was a less diverse selection of answers when associates were challenged to pinpoint the personal benefits of cross-fertilization (Table 20.3). Again and again the belief emerged that individuals had improved their interpersonal skills and thereby gained a better understanding of colleagues and, indeed, a greater insight into their own behaviour patterns. Many of them had implemented their newly acquired team-building skills within their organizations to the declared mutual benefit of themselves and colleagues. There was, however, once again a lack of clarity in their minds between benefits gained from cross-fertilization and those which resulted from being on an Action Learning programme. We shall return to this in our conclusions.

	Consortium (n = 7)	Open (n = 10)	In-company (n = 14)
A To yourself:			
Increased job satisfaction	1	–	–
Better interpersonal skills	2	3	3
Better team relationships	1	3	4
Communications skills	–	1	2
Improved performance/effectiveness	2	3	3
Better report writing	1	–	1
Listening skills improved	1	2	2
Better understanding of colleagues	–	–	1
Better understanding of organization	–	2	2
More confidence	–	3	–
Higher profile within organization	–	2	–
B To your enterprise:			
Improved performance	3	5	2
Increased knowledge and confidence	–	1	1
Enthusiasm infectious to colleagues	–	–	1
Benefit from project implementation	–	6	1
Company had major return on investment	–	2	–
Teamwork	–	1	–
Greater understanding by board	–	1	–
Total benefits	11	35	23
Average benefits per associate	(1.6)	(3.5)	(1.6)

Table 20.3 What have been/will be the benefits?

It was surprising to learn from associates on open sets that they believed they had been able to give a much wider range of benefits to the organization than those on either consortial or in-company sets. This can scarcely be considered a substantive conclusion. Perhaps it indicates that the way in which open programmes are sold to their sponsors, i.e. on the basis of implementation of a significant project and return on investment, gives greater salience to the benefits accruing and urges the open set participant to demonstrate that the benefits to their sponsoring organization have been achieved.

By contrast, the participants on in-company and consortial sets will often work to meet broader strategic company objectives. They reportedly often see the benefits more in terms of their own managerial development than in their specific contribution to the success of the company through the implementation of a single project.

Nonetheless, consortial and in-company set members interviewed felt strongly that they had the power to change things within their organization and to influence company strategy, due to their strength in numbers. This they clearly felt would not have been so easy had they been alone on an open set.

This was reinforced in the response to a direct question addressed to all associates as to whether they had a directly supporting superior or champion for their project. Well over three-quarters on consortial and in-company sets answered in the affirmative, compared with just over half on open sets.

INSIDE LOOKING OUT

Finally, associates were asked to express an opinion on what they gained and missed by participation in their particular pattern of set rather than the other two. This question was not included in the interview schedule mailed to the associates before the telephone discussion, as we did not want to influence their responses. It was added at the end of our telephone interview, enabling associates to give spontaneous answers.

Although those on open sets readily commented that they learned a good deal about other organizations and their functions, associates from in-company sets felt strongly that they had gained a better understanding of their own organization and its diverse functions. This had enhanced networking within their company and helped the gel to set more quickly because of familiarity with one another's backgrounds.

However, in-company respondents felt overwhelmingly that they had missed out on the wider perspective and the stimulation of an open set. In-company set members felt that their set could be too inwardly focused/incestuous and sometimes spent time on corporate 'bitching'. By contrast, all open set members felt that they had missed nothing by being in an open set rather than in a consortial or in-company set. Some indeed commented that there was a most welcome freedom from involvement in internal issues and frankness in all transactions.

There was a strong suggestion that consortial sets powerfully reinforced identification with one's own company (rather than the alienation often present on open programmes). They also benefited from intercompany comparisons because each enterprise had substantial representation from a range of areas. This was perceived as superior to a wholly open set and to the interdivisional patterns normally present on single in-company programmes.

CONCLUSIONS

The comments, observations and opinions reported above from associates, indicate that no generalized conclusions can be drawn concerning cross-fertilization in open, consortial and in-company sets. This has not surprised us. As indicated at the outset, IMC's received wisdom on the issue has been that cross-fertilization is contingent on a far wider range of matters than this simple consideration of three types of set structure was likely to reveal. Nonetheless, we list below something of what we believe we have discerned that may cast some light on the reports from Baston:[4]

- Cross-fertilization in the eyes of the associate tends to be seen in terms of personal skills, such as listening and interpersonal communication, and is, therefore, perceived as more beneficial to individuals than of direct benefit to their employing organizations. Ultimately, of course, such improved skills will undoubtedly benefit the company. Benefits arising from these improved skills may appear to be less significant due to their subtle nature.
- Open sets are more intellectually stimulating, due to the extensiveness of intercompany exchange that occurs between the diverse company cultures present. As such, they afford the best potential medium for stimulating cross-fertilization.
- In-company and consortial sets are more empowering in that the implementation of ideas becomes more likely due to the very high degree of organizational commitment.
- Consortial sets potentially can combine both worlds by providing an environment in which associates could experience both inter- and intra-company cross-fertilization, but our evidence does not support this observation.

FURTHER ACTION

If there was ever any doubt, there can no longer be: associates want to, and do indeed, learn from fellow set members by cross-fertilization. This is an extension of the sharing in finding solutions to common problems, or coping with adversity, which is the primary focus of Action Learning. The dividing line, if there is one, is not clear to associates. Nor do they see it as an issue of great significance provided they learn to be more effective managers. However, IMC can scarcely take this view for the future. If there are elements of Action Learning separable from cross-fertilization, then the efficacy of both could be continually enhanced by deliberate intent.

OPEN SETS ARE MORE INTELLECTUALLY STIMULATING

Our principal recommendation must therefore be for ongoing and continued research into this subject. This chapter reports no more than a pilot study, but it does offer pointers to further research – to proceed at a more advanced level. The pilot study has cast some light on a matter that has with increasing frequency been asserted – by providing preliminary evidence on how IMC MBA programme participants view cross-fertilization as a possible benefit in their learning.

Virtually every associate with whom we spoke emphasized total satisfaction in terms of what they achieved overall from their Action Learning MBA programme. But there is no comparative data on the incidence of cross-fertilization on other types of MBA programmes. We feel it would be valuable to be able to draw comparisons with other patterns that are thought to be more effective.

We feel that in any event better quality feedback from associates on cross-fertilization can be obtained in the following ways:

1. By brainstorming sessions at their concluding workshop after completing the programme.
2. By focusing on the issue in learning logs, and including it in their evaluative assessment of managerial learning – as a chapter on the incidence and implementation of cross-fertilization as experienced during the programme.

Finally, once the natural occurrence of cross-fertilization is better understood, steps should be taken by faculty to structure situations where it is more likely both to be fostered and acted upon. IMC has already taken steps, known as 'pan-setting', to bring associates together from different sets (with considerable anguish and mixed results) to facilitate cross-fertilization. Pan-setting blends open, consortial and in-company sets together in consideration of action for change and international business.[12]

Yet there must remain a haunting feeling that the cross-fertilization gauntlet thrown down by the opinionated folk Baston reports upon, is a feint. A more appropriate challenge might be to explore how best any sets of practising managers can learn both within and beyond their extant corporate cultures, whilst having available a strongly supportive environment to ensure the gaining of the benefits of that learning. Second, how does this match up against what can be accomplished in an unsupportive environment? Third, how, if at all, can pan-setting further the learning achieved?

We believe that understanding is more likely to arise from a holistic study of learning and action on MBA programmes rather than by parcelling out the element of cross-fertilization.

Finally, we believe that the effective functioning of any set of associates as a learning community is likely to play a role that is as significant, if not more so, than the environment external to the set itself.

223

REFERENCES

1 R.W. Revans, *The Sequence of Managerial Achievement*, MCB University Press, Bradford, 1984. [See Foreword]

2 J. Peters, 'Customer First: The Independent Answer' in *Business Education*, vol. 9, no. 3/4, 1988.

3 G.S.C. Wills, *Creating Wealth through Management Development*, MCB University Press, Bradford, 1988.

4 R.W. Baston, *The Company-based MBA*. Harbridge Consulting Group, London, 1989.

5 R. Rorty, *Contingency, Irony and Solidarity*, Cambridge University Press, Cambridge, 1989.

6 G. Anderson, 'A Fresh Approach to the MBA' in *Industrial and Commercial Training*, vol. 22, no. 1, 1990.

7 M. Devine, 'Company MBA' *The Director*, September, 1988.

8 J. Rogers, *Which MBA?*, The Economist Publications, London, 1990.

9 R. Boot, and J. Evans, 'Partnership in Education and Change' in *Management Education and Development*, vol. 21, pt. 1, 1990.

10 J. Espey and P. Batchelor, 'Management by Degrees', *Business Education*, vol. 9, no. 3/4, 1988. [See Chapter 21]

11 G.S.C. Wills, 'Managing Networking – The Design and Dynamics of IMC' in *Journal of European Industrial Training*, vol. 15, no. 2, 1991.

12 G.S.C. Wills, 'Action Learning Pan-setting' in *Training & Management Development Methods*, vol. 5, no. 2, 1991. [See Chapter 17]

Part IV
Programmes in Action

21 Management by Degrees*

James Espey and Pauline Batchelor

Management in Britain is slowly becoming less of an amateur affair and more of a profession. Gone are the days when the right accent and public school background were an automatic entrée into a management post. Senior executives are starting to realize that it is not enough for their managers to learn simply by doing the job, but that they need to be trained in all aspects of their business. To produce bright, challenging, lateral-thinking managers who can succeed in the contracting markets of the late 1980s, management development is essential.

The wine and spirit industry has perhaps been particularly prone to the amateur management syndrome – a liking for wine or a general interest in brewing, coupled with the right school tie and a few influential contacts, has produced much blinkered and inadequate leadership in the industry.

International Distillers & Vintners Limited (IDV) owns or controls over 20 wine and spirit marketing companies around the world. Its British-based operation, IDV (UK), is 'in the business of marketing a range of profitable, well-packaged, well-advertised, premium-priced liquor brands, be they agencies or own brands' (Mission Statement, 1983). Among its leading brands are Smirnoff Vodka, Bailey's Irish Cream, Piat d'Or, Malibu, Croft Original Sherry, and many other household names. Indeed IDV (UK) is currently the premier wine and spirit company in the UK.

In the early 1980s IDV (UK) already had a sound management development policy in the shape of a graduate recruiting and training scheme, whereby trainee managers spent time working in different divisions within the company, which gave them a breadth of vision and understanding of the complexities and day-to-day issues in the different areas. When James Espey was appointed managing director and chief executive in 1982, he was eager to build a more advanced management development programme on the existing foundations.

Before investing any money in such a programme, the chief executive first considered the possibility of modifying the existing recruitment policy by employing graduates who already had an appropriate business qualification,

*Originally published in *Journal of Management Development*, vol. 6, no. 5, 1987.

such as an MBA (Master of Business Administration). There were several drawbacks to this idea:

- Most MBA courses are geared much more to staff skills than genuine line manager skills; so the course contents were not ideal for IDV (UK)'s needs.
- MBA graduates tend to have done the course immediately after their first degree course. IDV (UK) considered that work experience was essential before the theoretical world of case studies and simulation exercises could have a real effect on an individual's development. The student needs to have learnt some of the real life issues of business and the complex factors that make for good business decisions.
- People who have studied for their MBAs after gaining several years of work experience are not easy to find. Many who would benefit from doing such a course have, by this time, financial and domestic responsibilities. They simply cannot afford to take 18 months or so off work to study. This is particularly true in the UK where managerial incomes are low by world standards.
- Those people who do take time off to do an MBA at a later stage should be treated with caution: they may be making a last desperate attempt to boost a flagging career.

It looked as though a new programme had to be devised for the development of managers within IDV (UK).

COMMITMENT OF TOP MANAGEMENT

One of the key requirements of a good management development programme is that it must be a top management responsibility. It is far too important a task to be left solely to the personnel department, whose role ought rather to be ensuring the correct implementation of the chosen training schemes. Decisions about the nature and extent of the programme must rest with senior management. The chief executive should be personally motivated by the management development programme, and the entire executive board must share responsibility for the scheme, instead of allocating it to the personnel department and forgetting about it.

Thus the first task for James Espey in 1982 was to persuade both the group board of IDV Limited and the board of IDV (UK) that an active management development policy would be highly beneficial to the company in both the short and the long term.

One of the problems about convincing any board of the value of management development programmes is that the costs are all too obvious (substantial course fees, not to mention the cost of managers' time and the disruption of their departments), whereas the benefits are less easily quantifiable. But there are positive ways of presenting the advantages of a good management development policy. Consider the cost of replacing a dissatisfied manager who leaves the company in search of a more demanding and stimulating job. The cost is significant, both in terms of money and of dislocation in the company. A good management development scheme should be considered not as a drain on resources but as an immense benefit in terms of lower staff turnover, better morale and better-directed people.

A number of the IDV (UK) board were sceptical at first, but went along with the programme as a whim of the chief executive's that was to be humoured. But when the board saw the tremendous changes in the individuals involved as they acquired a new breadth of understanding, the programme came to have its unanimous and unequivocal support.

CHOOSING A COURSE

Having gained board approval the next step was to decide on an appropriate course. The aim was to develop in managers the abilities to analyse company problems over a wide range of areas, to tackle problems on the basis of limited information and to gain a new initiative and breadth of vision – in short, to train them to become better executives so that they could make a more effective and profitable contribution to the organization. The obvious choice, therefore, was an MBA degree course. However, there were big drawbacks to sending managers away to study for up to 18 months:

- Jobs could not easily be held open for that long: other people would have to be found to fill the gap, leaving the absentee manager without a job.
- The likelihood of managers wanting to return to their previous jobs, or even organizations, after a prolonged absence was felt to be slim. The course was bound to change their attitudes and perspectives enormously. The company would therefore effectively be training managers for someone else.

Only one course seemed to offer what IDV (UK) was seeking: the MBA programme devised and run by the International Management Centre from Buckingham (IMCB). A number of factors were involved in the final choice:

- The course was structured on a part-time basis, so no long-term leave of absence was necessary.
- IMCB alone offered material that could be tailored to the specific needs of IDV (UK). No other organization at that time was willing to come into the company to produce an MBA programme together. The course was in fact a joint venture by IDV (UK) and IMCB, and was custom-built to the company's needs.
- The chief executive of IDV (UK) was attracted by the IMCB philosophy of

bringing education into the business, in the realization that conventional education was not delivering what the consumer required.

CHOOSING THE STUDENTS

Clearly the students had to be chosen carefully. About 60 managers applied to go on the course. IMCB vetted the applicants in terms of conventional MBA criteria. The company then considered other factors such as personality, practicality (i.e. the impossibility of releasing two key people from the same area), and so on. Finally 13 managers were selected to take the Action Learning programme – and all 13 eventually completed it.

The board considered carefully whether to put any obligations on the students in terms of commitment to the company, but eventually decided to make it a moral rather than a contractual commitment. It was hoped that the development and enrichment of these managers would increase their loyalty to IDV (UK), as the sponsor of the programme. And in the main, this is indeed how it worked out.

THE MBA PROGRAMME IN ACTION

The programme lasted 18 months on an official part-time basis. In reality it was full-time, as it was a living programme – the relationship between the students' work and their studies was so close that each affected and altered the nature and perspective of the other.

The programme was championed by James Espey as chief executive, and many of the IDV (UK) board were involved with it. One director had special responsibility for co-ordinating the programme, along with one or two personnel officers. Senior executives were encouraged to participate in the programme by giving lectures, which compelled them to think afresh and in a hard and analytical way about their own areas.

In addition a number of counterparts were appointed, i.e. people within the organization who had particular knowledge of a subject were 'twinned' with lecturers from IMCB. In this way the programme was an excellent balance of theory and practice – the students were never given the chance to retreat to the ivory towers of academe.

The students met for formal teaching once a week, for about four hours every Monday evening. A member of IMCB staff gave a lecture or established the basis for a discussion group. In addition there were a number of formalized away-weekends, directed and organized by IMCB.

Each student also had to produce a dissertation. The subjects were chosen by the students themselves, in consultation with the IMCB faculty and their counterparts on the IDV (UK) board. The company set two criteria for the choice of subject:

- that it should satisfy their academic needs in making a significant contribution to their MBA studies
- that it should make a significant contribution to the company.

The subjects were all scrutinized by Espey to ensure that they would make a beneficial contribution, and changes were made as a result.

Each student had an appropriate 'sponsor' at IDV (UK) board level. A client/customer relationship was developed between student and sponsor, involving terms of reference, priorities and strategy discussions. The object of the dissertations was to produce *actionable* recommendations.

BENEFITS TO IDV (UK)

Many benefits accrued to IDV (UK) as a result of its participation in the MBA scheme.

1. IDV (UK) effectively had 13 free consultants. All their project work was about the organization. The dissertations in particular were in-depth studies on different aspects of company policy; they covered communications strategy, the future of wine brands in the UK, own-label strategy, site selection in retail trading, wholesaling strategy, and so on – in fact, all the subjects that were of strategic concern to the company. And as the aim was to produce actionable recommendations, IDV (UK) received some valuable ideas.
2. The effect of the MBA scheme on staff was wide-ranging within IDV (UK). The students themselves broadened and increased their repertoire of alternative solutions which could be applied to general management problems, and enhanced their ability to think laterally. This is particularly important for a company like IDV (UK) which has a history of a stable management team, and therefore a relatively small input of external ideas.
   - Although only thirteen followed the programme they had a catalytic effect on others in the company:
   - On their peers, who saw the students' vision widening, leading them to become more challenging of top management. The students had ceased to see themselves in a straitjacket labelled 'Sales' or 'Marketing', 'Finance' or 'Production', and had started to challenge both laterally and upwards. This rubbed off on their colleagues.
   - On top management, because they needed to be more alert and think through policy decisions more carefully in the presence of searching challenges from the MBA set. In 1985 IDV (UK) had a valuable sales

think-tank on strategic issues which would not have occurred without the stimulus of the MBA programme.

In general, morale was strengthened and confidence in the company increased as a result of the improved management relations, both upwards and laterally.

3. In gaining a more complete vision of the company as a whole, some of the students recognized for the first time where their real skills and interests might lie. For example, one very promising sales executive asked to be transferred to distribution, where he is now running one of the biggest wine and spirits depots in the country. Thanks to the MBA programme, he was able to see an exciting career opportunity that would never otherwise have crossed his mind – and to act on it.

4. The MBAs were used as checks on the company's business plan. They had complete copies of the draft business plan (often a document restricted to a handful of top executives) and challenged the board on every item they had doubts about. It is all too easy for secrecy to be used as a weapon by an insecure or inadequate management to avert any challenge from subordinates. One or two members of the board did indeed have qualms about the open style of management that allowed students access to almost all the company's files, but they soon saw the palpable benefits of having more contributions to policy making. The only business that needed to be kept secret was possible takeovers or acquisitions – though this did not stop theoretical discussions on which company or brand should be acquired *if it were possible*.

5. A by-product of the MBA programme was the favourable feelings towards the company engendered in the participants. Not only were they better educated as a result of their studies, but were also better disposed towards IDV (UK). Their own motivation was increased and this enhanced their contribution to the company as well as giving them more satisfying and stimulating jobs.

6. The substantial long-term benefits lay in the improved quality of management decisions which these managers would have been unable to make without the advantage of an Action Learning MBA training. This augurs well for IDV (UK)'s future, in that they have established an additional cadre of good general managers.

DRAWBACKS TO THE SCHEME?

From the company's point of view the programme was an unqualified success. As the first venture of its kind, it had inevitable teething troubles, but these were easily ironed out because there was such a strong commitment to succeed

– commitment from the company, from IMCB and from the participants themselves.

From the participants' point of view, the programme put immense pressure on them as they struggled to balance their jobs and their domestic lives with their studies. But balancing such pressures is the very stuff of any top executive's life, and the sooner they learn to handle it the better they will be. The participants were all warned in advance of the demands the course would make on their time. Senior executives tried to make allowances in exceptional circumstances for the fact that a manager was effectively doing two jobs. Senior managers also observed the relations of the MBA group with their colleagues and subordinates. At first there was some rivalry and dissatisfaction which rapidly disappeared as it was repeatedly emphasized to the participants that they were not an élite cadre in the organization and that other managers would be expected to do the programme in the future (which did indeed happen).

ADAPTING THE PRINCIPLES

Clearly it might not be possible to have an Action Learning MBA course tailor-made for one specific company: an organization might be too small, and as the quality of the participants is a vital factor, there is inevitably a finite number of suitable candidates. The principles, however, remain the same: that for the right calibre of staff, such a programme is an invaluable long-term investment, and that a part-time programme linked as closely as possible to the company is the best method.

Different benefits can of course be derived from a mixed regional group of ten to twelve MBA students from a number of different organizations – certainly this provides students with a broader knowledge of other companies and their cultures.

It is even conceivable that executives from different parts of the world could, by distance-teaching methods, participate in these career-enhancing courses, with perhaps a two-week residential block of face-to-face tuition and discussions with their fellow students. In the modern age the idea of global education within a multinational organization should be seriously considered, so that all managers, wherever they happen to work, have the opportunity to be developed and stretched, making them both more valuable to the company and more fulfilled in their work.

CONCLUSION

There are many tools of management development, for example diploma programmes, short courses on specific aspects of the business, YTS schemes, graduate intake programmes and so on. A company must have a total programme of management development covering many aspects – and from IDV (UK)'s experience, the Action Learning MBA scheme is a vital component.

The Action Learning MBA programme at IDV (UK) taught its participants to think like chief executives – indeed, it is hoped that many of them will eventually become either chief executives or general managers. They gained a generalist attitude to their jobs rather than the parochial specialist attitude that is encouraged and reinforced by the divisional structure of most companies.

In effect, the Action Learning MBA programme accelerated the participants' abilities to become effective senior managers. In one way, it can be seen as giving, say, five years' worth of experience in one year of combined work and studying. The programme broadened the perspectives of management, and in a more thorough and reliable fashion than the haphazard nature of work experience alone.

IDV (UK) was delighted with the results of the programme. Its senior management hope that their experience will encourage other companies to make similar investments for the future. And the ultimate benefit accruing to IDV (UK) from the MBA programme? No less than the very success of the organization itself, where decision making and problem solving are now the domain of experienced, imaginative and well trained managers.

22 Organizational and Business Development through Action Learning*

David Seekings and Brian Wilson

The International Management Centre from Buckingham (IMCB) has been working with the Allied Irish Bank (AIB) in Britain for the past three years in a unique organizational business development project which has fundamentally altered the bank's approach to its British market. Although the project is not yet complete the bank is already benefiting from an upsurge in business activity and is expanding rapidly in Britain. What is more, the parent in Dublin is adapting the process for its use in Ireland.

In this chapter, David Seekings who, along with Professor Gordon Wills and William Giles, was involved throughout the programme, interviews Brian Wilson, General Manager, Allied Irish Bank, Britain, to find out what the bank felt about the programme, 'warts and all'.

Seekings: Brian, the bank has invested heavily in terms of time and money in what some of your colleagues still call 'the IMCB programme'. What was the rationale behind the project – and why did you opt to work with IMCB?

Wilson: To answer this question, I have to go back a few years. In the early 1980s, we in AIB Britain were faced with a situation of being a successful, if somewhat traditional, bank in a rapidly changing competitive environment. We recognized that we had to move radically if a profitable core business was not to be undermined.

At the same time we also recognized that the changes taking place in our marketplace offered opportunities for us too – if only we could be quick enough on our feet.

The bank decided that what was needed to respond effectively to changes around us was a fundamental reappraisal of our business, of the roles and skills of our people and their attitudes. In other words, we decided to use management

*Originally published in *Leadership and Organization Development Journal*, vol. 8, no. 5, 1987.

development, on a large scale throughout the organization, as the main weapon with which to address the challenge which our changing competitive environment posed. I was appointed group general manager around that time and given the task of spearheading this new approach. Perhaps it would be helpful if I put Allied Irish Bank in context by telling you more about us.

Allied Irish Bank has a balance sheet size of $13 million putting it on current standing at 195th in world rankings. We are Ireland's largest bank with an approximate market share in Ireland of 40 per cent of the banking sector. Our present size would put us 42nd in the European banking marketplace. We have been growing reasonably rapidly in recent years, both in terms of balance sheet size and profitability, and in 1983 we acquired in America a controlling interest in the First National Bank of Maryland which is based in Baltimore. Our stake in that bank is due to go to above 51 per cent towards the end of 1987 and if we consolidate our interest in Maryland that will move us in the banking league tables to approximately 150th.

The acquisition in Maryland has been a considerable success story for the Bank, as has been our growth in the British marketplace. However, we have also made another unfortunate acquisition of an Irish insurance company which turned out very badly for us and was subsequently reacquired by the state. I mention this just so that you can appreciate these are warts and all answers!

Allied Irish Bank made IR£102 million in 1986/87. It is a constituent of three banks which originally came together 21 years ago. One of our constituent banks, Provincial Bank of Ireland, which was founded in 1824, was, as we are not slow to point out, one of the pioneers of branch banking in the British Isles.

However, we really only commenced our expansion in the British marketplace in the 1970s. From small beginnings there we have grown a business to a point now which has a network of 65 branches (36 in branch banking), employs approximately £1200 people in Britain in 4 different business units, has a balance sheet of approximately £2 billion and contributes approximately 25 per cent of the group's profitability. Our business has grown rapidly in recent years and in the last four to five years we have had a compound growth rate and profitability in excess of 20 to 25 per cent.

Our business in Britain was, naturally, focused on the Irish community in Britain but we have long since grown in the wider market and now possibly 75 per cent of our business comes from the local community, though, naturally, we continue to recognize the importance of our ethnic connections and work hard on that side of our business.

Seekings: What problems faced you before you embarked on the project?

Wilson: I suppose we should start with the market environment. The last five years in Britain have seen a rapidly changing financial services marketplace. I use the word financial services advisedly. What we bankers traditionally thought of as the banking marketplace has now become a financial services arena with a whole variety of new players and a greatly increased level of competition. The new players included new entrants such as insurance companies, brokers, foreign banks like city banks going 'downstream' as, for example, in the case of Citibank Savings.

Competition was also increased by a series of regulatory changes including the Consumer Credit Act, the Building Societies Act, which for the first time allowed building societies to provide unsecured personal advances to the consumer marketplace, and the Financial Services Bill which is going to change the way all of us do business. It all adds up to picture of the decline of traditional barriers with an increasing free-for-all in the financial markets.

One particularly sobering financial statistic which perhaps best sums it up for us bankers is the fact that over the past three years demand deposits in branches of UK clearers have been declining by the rate of approximately 6 to 7 per cent per annum – at the expense of non-banks, e.g. building societies.

Seekings: I see the problem. How was AIB measuring up against this background?

Wilson: We had rather a mixed bag. We had very successfully built our business up during the 1970s to a point where, as I described to you earlier, we had over 30 branches throughout Britain and a reasonable customer base. However, we were faced with a number of worrying limitations. We had a limited product base, for example, no high interest current accounts or automatic teller machines (ATMs) and our traditional products particularly in the resource gathering deposit area had seen a tail-off in growth and in some areas were indeed eroding.

We also had four rapidly growing and vigorous business units which were starting to step on one another's toes. The argument was put forward that it was a huge market and that there should be room for everyone. In reality we found that much of our business was clustered together both in geographic and customer terms and there was a real danger of our starting to compete with ourselves. In our discussions with our staff, it was clear that they had a very sheltered and cosy view of our business environment. They were not sufficiently aware of the changes going on around them.

Their view of their customers was somewhat traditional too. We had been through a period of 'prospecting' in the 1970s when we gathered a number of new customers. It was now as if we saw ourselves as harvesting the fruits of that effort. Customers now 'came to us', and if they did not ask for something it meant that they did not need it – at least in the minds of some of our managers. This most specifically manifested itself in the absence of sufficient hard selling especially cold calling by our management teams.

Seekings: Faced with those concerns, what objectives did you set in designing your management development programme?

Wilson: It all had to start in the marketplace. We had to develop a real customer focus in the minds of our managers and staff and to enhance their selling skills.

This had to be our first priority. And not just an aspiration. We needed an understanding of what 'putting the customer first' really means in terms of attitude to work, to staff organization. In this respect, we needed to improve the technical skills of our staff in terms of selling, negotiation, appreciation of buying needs and so on.

In a large marketplace like Britain we needed a series of detailed business plans and marketing strategies to address the different geographic marketplaces in which we were operating. We decided on nine geographic plans, *not*, I would emphasize, *financial budgets*, to be put together on a highly participative basis by the people who would ultimately be responsible for their implementation: the managers in the branches.

We were trying to put planning back where it belongs: with those at the coalface who would ultimately be responsible for implementation. This meant, in fact, introducing a 'bottom-up' planning process to complement the conventional planning procedures of the bank.

Finally, it was crucial for us to develop a unified approach to our business in Britain. This was to enable us to maximize the scarce resources which we had at our disposal both in terms of support systems and skilled staff, to motivate our people to maximize business opportunities and to develop the team approach which we felt was so vital to our growth in the market.

Seekings: You decided to work with IMCB to develop the programme. Why did you choose what was, at that time, a very new, independent business school?

Wilson: We knew we did not want a conventional teaching programme, nor were we interested in working with consultants who told us what to do. We were attracted by IMCB's philosophy of Action Learning which, in its simplest form can be said to be learning by doing rather than being told how to do it. IMCB seemed to fit the bill: they were prepared to work with us to come up with a custom made Action Learning programme. There was never any question of our being 'sold' an adaption of an off-the-shelf product.

Seekings: How did you go about the programme?

Wilson: Well, there were a number of stages and, indeed, setbacks and I would like to describe briefly, with the full benefit of hindsight, and recognizing that this approach was particular to our circumstances in Britain and is not necessarily relevant to every other company embarking on such a programme.

We held, initially, a series of meetings with all our managers in the group in Britain, taking an afternoon for each meeting with a maximum of 10 to 12 managers on each occasion together with their line boss. At this meeting we requested the managers to prepare in advance a brief five-minute contribution outlining three areas where, in their opinion, the organization could improve.

The reason for this approach was to ensure that the meetings were participatory in character and did not have a one-way flow about them. We used the traditional technique of having discussion groups to focus on the issues raised which we grouped under a series of headings. The meetings were held with a fair degree of publicity around our system and they were valuable in a number of respects.

We were able to use the content from the meetings as a basic piece of input to the design of our management development programme. And we were also able to gain a valuable insight into the degree of awareness of the need for change in our system. In fact, what we encountered was an amount of complacency and a low level of awareness of threats which seriously concerned us.

All managers were then divided into a series of teams and sent on a two week start-up programme, split into parts and run by IMCB. The first week concentrated heavily on the development of new marketing skills understanding the fundamental role of the customer, touching on such issues as product, price, promotion, plans, buying needs, decision-making units, and the like. It also focused on issues of leadership and teamwork, using as a model the 'Margerison McCann' management wheel.

In the second week we introduced the concept of detailed business planning to each team and helped them design a framework against which they would segment their local marketplaces. We encouraged them to elect a leader from within their teams and we appointed a line superior to work as a mentor to each group. At this point, we set a 'profit gap' for each team. Having taken an average of performance over the previous three years, we then set a target or goal some 10 or 15 per cent greater than previously achieved. The purpose of this, as we explained to the teams, was to make the whole effort of planning worthwhile to set a high objective to shoot for.

Seekings: Were these demanding targets important to the process?

Wilson: Fundamental. We had to break the mould and force the teams to think of new ways of reaching their targets – it could not just be a 'let us squeeze more out of the existing lemon' exercise. The targets were received, not surprisingly, with a degree of reluctance by most of the participants as you might imagine; but we did stress to them that they would be free to come back if they felt that the target was unattainable and to set different goals for us.

With the support of the external facilitators (IMCB), each team was required to do detailed research of the business potential in their own area, segmenting the market and focusing on the attractive segments. You will readily see that what we were, in fact, introducing was an Action Learning programme in its most practical form.

Time does not permit me to give you a detailed description of the process; suffice it to say that having segmented their markets and undertaken the requisite research, we then introduced a requirement to each group to prioritize between the segments. To do this they had to spend a lot of time analysing the bank, and its products and, indeed, our competitors – from the customers' standpoint. It was something all of us found both difficult and illuminating. Having completed their analysis, we required each group to choose not more than three priority segments on which to focus. This caused quite a trauma for each group and it forced them to ask very hard and relevant questions about their business. It is very easy to design a plan which in effect focuses with equal force on all business opportunities around and, of course, often results in nothing being done at all in relation to the plan. By introducing priorities like these, we made our managers think very carefully about their business and the profitability and potential of the customers in it.

Seekings: How did the programme develop in practice?

Wilson: Well, but it was not without pain and difficulty. From the outset, it was quite a challenge, to keep the enthusiasm up for such a task among a group of people who were not used to the nature of the task involved and the hard work and research which it involved.

This required a tangible demonstration of commitment and belief on the part of senior managers and the other general managers and myself. We had to put ourselves around our system extensively. Of course, we had lots of setbacks. These included an industrial relations dispute in the middle of the programme which forced the whole programme to be set back for a period of six months and involved a re-start-up. The dispute created a lot of cynicism in our system, particularly from managers who were from different business cultural backgrounds.

Seekings: I know you are diffident about your own role. From my point of view I would say that your obvious, visible and whole-hearted commitment was fundamental to the success of the project. Without your drive and energy, the programme would have fallen down at the first hurdle. You also talk about the 'mid-life crisis'. What do you mean by this?

Wilson: By halfway through the process when people were right at the heart of the analysis and segmentation, many of the teams felt they were getting nowhere as they could not see a clearly defined finish line. This was Action Learning at its best. It was particularly important at this stage to provide tangible evidence of senior management support and reassurance so that people kept with the programme.

Equally important was the need to drive the process on to a firm conclusion and we approached this in a very formal way. We required each team to produce a reasonably 'glossy' planning document and informed them several weeks in advance of a deadline date and a meeting at which the general managers of the bank in Britain would attend with the team and at which they would be required to make a formal presentation on their plan. We deliberately arranged this meeting in their own geographic location rather than head office and made a point of stressing its formality and importance.

This may seem a small issue, but quite often managers in line functions are not used to making presentations or to all the work that goes into slide preparation etc., and the sheer psychological pressures and impact of preparing those presentations and practising for them in itself helped to drive home the importance of the plan and the processes involved.

Incidentally, as you well know, we also used the technique of providing each team with an external facilitator to help them with their presentations. You were able to point out to the teams many areas in which their presentation might appear negative or unduly critical and to relay the message to them about the need for positiveness, commitment and ownership of what they were presenting and proposing.

Our external IMCB facilitator was important in other ways: he was able to make critical comments against the objective background of the plan which he would not have been able to get away with in another environment. He was able to pick up on negative or critically focused presentations and persuade the managers to take a positive ownership and selling role towards what they were presenting.

Seekings: Was the process entirely 'bottom-up'?

Wilson: No, simultaneous to the area team process we had to start the development of formal 'top-down' plans from the heads of the business functions in Britain, hopefully designed to meet with and synchronize the 'bottom-up' plans coming from our branch system.

Seekings: I understand you feel that 'ownership' of the plans was an important issue?

Wilson: Absolutely. Too often plans are prepared by people who do not have to live with the results and follow-on consequence of their recommendations. Our 'bottom-up' – 'top-down' planning process was designed to confront this difficulty and to give direct ownership and participation to the implementers of the bank's new strategies.

Seekings: How did you respond to the area team presentations?

Wilson: This was an essential part of the process. In many organizations, and certainly in AIB, plans or reports are prepared with great care and attention to detail, received by senior management and then sometimes finish up in bottom drawers or with, at best, a tardy response. In this instance, we had set the deadline that general management and myself were required to receive the document a week in advance and I made sure they had read and studied each document carefully – a difficult enough task in itself, I can assure you. We then travelled to and received the formal presentation from the managers and had a two-hour question and answer session on each plan afterwards. We deliberately attempted at these sessions to be fairly forceful and penetrating in our questions so that each team felt they had been through a full process of critical appraisal and analysis. Following on the meetings, we ensured we wrote back formally to each team within three weeks with a full detailed written response to their plans.

Seekings: You mentioned your 'top-down' process. How did you dovetail this with the 'bottom-up' plans?

Wilson: This was a demanding task. We had to put together all the various components which had been built over the preceding months into a formal group plan for our business unit in Britain. This involved amalgamating the inputs from the individual branch manager plans from the nine geographic areas and making sure there was a good fit between these 'bottom-up' plans and 'top-down' plans, as we described them, of the head of the various business units of the corporate, retail banking, small business, etc. Needless to say, in an exercise of this complexity a perfect fit was not possible but there was a reasonably strong degree of synchronization and correlation between the group plans and those of the individual units. Indeed in the months preceding the finalization of the individual plans we had been attempting to anticipate the requirements and needs that were emerging from our system so that in our group plan we were being seen and were ourselves able to respond to the needs of our system and to the business direction in which we were going.

Seekings: So far, you have only described how managers were involved in the programme. What about the rest of the staff?

Wilson: This was clearly important – we did not want staff to think that we were doing something secret behind closed doors. We therefore developed an additional series of marketing effectiveness programmes. First of all a customer service programme with all the staff in our individual branches, involving them in the process, getting them to understand the issues behind the programme and to design specific tasks and selling programmes for each individual member of staff.

Incidentally, something which might be commonplace to retailers – but is not normal in banking – we now have weekly 'in store' training for all our branch staff. We also designed a cross-selling programme, the objective of which was to ensure that we obtained maximum added value from each existing or potential customer relationship of AIB's business units.

In many ways, this was one of the richest parts of the whole programme as we found, the further we went down the organization, the greater was the responsiveness to the management development programmes and the opportunity to participate in influencing the direction of the business which they involved. More junior managers we found had less cynicism and more idealism and enthusiasm than some of their more seasoned colleagues. It certainly gave us all great hope for the future.

Seekings: What did you achieve out of all of this?

Wilson: There are three types of gain I would like to focus on. The overall gains as we saw them, some specific gains and some which without any great originality I describe as 'other' or those particularly related to some benefits which we did not expect to be derived from the programme.

The most important overall benefit from our programme has perhaps been a focused direction for our businesses in Britain. This may sound somewhat trite, but it is very important in our experience. We now know what it is we want to do in the market. We have shared ownership, throughout our managers, for the direction in which we are trying to take the business.

We have also managed to define and agree with our managers the priorities on which we should be focusing in the marketplace and in the process we have achieved some important breakthroughs for bankers – for example, the idea of shedding unprofitable customers or focusing on those with greater potential. We now have our whole series of agreed strategies and tactics with which to address the priority marketplaces and a geographically based set of detailed plans with which to implement these.

A crucial gain for us has been the groupwide ownership which we have achieved of our plans and business direction. As you will have gathered, the process has been heavily participative and this has resulted in a very widely held understanding and association with what we are trying to achieve.

There are also a number of useful, specific and positive outcomes. Perhaps the most important among these, certainly for us as a bank, was the enhanced customer awareness which the programme achieved for us. The selling skills of our managers and staff were significantly improved. In particular, the more sharp-edged skills such as closing deals, negotiating constructively and identifying key decision takers in businesses, to name just a few.

Another significant gain was the increase in personal self-confidence on the part of our managerial staff. The work they had undertaken obviously gave them an enhanced awareness and knowledge of their local marketplace which is vital in attacking their business, but that increased knowledge and the conclusions which they have drawn from it has also significantly enhanced their own self-belief and willingness to take new initiatives.

We put a cross-selling programme into place for the first time which showed tangible business results. There has been an increasing knowledge and consequent improved relations between the managers in our different business units. There was a recognition of complementary skills and of the potential of working more closely together, particularly among those focusing on similar markets.

Seekings: How did the teams respond to the initial targets?

Wilson: Well perhaps the most obvious thing is that the business has gained a series of tough specific business goals which have now been set with the full ownership of management and staff because they are in effect their targets. The

243

profit gap to which I referred earlier has indeed been closed and in many instances teams came up with target objectives higher than the ones we had set them. In only one instance did a team come in with lower goals and we were prepared to accept these readily because it was in a tough geographic area. There is, we believe, a high motivation among individuals to achieve the targets set and this is reinforced by the team-building processes which we have success- fully introduced.

Seekings: You mentioned some unexpected benefits. What were these?

Wilson: There were several additional bonuses. The first was a considerably enhanced product demand from among our management and staff. This may sound strange to those who are not from the banking industry, but in previous times we in banking had a very simplistic view of the world as just lenders of money and did not appreciate the need to package this more effectively or to recognize that the private individual does not necessarily want or see a loan as an attractive product in itself.

With a relatively tight core of support systems and given the highly partici- pative way in which we went about the programme, this put considerable pressures on our system and forced the managers away from their offices for considerable periods. In turn, this required substantially increased levels of delegation in the system. The response of the more junior members of staff was very positive and the managerial capabilities of our managers were definitely enhanced.

A further gain for us was at least a temporary lowering of the barriers of suspicion between head office and support functions in our branch system. The work that our branch teams had to put into the design of their plans and, indeed, their presentations, gave them a much enhanced awareness of the complexities of change and the work that goes into such areas and, albeit temporarily perhaps, a more sympathetic attitude to their colleagues working in the support functions and at the centre.

Seekings: All this presents a very rosy picture. I cannot believe you did not experience problems along the way.

Wilson: We not only experienced problems, we also made mistakes along the way. First, we were very under-resourced. In Britain we had a very small head office function with most of our management team focused in the line, as indeed, it should be. Consequently, when we moved into this main development programme and the planning processes attendant to it, we put very great pres- sure on our systems and on our people. Inevitably some areas had to give, and at times there were some costs to be borne in terms of lost business opportunity or productivity.

A further difficulty for us, and this is a problem endemic in the banking industry, was the relatively limited quality of our management information systems. Banking traditionally is a very transaction-focused business and it has not in the past met the need to focus on the sort of management information which would be commonplace in other industries.

At one level this was a significant problem for us, but in another it resulted in some very creative work and solutions going on within our system and has made us focus more aggressively and actively on this area to some considerable effect, and we hope to see some significant gains in the future.

An ongoing problem for us was the pressures which the programme created in the day-to-day operations of our business. The programme was often used as a somewhat lame excuse to explain poor performance in other areas. The only acceptable response we found to this was, of course, to reject it totally as a reason and to stress to managers that what they were involved in was considered part of their day-to-day job.

Clearly, many of our managers found it difficult to reconcile short-term needs with long-term objectives. This was a considerable difficulty for those who had not been exposed to anything other than the usual annual budgetary processes in the past. Because of the different business units involved in our structure, we had to evolve the concept of a mentor, who was a senior executive for one of the business units, responsible for each team. He did not have a line role in relation to the team and the design and implementation of this position was difficult and never fully resolved to our satisfaction. Those were some of the problems we encountered. Let us look more specifically now at some of the mistakes we made in the introduction and implementation of the programme.

Passive leadership. For me, perhaps the most serious error I made in the introduction of this programme was to tolerate passive or uninvolved leadership from a number of key executives in the system. We discussed the programme extensively and came to a decision to introduce it. From that point on, I should have ensured that every member of the team took active ownership and participation. I paid a heavier price afterwards for those people from whom I tolerated indifference or veiled antagonism to the introduction of this approach.

Lack of senior management ownership. A second big error was not to allow a number of senior executives in crucial support functions to have an ongoing role in the programme. All senior executives in the bank were brought through the initial training phase, but many were not given ongoing roles afterwards. They subsequently became what we described as the 'watchers on the shore', quick to criticize the work of their colleagues and their absence from the office; because they had no ownership in the programme they had no reason to wish to see it succeed and they indeed found when they had subordinates who were involved away from the office, it became a positive irritant to them.

Limited communication. Because of this inadequate communication, there was a lot of suspicion and resistance on the part of junior members of staff which had to be overcome when the process finally did impinge upon them.

A third error we made was in the level of communication to staff in the organization as a whole. We foolishly presumed that our briefing system with our managers would ensure that the staff were informed as to where their managers had disappeared. This was a naive assumption on our part. In retrospect we should have had a much more fully developed programme of communication. I should also have spent some more time liaising with my senior colleagues in AIB in Dublin who were initially mystified and subsequently frustrated by the pressures which the work was imposing on our staff.

Too many changes. We also accommodated too many requests for changes or modification in programme design. At various stages we found some people looking for recreation facilities, others for more pre-course material and a subsequent group for less pre-course material. Some required changes in the hotel, some were happy with the hotel. The basic message I would draw from all this is, once you have a format and a basic location, unless some serious issues arise, stick to your game plan and do not allow yourself to be diverted from it.

Too long a 'time out'. We permitted too long a gap to occur after the completion of the various plans before we moved into the implementation phase. Perhaps, in retrospect, I was too tolerant in my assumption that people needed a break from the rigours of this more formal approach to our business. Once you allow people to step off the treadmill at all in a process like that, they quickly assume that it has just been a phase which they can put behind them and return to their old ways. I mentioned earlier how important it was to respond formally to our plans. Whenever we deviated from this, we found that we receive a disproportionate negative response from staff.

Little short-term delivery. Another mistake we made was not giving sufficient tangible evidence to the system of the new approach we had undertaken. This was particularly noticeable to junior staff. If we had delivered in the short term a number of, for example, new products, or evidences of the 'wind of change' we might have obtained more credibility at an earlier stage in the programme.

Seekings: That was a frank description of the problems you encountered during the programme. It is a well-known axiom that 80 per cent of business plans are never implemented. How are you overcoming this?

Wilson: Perhaps the most crucial decision we have taken in regard to our plans is to make every aspect of them specifically accountable with clear responsibility residing with individuals throughout our organization. In this respect we are clearly moving the whole process firmly into the line of our organization in a heavily participative way. The advisers and facilitators from IMCB who worked with us in the design and introductory phases have been moved back to the wings or eliminated completely and the system now clearly understands, through a series of specific goals, targets and review processes, exactly what must be achieved.

We also undertook a very wide-ranging capability assessment of the goals and targets we set ourselves in our plan. It was a very sobering exercise and it has set in train a number of remedial actions. I would certainly commend it to everyone designing or developing any new strategies in their business.

In developing our plans we have also continued to narrow the focus of our direct attack. I mentioned earlier the three priority segments that we concentrated on. We have, since then, sharpened our approach even more and in the year ahead have set ourselves limited but highly specific goals in regard to specific target business segments.

Finally, it is absolutely vital, in designing a plan like this, to ensure that the financial plans of the organization in the budgetary processes are linked in clearly to the longer-term strategic plans. This has been a important element in ensuring effective implementation.

Seekings: In reality, you have been using marketing development as a means of organizational and individual development throughout the bank. How do you feel your bank and the people in it have developed as a consequence of the programme?

Wilson: One significant change in the bank has been the increased two-way flows of information up and down our system. Most feedback from below in an organization is negative: 'I cannot do this because I am too busy, short of resources' and so on. Through the 'bottom-up' 'top-down' system and the consequent interaction of this, we have been able to obtain much positive feedback on our business, on the needs of our customers out in the marketplace, and on how we can overcome our problems.

The result of all this has been an increased level of business awareness in the bank in terms of the business direction we are taking and the priorities we must focus on. Our managers and staff are much less naive than they were both in terms of their own customers and, indeed, the competition.

We have also been able to enhance significantly the level of teamwork throughout our system and to improve the understanding of how teams function effectively. The follow-on from what has been a gradual breakdown in barriers of suspicion between different members of our organization is that they have begun to focus on the important priority of (the common enemy!) the customer.

In organizational terms, one of the more significant benefits has been the increased involvement of our staff in business activity. Traditionally, banking has been a transaction and administration-centred activity. We believe that our staff are now more involved in the more important areas of business in planning and in doing. Individuals have benefited too: their jobs have been enriched by their being involved in growing the business. We all work together more effectively, and our communication, selling and negotiation skills have been positively enhanced.

Finally, I believe we have managed to re-motivate a number of our managerial staff, who had perhaps become complacent or switched-off over a period of years, through the participative process involved and that participation carries much more ownership for the direction in which we are trying to bring business.

However, the ultimate test must be – what does all this mean to our customer and to our long-term profitability? We are in the process of asking our customers some searching questions about AIB and its service. Our long-term profitability? . . . Well, I remain optimistic.

Seekings: Thank you.

TAILPIECE

The AIB business development programme is extensive, far-reaching and on-going. It is not a short, one-off exercise – the bank is engaged in a rolling five-year plan. The early benefits are already showing through. AIB in Britain is making record profits and, while Brian Wilson stresses there is still much to be done, he can be well satisfied with progress to date.

One might be tempted to ask whether he could quantify the cost benefit of the programme. The response would probably be a smile and words to the effect that he does not know where the bank would have been had it not embarked on the programme, but that it would certainly not be where it is today!

23 Management Development through Action Learning*

James Kable

Most management development is a hoax. In well over 20 years of running management training courses, it is difficult for me to identify any permanent and productive changes in any organization because of those courses. I know the participants have benefited because they have told me so, but seldom the organization.

There have been many reasons for this. The first is that most people who go to management training courses are conscripts. They are usually under pressure at work and cannot afford the time away from work. But they are told to go anyway and they soldier on reluctantly in programmes lasting up to eight weeks. Another reason is that training in management is seldom planned as part of a continuous career development progression. People are chosen to go to courses in the most haphazard, almost diabolical, fashion. Over my 20 years in training, I have heard some bizarre explanations when participants are asked why they are attending the course. Let us look at some of them.

- *It is your turn to go.* Bill went last year and so it is your turn this year. The course may have nothing to do with your future career – but you are told to go, so you do.
- *Your boss wants you out of the way.* There are many reasons why the boss may not want you around the place for a while – a VIP visit, a chance to check your subordinate's performance, a cut in production. The least offensive way to move you out of the system is to send you on a training course.
- *The person who should have gone cannot go.* This is a common excuse. At the last minute, you are told that Charlie cannot go, he is sick. As the company has paid its money and cannot be refunded at such short notice, you are cashiered into the vacancy.
- *You have to be inoculated.* Most organizations regard management training as an inoculation process. You are supposed to be an effective manager but

*Originally published in *Journal of Management Development*, vol. 8, no. 2, 1989.

you are not 'managing' very well. So you are sent away to be purged with a one-shot injection of management development. This may be all you will have for the next five years. But once you have had it, you are assumed to be cured forever.

Thus many people who attend management training courses do not know what they are about, nor, very often, do they care. They are told about it at the last minute and their attendance is a complete waste of time and money.

Fortunately, it need not always be like this. For some people, attending a management training course can be interesting, if not exciting. But what happens when a manager returns from a training course, imbued with new knowledge, itching to try something learnt on the course and looking quite different? Colleagues back at work do not recognize this new breed of manager. They feel threatened and ill at ease. A lot of new trade-offs have to be made and they do not want to do that. It is too uncomfortable.

So pressure is applied to the recently graduate trainee to stay the same. These pressures are enormous. The trainee is outnumbered, outgunned and feels frustrated when it becomes impossible to implement some of the changes which were learnt on the course. The pressure often becomes quite unbearable. The manager must go back to the old ways of doing things, which everyone understood, or become ostracized. It takes a strong and resolute person to stand up to that sort of pressure. There are not many of them around.

Management development therefore becomes a hoax. At least, that is what I always thought.

ACTION LEARNING FOR REAL

Recently, however, and especially over the past couple of years, I have been using Action Learning as my conceptual base in all the management development courses I run.[1] I was introduced to this notion of adult learning through the work of Professor Reg Revans, the guru of the concept.[2]

Action Learning turns the learning process upside down. It emphasizes learning by doing. To this end, all management development courses which use this process have, as a main focus for all participants, a real project. The project is agreed with and selected by the organization which sponsors the trainee on the course. Throughout the course, managers then work through their projects with assistance from the other participants and qualified tutors who teach the various competencies required by the trainees.

One of my first applications of Action Learning in management development involved senior administrators from the University of Queensland and Griffith University. It was a unique occasion, the first time these universities had combined to implement a management development programme for their own staff.

The incentive was an Australian government report which analysed efficiencies within the tertiary education system in Australia and made a number of critical comments. The response by the two Brisbane-based universities was to set up this combined course.

It had to have an impact. The objectives were very clear:

1. The course had to be designed for university administrators specifically. It had to focus on their needs and their problems. Too often in the past they had been sent to management training courses, only to return frustrated and sometimes very angry because the material presented on the courses was irrelevant.

2. The conceptual content had to be pragmatic and therefore usable. Most of the participants had already been indoctrinated into a number of behavioural and quantitative models which they could not apply in their jobs. They did not want any more.

3. It was crucial that the course should be actively supported by the vice-chancellors of both universities. To this end, it was decided that they should be asked to attend the course as often as possible, and particularly when the project reports were being presented on the last two days of the course.

4. Finally, all participants had to be given the opportunity to work together on projects that were important to themselves and to their organizations.

The objectives were therefore quite clear and were determined early. The only way in which they could be achieved was through the application of Action Learning. No other technique came close.

The design of the course was a joint enterprise between the universities and myself as course director. To ensure a continuing communication, a small steering committee was set up which became the vital decision-making body for the course. The design of the course, which was discussed in depth with the universities through their membership of the steering committee, is shown below:

- Stage 1 – five-day residential
- Stage 2 – 12 weeks working on the job on the projects
- Stage 3 – three-day residential
- Stage 4 – two-day report and presentation session.

The characteristics of each stage of the course were as follows:

STAGE 1

During the five-day residential course the concepts of Action Learning were discussed and participants were encouraged to talk about their team projects. In addition, certain tutorial inputs were identified and sessions were run by experienced tutors covering material which participants would need to use in completing their projects.

STAGE 2

During the following 12 weeks, participants worked in teams on their projects. A tutor was assigned to each team to assist as required, and liaison was maintained between the team members, the steering committee and the project client. This was a senior administrator in the university, often the registrar, who was responsible for ensuring that team members had access to all the information and data required to do the project.

STAGE 3

A three-day residential session was held at the end of the 12-week period to enable additional material, identified since the first residential week finished, to be placed into the course. This material was often identified by the participants themselves as they worked through their projects – an example of Action Learning in practice.

STAGE 4

The final two days were devoted to project presentations, including an outline on a timetable for implementation. The results of this part of the course were quite remarkable. Presentations were professionally produced and elicited a number of recommendations that were subsequently put into practice.

ASSESSMENT

When the course was over, it was generally agreed that the Action Learning process had turned the course from an impractical, flaccid experience into an interesting, worthwhile endeavour. The participants worked hard because they wanted to do it, not because they were forced into it. The age-old problem of trying to turn conscripts into volunteers, which had required so much energy in the past, had disappeared. *This* management development course was no hoax. It was interesting and it worked.

The use of Action Learning principles in management development overcomes so many of the problems levelled at the effectiveness and value of management education provided by the more conventional approaches. There has been much criticism over a number of years about the present ways of doing things. In 1973, Henry Mintzberg said that 'although the management school gives students MBA and MPA degrees, it does not, in fact, teach them to be managers'.

Practising managers have known this for years. They have been crying out for a more effective method of management development but the academic world has been deaf to their pleas. The only business school in the world which has tried to redress this situation is the International Management Centres. With its headquarters in Buckingham in the UK, IMC actively pursues Action Learning in all its courses up to MBA level. It is a unique institution, often berated by academic colleagues but seldom by the managers for whom it provides a real service in management development.

CONCLUSION

So the wheel has now turned a full circle for me. Twenty years ago, when I first began my career in management development, I was enthusiastic and impatient to work with managers in an attempt to improve their skills. As the time went by, I became very concerned with the lack of any real change in the organizations which sponsored their managers on those courses. I began to be convinced that most management training was, indeed, a hoax.

Now I have regained my enthusiasm as I see the positive results achieved through the application of Action Learning. It is hard work and intellectually demanding if done properly. But it is worth the effort every time.

REFERENCES

1 J. Kable, *People, Preferences and Productivity*, Wiley, 1987.
2 R. Revans, *The Origins and Growth of Action Learning*, Chartwell-Bratt, 1982.

24 Developing Skills for Matrix Management*

Alan Mumford and Peter Honey

We are grateful to the Ford Motor Company first for the opportunity of working with them on the issues described here, and secondly for agreeing that we may write this chapter. We should, however, emphasize that the views expressed here are ours, and not necessarily those of our clients at Ford.

ORIGINS

Alan Mumford from the International Management Centre from Buckingham was originally invited to meet three Ford managers – two from their Industrial Relations (Personnel) function and one line manager who had been seconded to operate as 'employee involvement manager'. The particular part of Ford to be discussed was the Product Development Group, which is part of the Ford of Europe Organization. At that time PDG had around 4,000 staff operating near London and Cologne.

After a general briefing on their perceptions of Ford, the discussion turned to a more particular analysis of some current management issues. PDG had carried out an important comparative study on a Japanese car firm, and as a consequence had identified the need to change both the structure of the organization and the style of management. These changes had not been fully defined or agreed at the time of these first discussions, but subsequently PDG adopted a form of matrix management. This involved the creation of a programme management structure in which complete car programmes became the organizational base instead of the previous separate functional processes.

The other main input had been a large meeting of Ford managers worldwide attended by twenty of PDG's top managers. This worldwide meeting had looked at a number of problems and opportunities in Ford, and had moved into a discussion led by consultants on the desirability of, and necessary processes

*Originally published in *Industrial and Commercial Training*, Sept/Oct 1986.

for, a more participative management style. At the time of briefing Alan Mumford, the Vice-President Product Development and his team had been attempting to work to the principles of a more participative management process for the past six months. There was, however, some concern both within the top team and at levels below it that statements about a more participative management style had not yet been fully implemented. The top team, which had been exposed to some formal educational processes on participative management, thought it desirable that the levels below them should also receive some formal training. Discussions had been held with a number of organizations who might provide some such training. The proposal which Alan Mumford made, and which became the basis for the work described here, differed significantly in approach from the other proposals received by Ford. Firstly, it was his view that it was essential to look at the top team first rather than to propose immediately training for the levels of management below them. Secondly, he considered that the review should concentrate on the realities of what was being attempted and had been achieved so far, rather than starting with the 'well known' skills of participative management which Ford 'ought' to introduce.

Alan Mumford's proposed brief was discussed with senior Ford PDG managers and finally was agreed and circulated by the Vice-President product development. It is important to note that the principle of using an outside consultant in this way was itself discussed participatively by the top management group. It is also most relevant that, unlike some other areas in Ford, PDG agreed to start with its top team.

DIAGNOSIS AND REPORT

The main method of collecting information about what had been achieved and what was now necessary was through individual discussions with 24 managers in London and Cologne, supplemented with observation of the top team at work in several management meetings. A list of 10 topics provided full opportunity for discussion. Examples of topics discussed were:

- What do you understand by 'autocratic' and 'participative' in the Ford context?
- What progress and problems have you experienced in attempting to carry through the new principles agreed?
- Consider the managerial behaviour of your bosses. What do they do that helps or hinders you in the effective performance of your job?
- Consider your own managerial behaviour. What kinds of behaviour are rewarded, not rewarded, punished?

It had been agreed that the results of these diagnostic interviews should be given to the top management group in a specially arranged meeting, and that this should be done orally rather than through a detailed written report. This chosen process was designed to encourage participative discussion of the report as a whole. In view of some great sensitivities, a summary of the main findings and recommendations was given in advance to the Vice-President Product Development and the Industrial Relations Manager (the equivalent of Personnel Director). Neither of them attempted to influence the final report to their colleagues. The Vice-President said: 'Some of your feedback is uncomfortable to hear, but we need to hear it'.

The report was presented and discussed at a full-day off-site meeting. It is not appropriate to reveal here the full detail of that report. Given the great nature of the changes which they were seeking to make it was not surprising that they were encountering problems in implementing their good intentions. Some of the difficulties they had experienced were:

- Disagreement about the meaning in operational terms of words like participation, consensus.
- While the nature of approved managerial behaviour had been clear and consistent although not articulated before, the nature of a 'now desired' managerial behaviour was not wholly clear and had not been articulated.
- There was disagreement about the extent to which participative management processes had been adopted even by the top group. This was illustrated by one management decision which was claimed by some managers to have been arrived at by consensus, and by others not to have been so decided.

In his comments about the information he had received Alan Mumford identified a number of issues of which the most relevant to this article were:

- the need for a clearly defined and agreed definition of decision-taking processes, where he suggested the use of 'I tell', 'I share', 'we agree'
- the definition and acceptance of new desired managerial behaviour such as openness, confrontation, explicit feedback
- the definition of roles within the programme management structure.

He recommended two processes for the top management group itself. The first was a workshop for that group, and the second was the idea of an ongoing process consultant to help the top management group and other management teams below it. In addition managers below the top level would have a more extensive workshop based on the same principles.

The report was discussed by the top group in three separate sections: data, comments, recommendations. The Vice-President himself illustrated the decision-making processes identified by stating that the decision about the recommendations would be made by general agreement – a 'we agree' rather than an 'I tell' decision-making process. The final decision was to go ahead with the top group workshop, to put the idea of process consultancy on one side

256

for the time being, and to defer decision on the middle management workshops until the top team workshop had been experienced.

TOP TEAM WORKSHOP

Peter Honey joined Alan Mumford for the design and implementation of this workshop. The design of the workshop reflected primarily the concerns expressed by the top team during the diagnostic discussions and the subsequent review. In terms of the process used, however, it reflected the proposals made by us. It is worth emphasizing that the proposal we made, while being in our view both more realistic and therefore more effective, was also more risky to us as designers and to the participants.

It was clearly essential that the workshop should address the issue of clarification of terms and the absence of clear action plans identified during the diagnosis. We suggested, and the top management group accepted, two more ambitious objectives. First, we designed the whole workshop so that decisions during it were reached by clearly stated prior criteria for process. It would be clear whether a decision was being communicated by the Vice-President (I tell), or whether an issue was being shared (I share) or whether it was something on which full agreement was sought (we agree). It was also agreed that although the main purpose of the workshop was to work on and determine the issues of employee involvement and programme management, the team should also tackle some agenda items to provide an even more powerful illustration of the decision-making process. The objectives for the workshop therefore became to:

- set aims, objectives and performance measurements for employee involvement and Programme Management
- review and prepare plans for dealing with all main problems in EI and PM
- agree common language for EI and PM
- contribute to the design of next-level workshops
- use participative processes to reach decisions throughout, including those reached on some 'normal' agenda items
- experience the value of explicit feedback.

The process used for the workshop, held off-site over two days, was that the whole group was given a series of short inputs by one of us. After each input a task, for example definition of objectives for EI, was discussed in small groups. In the small groups we acted as process consultants. In addition, during the two days the top team shifted into its normal method of operation on several normal agenda items. Discussion on these items was managed by the Vice-President, who used the processes which had been discussed before and during the workshop. At the end of each agenda item process feedback was offered relating mainly to those issues covered during the workshop, rather than introducing additional even though important issues.

In terms of the work which we have done on different approaches to learning[1] it will perhaps not be surprising to hear that we asked all participants before the workshop to complete our learning styles questionnaire. We analysed the results before the workshop, and adjusted the process to provide more structured inputs, because of the high level of theorist preferences across the group as a whole. While we felt happy about the apparent response to the inputs we made and the proportion of time they took during the workshop, we were probably too ambitious in moving beyond the collection of data about learning and their use in the design of the workshop. Our attempt to provide a short session, for example, on the meaning of the data and the relevance of these issues in the longer term for management development, was not wholly successful.

Since we had agreed objectives for the workshop beforehand, it was relatively easy to assess its success. In fact all the workshop objectives were met with the exception of any real contribution to the design of next-level workshops. The design of the workshop was already ambitious because of its combination of processes centring on the core reality of management jobs. The point is made even more clear if we look at the difference between two of the things involved. When the workshop participants set objectives and designed plans for dealing with employee involvement and programme management they were undertaking real management tasks required for the effective development of management in PDG. To do so with process consultant feedback in an off-the-job environment might still be seen by some as a relatively peripheral managerial activity. For some participants the experience might be felt to be that of developing useful skills, and identifying useful plans, but not working on issues of fundamental importance. The decision to use as well the opportunity to discuss real agenda items was much more risky because these were at the heart of normal managerial concern. When this top team had to decide, as it did, whether to allocate more time to a big discussion of a potential budget cut at the expense of workshop time on Employee Involvement issues, issues about participative decision making became central for everyone.

One other feature about the managerial processes involved needs clarification. Although for the purposes of the workshop there was a distinction between 'normal' agenda items and those being discussed under the 'EI and PM' label, the workshop was designed to ensure that all these items became incorporated in the normal managerial life. This meant that decisions and the requirements for subsequent action arising during the workshop were all taken back and put on the agenda for subsequent meetings. This design feature was important not only in terms of the principles we were trying to help managers to use, but also helped to avoid some of the reasons for failures to act on good intentions about Participative Management in the past.

WORKSHOPS AT THE NEXT LEVEL

One of the decisions made at the top team workshop was that it had validated both the process and the credibility of ourselves for the next level of workshops, decision on which had been delayed at the completion of the diagnostic report review. This decision of principle was followed by a series of drafts and discussions between ourselves and the small group of Ford managers charged with sorting out the detail (from Industrial Relations and Employee Involvement). We had decided in terms of the likely numbers involved and the process we recommended that we should bring in a third colleague, Graham Robinson. The three of us formed in our view a successful working group because we shared a great deal, in terms of past experience of programme management, of our belief in the virtue of working on specific behaviours and experience in giving feedback to senior managers.

Our Ford clients decided that in addition to the workshops which we would run geared specifically to behavioural skills requirements, they wanted to introduce managers to wider issues of programme management through seminars run by Professor Hopeman of Villanova University, Pennsylvania. The process of designing the two events so that they complemented each other was obviously vital, and this was managed through a full exchange of materials, of design objectives and by attendance by Peter at a Hopeman seminar which preceded our workshop. We have not included here detailed comments on the design of the Hopeman seminars, since they are clearly not our material to quote. The main feature of the Hopeman seminars was the exploration of what matrix management aimed to achieve and the kinds of issues involved in successfully managing in that way. Clearly the design of our subsequent workshop presumed that people had benefited from the Hopeman seminar and this proved to be the case.

As compared with the top team workshop the subsequent workshops had an even more precise frame of reference. Whereas the top team workshop had dealt with both Employee Involvement and programme management issues the next level dealt solely with programme management. The reason for this was that at the time the second level workshops were being run the main organizational changes involved in programme management had been announced and indeed from the earliest workshops onwards were being implemented. The focus of concern both at top level and at the lower levels was therefore on the practical issues arising from programme management rather than on the combination of issues arising from both programme management and employee involvement. From the point of view of the design team this sharpened focus of attention was entirely acceptable since it again emphasized that we were dealing with current real and concrete issues, which managers had to manage well, rather than perhaps equally desirable but vaguer issues of general management styles. In practical terms too we felt that the principles involved were the same, and that the behavioural skills were essentially the same under either heading. The focus on one particular aspect made it more likely that we could achieve something significant in two days, whereas a wider focus with the same time limitation might mean we achieved less.

The objectives and detailed design of the workshops were discussed with representatives of the top team. The objectives were that by the end of the workshops participants would have:

- identified the key behavioural skills for the successful implementation of programme management and practised and developed them during the workshop
- clarified their understanding of the different management approaches (directive, consultative, collaborative, and delegative) and recognized the operational situations in which they should be used (*Note*: the change from the three definitions used with the top team was made to fit into a wider Ford environment)
- obtained an understanding of the characteristics of effective working groups and reviewed the effectiveness of their participation in a working group.

These objectives were sustained for all fourteen of the workshops which we ran in the United Kingdom over a period of three months. (A German-speaking consultant subsequently ran workshops in Germany.)

The main design features of these workshops were again that they concentrated on the actuality of what these managers would be required to do, that they involved managers in working on the real tasks of defining programme management, with help from a process consultant. One important issue of principle decided beforehand was that we should deal with actual programme management teams as far as possible, as compared with the alternative of mixing people across teams. Again the decision which we strongly advocated was that this should be as far as possible an occasion of reality rather than simulation. Clearly the choice of real teams produced problems both in terms of releasing all managers at once, and also overcoming the view that working in real teams would be too risky and dangerous.

As with the top team workshop, the role of faculty (Peter, Alan and Graham) once the workshops were under way was to combine a series of short inputs which we shared between us (only 20 minutes and 2 inputs in total over the 2 days) with a process consultant role within the small groups. In addition there was a further role for us. Part of our proposal to Ford before setting up these workshops was that they should develop the resources to run such activities themselves. We therefore took on the task of helping three Ford managers from the Industrial Relations Department to learn how to run these sessions, and specifically how to give process feedback. From the point of view of IMCB we had operated from the beginning with the commitment that we should involve the relevant Ford staff managers in a full understanding of what we were doing and how we were doing it from the diagnostic stage onwards. As a matter of principle we think it right that a client should be enabled to take care of himself, instead of having to rely in perpetuity on the outside experts who have carefully hidden some of the expertise away from the client.

The workshops were run off-site over two days, with no significant work during the intervening evening. The numbers attending the workshops ranged from 25–45 and the design of the programme deliberately provided for people to work in two different groups during the two days. This design feature was to ensure, as is often the case, simply that people have an opportunity to mix with as many colleagues as possible. One of the characteristics of matrix management is that people have to operate in two different management groups, and have to convey views and represent issues from one group to another. Our design therefore used a two-stage task process and provided for participants to be placed in two groups to give them that experience.

Each workshop used a five-stage approach for three main tasks:

1. A short briefing session where the task was given, together with any introductory points and supporting documentation.
2. A preparatory phase, typically lasting an hour or so, in five groups (A, B, C, D, E) of 5, 6 or 7 members.
3. A core phase in three larger groups (X, Y, Z) with approximately equal representation from each of the preparatory groups.
4. A process review phase, lasting 45 minutes, done separately in the core groups and facilitated by one of us.
5. A plenary session where each core group reported back on the results of the task and learnings from their process review.

This cycle of events was repeated for all three tasks which in summary were as follows.

TASK 1

In the light of your knowledge of, and experience to date with, programme management, decide which 10 behavioural skills are most important in helping ensure PM is a success in product development. (Each group was given a list of 25 skills and invited to use them as thought starters.)

TASK 2

Identify experiences you have had in product development with each management approach (each group had been given precise definitions for the Directive, Consultative, Collaborative, and Delegative approaches) and, assuming that all four approaches are appropriate at some time, develop guidelines that managers in PD could use to decide when to adopt which approach.

TASK 3

You are in competition with the other groups to produce the best 15-minute presentation on what actions you propose to take to create effective group working in Product Development after this workshop. (An additional 'complication' in this task was that despite being in competition with one another, the groups had to co-operate in agreeing the criteria to be used to judge which presentation was best and the mechanics of how the adjudication was to be carried out.)

There was an important fourth task, designed to produce individual and group commitment to action after the workshop.

TASK 4

Think back over the whole workshop and the action plans that have resulted from each of the process reviews (the relevant flipcharts are up on the wall in your group room). Decide what you, as an individual, are going to do to implement the lessons of the workshop when you return to work.

This individual work cascaded into some group discussions on appropriate subsequent action which were announced and reviewed in the final plenary session.

During group discussions the faculty member would make process interventions as he thought appropriate, but worked to the priority of allowing the group to manage itself or indeed not to manage itself. Process interventions were made by individual faculty members according to a briefing note agreed between us beforehand. Although each group would be different in its approach and in its problems in relation to particular tasks, we felt it necessary that faculty members would be working to a broadly agreed view about timing and intervention, even though these would be within differing situations within the group. In addition to making process interventions, faculty had an important role to play during the process reviews at the end of each task. These sessions were structured to the extent of following a laid-down procedure.

The recommended procedure for reviewing was as follows

1. Compile (on flips) 2 lists
   - what went well
   - what could have gone better.
2. Collect feedback from your observer and add any extra points to the 2 lists.
3. React to the feedback by asking questions of clarification and/or for the

observer's suggestions (resist the temptation to become defensive or to argue with the observer).

4. Select from the list one or two issues to focus upon.
5. In the light of the selected issues, gather suggestions for action (from everyone, not just the observer).
6. Plan actions so that everyone involved is clear what they have to do. Be prepared to experiment with different approaches rather than planning something safe and unremarkable.

These review sessions were a vital ingredient in the double-value formula for the workshop, besides being the main vehicles for learning from experience. Interestingly the idea of conducting process reviews back at work, after significant meetings for example, featured in many of the action plans taken away at the end of each workshop.

Clearly another significant aspect of the design from the point of view of the participants was the nature of the tasks they were set. It would have been relatively easy to invent some unreal tasks for the participants to undertake and to monitor and give feedback on their performance. We chose instead the 'double value' formula which was to identify real tasks within the programme management context. We therefore designed the process so that their tasks were to identify the skills required in effective programme management, the different decision-making processes involved, and the issues of working effectively in groups. Identifying, clarifying and negotiating these amongst themselves would, we believed, ensure a greater level of understanding and commitment to the required skills, than simply presenting them with a list of skills and then providing some simulated experience of working on them. It is not, for example, difficult to get intelligent managers to 'accept' that effective listening is a skill required if you wish to have effective participation (and is clearly less required if your management process is authoritarian). It is in our view more helpful to cause people to work on what effective listening really means by involving them in a discussion in which they have to listen to other people describing what effective listening is.

It will be remembered that we are dealing mainly with real management teams and in each case a member of the top team responsible for that particular team was involved, first, in launching the workshop and, secondly, in participating in the final session in which specific action plans for that team were presented to and often agreed with him. These final action planning sessions were both the most productive and the most risky parts of the workshop from some points of view. They could be seen as the most active since they generated the most specific managerial actions for continuing after the workshop. Equally, however, they could be risky if they led to the identification of actions which were either in qualitative or quantitative terms too much for the team to tackle satisfactorily afterwards. In one or two cases it was clear that the process generated more than the team and its leader could manage. This final task was amended during the course of these workshops in order to reduce the possibility of unacceptable stresses of this kind. It became instead a commitment to personal action and sharing of views on personal action across the groups, rather than an attempted total management action plan on programme management by each team.

WORKSHOPS WITHIN A WORKSHOP

We have mentioned already our substantial commitment to developing the internal resource to be able to undertake these activities. The processes we used for this were to require each Ford trainer to produce a personal learning plan before he became involved in the workshops. We used our learning styles questionnaire in order to facilitate this. The trainers had all been involved in the design of the workshops and indeed had significantly contributed to the design. During the early workshops they sat in with us during the input sessions and more significantly during the group sessions. The first step was for them to observe us in action, using our own checklists and guidance notes subsequently to discuss with us the interventions we had made, the strategy we had adopted, things they would have done if they had been responsible for the feedback. The next step was to take over responsibility for one of the small group process reviews during the two days and to receive feedback from a faculty member in the group on their performance. The final stage was to take full responsibility for feedback during the whole of a workshop again under the wing of one of us. Then the judgement was made on when they could fly on their own and take up a full position as a process consultant without the presence of one of the experienced faculty. The trainers had experience of working with each of the experienced members of faculty before being launched on their own.

There were some differences in the speed with which they were able to take up some of the more difficult issues, but eventually all three received our approval to take up a full role. The final judgement on this was very important to us, since we thought we had a responsibility to three parties. First, we had to be clear that line managers would receive effective help from the individual concerned. Second, we did not want to place the individual trainer in a position which he could not manage well. Finally, we had a concern to sustain the quality of a workshop in which we had invested a great deal of our own intellectual and emotional equity.

CONCLUSION

This chapter deals with only part of the main change project undertaken by Ford of Europe PDG. Much more was happening day by day within the organization at the time, to energize and support the objectives and processes described here. More has happened since, with the off-the-job development of process consultancy skills in a further workshop, a workshop specifically for trade union representatives and a process consultancy role with joint management–union working groups.

Our intention in describing this part of a complex whole was to give further evidence on the opportunity to change the boundaries[2] between 'real management development' on the job, and 'unreal management development' off the job. This kind of work on real management issues is the core of IMCB's approach to management development. We proposed, and our clients in Ford had the courage to accept, a much more real form of management training. We are not suggesting that this particular process is always suitable even for change events with similar objectives. We have, however, tried to show reality can be used as the main theme – in the right circumstances and with the right managers involved.

REFERENCES

1 P. Honey and A. Mumford, *Manual of Learning Styles*, Honey, 1982.
2 A. Mumford, 'Effectiveness in Management Development' in *Journal of Management Development*, vol. 3, no. 1, 1984.

25 Developing the Top Team*

Alan Mumford

This chapter presents the following five points:

1. Developing people at the top of an organization is challenging, but provides returns to the organization commensurate with the challenge.
2. Development is best viewed as a process which integrates work on organizational issues with carefully designed learning experiences.
3. Learning through the job does not have to be informal and accidental, but can be designed and understood by executives and directors themselves.
4. When those at the top of the organization have participated in an integrated work and learning experience, they are more likely to initiate, design and participate in such processes for those who work for them.
5. The roles of human resources specialists, and particularly training and development people, must expand to include the design of effective development experiences through the job, in addition to their traditional role as supporters of management development systems such as appraisal, succession planning and assessment centres.

The purpose of this chapter is both to illustrate through specific examples these general propositions and to provide individuals with ideas which they can implement, both for themselves as individuals and for their managers.

WHAT DO WE MEAN BY DEVELOPMENT?

It is a common experience that, when asked how they developed for their jobs as managers or directors, individuals will reply that they 'learned from experience'. A few years ago some colleagues and I interviewed 144 directors in 41 UK-based organizations. Although some of them worked in large organizations with well established formal management development processes, their answers were in most cases the same. They described a variety of experiences they had had on their way to the top. Jobs they had done, projects on which they

*Originally published in *Journal of Management Development*, vol. 10, no. 5, 1991.

had worked, specific tasks they had undertaken, bosses or colleagues with whom they had worked. Formal management development processes, whether described as the total system which might move people from one job to another, or the appraisal process, or attendance on courses, were very rarely highlighted, even where directors had participated in such formal processes. As a result of this research, I offered a new model (see Table 25.1) for management development.[1]

Type 1 'Informal managerial' – accidental processes

Characteristics:
   Occur within managerial activities
   Explicit intention is task performance
   No clear development objectives
   Unstructured in development terms
   Not planned in advance
   Owned by managers
Development consequences:
   Learning is real, direct, unconscious, insufficient

Type 2 'Integrated managerial' – opportunistic processes

Characteristics:
   Occur within managerial activities
   Explicit intention is both task performance and development
   Clear development objectives
   Structured for development by boss and subordinate
   Planned beforehand or reviewed subsequently as learning experiences
   Owned by managers
Development consequences:
   Learning is real, direct, conscious, more substantial

Type 3 'Formal management development' – planned processes

Characteristics:
   Often away from normal managerial activities
   Explicit intention is development
   Clear development objectives
   Structured for development by developers
   Planned beforehand and reviewed subsequently as learning experiences
   Owned more by developers than managers
Development consequences:
   Learning may be real (through a job) or detached (through a course)
   Is more likely to be conscious, relatively infrequent

Table 25.1 Model of types of management development

It is clear to me that for all too long management development and training specialists have operated on a definition of management development which is focused entirely on what is described as 'Type 3'. It is my view now that we need a definition of management development which embraces all three types of activity, instead of focusing simply on the formal aspects. So my definition of management development now is: An attempt to improve managerial effectiveness through a learning process.

This definition amends the one used by myself and others probably over the last 15 years, which included the words 'planned and deliberate' before 'learning process'. Managers know, and we recognize if we choose to look at the situation, that much of their learning is not planned and deliberate, but does develop their effectiveness.

It is of course possible for management development specialists to say that they are especially concerned with 'planned and deliberate learning processes'. In one sense I support that view – I am certainly in the business of encouraging more conscious and more effective learning processes. In another sense, however, management development people ought to consider whether the concentration so many of them have had on the Type 3 processes has been necessarily appropriate and effective. If we exclude ourselves from the unruly and often chaotic real managerial world in our definition of management development, we exclude ourselves from the majority of experiences which lead managers and directors to develop their skills.

My definition of development is also inclusive in the sense that I embrace all kinds of learning activity within it; I see development as the total process, training/education and informal learning both being contributors to it.

Finally, some authors whom I respect have distinguished between learning and development. While I certainly believe that there are different levels of learning, different stages with different intensities, I am not happy that the words learning and development helpfully distinguish these aspects. So for me the words are interchangeable. I prefer rather to talk about the difference between incremental and transformational learning opportunities. The first are those geared to improving performance within a relatively stable personal and organizational environment. The earth-shattering total changes related to massive switches of organizational culture, or personal behavioural changes of great magnitude, I refer to as transformational opportunities.

THE TOP TEAM

My original research, its follow-up, and the work I have done within organizations have focused on people at the top of organizations. In the original research indeed they were all main-board directors. My subsequent research and activities have covered people at director level in subsidiary or divisional activities as well. It will be clear that a great deal of my work could in principle be applied to a variety of managers, although the specific illustrations here are about the people at the top. As the song says about New York, if you can make it here you can make it anywhere.

LEARNING OPPORTUNITIES

The statements made so far, based on research and subsequent experience, are 'generally' true. How true are they for you? You will find the following exercise helpful in attempting to answer this question.

PERSONAL EXPERIENCES OF LEARNING

1. Look back over your career and identify:
   - your two most significant/important/helpful learning experiences
   - your two least significant/important/helpful learning experiences.
2. What was there about the experience that made it so helpful or unhelpful?

Here are some examples given by directors discussing their experiences with me:

> 'I have in my mind and occasionally write down a list of things I want to achieve during a meeting or on the achievement of a task. At the end of a day I review how well I have done. I look as objectively as I can at what I have achieved and what my contribution has been, as well as that of others, the success or failure on things I set out to achieve.'

This director was unusual in the conscious, relatively structured way in which he learned, and we shall look later at the kind of learning approach he represents.

> '*A project*: I was given responsibility for investigating whether to set up a new company in France. I learned a lot from the project. Certainly, dealing with the French was a valuable experience which has come in useful subsequently. Even more, I learned something about how to set up a project. I was given no proper terms of reference, no budget, and people I went to for help at a senior level did not know that I was doing the project.'

> '*Problem solving*: I remember my first experience, discussions about whether we should extend our operations into a country we had never worked in before. We started with big figures about all the markets we were not in and then we looked at the problems involved. I was very enthusiastic about going to a particular country, then one of my colleagues went over his experience of working there for another organization. It was like having a tutorial about the realities of managing abroad.'

These are just three among a wide variety of experiences we have discovered in talking to directors. A more extensive list is shown in Table 25.2.

Research over the last 20 years on what managers, and particularly senior managers, do has constantly shown that it is very much situation-specific. This means that, since the content of what managers do varies substantially between different kinds of organization (think of being a director of research in a high-technology company, compared with being the sales director of a publishing company, for example), learning needs and learning opportunities are also very much situation-specific. It is the nature of the job which makes learning from it both so available and so necessary and yet so difficult to plan, direct and control. Jobs are immensely rich in learning opportunities, as the list in Table 25.2 illustrates. Yet most managers do not recognize the diamonds; they are hidden away and often remain undetected because no one knows what to look for.

Information opportunities	Formal opportunities
Stretching the job	Being coached
Boss	Being counselled
Mentor	Having a mentor
Colleagues/Peers	Job rotation
Subordinates	Secondments
Network contacts	Stretched boundaries
Projects	Special projects
Familiar tasks	Committees
Unfamiliar tasks	Task groups
Task groups	External activities
Problem solving with colleagues	Internal courses
Domestic life	External courses
Voluntary work	Reading
Professional groups	
Social committees	
Sporting clubs	
Reading	

Table 25.2 Learning opportunities

It is because learning through the job is so realistic and so little studied that it is potentially such a productive area for further work. With my colleague Peter Honey, I have produced a leading resource aimed to help managers with this. The *Manual*[2] provides a variety of exercises and diagnostic instruments, which the training and development adviser can use to help managers. It is now accompanied by a workbook for managers themselves.[3] Many readers may also be familiar with the deservedly popular resource by Pedler and his colleagues.[4]

My colleagues, Peter Honey and Graham Robinson, and I were given the special advantage of following through the original director research with a smaller group of directors. We visited them at roughly three-week intervals over three or four months to discuss with them, first, what they had been doing as directors in that period and, second, what they had learned from it. The results of this have been published in a guidebook,[5] which contains a number of suggestions on how and why directors learn from experience. Perhaps our most interesting discovery was that we found directors using what we called four approaches to learning from experience:

- intuitive
- incidental
- retrospective
- prospective.

270

This analysis not only is understandable by the directors with whom we work; it is also usable – they can be helped to learn more effectively from their work experience. In terms of the model of management development presented earlier (Table 25.1) it is one of the ways in which we can encourage people to undertake Type 2 learning.

It will be noted that I have started with a focus on opportunities for learning in, around, and through the job. It is for most directors the most useful initiating process. Managers and directors are primarily concerned with achieving results for their organization. Learning is very rarely seen as anything more than an occasionally important contributor to this process. Learning is a discretionary activity. If, therefore, we focus a prime part of our attempt on encouraging directors to learn on the activities which are foremost in their minds, we are more likely to secure effective results.

LEARNING OFF THE JOB

The last sentence of the previous section provides us with a bridge to statements about the design of effective programmes off the job. Courses, workshops and seminars ought to be based on the reality of the work done by people in the top team. There are two aspects to this.

The first point is that a great deal of the analytical work about what managers do, certainly the most persuasive reports on such work, has been done at top level. The work of, first, Henry Mintzberg[6] and then John Kotter[7] gives an excellent basis for understanding what senior managers do – very different from the standard precepts still apparently used in some management training and educational institutions.

The second aspect is that, especially when working on an in-company basis, it is possible, desirable, and immensely productive to work directly on the opportunities and problems of the members of the top team as individuals and as a group.

The most effective design process is one which puts these two aspects together. Some illustrations from my own experience are outlined below.

PROGRAMME FOR DIRECTORS OF PILKINGTON

The content of this programme was designed through a two-day diagnostic workshop. In this workshop representative directors worked through a variety of analyses of the issues and problems facing both Pilkington as a whole and its different parts. They looked at the different roles carried out, for different reasons, by people at the top. They looked at skills. The combined process was intended to, and did, achieve the desired end of putting together a view of the problems that Pilkington directors needed to solve and the skills and knowledge which preferably they would have in order to contribute to those solutions.

SWAN HUNTER PROGRAMME

In this case a different process was followed, though with similar beliefs about how such a programme should be designed. For this company, the programme was run for the complete board of Swan Hunter Shipbuilders. The content was arrived at by individual diagnostic interviews with each member of the board. As a result of the interviews, each director (including the chief executive) identified a personal development plan. It was my task both to help them identify these plans on an individual basis, and to generate a total review of needs which seem to apply to the board as a whole. As with Pilkington, one of the main themes in the initial interviews was to encourage them to discuss the problems and opportunities facing Swan Hunter.

I have given first and separate emphasis to this question of how to diagnose what should be done for a group of directors at the top. As will be seen, it is quite different from any generalized process of running a programme for directors based on commonly accepted views of what directors do. In both cases there were significant differences of need, or different emphases, compared even with the list suggested in my own work.[1]

Naturally this process will take more time and may cost more money than quicker approaches through the general principles. However, clients have to weigh up the benefits of accuracy and commitment which such a process generates.

It is perhaps particularly interesting to look at the kind of content produced for the Swan Hunter board because, although working with the team at the top can be very exciting, it is also clearly quite risky. You need to have designers and implementers for the programme who are credible in the eyes of people who are used to experienced, high-quality people familiar with the real issues in industry and commerce. In the case of Swan Hunter we worked on real opportunities and problems under the following headings:

- the job of a director (compared with that of a senior manager)
- opportunities and problems for Swan Hunter
- improving our strategy
- the board as a team
- directing change
- selecting and developing key executives.

Under each of these headings the tutor engaged in preparation with directors of Swan Hunter to ensure that both the content of and priorities for a two-day workshop on these subjects covered the matters of main concern. In each case, participants were asked to work on their own activities and opportunities within the organization. As an example, instead of just running a session giving wise comments on how to manage change, participants are asked to review their own experiences of change in the organization, why it was successful and unsuccessful, and how they propose to direct a forthcoming change.

Two other themes run through the programme. In this case there are five two-day workshops, over a nine-month period. (Elsewhere I have run programmes with four-day workshops over a shorter period.) In addition to the declared theme for each workshop as indicated above, we have a running series of interventions on what they are learning, how they are learning it and what they are going to do about what they have learned. I say more about these processes in the next section.

Finally, each member of the board identified for himself a significant project. This takes up some issue both of personal significance and of importance to the organization as a whole. The project runs through the programme in the sense that participants work on their projects during the periods between workshops, reporting on their progress (and occasionally explaining less progress than they planned!) at each workshop. Although each project has an important organizational value in itself, it has the further developmental value of stretching and expanding an individual director's knowledge and experience. I call this the double-value approach to management development. In the context of the total programme, projects have the additional benefit in some but not all cases of providing a test-bed for some of the things which we are discussing in the workshops. One of the more obvious (to me as a designer but not necessarily to the participants initially) is that the session on directing change provides information and experience which is valuable for them when they come to review how they are to implement the project on which they have been working.

It has never been difficult to identify appropriate projects or problems in any of the director programmes I have run; organizations are full of important issues which senior people 'do not have the time to tackle'. It is precisely one of the virtues of this kind of programme that it provides not time but energy, commitment and a management process to monitor progress. However, the projects are unique and confidential, so examples are not included here.

I have mentioned the issue of double value. Notoriously, management development courses are not evaluated. One of the advantages of a programme of the kind I have designed and run is that some at least of the benefits are easily identifiable. This is most particularly but not uniquely true for the project. A project which has been undertaken and completed always has results which can be measured. Those results in our experience themselves justify the direct investment cost of the programme, and the opportunity cost of sending directors on it.

By this stage some at least of my readers will be saying, 'He is describing an Action Learning programme!' It is indeed the case that the general philosophy of the International Management Centres (IMC), and its approach to learning through structured experience, has been based explicitly on the philosophy – and sometimes the vehemence – of Reg Revans. However, in eight years' experience as an independent business school, we have added to the ideas about Action Learning which existed in 1983. The original Revans equation describing learning was:

$$learning\ (L) = programmed\ knowledge\ (P) + questioning\ (Q)$$

Our experience has caused us to revise this equation, while continuing to acknowledge the fundamental position of Reg Revans as the originator of the whole force and philosophy of Action Learning. Our revised equation is:

$$Q + P + Q = L$$

The fundamental idea here is that it is the manager's questioning, whether through a formal programme or through the incidents of his or her work, which creates the need for or desire for knowledge and skill.

The other part of our modern reformulation of Action Learning is the use of the four Is:

- interaction
- integration
- implementation
- iteration.

This picks up the essential proposition that isolated training and development events, even when superbly designed through a process such as those described above, will remain isolated – another I – unless they are designed to be integrated and contain implementation in the way shown. The 'iteration' point comes in because the design of a programme should emphasize the learning processes which will bring about continued learning, even outside the programme itself.

THE LEARNING PROCESS

Again I have provided a bridge to the next subject. The idea that individuals should be responsible for and take charge of their own learning has been part of the management development scene from the early 1970s. One of the important characteristics of Action Learning, as advanced by Reg Revans, was precisely that it took attention away from the tutor and put it on the learner. In addition, while attention to real problems and issues is a fundamental feature of Action Learning, it is the discussion of these problems and opportunities in a group (Action Learning sets) which converts the situation from being a normal managerial problem-solving activity to a problem-solving and learning activity.

However, one of the main defects of much traditional management development has been that it provided what are thought of as development opportunities, while not providing either understanding of, or skills in, the learning processes necessary to support those activities. For example, to move somebody within the context of a formal management development scheme, from one department to another on the grounds that it is good development, is not enough. All too many management development schemes merely provide a variety, by such means, of Type 1 processes – they give more opportunities for informal and accidental learning. Similarly Action Learning, though productive in terms of problem solving and identified benefits, all too often has emphasized the action and given no significant attention to the learning process.

If we are to talk realistically about people learning and developing from real experiences we must provide them with a better understanding of how and why they do so. In the full-scale director programmes that I run, therefore, I share with participants knowledge about the design of the programme and about their own preferred ways of learning. The particular vehicles for this are the Honey and Mumford versions of the learning cycle and learning styles;[8] an alternative is to use the work of David Kolb.[9] Explicit attention to learning processes and the different preferences individuals have for the way in which they learn is both exciting and productive for individuals. It helps to explain the differences we find when we assess the results of exercises such as the one suggested at the beginning of this chapter (past learning experiences). It provides an identifiable way of exchanging strengths and relative weaknesses within a group. It generates in some, though not all, the desire to improve the range of learning preferences which an individual may have.

This whole process is important not only within the context of the programme itself – helping individuals to understand and perhaps to change their reaction to certain sessions within the programme. It is also important because it provides exactly that link with the real world of learning which exists outside the relatively structured and protected world we have created in the workshop. When we say we want individuals to take charge of their own learning this surely involves:

- understanding by the individual of his or her learning processes
- awareness of the variety of learning opportunities, and the ability to choose among them those most congruent with what the learner wants to do (sometimes the learner will want to take opportunities which fit preferences, while sometimes he can choose to do something which builds on current preferences)
- Enabling individuals to recognize the different stages of learning opportunities they encounter on the job, which is where most learning opportunities will continue to arise.

THE MANAGEMENT DEVELOPMENT SYSTEM

I have said nothing here about management development systems such as succession planning, appraisal and assessment centres. One reason is that I cannot cover everything in a single chapter. I have attempted indeed to cover the full range of management development activities in my last book.[10] Here my priorities have been chosen because I am clear that our focus ought to be on learning and development first and on systems second. The human resources function has given far too much emphasis to setting up systems. Not only has it done so all too frequently without any attempt subsequently to monitor and evaluate the success of the system. Even worse, focus on the system has apparently caused people to be unaware of the fact that they have lost sight of the primary purpose. The primary purpose is 'to improve managerial effectiveness through a learning process'. This is where we came in at the beginning of this chapter. Systems which provide opportunities in the sense of planned job moves or attendance on courses are certainly desirable, especially when they are designed according to the principles of effectiveness and reality. However, they lose much of their point and justification if they provide opportunities without providing the support necessary for effective learning processes.

MEETING ORGANIZATIONAL OBJECTIVES

Implicit in my argument is the view that management development not only should meet organizational objectives but also should be based on them, in the sense of tackling real organizational issues and problems. It may also be clear that in my view the role of human resources, management development and training specialists can be redesigned to offer greater opportunities and greater risks. The opportunities are those of becoming involved in helping to identify appropriate business-related opportunities. They are the opportunities suggested by becoming an adviser on effective learning processes, instead of the bureaucratic administrator of courses or schemes.

REFERENCES

1 A. Mumford, *Developing Top Managers*, Gower, Aldershot, 1988.
2 P. Honey and A. Mumford, *The Manual of Learning Opportunities*, Honey, Maidenhead, 1989.
3 P. Honey and A. Mumford, *The Opportunist Learner*, Honey, Maidenhead, 1990.
4 M. Pedler, J. Burgoyne and T. Boydell, *A Manager's Guide to Self-Development*, McGraw-Hill, Maidenhead, 1986.
5 A. Mumford, P. Honey and G. Robinson, *Director's Development Guidebook: Making Experience Count*, Employment Department, London, 1990.
6 H. Mintzberg, *The Nature of Managerial Work*, Prentice Hall, Englewood Cliffs, NJ, 1980.
7 J.E. Kotter, *The General Managers*, The Free Press, New York, NY, 1982.

8 P. Honey and A. Mumford, *The Manual of Learning Styles*, 3rd ed., 1992, and *Using Your Learning Styles*, 3rd ed., 1995; Honey, Maidenhead.
9 D. Kolb, *Experiential Learning*, Prentice Hall, Englewood Cliffs, NJ, 1984.
10 A. Mumford, *Management Development: Strategies for Action*, IPM, London, 1989.

26 Leading Courageous Managers On*

Lesley Gore, Kathryn Toledano and Gordon Wills

First the bad news. Our publishing enterprise is threatened over the next decade with massive changes among its suppliers, in the formulation of its products and in its channels of distribution. We are owned and led by a team of partners who have built the enterprise to what it is today but have no burning zeal to see it into another quarter century of growth and development – who would at their age? They talk frequently of selling out to realize their capital, an outcome which would surely mean the end of the culture they and we have created and nurtured over the past 27 years. Meanwhile, they clearly enjoy the fruits of their labours.

Now the good news. Our owners know the bad news to be true. They consider it their personal responsibility to enable those who might wish to prosper with and through the enterprise over the next quarter century to address and surely overcome the challenges. In cold hard terms, however, we must produce a scenario for the owners that is a better offer than selling out their stakes to people who might/probably would unscramble our enterprise and its culture.

Until ten years ago the owners managed as well as led the enterprise. The rest of us enjoyed the culture because the owners were infrequent attendees at the offices. The enterprise was their hobby, a sideline to their professional work as university management academics. We were not overmanaged, but we did have to produce what was perceived as the critical management information for the owners on a routine basis.

Ten years ago the enterprise started to become noticeably bigger. We moved to new offices and not everyone knew everyone any more. Today we have £15m annual sales, and 150 or so full-time staff headquartered in Bradford, England but with three more offices and a host of agents across the world. We buy in a great many services ranging from authorship and editing to copywriting and promotional lists, printing and shipping. Not big; but big enough not to be small any longer. It was obvious the owners either had to manage it more, or somehow or other find others to manage it more for them. Fortunately, or wisely for us, they decided to find others to manage the growing organization while they

*Originally published in *Empowerment in Organizations*, vol. 2, no. 3, 1994.

concentrated on learning to lead it. Finally, and most importantly for this analysis, they decided to give anyone and everyone within the enterprise the opportunity to develop into managerial roles if they so wished, and to the full extent of their abilities. This was a considerable but not unduly worrisome act of faith and trust for them. Trust was easily given because everyone did still know everyone in the supervisory and middle management areas, and thought well of one another. Faith was a two-way commitment between a group of six university academics and some 30 administrative and marketing promotions staffs. If the right opportunities were identified and appropriate support was given, they could become whatever it was that would be needed, plus or minus a few specialist skills as yet unknown.

With a few honourable exceptions, management recruitment outside has not been necessary. Together we have built our enterprise to its present state as the largest academic management journal publishing house in the world, with some 130 journal titles. We always assumed we could do it of course. And the reason why it was not especially worrisome to the owners was that they were all management teachers, and believed their own rhetoric. They believed it was possible to develop intelligent staff to tackle the challenges of the managerial job at MCB University Press, provided they developed their leadership skills as owners. Immediate and sustained results were achieved.[1]

LEADERSHIP STRATEGIES EMPLOYED

This chapter will explore in some detail the leadership strategies which the owners have pursued to enable courageous managers to emerge and flourish. It will sound a lot tidier and better thought out than it has been, but the learning processes accomplished require clarity in presentation. We have never used the word 'empowerment', but from reading the literature today, including our own new journal called *Empowerment in Organizations*, it would appear we could readily have done so.

The four key strategies have been focused on:

1. Management Action Learning.
2. Systems development.
3. Mentoring and coaching.
4. Structural change.

At no time have we been an organization that believed it must introduce 'empowerment' to overcome any serious malaise. We are unable therefore to identify with much of the literature about mistrust, frustrated line management or fear of giving up power by supervisors or managers.[2-4] Neither can we accept the perspective Hand[5] offers, that management has the authority to improve the processes but is blind to the problems; and the staff have the knowledge of the problems but are powerless to resolve them. Nor do we find his simplistic solution that the use of 'teamwork and empowerment can change all this' of very much operational use as we make the journey. Each and every enterprise we presume has to find its own resolutions in its own socio-technical and market context, and contextualization is the hard part.[6]

Finally, before we enter into detailed consideration of our four strategic thrusts, we wish to emphasize that we see nothing as absolutely right or wrong with the sequencing of the actions we took. Again it was context that determined how we proceeded. Their apparent separation was normally very much clearer at their commencement than as time has passed. There was no grand plan, although we believe that by staying sensitive to key issues for our enterprise we seem to have clearly addressed the important themes.[7]

MANAGEMENT ACTION LEARNING

Our first main programmes of management Action Learning took place in the early 1980s. All middle managers reporting to the owners, who were effectively the senior management team at that time, were required to join a programme and known as SEMAP I – Senior Management Action Programme. The owners' experience as first-wave UK university business school academics in the 1960s and 1970s had convinced them that Action Learning approaches after Revans[8] were likely to be the most appropriate for our staff. On the international scene they had, in 1982, already been responsible for the launch of the International Management Centres – wholly devoted to Action Learning approaches.[9,10]

Each manager was required to choose an important issue for the future growth and development of his/her role in MCB University Press, and then undertake a programme of Action Learning study over nine months – sharing the journey of analysis, evaluation and the conclusions with fellow middle managers in a set from right across the enterprise. An accomplished outsider from International Management Centres was invited to act as facilitator to the whole process, and eventually reviewed it.[11] No other use of outside resources was made by the owners, although the managers concerned made extensive sorties outwith the organization to gain their better understandings. Sutton[11] reports *inter alia* that the owners reserved the right to veto some of the Action Learning project notions arising – not unkindly, but simply because they were felt to be inappropriate. While Sutton believed this was bad Action Learning, the owners were reportedly not convinced they need encourage such freedom!

McClelland[12] assures us that by tackling management development in this way the owners were 'gaining competitive advantage through strategic management development' in a way few businesses employing less than 7500 staff in the USA do even to this day. Their most common steps to develop managers are to send them outside the organization, and for the smaller organization this pattern is almost universal. We did not, however, see our approach as 'shifting the primary focus', as McClelland suggests, 'from individual to organization effectiveness by placing emphasis on the need for managers who can deal with strategic as well as tactical issues'. Nor were we undertaking anything as ambitious as 'a complete assessment of management skills, knowledge, experience and formal levels of education'. Heaven forbid. Rather we saw ourselves as broadening each of our middle manager's understanding of what others did, and doing so on the basis of Action Learning projects, that would be implemented to change and develop the way the enterprise addressed the issues for which the managers concerned felt responsible. And the process made us turn to one another rather than the owners for assistance, guidance and support as we went.

The projects were not trivial. For instance, one envisaged merging two disparate production systems, and stated how to do so. The owners said: 'Fine. Get on with it'. Another looked at a new campaign to improve renewals driven by the new computer systems. Again, the owners said: 'Yes, but how about this as well?' and set up a continuing taskforce, reconvened annually to evaluate and energize renewals. It is still at work over a decade later with sophisticated lifecycle modeling.[13]

The report-back sessions to the owners were held in the appropriate country house in the Lake District. The greatest fears reported then, and still to this day, were the deep individual anxieties of novices making formal presentations to supposedly fearsome management intellectuals! Focused skill development was provided and still always is in such circumstances. But it is worth remembering that the self-confidence acquired from communications skills development is indispensable to success for every manager in every role.

Tom Watson Senior, founder of IBM, is widely quoted as saying: 'Companies must respect individual employees and help them develop their own self-respect. They must never be psychologically abused'. How apt that dictum in the context of personal communications skills.

SEMAP I was swiftly followed by our first in-house Action Learning advanced diploma/bachelor of administration programme. Some 20 per cent of the full-time staff attended either half or all of its workshops successfully. The full bachelor programme lasted two years and provided focused education and training for mature individuals across the main functions and in the skills areas highlighted as vital from SEMAP I.

To summarize, the first stage of management Action Learning was straightforward, with hindsight. The owners required us to action learn our way forward into the key issues affecting our role in the future in debate and discussion with colleagues right across the enterprise. Follow-through was with focused knowledge and skills development at bachelor level. This was followed by the active encouragement of all the emerging senior managers to follow Action Learning MBA programmes, and to date, around the world more than half of them have done so. Two are now proceeding to their more advanced Action Learning DBAs.[14]

So much general education and training frequently gave rise to requests for professional skills development within the several areas of the enterprise. This was always encouraged not instead but as well. Any reasonable request was accepted. A company-wide supervisors' programme was run using external facilitators. A cadre of marketing services staff spent a year on the British Direct Marketing Association's diploma programme run at the University of Bradford. Computer database marketing training, training for new production systems and in finance, and full-scale computer studies over four years in one instance all proceeded. Ten per cent of payroll now goes on our above-the-line training investment.

SEMAP II next took shape as a most important stage in the development of courageous managers was reached, and has been extensively documented.[15] Its focus was clearly stated as 'enabling managerial growth and ownership succession'. Using Action Learning, virtually every manager and supervisor and staff member in the enterprise was involved in either the senior set, or on two other levels known as A–MAP and B–MAP. Projects were chosen from across the enterprise on the initiative of the staff concerned, and worked on for six to nine months. And to the surprise of many – not least the owners – the main issues identified were information systems and logistics flows.

The production staff, once again, wished to move forward with further new technologies now available. They wanted to adopt a strategy for the capture of knowledge electronically that would enable their database of articles to be accessed in whatever manner customer demand was likely to ask in the coming decade. The investment, including training and transfer, was approved at around £500,000 on the advice of the staff concerned, who themselves called in the Printing Industry Research Association, PIRA, as their consultants in the process.

A literati club, being an authors' and editors' database, was proposed and implemented. A promotional logistics information system was developed to improve the efficacy of the largest expense area in the enterprise, and a host more ideas were conceived. At six- and twelve-month intervals after the main report-back workshops, the staff concerned were required to evaluate whether their proposals had been acted on, and if not why not – on direct report to the owners.

The significance of SEMAP II, with A–MAP and B–MAP, was, however, far greater than simply the projects conducted albeit that they were of great significance, with their implementation liquidating the investment in the programmes within a year. It translated into our next strategic thrust into systems development – coinciding as it went with the publicity surrounding the similar endeavours of Stayer[16] at Johnsonville Foods in the USA.

SYSTEMS DEVELOPMENT

The use of systems in our enterprise is, of course, as old as the enterprise itself. The difference between our systems strategy since the late 1980s and our previous approach is that we now develop and use them quite deliberately to make our managers more courageous. Previous systems had been designed either to increase productivities and efficiencies – such as the use of computer bureaux to process orders and despatches – or to provide intelligence to the owners concerning, for example, the cost effectiveness of promotional activities.

It was this latter area that first saw the awakenings of interest in systems that could enable our managers to learn incrementally.[17] Managers in the marketing services area, who today reinvest nearly 25 per cent of each year's gross revenue in the search for new sales either to existing customers or prospects, resolved to develop their own marketing database. None of the owners knew anything about such an activity professionally, although one with especial interest in information management immediately came to their assistance and as a sponsor. They organized their own search for an appropriate database package and downloaded the subscription/product-based lists from the organization's computer. Then they began to manipulate and work it to achieve their own purposes – clustering activities around a series of pre-agreed campaigns, and a campaign by campaign review cycle.[18] This non-owner initiative was the first occasion on which staff, unprompted, had led the owners to a better-managed business. The baton had begun to change hands and the owners' response was extremely positive. Spontaneous combustion had occurred. (We are not overlooking here the fact that the several Action Learning programmes had triggered all manner of management growth and indeed launched our highly successful acquisitions strategies; but the owners had led them out initially, and that is the distinctive point to be made.)

The marketing database was an almost immediate success – it took only a year to convince the Doubting Thomases among the managers' colleagues to make proper use of it. The owners willingly and dutifully gave it their strong seal of approval. However, its contribution to systems and strategic marketing in our enterprise was only at the beginning. The owners resolved to extend the modelling of information needs and flows across the entire organization, and to commit whatever resources were necessary to building systems that would enable our managers to run the enterprise.

While a holistic model was set down on paper for debate, at no time did the owners envisage anything other than a series of relational databases. And within such a framework, it was always to be, and still is, the intention that prototyping of systems away from the mainstream development would normally be encouraged. Mention has already been made of how the SEMAP II programme had given rise to a promotional logistics information system and, of great importance for the future of the enterprise, a reshaped electronic production system. To these were added two customer clubs, and a club specifically for authors. Although a more modest investment than the reshaped electronic production system, the clubs were of very great importance for our courageous management.

The customer clubs covered the librarians and human resource professionals who were subscribers to our journals – populations of some 7000 each. For each club, detailed profile information was collected and all relationships were chanelled through specific teams of staff. These teams became our 'experts' on the needs and wants and behaviours of those groups of customers. Rather than the owners having opinions or views – which of course they did – and using these as a basis for action, managers were now gathering their own intelligence which readily suggested what actions to take.

Librarian key customers purchase on behalf of academic colleagues across their institutions. To influence them and to serve them demands a different strategy from that required for human resource professionals – they buy for themselves, albeit with company funds. Their careers evolve and develop and as they do their needs for journals evolve. Librarians are much more likely to sustain subscriptions to a given journal for a longer period.

The authors' club, known eventually as the Literati Club, had been proposed originally as a straightforward database to make the production task simpler to manage. It has progressed to become one of the main engines for our current quality initiative in the enterprise, providing sample bases for benchmarking studies. It has become a routine resource for managers other than the owners (who, it must be remembered, are university academics) to grow in confidence in seeking good contributors, new editors, ideas for new launches and more besides. Most recently it has become the source of intelligence for the conduct of author development workshops worldwide and for field sales visits at institutions where sales analyses show our products are under represented.

These clubs not only enable our managers to act courageously; they are now smarter and more intelligently briefed than the owners ever were.[13] It has been the success of these clubs in demonstrating how much more wisely well-designed information systems enable us to proceed that has most recently led to the enterprise's largest investment ever in systems development, our computer-based integrated customer environment (ICE).

The conduct of the clubs using the marketing database download, and the conduct of the cross-selling campaigns, were tedious and inefficient. In comparison, the Literati Club's standalone system was jealously regarded. It was clear that sooner rather than later a new system for customer development would be needed. Its design was created from grass roots upwards and only to help implement it were consultants brought in. Everyone was asked for their wish lists, and a company-wide taskforce deliberated for a year or more.

At this juncture we went briefly off the rails. The customerization taskforce was a representative concern rather than a team of committed enthusiasts.

Nothing happened until we returned it to the enthusiasts' hands, then even they made a false move too. Daunted at the size of the task of introducing an integrated customer environment embracing marketing needs, subscriptions control and financial collections, the enthusiasts invited in outside consultants who proposed to tell us what we needed. The owners intervened to say 'no, thank you'. The managers had to rise to the occasion no matter how daunting it might be! And if an extra in-company staff member was needed, so be it. The outcome, the ICE, had to be what its managers and operators specified and owned. And so it has been that the managers concerned have invested close on £1 million to acquire the ICE which they say they, not the owners, want and need.

MENTORING AND COACHING

We have never been wholly clear in our minds at MCB University Press whether the owners and increasingly, of course, the new senior managers as a group, needed to mentor and/or coach their colleagues. The two processes surely differ. Mentoring is frequently defined as a listening activity and a questioning activity rather than the more prescriptive stance taken by a coach.

The owners and senior managers shared in an in-house mentoring workshop in 1990. As a result, we had a somewhat clearer understanding of what is involved. Rather than leading with coaching and then evolving to mentoring, we resolved to offer both behaviours at the same time and, if forced to state a preference, to favour the deep end or stretching approach of mentoring. In other words we wanted individuals to do as much as they felt comfortable with, plus some stress, to the point where if they needed help they asked for it. Only if they got into trouble was coaching to be thrust on them, as with the decision to return the ICE systems project to the internal managers to lead.

Throughout the past decade, all in the emerging senior management team have had an owner/partner or company director as their mentor. It is that individual who each year conducts a self-driven appraisal and career review, and who also argues for the issues raised by the senior manager in the ultimate decision-making forum of the enterprise – the board of directors. Some of these dyadic relationships have worked well, some less well. They have at various times moved around by pressure of organizational role change rather than careful matching of the two involved. On their own, they could never have been sufficient for the task. The deliberate activities already described under management Action Learning that required senior managers to work at and share problems and issues – not least how they related to the owners – was vital too, and very effective.

Coaching in the main has come into play where Burdett[19] suggested it should. Managers used to managing 'what is', needed guidance to adapt to 'what can be or the art of the possible'. Managers used to managing with formal authority were sometimes 'reluctant to move into collaborative relationships as the basis for getting things done'. The Action Learning challenges demanded of all concerned created areas of dissatisfaction with the status quo while, at the same time, 'affording a context in which that dissatisfaction could be addressed'.

For example, for several years there was far too little dissatisfaction for the owners' comfort in production. The SEMAP II programme transformed that and unleashed, just as SEMAP I before it had, an appetite for development that is now as hungry as that in the marketing and customer development areas. Indeed, production was first to come to terms with the great transformations of its work practices, most recently eliminating any own-warehouse activities in journal despatches.

Having created and focused on dissatisfaction, of course, the coaching and mentoring role seeks to ensure that it is suitably addressed. Each dyad will have found its own *modus operandi*. The secret seems to be not how proactive or reflective the mentor or coach may be, but whether the focus of the relationship is manager centred and intended to reach consensus.[20]

Most recently, the senior managers themselves have launched what is called our career management initiative. Twenty members of staff have personally requested that a senior manager should help them evolve and develop their career at MCB University Press. The allocation as between senior managers was made on their own initiatives and the owners were not involved. Once again we see an instance of senior managers showing the owners how to run the enterprise more effectively, and receiving wholehearted support for their initiative. It is already showing good results after six months, with all clearly aware of what aspirations the 20 have. They are ready either to assist them to achieve them or to counsel why a particular ambition cannot be speedily achieved and what steps have to be taken as necessary preparation to succeed eventually.

The owners have forced a further issue however. They have insisted that the senior managers take more responsibility for the 'general' development and training of their colleagues over and beyond the focused skills needed for their current and immediately perceived roles. Management Action Learning programmes at MBA and bachelor levels are again being offered to all levels of staff, but this time under the aegis of those who have already learned their way to those awards. Known as our Enterprise School of Management, conducted in partnership with the International Management Centres, it has seen the development of a consortium approach with our enterprise's suppliers and of a new curriculum at bachelor level, focusing on publishing in its broadest scope. The next generations of middle managers are not only being trained, mentored and coached by their senior colleagues, they are being 'generally' educated under their leadership as well.

What we are seeking to create is an environment where the workplace is constantly challenged and stretched. We are seeking in every way to stimulate the people with whom we work without intimidating them. 'Being a learning organization *per se* is not enough. The talents of each and every individual must be developed'.[21]

STRUCTURAL CHANGE

The formal structure of our enterprise was established in 1977 and remained unchanged until November 1993. The only element of doubt we regularly had about it was how best to attend to new launches and acquisitions. The reason we remained unchanged for so long was because it had been outstandingly commercially successful the way we were. The structure had been based on self-managed publishing/market missions – extremely fashionable then – in the heyday of output budgeting. For the ten previous years, foundation to 1977, it had been built around owner self-managed venture groups for each journal. So we have a not inconsiderable tradition of self-management in our enterprise.

The challenge to improve our structure emerged in high relief as the owners withdrew from their critical senior management roles as publishers, and invited those who had been their executive associates to take up the tasks. While the new incumbents had much of the knowledge required to do most of the job, it was inappropriate for the enterprise at large to ask it of them. The power and authority vested in an owner *per se* had given the role of publisher more than its nominal tasks, and that could not be transferred. Colleagues wanted to flatten the structure at senior levels as the owners moved upwards, just as it had been flattened by the owners previously at middle-manager levels, not to create cardinals among themselves.

The first fault lines emerged as previously indicated in the area of new launches and acquisitions. The publishers working as owners had always shared decision making in these matters as well as having responsibilities for their autonomous operational domains. First, an Acquisitions Unit and then a New Launches Programme were spun out of the orbit of the non-owner publishers, alongside the publishing/market missions, to be managed by the owners.

The second fault line was more demanding. Future versus present issues could be handled comfortably in parallel, but a challenge to make the enterprise customer- as opposed to product-oriented could not. The emergence of the marketing database approach for promotional campaigns and development of existing customers was the death knell of the 1977 model. The marketing database was so evidently cost beneficial that support for it grew with ever-increasing commitment to the need to give the whole enterprise a customer focus; the ultimate step indeed on this road was the creation of the ICE system. The organization had to be restructured as ICE came on stream.

What we have since come to realize was that, by following the logic of a customer focus, and establishing a new structure which none of the owners had ever operated in their time as senior managers, there was an opportunity on the grand scale for the new senior managers to call the shots. And they in their turn had the opportunity to do the same for their colleagues, who were taking up roles they themselves had never filled.

The need for the great structural change was perceived among the owners and leaders. It was promulgated in broad outline as VISION '94 in December 1992. It sought to align our structure with the future purposes of our enterprise.[22,23] Senior managers were then required to join in SEMAP III throughout the first nine months of 1993 to explore and test out the VISION for 1994. They were required to resolve how they would want to organize its implementation.[24] The top roles were offered by the owners to the key players in the former structure. Profit-related pay (PRP) was introduced for 1993 trading, and since continued, to ensure that so far as possible the enterprise did not take its eyes off the current year's bottom line while planning and thinking its way into 1994's new look. The only caveat entered was that at the outset the headcount was to remain constant, with any large gaps filled by contracting out.

At the same time, to ensure that the new structure and thinking reached well beyond the senior managers, 20 staff members commenced Action Learning bachelor programme from across the enterprise, with their assignments and dissertations focused on areas of VISION '94 as debated with their senior managers. Three of the senior managers themselves joined an Action Learning MBA programme, again using their assignments and dissertations to focus on the development of the future in terms of empowerment, field sales campaigns, agent relationships, electronic publishing, facilities management and much more besides.

SEMAP III projects reflected the determination of VISION '94 to take a sharper look at our world markets – over half our revenue is from outside the UK. Schemes and actions emerged for greater penetration of selected continental European countries, and for the development of region-specific new launches and pricing strategies in Southern Africa and South America.

The integration of Publishing Logistics led to close focus on editorial procurement, a quality initiative for articles themselves, production tracking, journal despatches and copyright clearances. The determined customer focus of the new structure led to an evaluation of the quality of service offered in customer service – a strategy looking for 'moments of truth' in the process, each to be better managed. The wholly new area of sales prospecting in contradistinction to customer development examined the key training requirements for that field – a precursor to the subsequent demands for a bachelor programme based in publishing itself. Production similarly looked to ways in which its now arriving new technologies could enhance its performance, particularly by the development of middle-management competences in the department.

Each of these projects can again be seen to be at one and the same time creating and addressing dissatisfaction within the enterprise. The original restructuring that had taken acquisitions and new launches out of the publisher's domain was sustained but with a strong caveat. Now brought together in a Business Development Centre, they were required to create no separate focus for developing the future. They were on the contrary required to take the initiative to bring together, across the organization, multifunctional teams to address the issues that were important, and then to effect the outcomes. For instance, as soon as an acquisition was mooted or a new launch explored, those concerned to see it was absorbed and/or implemented must be involved from the operational areas of the enterprise.

One year on, with VISION '94 now firmly in place, two further dimensions have been added to this structural proactivity. The Head of Publishing Logistics has been asked outwith her operational responsibilities to initiate multifunctional teams to review and develop medium-term strategies for cohorts of journals within our total range, e.g. best sellers, best contributors, or acquired titles three years on. A new role leading out, our Electronic Publishing Initiatives (EPIs), with the mandate to operate using the same patterns as the Business Development Centre, has also been established for a senior manager.

Our belief is that every individual in the enterprise must be as involved as possible in creating and sharing in the electronic publishing transformation of our product range and more besides in the coming years. The individual taking up the EPI role is one who has a distinguished track record as intrapreneur within the enterprise. As such there is no danger of losing the advantages of prototyping approaches to such activities which have enabled us to succeed well thus far. Nevertheless, we believe the time has come when the heart and substance of our existing technologies providing hardcopy publishing seem to be on the threshold of a discontinuity. We do not know what the outcomes will be when the situation stabilizes but we are ready to put ourselves out of one technology into another if that is what some or most of our customers require, and we can discern how to achieve it profitably. Everyone has a right to be involved in the excitement and it would be folly not to let everyone contribute as best they are able. As we observed in the opening paragraphs of this chapter we believe all our futures are at stake.

The success of the approach adopted during the implementation of VISION '94, i.e. promulgating a new vision and structure and inviting the senior management to explore how it wanted to implement it, has staggered us all. It will be clear from our analysis that by almost any definition our enterprise has enjoyed a very considerable pattern of empowerment, been a learning organization and used strategic management development over the past decade. But this was a totally new experience for the owners and senior managers alike. 'The battleship', as Carr[25] describes it, 'had become a fleet'.

Resistance to change? Why? By the end of 1993 the staff simply could not wait to get started. And that was before the fruits of the ICE system were going to be available – not ready until August 1994. The changeover was so smooth it was hard to credit that what had gone out of the window was the way of organizing ourselves that had built the enterprise to what it had become, the structure that had enabled the owners to build a truly international academic management publishing house. Apart from the vision formulation and a determination to set in place the programmes of management Action Learning, the owners had transferred responsibility to the senior managers. They had created an environment in which managers had been keen and able to identify and solve complex problems on their own. The managers concerned chose to create power for themselves. As Harari[26] reported from another educational publishing company, any owner could say: 'I don't know what my people are doing but, because I work face to face with them as coach, I know that whatever it is, they are doing exactly what I'd want them to do if I knew what they were doing!'

By June 1994, for the owners' think tank sessions, the senior managers were able to report no great interface problems between their new areas of responsibility in the new structure. What they did not say, and what the owners have readily conceded gives them very great pride, is that a host of temporary teams and taskforces have been spawned, worked matters through and disbanded over the past 18 months.[27]

A host of individuals, at all levels, have called together colleagues from across the enterprise in a lattice of relationships to address issues from the design of reports to the creation of a new sample copy strategy or the relaunch of an ailing journal.[28-30]

They had little hesitation in so doing because they could see no real barrier to doing it and it was the obvious thing to do to solve their problem. Nobody had any ready answers to offer because it was all going to be different.

LEADING THE COURAGEOUS ON

As we observed at the outset, we have some bad news, some threats to overcome. In the context of what has been described, of what the owners have done and led us to do over the past decade, we believe we are reasonably well equipped to evolve a better scenario than selling off the enterprise to other owners. We believe we will be able to address the challenges of electronic publishing in a profitable way. With a continuing coaching and mentoring role from the owners and our permanent commitment to Action Learning development, we have reached the stage where we can sustain our systems and structural growth and development.

The issue of financial ownership succession is of a different order of magnitude. We need help from within and without. What the owners did for systems and organization structure they need to do now for financial structure. It is clearly up to the senior managers to open the debate and for the owners to be responsible for mentoring and coaching some desirable outcomes – either ownership by a new group of investors who accept and endorse the talents of the enterprise, or an increasing share in financial ownership by those who are zealously concerned to carry their own careers forward within MCB University Press into the next millennium. The owners have long since established a trust fund holding 5 per cent of the equity for all staff at large. Profit-related pay began in 1993. What next makes sense?

WHAT SOME OF OUR COLLEAGUES HAD TO SAY

PAUL MORRELL – OPERATIONS MANAGER, PRODUCTION SERVICES DEPARTMENT

Paul is 34 and joined the company 13 years ago as a typesetter and was promoted to Typesetting Manager as the department grew in size. He had completed only one development programme, an in-house supervisor's training course, but recently joined the Bachelor programme.

In 1992 the Director of Production Services recommended that MCB invest in new electronic typesetting production equipment to replace an increasingly inflexible and outdated system. An initial investment of £300,000 was agreed by the board to provide a production system that would allow MCB the ability to generate journals more efficiently and to offer a greater range of opportunities for electronic titles in the future.

Paul was involved from the outset in the decision on the most appropriate hardware system and software package. Paul went to seminars, visited exhibitions and systems on site at other companies. He reviewed his findings in discussion with his senior manager and they jointly agreed to adopt Apple Macs with QuarkXpress software.

Paul was further involved in planning the introduction of the new kit phased over a period of 15 months with typesetters trained two at a time, while the requirement to produce over 600 journal issues was also maintained! All training was completed three months ahead of schedule and only 12 issues came out late.

The introduction of new kit was an important trigger creating an opportunity for the empowerment of Paul. His approach to work had shifted – he was less bolshy! From Paul's perspective, two events were instrumental in this marked change: the supervisor's training course and mixing with other production professionals at seminars and exhibitions.

> The supervisor's course opened my eyes to a lot of things. That was the first time I was asked to look at myself and . . . learning [how] to change other people's [decisions] you have probably got to change yourself as well.

Paul's current role, now that the new equipment has been installed and all staff are fully trained, includes keeping abreast of new technological developments, assessing their suitability and, if appropriate, recommending their adoption. He plays a key role in influencing the further development of the department.

> It has certainly changed my role in the way I look at new investments: how cost effective they are, the comparison of one system to another, changing the way in which the department is run.

Paul has directly influenced the technological and organizational innovations in the production services department as a result of his training and career development. His perceptions of ownership of this area already benefit the company through his continued assessment of our opportunities to profit from technological initiatives.

GILLIAN CRAWFORD – LIBRARY LINK MANAGER, CUSTOMER DEVELOPMENT: LIBRARIANS

Gill is 25 years old. She has been employed by MCB for six years, starting as an assistant in Office Services and progressing through various marketing appointments to her current role as Library Link Manager. She is responsible for the company's relationship with existing librarian customers world-wide, reporting to a senior manager.

She was promoted to this position having demonstrated assertive behaviour in undertaking previous tasks and responsibilities and she has completed the British Direct Marketing Association's Diploma. Once given the opportunity she has readily and rapidly taken on significant responsibility, e.g. recruitment of staff, development and allocation of promotion budget and marketing schedules, and the production of a portfolio.

The Customer Development: Librarians' department was initially set up in November 1993 with given parameters as to how Gillian's part should be structured:

> The department would have been structured differently if I'd been empowered to do so – it's a problem managing something you haven't set up.

Seeking greater effectiveness in terms of promotion to librarian subscribers, Gill floated the idea for the production and use of high quality 'selections' of articles as sample copies of journals during a discussion with one of the business partners. He encouraged her to develop the idea and to gain support from interested parties in other departments. Having gained their feedback, she personally had the proposal approved by the board. She did however encounter problems along the way:

> To be the driving force behind a new initiative can sometimes cause difficulties such as barriers at the interface level and resentment from other members of staff, particularly if they are more senior. Recognition, not necessarily financial, of initiatives is desirable.

Gillian believes that she has gained personally from being empowered:

Project management experience, confidence in expressing ideas and learning to be an intrapreneur . . .

and perceived the organization as having gained from her experience by:

gaining a more confident member of staff able to make good career progression, together with new ideas for marketing to librarians.

MARIAN BOND – REGIONAL DEVELOPMENT MANAGER, EUROPE AND MIDDLE EAST

Marian is 30 and was recruited in November 1992 to assist in the development of MCB's marketing database. She quickly demonstrated her ability and in mid-1993 was asked to take on the role of Regional Development Manager (RDM) reporting to a partner responsible for Europe and the Middle East. This was a new role, although RDMs were already in the Asia Pacific and North America, working for other partners. Individual RDMs have widely differing portfolios of responsibilities reflecting the different growth strategies that are appropriate for different markets.

Marian was expected to liaise widely throughout the organization to achieve her goals in concurrence with, but yet not constrained by, others. Many interface communications were via taskforces addressing particular issues.

To begin with it frustrated me greatly that we are not encouraged to be prescriptive – you have to sell the idea and allow them to buy into it.

Marian's work in other organizations prior to joining MCB has involved taskforce situations, but her experience was that these had been prescriptive within given parameters.

Within MCB it's a development process, meeting as a forum and bringing skills to the table to decide what you are going to do. The means by which a problem should be tackled or the people who should be involved are not predetermined. The actual exposure to the different interfaces and the team-building process improves one's understanding . . . I find that type of forum motivates me greatly. I want to become involved and responsible and take away an action agenda.

Having agreed the key issues for the region in discussion with the partner, Marian kept him informed with regular reports and informal reviews. How she was to achieve her personal targets relating to those key issues was down to Marian and she chose to do this through setting personal objectives and action schedules.

Thereafter, it was up to myself to put the plan together . . . the partner's concern is at a strategic level.

DEBORAH KAVANAGH – LIBRARY LINK SERVICES MANAGER, CUSTOMER DEVELOPMENT: LIBRARIANS

Deborah is 29 and joined MCB seven years ago as a computer typesetter, setting academic courseware. After two promotions, first to control and then co-ordinate the courseware, Deborah was promoted to manage the Anbar Library and document delivery service and the Docutech production activity, reporting to a senior manager.

The activities within this role have offered Deborah a number of empowering opportunities:

> ... interviewing and recruiting members of staff: developing and automating the Anbar Library, the setting up of a capping system within the Anbar Library and the development of the electronic bulletin board working with technical consultants.

MCB's development of an electronic bulletin board as a means of communication with the academic and library community is one of the key activities in its electronic publishing initiatives. Deborah learned skills that were new both to her and the organization as a direct result of this responsibility.

Deborah has gained from being empowered by:

> Feelings of esteem, greater confidence in myself and a better understanding of people's needs.

Deborah has been able to progress many activities efficiently and speedily in a role that was new to her and to the organization and made valuable input to the development of new systems. She feels now that she is a more valued member of MCB and that her outlook for the future is more promising.

She has also felt able to empower others, e.g. giving one member of staff the responsibility for co-ordinating the photocopying of articles. She is motivating her newly acquired team by involving them more in the day-to-day running of the department by holding frequent meetings. She has just completed her Bachelor programme in Action Learning.

TONY PEARSON – SYSTEMS SUPPORT MANAGER, INFORMATION & COMPUTER SERVICES

Tony is 25. When his career as a professional footballer came to an end through an ankle injury six years ago, Tony entered MCB in the Customer Services Department. He progressed from there to the Human Resources Mission and is now located in the Information & Computer Services Department.

It is interesting to note that Tony decided to change career path four years ago from that of publishing to computing and was sponsored by MCB to develop this aspiration 'from scratch'. He has been encouraged to develop intuitively within MCB following his own path of specialized computer development and is currently completing a BSc computer studies, after attaining HNC and HND, rather than in-house Action Learning programmes.

Untypical of most managers at MCB, he has not had any specific management training, preferring the specialist path, but feels he is learning by experience and knows what is 'culturally out of order or in step'. He manages by his perceptions of what is the right thing to do and feels able to rely on his intuition:

> This is very much a one-off organization in the structure of the place. People are sometimes empowered by default. Often planning does not go behind it and it is experience opposed to specific training which I suppose pulls you through.

The trigger for Tony's current empowered state was his manager's redundancy, in December 1992 (this is what he considers empowerment by 'default'). The IT department at that time consisted of two employees, Tony and the outgoing director of systems and information. At that time Tony had the systems expertise to keep the company's mini-computer running and was trusted to do this and able to set his own priorities. He had to hold the fort for some three months while new skills and experience were sought in the marketplace – 'very much out on a limb and often I had to just fight back and enter unknown territory'.

A computer manager was appointed at the end of March 1993 to head the Information & Computer Services department. By then, the emphasis of the department had changed to prioritizing the much-needed integration of MCB's various information systems. The computer manager has, since his appointment, been totally involved in this, aided by Tony and external consultants.

Currently in the process of sharing his knowledge of the MCB system with his manager and other employees within and outside his department, Tony is still the only person with specialist knowledge of certain aspects of MCB's systems and that knowledge empowers him.

The department now has four permanent staff and the computer manager is happy to empower his staff in the decisions relating to those functions where they have a greater knowledge than himself.

Tony feels accountable – dealing with suppliers, and all levels of MCB management. He has responsibility for decision making within a budget 'without having to go through particular channels'.

When questioned about the most appropriate managerial style for him to behave in an empowered way Tony responded:

> It is having the confidence in the people you employ to do a specific task you assign in a specific period and not worry about the details, and it's nothing more than that really. We get the man management skills that go with that. There is no need for anyone to look over my shoulder with my job, nor would I do that with people who I feel I can give tasks to.

His perception of how the company's culture allows empowerment is that:

It encourages it in that there are no secretaries, so for example we do our own typing. What that means is you have to communicate more with people to find out how to do things. You find out much more quickly what people do for a living. Nobody is pigeon-holed in quite the same way as they would be elsewhere – there are pigeon holes but they are not as clearly defined as they might be. There is much more of an open-door policy than other companies. What that means is that people are not afraid to find out more about the business than is really relevant to them. As soon as you realize that, then you are not afraid to grasp the nettle.

MCB-UP has benefited by empowering its 'footballer acquisition' of six years ago who, in his own words, is now:

A good, all-round computer professional, who not only has the definitive in-depth knowledge of the organization's systems and data, but also has the experience of dealing with others at all levels of the company in a range of matters both technical and managerial.

As to the future: does Tony feel he is in a position to push for more of the same, or does he feel he is being pulled with people having higher aspirations for him than he can fulfil?

I would not think twice about grasping! I would hope the opportunities are there. It is not a problem.

ALISON DENBY – RESEARCH AND DEVELOPMENT EXECUTIVE, BUSINESS DEVELOPMENT CENTRE

Alison is 24. She has been with MCB for five years, commencing in production, moving to customer services and now in the business development centre.

Does Alison feel that in her role within the organization, she has been pulled into an empowered role or has pushed for it?

It's a combination, quite a lot of pull with some push and enthusiasm.

Auditing acquisitions is one of the main areas where I am given the opportunity to do something my own way. I had been involved in audits before, but never actually running them and planning them myself. I was given the opportunity to do all that with help and support where needed but had to decide how to do it myself and how to organize a team.

I was not very comfortable with my first handover audit at all because I was empowered to co-ordinate, but a senior manager was also at the audit for support. This led to leadership and control conflicts as I was unable to 'pull rank' and take total control.

I was very scared to do one completely on my own, but once I had done it and come back and done the report I was happy and felt more confident to go forward to the next.

With the nature of our research to find acquisitions it is very difficult because sometimes you do not get anywhere for weeks on end and then all of a sudden you do get somewhere. You go through patches of finding it difficult to keep motivated until something happens which gets you going again.

I think more than training and development has helped me, it has been a combination of training, company culture and interdepartmental communication.

The external work I have done for my BA degree at Huddersfield University has helped a lot because I have got to know more about the subject matter that I am talking to editors or prospective editors about. I have integrated with academics from outside the organization and that has helped me on journal launches.

MCB's culture encourages interdepartmental communication. Integrating with other people within the organization through the work I do in business development has enhanced my understanding of the organization and the business. This enables me to be more assertive when solving problems, rather than relying on my manager for answers.

I recently had what seemed a good idea for a new launch – part of a subject we are doing at university. I have been encouraged by my colleagues to take it on to the next stage.

I am hoping to have at least one of my ideas developed into a new journal launch for 1995. This is one of the targets I have set myself personally. I would feel good about that, especially when it sold subscriptions well.

CATHY MOSTYN – DIRECTOR SALES OPERATIONS/PROSPECTING

Cathy is 39 years old. She joined the company 15 years ago and has had a varied career since then, progressing through several departments, e.g subscriptions control, production, librarians mission and human resource professions mission. She is now heading sales operations, a department with ten employees responsible for obtaining new sales for MCB products worldwide with a promotional budget of £2.5m.

Regarded by most peers as one of the company's most effective team managers, 'streetwise', competitive, and a good communicator, how does she empower her team?

> Empowerment was not at the back of my mind at all until recently. The first time I decided I consciously wanted to empower was when compiling the human resource written case analysis on motivation for my Action Learning MBA programme. I tried to make the team responsible and recognized as doing a good job.

When subsequently setting up her new team to develop new sales worldwide in November 1993 she changed from having one member of staff reporting to another to using senior members of staff as facilitators.

> They get into their own teams and the senior members are facilitators for discussion. They all have different styles, but I do not want them in the team if they do not fit in and would fight against introducing anybody who would upset the applecart.

How does Cathy build confidence in someone?

> A lot of it is style. You have to make someone feel good about doing something good.
>
> I only remember having carpeted one person for making a mistake. I think you can take teamwork too far, however. The idea of discussing errors by people I trust in a team setting does not appeal. I think a quiet word on the side works better.

297

It throws you for a little while and it hurts. Unless it continues to happen, it should be dealt with personally and not dwelt upon.

The process of planning, organization and implementation is bottom up with a few exceptions. The sales budgets are put together by each individual team member and discussed and agreed on an individual basis with Cathy.

They put their targets together and they have to achieve them. At the moment the team are measured on getting the work out and on achieving their targets.

We are, however, now moving away purely from the quantity measures and moving to quality. Getting them to think of quality in addition to quantity. We are now looking at putting mechanisms in there to control process not people and the people will be involved in working those out.

THREE MEMBERS OF CATHY MOSTYN'S SALES OPERATIONS TEAM – SARAH CARTER, SHARON JONES AND PAT GLEDHILL

Their main empowering experience in the last two years was being made individually responsible for setting their own promotional budgets and targets.

We now understand how those targets got there and why those budgets are X amount. Before it was just, 'Here is what you are going to spend' and we never really understood where that amount came from, and what the calculations were to get to that amount. We understand the whole process of it all now. We feel we have control and responsibility.

I think it has been good in that we are more enthusiastic about reaching the targets, because we know that we have set them and we feel that we have got something to prove as individuals.

I have learned more this year than I ever learned doing it the other way. Just in a matter of a few months, going through that process, I learned more than a full year previously.

When we were first given the task it was a case of go do it, we were given no guidelines, no past formula or anything, it was just do it. At first it was 'Help, where do we start?' So we asked each other how we had done certain stages, and learned from one another.

I have understood more about the finance function since we started to work this way. You are more in control of your budget and you know what its limitations are, and how flexible it can be, and how that fits in with the Finance Department, such as quarter ends, etc.

Obviously we had to justify everything we had done. If Cathy did not agree, or had another suggestion, this was discussed before anything was put in place.

I actually feel closer to Cathy now. I feel as if I can go into her office more than I could before, but we try to try things out first before going to Cathy. If we have an idea that is different, or a suggestion to try, we either just go ahead and implement it or, if it is something out of the ordinary that might cost a bit more, we just have a word with Cathy.

A critical new development is that some of the team are now involved in managing subcontractors, so are managing other people externally, doing the work for them. How do they feel about that?

The fact that I am being trusted to give the right feedback and the right information and give them the OK on what they have eventually decided is really enjoyable and I have learned from it. Not just learning that I know more than I realize because I am doing it every day, but just learning the process of letting somebody else manage the campaign which has freed me up to do other things.

It is a fresh mind. We are working with Direct Answer in the US – Karen tells me what works in America and I am learning from that and can apply it to other journals. These are all things we have not done before. It adds more interest to your job.

I think MCB are getting more out of their staff. They are getting people a lot more involved in the company. We are setting targets and budgets so we are getting more involved in the company's performance, what we have to achieve at the end of the year.

MCB has a great 'knack' for making you want to do well. I have never worked anywhere else and taken work home – by choice!

It is quite pleasing to be trusted. If your senior manager thinks you are capable of doing something then you think so yourself. You do not question yourself, they trust you. It also gives you the confidence to question what is being asked of you. Before we might have done things without knowing why. Now we go back and ask.

REFERENCES

1 P. Weis, 'Achieving Zero-defect Service through Self-directed Teams' in *Journal of Systems Management*, February, 1992, pp. 26–36, whom we thank for suggesting the notion of 'courageous managers'.

2 D. Simon, 'Managing Cultural Change at BP' in *Target: Management Development Review*, vol. 4, no. 3, 1991, pp. 16–19.

3 D. Andrews, 'The Trust Factor: The Hidden Obstacle to Empowerment' in *APICS – The Performance Advantage*, May 1994, pp. 30–2.

4 R.E. Temple and R.W. Droege, 'Internal Customers Need Delighting Too' in *Managing Service Quality*, vol. 4, no. 1, 1994, pp. 14–17.

5 M. Hand, 'Freeing the Victims' in *Total Quality Management*, vol. 5, no. 3, June 1993, pp. 11–14.

6 J. Kotter, *The General Managers*, Free Press, New York, NY, 1982.

7 R.E. Ripley and M.J. Ripley, 'Empowerment – The Cornerstone of Quality: Empowering Management in Innovative Organizations in the 1990s' in *Management Decision*, vol. 30, no. 4, 1992, pp. 23–43.

8 R. Revans, *The Origins and Growth of Action Learning*, Chartwell-Bratt, Bromley, 1982.

9 J.V. Peters, 'Customers First – The Independent Answer' in *Business Education*, vol. 9, no. 3/14, 1988.

10 G. Wills, *Your Enterprise School of Management*, Revans' Professorship Report: 1992, MCB University Press for International Management Centres, UK, 1993.

11 D. Sutton, 'The Problems of Developing Managers in the Small Firm' in *Training and Management Development News*, vol. 1, no. 1, 1987.

12 S. McClelland, 'Gaining Competitive Advantage through Strategic Management Development' in *Journal of Management Development*, vol. 13, no. 5, 1994, pp. 4–13.

13 B. Bruce, T. Jordan and G. Wills, 'Realizing the Benefits of a Marketing Intelligentsia' in *Marketing Intelligence & Planning*, vol. 12, no. 6, 1994, pp. 21–34.

14 R.J. Newton and M.J. Wilkinson, 'Project Morale: The Empowerment of Managers in Their Everyday Work' in *Empowerment in Organizations*, vol. 2, no. 1, 1994, pp. 25–30, explore a similar approach using Action Learning at Ashworth Hospital.

15 G. Wills, 'Enabling Managerial Growth and Ownership Succession' in *Management Decision*, vol. 30, no. 1, 1992.

16 R. Stayer, 'How I Learned to Let My Workers Lead' in *Harvard Business Review*, November/December, 1990.

17 C. Argyris, 'Double Loop Learning in Organisations' in *Harvard Business Review*, September/October 1977, pp. 115–25.

18 G. Wills, B. Bruce and T. Duncan, 'Creating a Marketing Intelligentsia' in *Marketing Intelligence & Planning*, vol. 9, no. 4, 1991, pp. 1–20.

19 J. Burdett, 'To Coach or Not to Coach? That Is the Question', Parts 1 & 2, in *Industrial and Commercial Training*, vol. 23, no. 5, 1991, pp. 10–16 and no. 6, 1991, pp. 17–23.

20 A. Mumford, *Management Development Strategies for Action*, Institute of Personnel Management, UK, 1989.

21 D. Casse, 'People Are Not Resources', *Journal of European Industrial Training*, vol. 18, no. 5, 1994, pp. 23–6.

22 W.C. Harker, 'Alignment for Success in the Nineties' in *Business Quarterly*, Winter 1991, pp. 107–12.

23 N.H. Chorn, 'Organisations: A New Paradigm' in *Management Decision*, vol. 29, no. 4, 1991, pp. 8–11.

24 C. Carr, 'Managing Self-managed Workers' in *Training and Development*, September 1991, pp. 37–42.

25 C. Carr, 'Empowering Leaders' in *Training and Development*, March 1994, pp. 39–44.

26 O. Harari, 'Stop Empowering People' in *Small Business Reports*, March 1994, pp. 53–5.

27 R.F. Lynch and T.J. Werner, 'A League of Their Own' in *Small Business Reports*, April 1994, pp. 25–42.

28 F. Shipper and C.C. Manz, 'An Alternative Road to Empowerment' in *Organizational Dynamics*, vol. 20, no. 3, Winter 1992, pp. 48–61.

29 L. Martin and J.F. Vogt, 'No Sense of Trespass: Empowerment through Informational and Interpersonal Licence' in *Organizational Development Journal*, vol. 10, no. 1, 1992, pp. 1–8.

30 J. Belasco, 'Empowerment as a Growth Strategy' in *Management International Review*, vol. 32, no. 2, 1992, pp. 181–8.

27 Rediscovering Standards*

Abby Day and John Peters

If your organization is one of the many today hoping to receive a BS 5750 certificate, the good news is that earning the certificate is the easy part. There is one route, favoured by many, which is an almost foolproof method designed to enable that certificate to be nailed to the wall; fake it. There are scores of able consultants who will willingly allow you to part with large sums of money to hire them to write documentation sufficient to convince a third party auditor such as BSI. All you have to do is trade the costs of consultancy, audit and registration against the benefits of holding the standard – or against the costs of not having it. Certainly, we hear about the bullying of small suppliers by big customers, who turn around one day (sometimes to a customer they have dealt with happily for years) and say 'Get registered to 5750 or we will not deal with you any more'. That's when 5750 is a necessary evil, yet another bureaucratic barrier of paper work and red tape in the way of businesses going about their business; nothing to do with 'quality'!

But is this really true, or can 5750 be an important step on the eternal path of continuous improvement? To address this, we need to go back to first principles.

DEFINING QUALITY

What is 'quality' anyway? We might be tempted to rush to the library to find out what has been written so far about quality, what the paradigms are, new and old, what the seminal and evolutionary works are – what, for goodness sake, is the body of knowledge? We might as well save our energy. For something that has become a worldwide business obsession, heavyweight thinkers about quality are thin on the ground. There has been little or no progress in the theoretical underpinning of the discipline. Much as we seek to avoid theoretical abstractions, there is nothing so practical as a good theory.

*Originally published in *International Journal of Contemporary Hospitality Management*, vol. 6, no. 12, 1994.

Quality is such a gravy train today, that too many academics are so busy scrambling aboard to be bothered to know who is driving it, or how. That is why the theoretical base from which quality practice is derived consists almost entirely of elderly Americans, namely Messrs Deming, Crosby and Juran.

WE KNOW IT WHEN WE SEE IT

There was once a trial where the defendant was being accused of selling pornographic material. His lawyer was conducting a clever defence by arguing that there was no common definition of obscenity, therefore his client had no way of knowing that the materials he was selling were indeed obscene before the law.

At one stage he asked the judge what his definition of pornography was, to make the point still further. 'Young man', the judge said, 'you may not know how to define it, and I may not know how to define it, but we both know it when we see it!'

Quality is rather like pornography in this respect. We may not be able to define it easily, but we know it when we see it. We know what good quality service in a restaurant feels like, and we know what bad quality service feels like. But how do we know this instinctively? We can distinguish between a well-written paper and a badly written one, but how? We can imagine how to make our working environment a high quality one, and how to make it a lower quality one, but what exactly would that mean? Further, would it mean the same to everyone?

For a quality manager, these questions are familiar. Those concerned with quality of output in organizations are required to go further than simply to say 'We don't know what it is, but we know it when we see it'. And so, standards are born – technical and/or managerial specifications about products and services which allow us to replicate them with a predictable degree of consistency.

THE PHILOSOPHY OF QUALITY

Prior to setting standards it is necessary to establish a shared understanding of quality. Here are some common definitions of quality:

- Fitness for purpose or use.
- The totality of features and characteristics of a product or service that bear on its ability to satisfy stated or implied needs (BS 1778/ISO 8402).
- The total composite product and service characteristics of marketing, engineering, manufacture and maintenance through which the product and service in use will meet the expectation by the customer.

The three definitions overlap to some extent – quality is caused by an interaction; it needs two parties (subject and object) for quality to come into existence (an interaction between a customer – a subject – and a product or service – an object); and the definitions imply that quality in itself does not exist. It is only brought into being when a customer consumes a product or service, and so can experience the inherent quality of that product or service.

Does this mean that quality is what our customers tell us it is? For practical purposes, the answer is yes, and that is when it becomes complicated. Whenever we involve people, rather than machines, it becomes complicated. One way of simplifying it is to review human experiences in terms of two types of quality patterns.

STATIC AND DYNAMIC PATTERNS

In his novel *Lila*, author Robert M. Pirsig (previously known for *Zen and the Art of Motorcycle Maintenance*) described the experience of buying a new record. We have all had that experience, where we rush home with the record, or disk, today, and play it over and over again until we are sick of it. With each repeated play, the song seems to lose something. What happened? Was the song good at first but became less good with each play? Pirsig explains:

> The first good, that made you want to buy the record, was dynamic quality. Dynamic quality comes as a sort of surprise. What the record did was weaken for a moment your existing static patterns in such a way that the dynamic quality shone through. The second good, the kind that made you want to recommend it to a friend even when you had lost your own enthusiasm for it, is static quality. Static quality is what you normally expect . . .
>
> Static patterns are dead. That which does not change cannot live. But . . . life cannot exist on dynamic quality alone. It has no staying power. To cling to dynamic quality alone apart from any static patterns is to cling to chaos.
>
> Static quality patterns are dead when they are exclusive, when they demand blind obedience and suppress dynamic change. But static patterns nevertheless provide a necessary stabilising force to protect the dynamic process from degradation. Although dynamic quality, the quality of freedom, creates this world in which we live, the patterns of static quality, the quality of order, preserve our world. Neither static nor dynamic quality can survive without the other.

Static quality is what we normally expect. A customer getting on to an aeroplane *expects* the wings to stay on. A customer walking into a hotel room *expects* a bed free of cockroaches. But we have not arrived at 'quality' yet. The wings staying on, or the absence of cockroaches, does not create quality.

We normally reach quality through human interaction which *'delights'* (to use a piece of quality management jargon) the customer. The cabin staff member who goes out of his/her way to find you a special meal or to make sure your children are comfortable. The hotel receptionist who remembers your name. This is *dynamic* quality.

You can, indeed you must, systematize static quality. However pleasant and delightful the stewardess, if the wings fall off the aeroplane, the flight will be a low quality experience. Static systems do not create quality, but their absence creates a lack of quality. The first job of the general manager (specifically 'general manager' and not 'quality manager', for these are general, business management issues) is to identify the necessary static quality systems for his or her business and ensure that they keep going right – and we must do whatever it takes to achieve this, as static systems are a platform on which to build quality.

The second job of the general manager is, having identified the static factors and protected them, to identify the 'moments of truth' in encounters with customers, and what might produce a perception of quality. You cannot, must not, systematize dynamic quality. The first time someone in the USA told you to 'have a nice day' may have been delightful; by the 288th time it was just expected. All you can do is to understand what the customer might perceive as moments of quality creation, and *'create the space for them to happen'*. If your staff are spending their time and creative energies troubleshooting static quality problems – trying desperately to kill the cockroach while the receptionist stalls the customer at the check-in desk – they are going to have nothing left to create dynamic quality.

Static systems change over time, albeit undramatically. The rules of the game, or what is needed to stay in the game, change. A few years ago, a bar of soap and a bottle of shampoo in a hotel room might have delighted a customer, because it would have shown an unusually high level of service. Now we look for ever more exotic items to put in the little baskets to tickle the jaded appetites of our guests. They have become stay-in-the-game items; their absence produced negative quality. What once was dynamic has moved into the static.

Dynamic, quality-creating moments of truth need to be fresh daily. We easily recognize the difference between the real smile and the forced; they may both be more pleasant than a scowl or a blank look of indifference, but one may create quality, and one will probably not.

MANAGED SYSTEMS REVISION CYCLE

Continuous improvement, then, is not quite what it seems. Static systems need continuous *monitoring*, to keep an eye on what the stay-in-the-game factors are, but step change improvement. Static systems are the glue which hold an organization together. You cannot continually tinker with them or the organization will fall apart. You cannot keep them for ever either. There has to be a managed systems revision cycle, reviewing and changing them at just the right time. When that time is, is particular to your organization in its own context. The dynamic needs a forum for sharing what works and what does not. Dynamic systems exhibit true continuous improvement, as they cannot be preserved. Any attempt to capture or systematize the dynamic will kill it. We can only create space for it, and train our staff to understand moments of truth, and the benefits our customers really want.

THE ROLE OF STANDARDS

Now we can return to standards, and to BS 5750. A quality management system (QMS) is a business management system. That is all it is. Its aim is to protect the factors in your business which need to keep going right, in a systematic and efficient way, and to create the space to delight your customers so that they will keep coming back. It is a means to an end, and the end is profit, survival, or whatever your ultimate business objective is. That end will be achieved by gaining and keeping customers, and servicing them as economically as you can, and that is what the quality management system should help you to do.

To put your QMS in place, properly, is therefore as simple or as complicated as identifying what your core competences and your key business issues are (and will be in the future); identifying what are the most important benefits your customers seek (and how these might change); stating what you are going to do to make sure they keep going right; then doing it.

If you have done that, thoroughly, thoughtfully and carefully, you have a quality management system that is real for you. At that point you can, if you choose, invite a third party auditor, such as BSI, to examine the evidence of your system, which is the plan and documentation you have prepared, and ask them to give you the certificate for the wall.

In truth, BS 5750 is not a quality management system at all. It is a reliability and consistency assurance system (though no less valuable for that). It does mean therefore that if you specify that you will give a terrible service to your customers, and document how you do that, systematically, you will get your BS 5750 certification (as you are going out of business). The standard is non-judgemental as to the quality of the business itself and its success.

This means that you should not entertain a consultant who comes armed with the BS 5750 manual, or with someone else's quality management system documentation and tries to sell you a QMS. You are back to faking it. If you take that approach to achieve the 5750 standard, you must thereafter ignore those documents, or every horror story about bureaucracy and the standard getting in the way of your business will come true. BS 5750 is a reliability assurance mechanism. You cannot start with it, otherwise you are assuring nothing but forms and paperwork. You must start with the reality of your business.

QUALITY IN CONTEXT

That is the 'what' of quality management. But what about the 'how'? Writing plans, even technically or theoretically brilliant plans, is relatively easy. Implementing them is much harder. But the one thing we know for sure about implementation is that ownership is the key. The more people feel that they own responsibility for outcomes, the more likely they are to work hard towards producing them.

Quality cannot be owned by a quality manager, or a general manager. If one person or a small team tries to catch quality miscreants, or inspect out bad performance, they will ultimately fail. The static systems will by definition not be working, and the policing of them will drive out the dynamic. Quality has to be everyone's business, because everyone in an organization touches a customer in one way or another. That is not to say that an individual or small team should not take strategic responsibility for quality. They must, just as in the end an individual or small team must take strategic responsibility for strategy and overall business policy. But an imposed, controls- and rules-based quality management system will not work, because it will not be quality. It will be, at best, reliability and consistency.

ACTION LEARNING YOUR WAY TO QUALITY

We work on deriving and implementing quality management systems through a developmental approach called Action Learning. Action Learning puts a framework around the most effective way we learn, which is from experience, by doing things for real. Learning from experience is effective but highly inefficient; as someone once said, experience is what you get when you did not get what you wanted.

Action Learning says that if you put together people who have a problem or challenge which they care about; guide them to any known precedent, sourced in books or articles which relate to the problem; help them through adapting and applying that precedent to their own context; help them to frame the right questions which will assist them to tackle their problem or challenge; and take them through the successes and failures of implementation, then you have real learning. Put another way, it is like learning to ride a bicycle. You cannot learn to ride a bicycle by hearing a lecture by an expert bicycle rider, or reading a case study about bicycle riding (although both might inspire you to want to learn). In the end, you have to get on the bicycle and experience it yourself.

Taking an individual or small group through an Action Learning approach to quality management systems gives them the opportunity to replicate the process through the whole organization. It needs skilled facilitation to make it work (which may be someone from within the organization, if that specialist skill exists, or outside it) but, aside from that, the learning and its outcomes are entirely owned by those who own the problem or challenge.

Action Learning your way to BS 5750 sounds an unusual marriage, but is in practice the only effective route. For quality management systems are about learning: individual and organizational. An effective QMS involves learning about the business, about customers and suppliers, about the changing environment around us; and then capturing that learning, organizationally, in a system which puts it into operation.

QUALITY BY DEGREE

Quite recently, we launched the world's first and only, as far as we know, Action Learning-based qualification programme in quality management: the Diploma in Quality Management (DipQM), in association with the independent business school, International Management Centres (IMC), and the British Standards Institution. The DipQM involves two main organization-based projects: the establishment or refinement of a quality management system: and a strategy towards total quality. The first programme, which started in June 1993, attracted participants from large and small, service and manufacturing, public and private, and included the NEC Corporation, British Railways, TSB and Abbey National among them.

The QMS projects arising from the diploma illustrate some of the benefits of thinking through and learning about quality management as a business management system. The participant from British Rail is working out a management system for the emerging business entities called train operating companies – the parts of the railway due to be put out to tender and possibly franchised to private operators. His output from the diploma will be the first of the TOC management systems, to be replicated around the rest of the railway.

Another participant has taken the various management systems in his organization, on the environment, on customer service, on health and safety and so on, and is seeking to unify them into a total integrated business and quality management system. A third is seeking culture change in her firm around quality management system interventions.

We are seeing the evolution of the role of quality manager from inspector and controller towards strategist, consultant, facilitator and educator. To conclude, it would be useful to look at the evolution of the discipline of quality management itself.

TOWARDS TOTAL QUALITY

Total quality is a much used term today, and there are many organizations which trumpet the fact that it is 'a TQ organization', or says 'Our aim is quality in everything we do' or some similar platitude, without knowledge of what it means. Achievement of total quality is not for mortals. It is a journey, not a destination.

But any journey needs milestones, to indicate how far down the road you have travelled, and whether you are going the right way. Certainly among those milestones are success, profitability and return on investment in quality. If we do not encounter these milestones on our road, we are walking the wrong road! Quality, and the business of the organization, cannot be separate things, separate targets.

We will see, rightly, investments in quality tied much more closely to bottom-line returns. Like training and development, it is not enough for it to be 'nice to do'; it must be necessary to do, as a part of our strategic direction and intent. Quality managers, and those associated with quality, must learn the language of financial controllers, managing directors and shareholders (as, similarly, must trainers) and sell the benefits to them.

Those needs bring us full circle, back to standards. It is interesting that BSI, the main standards setting body in the world, has Japan and the USA among its fastest growing markets. Japan, the home of total quality, interested in British standards?

The leading edge in total quality a few years ago was benchmarking, to take the best of what your competitors and others were doing and try to match it. Today, it is self- and customer-derived performance measures. This is where the world's excellent companies are, and such measures can follow from properly thought through standards. We have gone beyond the imitativeness of bench-marking, which is at best matching what your competitors were doing yesterday, and on to setting and achieving performance measures and service standards for present and continuing success. That is why the Japanese are discovering, or rediscovering, standards amidst a philosophy of total quality, and that is a way we can really achieve the most from quality management systems and standards setting.

28 Operationalizing Total Quality*

John Peters

Every organization adopts a different approach to making steps towards total quality. Approaches will quite naturally vary depending on the start-point, the organization's context, its history, tradition and culture, and so on.

We can however, point to an emerging set of approaches which appear to reach a kind of consensus. A content analysis of the various case reports points to the following seven variables which appear to be virtually consistent with successful progress down the road towards total quality:

1. Quality is driven by the key success factors (KSF) of the business. There must be a perceived 'meshing' of the need for quality and the organization's strategic imperatives. Whether there is or not will be a crucial variable in the generally acknowledged truism that, to be successful, a quality improvement drive must be wholeheartedly backed by top management.
2. Total quality requires a heavy investment in training, development and 'learning'. This investment may be in the form of externally contracted help (courses, consultancy, business education) or internal time allocation (a number of hours per week on 'quality time', multi-level improvement processes and projects, etc.) or, most usually, both. The amount of investment will normally be a function of the perceived benefits arising (for example, reduction in the costs of non-quality) and/or the relationship of quality and KSF (see 1 above).
3. Quality improvement, albeit a continuous process in theory at least, requires in practice a series of deadline-driven projects, which act as 'waymarkers' to demonstrate that progress is being made. Crosby's Zero Defects Day is one; ISO 9000 registration is another. Case examples of quality improvement invariably detail a series of activities or steps, which prioritize themselves within the generalities of organizational life.
4. Quality improvement is linked to the derivation of and measurement against a series of performance measures. This relates to 3 above in providing a progressive structure against which improvement can be ensured. These are

*Originally published in *The TQM Magazine*, vol. 6, no. 4, 1994.

frequently process control measures, such as variations from a pre-set mean and steps taken to reduce them, but can also be realized in the measurement of tangibles such as misplaced orders, reworks, warranty claims, scrap; or less tangible issues such as customer retention.

5. Total quality progression involves an almost constant stream of initiatives, which serve the purpose of keeping the quality drive 'fresh'. The physical laws of entropy suggest that systems degrade over time unless acted on otherwise. Theoretically total quality can become an organization's overriding culture, suggesting that it generates its own momentum, but in practice this does not seem to have been realized. In dynamic environments, it is reasonable to suggest that a never-ending series of initiatives aimed at a constant readjustment and realignment with the marketplace is necessary.

6. Quality improvement initiatives involve some form of ritual celebration when milestones are achieved; from internal awards of badges, rosettes or trophies, to prizes for best participation in quality, to the opportunity to make project presentations at significant corporate events (board meetings, international conferences, etc.), to financial participation in costs saved/revenues generated from quality improvement projects.

7. Total quality improvement always involves some way of addressing the business in terms of its key processes and, at some stage, an orientation towards customer-friendly delivery systems. That is to say, business processes are addressed to optimize their efficiency (which often involves simplification) and also to 'see the organization from the customer's point of view' (to improve customer service standards).

As a general extraction of success principles, this may be of some benefit to managers involved in quality improvement drives or programmes. But can we produce a kind of road map to allow people to see where they are on the journey?

Our work in detail with 28 organizations over the past year has indicated that this might be possible. The next part of this chapter will describe five levels of progress, and indicate progression steps from one to the next.

DIPLOMA IN QUALITY MANAGEMENT

The Diploma in Quality Management (DipQM) was launched by an independent business school, International Management Centres (IMC), in 1993, with the British Standards Institution (BSI) as a partner in delivery and design. To date, 28 individuals from a range of organizations have joined the programme. In 1994, Bournemouth University also joined to make a tripartite delivery structure, involving joint certification, progress within both Bournemouth and/or IMC towards further qualification if desired, local (south coast UK) delivery, and future programme refinement and development.[1] The author is director of quality/programmes and associate professor of IMC.

In brief, each participant creates both systems improvement/revision plans and actions, and total quality strategy plans and actions. These make up the academic submissions by which the diploma is awarded (the educational approach being Action Learning/Action Research, which demands participation in, as well as analysis of, problems and challenges).

A detailed analysis of the organizations participating as written up by delegates in their various submissions has revealed a five-level quality improvement taxonomy which will be discussed below. Organizations represented ranged from the very large (NEC Corporation, Abbey National) to the very small (fewer than 50 staff); from public (a housing action trust, the Health and Safety Executive) to privatized (British Telecom, British Gas, Yorkshire Electric) to private; and included both manufacturing and service organizations. As such, they are a random, self-selected representation of organizations interested in quality improvement.

The taxonomy to be described is structured around point 7: the addressing of the business processes in an organization.

LEVEL ONE: IMPROVE EFFICIENCIES WITHIN SUBPROCESSES/SUBDEPARTMENTS

A Level One organization is focusing on cost/efficiency improvement by creating intra-function or department teams aimed at improving subprocess efficiencies. Examples would be: to improve the filing system for personnel records, by asking the records staff to devise an improvement, which would be signed off by a department head, or to reorganize an office or assembly line configuration to increase ease and efficiency.

In either case, such initiatives will not be seen to impact significantly on the rest of the organization.

In practice, they vary little from the F.W. Taylor-inspired 'Scientific Management' or work study movement, aimed at individual or group work flow optimization. The difference is in philosophy or intent, as quality improvement initiatives usually seek to 'empower' lower-level staff to improve their own work situation, albeit normally in a directed manner.

LEVEL TWO: IMPROVE EFFICIENCIES WITHIN PROCESSES/DEPARTMENTS

A Level Two organization addresses the same issues, but throughout a process or department. An example would be to improve the functioning of the personnel department by addressing work flows within the whole department.

There is little or no difference, apart from scale, between Levels One and Two. Both maintain the organizational structure status quo, and neither threaten managerial freedom.

311

Levels One and Two appear to arise in organizations where quality improvement has made its way on to the senior management agenda, but neither the will nor the perceived need exists to examine the fuller organizational processes.

Levels One and Two will typically be driven by the quality manager in a facilitative/coach role, working with and for each department head. In themselves, Levels One and Two have little or no impact on full organization strategy or policy issues (a statement which can be legitimately applied to the quality circles/quality control circles/zero defect team movement). However, Level One and Two organizations have realized cost savings and delivered quality improvements, often at significant levels.

LEVEL THREE: IMPROVE EFFICIENCIES BETWEEN PROCESSES/DEPARTMENTS

Levels One and Two are relatively easy and 'safe' for organizations to adopt. Several members of our survey group, however, have found that *intra*-process improvements do not help – in fact, can hinder – *inter*-process efficiencies.

We can reasonably propose that any intervention aiming towards total quality must at least have a plan or vision for Level Three while embarking on Levels One and Two. If not, tensions will invariably arise as intra-process optimization activities start to squeeze the other processes and departments on which they impact. We have also found that the intention of 'empowerment' founders on the rocks of departmental territory protection when such a squeeze takes place. These have to be negotiated, carefully, at management committee or 'steering group' level, and frequently mediated by a senior executive/management director.

This transition between intra- and inter- department quality is a key stage, and one we have observed to be a main stumbling-block. If the heat of mediation between discontented departmental barons becomes too intense, it may be easier for a frustrated chief executive officer (CEO) to abandon the whole drive towards total quality, in the interests of keeping the peace.

Unless our previously observed criteria of alignment with strategic intent, coupled with the perceived need to act driven by external market pressure or cost reduction imperatives, are in place, abandonment is highly likely. We can distinguish, again based on observations from our control group and others, between senior management who 'get interested' in quality (by reading a book, talking to others, etc.) and those who 'feel the need' for quality. The 'get interested' group have the highest propensity to 'get not interested' when departmental tensions arise. The 'feel the need' group are more likely to work the problem through strategically.

Our observations are that quality managers must make the breakthrough with their top management into 'feel the need' by whatever means available, if they are to avoid the frustrations of unfinished TQ initiatives. We have seen candidates on the DipQM programme approach this by articulating the key success factors for the organization and packaging their TQ plans appropriately. In some cases, this means TQ is not branded 'total quality' at all, but 'customer retention' or business improvement.

Level Three organizations need to have mapped their organizational work and information flows, observing that some are multifaceted (e.g. human resources to all) and some single-faceted (e.g. goods inwards to manufacturing); some are tangible transactions (manufacturing to distribution), and some intangible (provision of information); some are voluntary (training and development, works outings) and some coerced (status reports).

Level Three organizations usually adopt some form of 'internal customer' approach, which may be expressed as service level agreements at a quasi-contractual level from departmental provider to departmental customers. They are realized by department head teams, or inter-departmental (cross-functional) teams working on the *relationships* between functions, rather than on the functions themselves. This is a key differentiator.

To restate: our observations have shown that, while Level One or Two thinking and actions can create improvements, they will not create a progression to TQ. A quality manager must have at least Level Three thinking, and be armed with requisite tactics, political acumen, and relationship management plans.

LEVEL FOUR: ADDRESS THE PROCESSES THEMSELVES

At Level Four, the concern switches from efficiency, within and between the processes, to addressing the efficiencies of the processes themselves. At this level we enter the emerging science or art of business process re-engineering (BPR).

If senior management is not very heavily committed to this level, BPR planning or the idea of 'organizational transformation' will undoubtedly fail. A quality manager either must have a committed top team (of the 'feel the need' variety) or must sell to the top team. To address the processes themselves involves the disturbance of departmental power blocks, albeit with reorganization into new, process-focused power blocks if need be.

The integrity of the management systems and information systems is a key challenge here; a non-integrated and non-integrative system (from information to pay and reward) will hinder progression to Level Four.

The involvement of consultative skills, whether internal or external, may be called on at any level but, in a move to Level Four, these appear to be crucial. A disinterested eye is of the utmost importance in unravelling organically developed work/information flows and practices, and restructuring them into new patterns, without the political interest immersion in an organization inevitably brings.

Our DipQM candidates working as internal consultants at this level have been able to do this, and been seen to do this, through the discipline of an academic programme and the attendant methodological rigours imposed by external markers.

Interestingly, the field of logistics management is well suited to the provision of Level Four expertise. Strategic logistics has, for many years before BPR was coined as a phrase, addressed process flow issues 'from conception to consumption'. Our own consultancy work in QM draws deliberately on logistics expertise for this very reason.

LEVEL FIVE: ADDRESS THE FULL PROCESS

Level Five is, for most organizations, a vision of the future. It involves a reconception of the organization without boundaries at the back end, where suppliers enter, and at the front end, where customers leave.

A useful reference for Level Five thinking is *The Virtual Corporation*,[2] which sets out both organizational case examples and visions of technology-driven total process integration.

We have observed some faltering examples of Level Five thinking and practice among our control groups; for example, an electronic data interchange (EDI) triggered response at the point of sale in a large retail store which creates an automatic restocking order and delivery from its packaged goods supplier, in turn creating a supply of bulk ingredients from the packaged goods firm's supplier, which in turn triggers a new manufacturing cycle in that firm, and a re-order of raw materials from the supplier at the end of the chain.

In its ultimate expression, the ties between supplier and customer at all stages would become very hard to break, and the levels of trust involved (and the unusualness of this as an operating paradigm) are so high as to make Level Five alive in vision only.

We suggest, however, that a quality manager with Level Five thinking will be better able to enable Level One activities to take place to optimum effect.

CONCLUSIONS

This chapter has presented some observations gathered from two main sources:

- case examples of TQ organizations as described in this and other publications in past years, and
- observation and analysis of 28 organizations whose quality managers are participating in a qualification programme under the author's direction.

To present the full methodology involved in this research may be appropriate elsewhere. The intention of this chapter was to construct a useful broad 'check-list' of necessary ingredients for TQ initiatives, and a 'road-map' of stages of evolution of organizations towards TQ; both of these to be of use to the quality manager working towards TQ in his/her organization.

The checklist of ingredients is:

- Quality must be KSF-driven
- TQ requires heavy investment in training and learning
- Successful TQ initiatives are broken down into tangible, discrete but linked project or activity steps
- Quality improvement is underpinned by measurables
- TQ has not to date been seen to have gathered its own momentum, and must therefore be constantly 'refreshed' by new approaches
- TQ initiatives involve ritual celebrations of achievement
- TQ must address, in some form, business processes.

The road-map distinguished five levels of organizational progress towards TQ:

- Level One: operational sub-process improvement
- Level Two: operational intra-process improvement
- Level Three: inter-process relationship improvement
- Level Four: process redesign/re-engineering
- Level Five: total process reconception.

Our observations are that Level Three is the minimum which a quality manager must work conceptually to make TQ a reality, and to deliver anything more than finite cost and efficiency savings. A Level Three organization can be expected to show continuing benefits from quality.

We would expect quality managers to be able to embrace Level Five conceptually, albeit that achievement of Level Five may be some way in the future. The importance of focusing on customer processes and customer strategies in serving them and retaining them suggests that Level Five thinking is the most appropriate guiding philosophy for wherever the organization happens to be at present on the endless road towards total quality.

REFERENCES

1 A. Day, and J. Peters, 'Rediscovery Standards: Static and Dynamic Quality', *International Journal of Contemporary Hospitality Management*, vol. 6, nos. 1/2, 1994, pp. 81–4.
2 W.H. Davidow, and M.S. Malone, *The Virtual Corporation*, Harper Business, New York, NY, 1993.

29 Achieving Success in Postgraduate Action Research Programmes

Cliff Bunning

More and more managers and others within organizations are seeking post-graduate education via fieldwork projects, using action research, rather than via coursework programmes. The purpose of this chapter is to provide some guidelines so that those commencing such endeavours will be aware of some of the shoals and reefs that can be encountered in perilous journeys of this kind. The purpose is not to dissuade but, by being forewarned, to avoid some of the difficulties that others have laboured with and, in some cases, foundered on.

The task of successfully completing a piece of action research for academic purposes consists of five aspects: commissioning the work, literature review, fieldwork, personal functioning and writing. Each is dealt with separately in what follows.

COMMISSIONING THE WORK

Three topics will be dealt with in this section: choosing your project, choosing your academic supervisor and your approach to what you are embarking on.

YOUR PROJECT

With respect to your project, the two main considerations will be where you are going to do the research and what it is going to be about. These two aspects are generally interactive. Although it would be elegant to choose your topic of interest and then seek a suitable co-operative locale, and some are fortunate enough to be able to do that, often the reverse process is evident – you have limited choice of locale and have to take their particular interests as your agenda. For some people, both location and topic are set by others, in that they are sponsored by their organization, which determines the locale, and the topic is equally pre-ordained by current organizational priorities. This is not necessarily bad, it depends on how much of a compromise you feel you are making.

Serious research, particularly for a doctorate, is a very draining experience. You can easily fall out of love with your project and the work involved in it, even if you were keen at the start. To be ambivalent at the start is therefore a presage of a motivational problem further down the track.

The motivation of the intended client system must also be considered. It is not unusual for the people in the organization, or that part of the organization in which you would like to work, to agree to co-operate with your research project either:

- without understanding not merely the work that will be involved, but the potential intellectual and psychological demands and cultural disruption which is associated with emancipatory action research, double loop learning, reflective critiques of unexamined paradigms and so on, or
- agreeing because of pressure from above or from you, so that they are saying 'yes' when they are really feeling 'no' or 'I don't think so'. There is so much pressure on you as a postgraduate student to achieve an acceptable fieldwork agreement (because otherwise the academic programme cannot go forward) that you may well accept agreement from others knowing it is far from wholehearted. Be aware that, particularly for defensive people, the degree of commitment is likely to drop rather than increase as the work, the time commitments and the challenge to the *status quo* unfold, and this can imperil your project after perhaps months of work.

Creating an informed psychological contract, as well as a written agreement for serious research should not be rushed, any more than other important personal or organizational decisions should be rushed. The difficulty in forming the contract is that, if you are going to be genuinely emergent in your design and collaborative in your management of the project, you cannot say in detail in advance what you are going to do or even what the project will achieve, except in general terms.

The contract is one which involves mutual trust; you are embarking on a joint enterprise of exploration, discovery and learning. The commitment, apart from physical matters such as time and resources, is to 'lift the lid on Pandora's box' or to use a more dynamic analogy, agree to take a raft down some rapids where the trip and even the destination cannot be reliably predicted, except by introducing a false certainty which is misleading and unprofessional.

To use a modern expression, in action research, the journey is the goal, because the journey of discovery, reflection and enhancement is intended never to arrive at a destination that legitimizes stopping the process of being on such a journey.

YOUR ACADEMIC SUPERVISOR

An equal number of perils are associated with the matter of who is to be your academic supervisor. This depends upon how long your overall project including writing up is intended to be. For a project that will last six months, it is quite important. For one that will last two to three years it is vitally important.

The difficulty is that students often have little or no choice of their academic supervisor. Once the topic and the methodology are considered, plus availability of possible supervisors, the choice may be made for you. Nevertheless, some basic issues are relevant:

- Does the supervisor sound enthusiastic?
- Does he/she believe they have the time for regular contact?
- What is their concept of academic supervision?
- Do they see themselves able and willing to assist with holistic issues (e.g. how your own functioning or non-functioning is affecting your research) or do they wish to confine themselves to the technical aspects of the project?
- How committed do they seem to be regarding your learning and growth, as distinct from merely completing the academic requirements?
- Is there rapport or the potential for rapport between the two of you?

A question that arises is: 'Does the proposed academic supervisor have to be an expert in both your content issues and your research processes?' The answer is that process is strategic, because research degrees are primarily about learning to do valid research, which is a process. Familiarity with your general content area on the part of the supervisor is necessary but he/she does not need to be an expert in that area. Sometimes the dilemma is solved by having two supervisors, one for process and one for content. An expert in action research or soft systems methodology, for example, can supervise you in a content area which he/she knows little about and is not qualified to have an expert opinion.

A similar process of psychological contracting such as between yourself and your supervisor should take place between yourself and your principal client and between you and your potential co-researchers in the project.

YOUR APPROACH

Your own situation and approach is of equal importance when commissioning the work. Your co-researchers, no matter how well-intentioned, are not likely to realize what they are letting themselves in for unless they have prior relevant experience, and that is equally true for you. Nonetheless, or perhaps because of that fact, some review of your own motivation and general situation is important so that you can be aware of potential problems before they occur.

Issues which should be reviewed with your supervisor include:

- Your reasons for enrolling (distinguishing between intrinsic reasons, such as desire to acquire knowledge and skills, and extrinsic reasons like prestige of the qualification, pressure from other parties).
- Your willingness and ability to commit a significant number of hours per week, every week to the library work, fieldwork and writing, assuming you are doing the programme as a part-time endeavour.
- Your ability to attend the workshops, set meetings and the meetings with your academic supervisor.
- What activities you are forgoing in order to carry out those listed above, as everybody's life is already full.
- Your current reading skills in terms of speed and retention – vast quantities of articles and books will need to be reviewed.
- Your current writing skills and experience in writing academic material to publishable standard.
- Your current level of stress and the degree to which you can cope with challenging or stressful situations.
- The attitude of your boss (if employed) and the key figures in your private life to this major diversion of your time and attention for the period contemplated.
- Your own level of personal enthusiasm.

The issues raised earlier about the potential disruption of action research programmes to the clients' values, beliefs and paradigms applies equally to the initiating researcher. Professional development involves knowing (gaining information), doing (acquiring skills) and being (developing one's beliefs, values, self-acceptance etc.).[1]

The question revolves around whether you have an instrumental, single-loop approach to the project (I would like to learn more and acquire some research and writing skills) which reflects a knowing and doing orientation, or whether you are open to and, indeed, seeking to commence a journey of self-discovery and self-development of a kind that cannot be foreseen, which raises being as well as mere knowing and doing issues.

The whole process is represented in Figure 29.1.

Some students enter a post-graduate programme with an intent only to learn more about the content issues they are interested in (2). Some may also wish to learn more about action research techniques (4) and perhaps even to acquire personal functioning skills such as better writing, interpersonal functioning etc. (6). All of this can lead to valuable learning, but only within existing beliefs and assumptions. This type of learning can be referred to as single-loop, instrumental or knowing/doing learning.

Transformative learning takes place when you allow yourself to re-examine your fundamental beliefs, attitudes, assumptions and values in three domains: the content issues (1) – which you may have had many years' experience in and possess therefore quite firm views, the process issues (3) – how to address

319

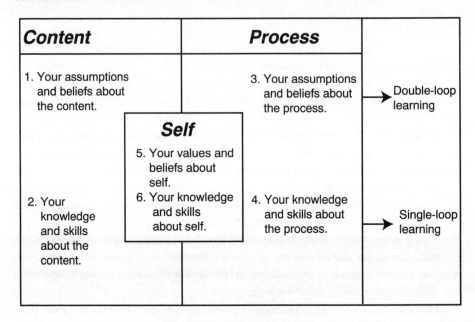

Figure 29.1 Domains of learning

social and organizational problems and change issues, and personal functioning issues (5) – who you are and your role and place in the outer world etc. This focus is referred to as double-loop, generative, transformative learning, or being issues.

Action research projects, unlike more traditional reductionist projects, place great emphasis upon your values, beliefs and behaviour as a researcher because you are interacting continuously with, and influencing the outcomes of, the research. Via reflexive critique[2] and other methods, your own functioning is necessarily included in the research, so an instrumental, extrinsically motivated, arms-length approach to the whole enterprise simply will not do.

The above points make it evident that commissioning an action research project is an important undertaking with many aspects that need careful consideration and negotiation. Inevitably some aspects will be less than ideal, because action research is done in real, rather than artificially controlled experimental, situations. So it behoves you to work carefully through all the issues, compromises and unknowns, so that you can form a realistic appraisal of whether a particular configuration of variables is viable. 'Marry in haste and repent at leisure' could well be adapted to 'Start research in haste and repent at leisure'.

LITERATURE REVIEW

You will acquire relevant literature throughout the life of your project, and indeed will seek out literature on topics which emerge as relevant as the research unfolds. Nevertheless, there is an initial task to acquire and review literature relevant to your expected main content themes, as well as your intended process methodologies before becoming active in the field. The reason is obvious. Literature is meant to inform action, and to do that, it needs to be read and understood before action is planned and carried out.

Many students are often not clear about their content focus until arrangements are firm for the fieldwork project, yet it is an unusual client who, having agreed to collaborate in some research on an issue of organizational significance, is then willing to wait three months whilst you collect and critically appraise the relevant literature! If this can be agreed to, then all the better. Otherwise you may be forced to review your literature parallel with your fieldwork. If this is the case, then it should proceed with the utmost urgency.

Fieldwork activities are often much easier and more interesting to do than seeking out and critically reviewing relevant literature and students may therefore avoid the latter, claiming pressure of work. This is an example of where a good academic supervisor can influence the student to address matters in their correct priority.

I have written elsewhere[3] on how to engage in a large literature review. Suffice to say it is necessary to have a well organized system to identify, secure, codify and retrieve the essential material from anything from 100 to 300 separate articles and books. Without a system, you will surely be overwhelmed; with an effective system, it can be done with relative ease.

The second role of literature, apart from assisting at the strategy planning stage, is to provide richness and depth to the reflections and generalizations that arise from the fieldwork. Knowledge of others' work can help you see the significance of your own experiences. If you are developing grounded theory, it is particularly important to know who else has formulated constructs or models in your area of theorizing.

Some students acquire their literature reasonably early in their project but then fail to process it to a degree where they learn from it, and so gain new ideas and strategies which directly influence what they do in the field. Therefore you should write up your draft literature review chapters before, or early during the fieldwork. The only exception is for smaller projects where you intend to integrate your literature with description of your project details. In such a case you need to make notes of key points that you can use before your action is too far advanced.

FIELDWORK

Fieldwork strategies vary depending upon the particular action research paradigm that you are operating from. This chapter is written from an emancipatory action research perspective, the goals of which include not only an improvement in the situation which is the subject of the intervention, and the development of some local theory, but also the empowerment of the members of the system in terms of their increased capacity to be self-managing.

The first task, after the project has been agreed to, and one of great strategic significance, is the forming of the group of co-researchers who will work with you. In a small project within your own work area, the composition of the group might be almost pre-ordained. However, if you are an outsider to the organization, and if your project has a wide sweep to the topic and the organization has a significant number of people working in it, then choice of co-researchers is involved.

You would normally seek a heterogeneous group, because in action research you seek to work with multiple social perceptions of reality and it is best if the main viewpoints can be represented directly in the project planning group. Invitations might be issued or volunteers sought representing the various organizational functions, levels, roles, ages, gender and ethnic mix such as are extant in the areas of the organization in which the work is to be done. A group of four to eight persons is ideal, because less than four has a narrow range of viewpoints and is vulnerable to absences, and more than eight creates complex group dynamics phenomena.

I have written elsewhere[4] about the critical influence that the personal orientations of the members of the action research team have on the decision-making within that team. In general, one is seeking persons who are inner-directed, developmentally-oriented, somewhat reflective by nature and interested in effectiveness issues more than efficiency issues.

Because you work with a group of internal co-researchers, there is much less personal influence by you over the particular focus and the methodologies to be employed. Although you will naturally exercise some influence as the 'expert' researcher, you should seek to empower the group in these matters so that they play a significant part in making project decisions, rather than have them eventually disowning the project as belonging to you.

This giving away of control can be very scary when you know that it is you, not them, who will be held accountable academically. However, if you feel this anxiety, you need to reframe your perception of the situation. The fact is that your academic project (attaining a degree or doing a research module within a degree) is not the same as your organizational project. It is quite possible, even at the doctoral level, to lodge an outstanding thesis on some fieldwork which was a failure from an organizational point of view. Your first responsibility as an action researcher, or Action Learner, is to be aware, to be critical and self-critical, and to be non-defensive. Your second responsibility is that what you, personally, do is of a professional standard (e.g. your literature review, writing, design of data collection instruments etc.). You are not, and cannot be held accountable for the decisions of others, and so you can share power with them freely without feeling that your own academic interests are at risk.

Another important point regarding fieldwork is your degree of commitment to a successful and easy completion of the academic project versus your degree of commitment to your own personal learning and growth. There is a big temptation to use methodologies for your fieldwork that you have used before and know you can use successfully. But if you know how to design surveys or do focus groups, then what is the value of doing the same thing again? By contrast, techniques like computer-based text analysis, soft systems methodology, repertory grid interviews or ethnographic observations may present some interesting and growth enhancing alternatives for you, provided they suit the issues.

Detailed methodologies such as stakeholder analysis, recording of data, and triangulation, have been dealt with elsewhere.[5]

PERSONAL FUNCTIONING

Four topics will be dealt with under this heading: journal keeping, relations with your supervisor, set participation and reflecting.

JOURNAL KEEPING

Action research methods rely on 'soft' or subjective data and acknowledge the researcher as a significant variable within the research context. Consequently, journal keeping is a vital part of data collection. Whether it is called a learning log, a diary or a journal, regular entries, preferably immediately after each activity, provide an invaluable record of activity undertaken and your own and others' immediate reactions.

Some students keep two journals: one to record facts and activities like meetings and important telephone calls and the other, a more reflective journal of learnings, insights, personal feelings and concerns.

A large number of students fail to keep a proper journal at all, having only scrappy and sporadic entries, and so face problems when writing up their fieldwork. They are also quite unable to demonstrate their use of reflexive critique, because they lack the 'here and now' entries showing how they thought and felt at various times over the preceding months. As with other aspects of self-managed activity (which is what research is) the cause is often a lack of personal discipline – an unwillingness to defer other gratifications and engage in something they might find tedious in order to achieve a benefit later. Some students avoid their writing block by dictating into a hand-held tape recorder, especially when they are driving, so that it need not take any extra time.

However, keeping a journal can be a joy to some people, an opportunity for quiet reflection. But such people are in a minority, and the majority of us have to apply personal discipline or later pay the price for our self-indulgence.

RELATIONS WITH YOUR SUPERVISOR

Relations with one's supervisor are often the source of complaint on the part of the student. Stories of research supervisors who are impossible to book a meeting with, who fail to prepare themselves for meetings, who disappear on sabbatical leave or seek to take over the research agenda in order to achieve personal publication for themselves are legion. In all fairness, however, it must be said that academic supervisors have an equal number of stories to tell about the shortcomings of students!

A supervisor of action research is typically coming from an adult education model of relationships, and so is seeking to empower the student, rather than control them or create another person in their own image. The dilemma for a caring academic supervisor is how much authority should they seek to muster when the student is missing agreed deadlines and failing to write, because that is reverting to a parent/child relationship. The other difficulty is that if you, as a supervisor, do establish a collegiate relationship which is forgiving of the foibles of the student, then when you seek to exercise authority, it is often not believed, but seen (quite rightly) as an act being put on for the student's benefit.

My own learning as an academic supervisor is that if students are disrupted by physical events such as changing jobs, a new baby, or some short-term work crisis, then, given extra time, they normally return to purposeful activity when the external disruption passes. However, and more importantly, I have also learnt that giving someone who is in avoidance mode extra time is never in their own best interests. It just colludes in the denial of reality. The cause of the avoidance needs to be openly and directly addressed and resolved or at least ameliorated. I have written elsewhere[6] about the various causes of avoidance and possible ameliorative strategies.

Another issue is the degree to which the student is emotionally stable or emotionally excitable. As you learn in action research, all judgements say as much or more about the judger as they do about the object judged. Although some of the judgements that your academic supervisor delivers on your work are incontestable academic protocol, others perhaps most, may be opinions, albeit expert opinions.

It is easy to contest feedback and beg to differ and, even worse for you, to develop negative attitudes to your supervisor. Most unhelpful of all is deciding to avoid contact with your supervisor as much as possible, without trying to address the matters of dissatisfaction. Except for a few recluses, we all live in an interdependent world and need to be able to collaborate with others effectively in order to achieve our own goals. This is especially true of your relationship with your academic supervisor. You are far more dependent/vulnerable in the relationship than the supervisor so, unless it is a matter of great principle, it is better to conform to your supervisor's requests and orientation. Not only is this likely to lead to better outcomes for you, but it is possible that he/she is trying to tell you something from another perspective or paradigm, the wisdom of which will not become evident until much later, perhaps long after the programme is over.

YOUR SET PARTICIPATION

In Action Learning, it is essential that you are a regular participant in set meetings with other Action Learners, because Action Learning is, at heart, a social learning model. A main source of learning is the challenge and support that you receive from other set members. It is not mandatory for you to have a group from within the client system or systems who help you design and manage your project, but it is something to consider.

By contrast, when using an action research paradigm, it is essential that you have a group of co-researchers representing those affected by the project, but it is not essential you attend set meetings of others doing action research in other places, although this is obviously desirable.

Learning sets and groups of co-researchers are not unique phenomena, subject to special laws and forces peculiar to action research. Everything you know about team building and group dynamics is relevant. If a group is not functioning very well, then you need to address the issues, rather than hope that some self-correcting mechanism will magically come into operation. Team building at the start of any group, particularly an action research group of co-researchers, is almost a necessity.

The most serious problem relative to sets is non-attendance, which can be part of a larger avoidance pattern. If you haven't done much since the last meeting, then there is a temptation to miss the meeting so you will not be held accountable and so become embarrassed. However, this cuts you off from the stimulation and remotivation that is frequently experienced at set meetings. So always go, especially if you have done nothing.

REFLECTING

An intrinsic element in learning from experience is reflecting and then drawing generalizations from those reflections. Reflection is not widely valued in our society, least of all by males, who inherit a social script which has a strong action imperative. For some, reflection is tied up with the process of diary keeping, whilst for others it is done driving to work or during exercise. You certainly do not need to be physically passive to reflect. One way or another, you must give yourself time to think about your research, both concepts and fieldwork activities, on a very regular basis, preferably daily.

As Figure 29.1 indicates, there are six principal aspects about which you can and should reflect:

- content issues at the operational level
- content issues at the paradigm level
- process issues at the operational level
- process issues at the paradigm level
- your own functioning at the doing level
- your own functioning at the being level.

Mezirow[7] provides an excellent coverage of the various aspects of reflection.

It is often assumed that just because experiential learning is based on immediate real-life experience, it is valid and valuable. In fact, you can reflect upon your experiences and generalize upon them in ways that lead to conclusions that are both invalid and quite disabling for you personally.

Defensiveness is the most powerful contaminant of experiential learning, because if you are defensive, you will draw conclusions that leave you blameless and others the culprits, regardless of the facts. Other corruptors of learning are drawing conclusions from too few instances, failing to consider alternative explanations, and displaying bias either in what data is attended to or how it is interpreted. The latter problem is typically caused by operating from within your existing paradigm or cognitive map and so being blind to other ways of seeing and interpreting the situation.

It is for these reasons, as well as others, that action research emphasizes planning and reflecting on action in a group context. Unless the whole group has the same learning disabilities, there is hope that individual deficiencies (including your own) in reflecting and generalizing will be corrected by the contrary opinions of others. But this happens only if you encourage dissenting views and listen to them openly when they are expressed.

Mulligan[8] has drawn attention to the internal processors which are necessary for effective experiential learning. They are:

- *Will*, which helps us turn our intentions into reality, and in everyday learning situations is needed to organize and order the learning process and to balance the need to learn with other needs which may block learning.
- *Memory*, which is the key to past learning. This processor is particularly vital for the storage of current experiences as this source of potential learning is not presented in orderly form, as with lecture presentations, and comes with no chapter headings, bold letters, or prioritized keypoints.
- *Reason*, the process which by use of constructs, internal frameworks or

models, endeavours to make sense of experience. Learning will often involve unlearning something already learnt or, at least, suspending belief whilst we apply reason to the new experience.

- *Feelings*, which, from a learning point of view, are valuable; it is what we do with them which helps or hinders. Emotional impact can help to create a lasting memory of an event or it can lead to blocking of memory.
- *Sensing*, which covers the five means by which we acquire information from our environment. It is important in experiential learning that we allow our observations to confound our treasured beliefs, and this depends upon keen and undistorted sensing.
- *Intuiting*, which like sensing, is a perceptual processor and the key to what is tacit or missing in a situation. It is complementary to the sensing function, but works in the opposite way by defocusing on sensory detail and relying on more holistic inner sources.
- *Imagining*, which is the key to the future and the precursor to creativity and action. It helps us transcend current experience of reality and combine the possible with the impossible.

In reviewing this whole issue of personal functioning, from my experience the biggest roadblock for research students is avoidance, particularly avoidance at writing up the literature and the fieldwork. Second to that disability is failure to keep adequate diary notes, along with a general reluctance to put time and energy into reflection.

WRITING

Writing is the final research act, and thus the downstream recipient of all the deficiencies in the upstream processes of getting started, doing your literature review, doing your fieldwork, keeping good records, and your own personal functioning over the life of the project. It is inevitable that, if there are problems, this is where most of them show up and cause a failure to produce written text by the various deadlines set.

It is evident from observation that many people, perhaps most, dislike writing. The number of people who put off even writing to their friends is evidence of that. When it comes to a requirement to write a 20,000, 30,000 or 50,000 word dissertation or thesis, paralysis is widespread.

Blocks to writing come from many sources, including not being able to create by yourself a conceptual overview or chapter outline about how the whole material will be organized, laziness, and difficulties with English expression and sentence construction. However, the main problems are psychological and can include any of the following:

- a strong preference for action, rather than passive activities like writing
- a fear of being criticized, and avoiding this by not producing anything that can be judged
- comparing your first draft to the published material of others which has been through innumerable improvement processes, thereby triggering negative headtalk about your own writing ability
- a fear of closure, so deliberately prolonging the academic process by seeking more literature or forever reworking drafts
- self-indulgent wilfulness, so that you only do what is immediately pleasurable.

Obviously each person's blockages need to be identified and addressed specifically, but the overall answer is to exercise personal discipline. Setting targets and forcing yourself to meet them may be using a blunt instrument, but even counselling about avoidance in all its forms is problematic, and may take months to pay off. The key to writing success is to start writing before the fieldwork commences, and never to be more than a couple of weeks behind the fieldwork in your write-ups.

Never consider you have to write a thesis. Right now you need to write one section of one chapter: 'The longest journey starts with a single step'.

What you must continue to tell yourself is that nobody ever gained a degree for doing fieldwork or assembling some good literature. You gain a degree for what you write about what you did. If there is no write-up, there is no basis for awarding a degree, regardless of the elegance or results of your fieldwork.

CONCLUSION

Action research can be a joyful and a transformative experience. Sadly, it is sometimes spoiled by the mismanagement of some of the many links in the chain from thinking about doing an action research project to achieving your award at the end of it. This chapter is intended to indicate some of the more common potholes on the journey. If you can avoid them, you will move forward in a way which is beneficial both to yourself and to others (including your supervisor!).

REFERENCES

1 C. Bunning, 'Personal and Professional Development' in *Tutor*, vol. 40, 1992, pp. 28–32.
2 R. Winter, *Learning from Experience. Principles and Practice in Action-Research*, The Falmer Press, London, 1989.
3 C. Bunning, '*Some Notes on Writing a Major Literature Review*', occasional paper, International Management Centre, Brisbane, 1993.
4 C. Bunning, '*Personal Characteristics Conducive to Effective Participation in Action Research*', occasional paper, International Management Centre, Brisbane, 1995.

5 C. Bunning, '*Professional Development Using Action Research*', occasional paper, International Management Centre, Brisbane, 1995.
6 C. Bunning, '*Dealing with Procrastination and Avoidance*', occasional paper, International Management Centre, Brisbane, 1995.
7 J. Mezirow, *Transformative Dimensions of Adult Learning*, Jossey-Bass, San Francisco, 1991.
8 J. Mulligan, 'Internal Processors in Experiential Learning' in J. Mulligan and C. Griffin (eds) *Empowerment through Experiential Learning*, Kogan Page, London, 1992.

Part V
Does Action Learning Work?

30 Measuring the ROI from Management Action Learning*

Gordon Wills and Carol Oliver

It is widely believed, and we are among the believers, that management development programmes are a good investment. We believe they are good for the people who participate. We believe we know from regular experience that they are good for the people who stay behind and who, by default, then gain more scope to flex their muscles and brains when the favoured one is away. But there are seemingly no analyses where such beliefs are systematically checked out with data of the hard programme ROI, at the end, then one year and five years later.

Between 1992 and 1995, we tracked what occurred when over £3 million was invested on MBA programme fees to develop 300+ managers, in 12 countries around the world. Questionnaires were completed and their contents debated for six hours at graduation time which was held consecutively in Kuala Lumpur, Surfers Paradise, at Ripley Castle in Yorkshire and Amsterdam. The MBA programmes were organized by International Management Centres (IMC), the leading Action Learning multinational business school following the principles set down by Reg Revans over 50 years ago.

This study (n = 101) covers just one part of what has now, over 12 years, become a £30 million tranche of investment made for over 5000 managers by nearly 1000 enterprises in 31 countries using the processes of Action Learning with IMC.

Best estimates indicate that the 300+ managers spent 2500 hours each, 750,000 hours in total, talking with one another, with colleagues, sharing their managerial problems and challenges and helping one another to come to terms with actions which needed to be taken. IMC faculty members, skilled and knowledgeable in their own areas, participated in their meetings. Their role was to help the managers to be aware of what was already known in the areas where they were seeking to improve and to help them to discover new knowledge where

*Originally published in *Management Development Review*, vol. 9, no. 1, 1996.

necessary. The 5000 managers in the overall programme spent nearly ten million hours at the task.

Just under half the 300+ managers went on to implement most or all of their recommended courses of action with the support of their sponsoring organizations. These typically required investments which were well in excess of five times the programme fees and on not infrequent occasions in excess of £1 million. These investments in their turn yielded satisfactory returns, through major cost reductions and new revenues.

- 'My employer gave me full opportunity, responsibility and freedom to implement my projects.'
- 'My employer invested £1.2 million to fully implement the project. We gained a threefold return in the first twelve months.'

In addition, of course, a wide range of non-financial benefits were cited. This analysis suggests that the 300+ managers triggered at least £10 million of investment to implement their action plans, with ROI expected of £50 million. Judgemental extrapolation suggests the 5000 probably triggered over £100 million with half a billion pounds ROI. Certainly some programmes!

This particular quantum of managerial development by Action Learning, *par excellence*, exemplifies the case for investing an enterprise's funds in such programmes regardless, and we say regardless advisedly, of whether the manager now with an MBA qualification stays with or leaves the sponsoring enterprise. And regardless of how much the individual *per se* may or may not have learned. Which is not intended to belittle individual learning for a single moment. Our purpose here is to argue that soft benefits do not need to be educed to justify management development of the Action Learning variety. More and more of it should be done within any and every enterprise until the marginal hard ROI equates with other projects in hand. Educationists should cease being afraid of measuring and propagandizing the hard benefits they provide to enterprises.

DID THE MANAGERS LEAVE?

Well no. Of course not. Most of them stayed put, relishing their new intellectual understanding and involvement in their enterprise. Would you leave an enterprise that has sponsored you on an MBA programme that gave you the broader helicopter view of the business way beyond your previous experience, enhanced your self-confidence, presentation, listening, team and overall people skills, given you understanding in particular of financial issues, helped you to become more action-oriented on the critical issues affecting the enterprise, and more timeous and objective in the conduct of your role? That is exactly what they reported had happened:

- 'We found the best solutions often came from those closest to the job. It was dangerous to have our own preconceived ideas or to think we knew best.'
- 'As an action learner I was able to gather information more easily than as a manager; others wanted to help me – even commiserated with me.'
- 'We gained confidence to talk to people at all levels in the enterprise.'
- 'In developing our projects we learned what the other parts of the company did, their purpose and methods of working.'

All this, it can be seen, was accomplished in the context of the organization itself, and their dissertation project (while academically rigorous) had to be based on the key ingredients of the future strategies of the enterprise. The conclusions reached normally made their way directly to the boardroom. IMC invariably involved top managers in the process as mentors and sometimes as adjunct faculty. IMC ensured that bosses were fully aware at all stages of the Action Learning approach. Subordinates, colleagues and families who took up some of the manager's load while diverting 2500 hours to the programme were, by and large, grudgingly supportive too.

Ninety-three per cent of managers were still with their employer at the end, and 48 per cent had been promoted during the 24-month programme.

The MBA dissertation project was seen as the runaway winner among all the assignments in terms of personal and organizational benefit. It also took the most sweat and tears to create. After that, each of the specialist areas of management intelligence, corporate integration, human resource management, finance, marketing and operations had its own following. These preferences were reassuringly based first on usefulness to the enterprise and eye-opening potential, and only latterly on the faculty member's particular style and approach to supporting the learning processes. Very few were dismissive of any areas, but where there were regrets it was that the debate had not been vigorous enough.

WHICH LEARNING RESOURCES WERE MOST VALUED?

All manner of resources are available to a work-based learner. Yet the greatest contribution of all came from what Revans describes as 'comrades in adversity'. These are the fellow members of the small learning cell that Action Learning uses, known as the set. On a semantic differential scale, it averaged 3.90 with a maximum score of 5 available:

- 'Feedback from the set, the level of interaction and exchange of ideas were both fun and enlivening – as well as invaluable.'

The second greatest contribution came not from the subject area experts but the set adviser, or linker/facilitator, with a score of 3.82, which was followed by the tutors, with the expertise at 3.75. Next came the course materials issued and found in support (3.66), colleagues at work (3.18), bosses and mentors (3.06) and finally library services with 2.83.

One of the most valued but underestimated resources which managers use is feedback from tutors through the marked assignments that go towards the ultimate award of the MBA. It is, of course, a crucial moment for faculty to make sure the measures of quality really do justice to the context in which the manager concerned works and seeks to act and improve performance. With programmes in 31 countries over 12 years ranging from South Pacific islands and African homelands to the more mature Dutch, UK or Australian economies it is no small challenge. The verdict given by two-thirds of the managers was that the process was 'good or very good':

- 'After having done all nine assignments, the habit developed of going through the four learning stages is continuously with me.'
- 'Receiving my first A grade for an assignment was the greatest highlight.'
- 'I struggled with my organizational management assignment, but when I got a good grade it gave me confidence, it was a turning point. I knew I could do it.'

HOW TYPICAL WERE THESE MANAGERS?

There are few ways in which we can assert that the managers who devoted 2500 hours each to these IMC programmes to gain the MBA are normal. Normal managers simply do not do this sort of thing. They do not seek and relish the intellectualization of their role as a manager. They live off their wits and their experiences. And why not?

Action Learners believe that wits and experiences can be very considerably improved on when they are shared in a rigorous and disciplined way.

Yet it would be erroneous to believe that IMC's managers were a scholarly segment, although 82 per cent did indeed have bachelor level university education (44 per cent) or its equivalent in a professional area (38 per cent). Eighteen per cent were straight from their experience – often performing outstandingly on the programme as well as in their workplace.

At the end of the programme all were adamant that they had, for the first time in their lives, learned what learning was. It was continuous, of course, but most excitingly, they had learned that all managers, all team members, have potentially different styles and preferences for learning and for working. Unless each manager knows, understands and accommodates these differences the workplace cannot hope to perform to its best. In this respect they believed they were henceforth and irrevocably a different sort of manager.

WHAT DID WE ALL DO WRONG?

If the whole Action Learning project sounds like an outstanding success, that is simply because it has been. Our weaknesses at IMC were mainly associated with faculty members who found it difficult to meet the expectations of demanding, action and context-based managers. The second criticism was at the place of work, with top managers and colleagues giving less support than was hoped for. The third complaint was of IMC's organizing skills for sets around the globe. And finally, managers looked at themselves and criticized their own inabilities to manage their time effectively.

Our response to each of these, which have been recurring themes for the whole 12 years, has been to empower managers to hire and fire their faculty, to provide boss mentoring development workshops whenever possible, to evaluate and re-engineer our own support organization (most recently leading us on to the Internet at URL http://www/mcb.co.uk), and to introduce time management tutorial workshops at the beginning of all our programmes. These four themes of criticism seem endemic to the process itself and accordingly set to remain with us for ever. Forewarned thus, we have a continuing search to alleviate these complaints permanently on our managerial agenda.

ONE YEAR AND FIVE YEARS LATER

Since 1982 it has been a requirement of all IMC graduates that they must renew their professional competences at least every five years and attest to how they have achieved it. It is known as the Five-Year Continuing Renewal. Experience has shown that five years after a main Action Learning project is normally too late to seek to evaluate its specific benefits. Events will have moved on and almost always career promotion will have removed the individual concerned within or beyond the enterprise which sponsored participation on the programme.

After one year, however, where we have introduced a progress audit option for graduates known as A+, we have had much greater success in seeing the extent to which their end-of-programme assessments have held up. They afford the supporting evidence we need in the round, albeit with pluses and minuses present. For some, the hoped-for implementation did not happen with: 'the organization is now focusing on alternative structures and the original idea has been discounted'. For others, the outcomes were better than expected: 'They actually implemented'.

CONCLUSION

Our conclusion must accordingly be that while soft benefits will continue to deliver well after the programme is over, through changed behaviours, growth in confidence and the like, most of the sensibly attributable hard ROI is realistically traceable by thorough, evaluative survey methods on completion and during the 12 months following a programme.

Training and development managers should, in our opinion, do a great deal more evaluative research to measure the organizational and particularly the financial impact of programmes. In this way, a budgetarily supportive culture can emerge to supplement the generalized feeling of goodwill towards development of staffs.

FURTHER READING

'2nd Quinquennial Review of MBA: November 1992' in *Design & Process Newsletter*, International Management Centres, Buckingham, 1992.

Barker, J., '1991 David Sutton Fellowship Report' in *Design & Process Newsletter*, International Management Centres, Buckingham, 1991.

Bennett, R., 'Effective set advising in action learning' in *Journal of European Industrial Training*, vol. 14, no. 7, 1990. [see Chapter 16]

Caie, B., 'Learning in style – reflections on an action learning MBA programme' in *Business Education*, vol. 9, no. 3/4, 1988. [see Chapter 10]

Coates, J., 'An action learning approach to performance review and development' in *Business Education*, vol. 9, no. 3/4, 1988.

Cusins, P., 'Action learning revisited' in *Industrial and Commercial Training*, vol. 27, no. 4, 1995.

Espey, J. and Batchelor, P., 'Management by degrees: a case study in management development' in *Business Education*, vol. 9, no. 3/4, 1988. [see Chapter 21]

Gore, L., Toledano, K. and Wills, G., 'Leading courageous managers on' in *Empowerment in Organizations*, vol. 2, no. 3, 1994. [see Chapter 26]

Margerison, C., '1991 Revans Professorship Report' in *Design & Process Newsletter*, International Management Centres, Buckingham, 1991.

Mumford, A., 'Developing managers for the board' in *Business Education*, vol. 9, no. 3/4, 1988.

Mumford, A., 'Effectiveness in management development' in *Business Education*, vol. 9, no. 3/4, 1988.

Mumford, A., 'Learning in action' in *Personnel Management*, vol. 23, no. 7, 1991.

Mumford, A., 'A review of action learning literature' in *Management Bibliographies & Reviews*, vol. 20, no. 6/7, 1994.

Mumford, A. and Honey, P., 'Developing skills for matrix management' in *Business Education*, vol. 9, no. 3/4, 1988. [see Chapter 24]

Peters, J., 'The new MBA – what it means for managers' in *Business Education*, vol. 9, no. 3/4, 1988.

Prideaux, G., 'Pan setting II' in *Training & Management Development Methods*, vol. 5, 1991.

Prideaux, G., 'Making action learning more effective' in *Training & Management Development Methods*, vol. 6, 1992. [see Chapter 15]

Revans, R., *The Origins and Growth of Action Learning*, Chartwell-Bratt, Bromley, 1982.

Revans, R., 'The learning equation: an introduction' in *Business Education*, vol. 9, no. 3/4 1988. [see Foreword]

Seekings, D., talks to Brian Wilson, 'Allied Irish Bank in Britain: organizational and business development through action learning' in *Business Education*, vol. 9, no. 3/4, 1988. [see Chapter 22]

Smith, A., '1992 David Sutton Fellowship Report' in *Design & Process Newsletter*, International Management Centres, Buckingham, 1992.

Sutton, D., 'The problems of developing managers in the small firm' in *Business Education*, vol. 9, no. 3/4, 1988.

Sutton, D., 'Action learning in search of P', *Industrial and Commercial Training*, vol. 2, no. 1, 1992. [see Chapter 5]

Thomas, J., 'Researching learning to learn' in *Design & Process Newsletter*, International Management Centres, Buckingham.

'Total Quality Assurance', *IMC's 4th Annual Professional Congress*, Buckingham, England, November 1992.

Wills, G., 'A radical alternative in management education' in *Business Education*, vol. 9, no. 3/4, 1988.

Wills, G., 'The customer first – faculty last approach to excellence' in *Business Education*, vol. 9, no. 3/4, 1988.

Wills, G., 'Wealth creation through management development' in *Business Education*, vol. 9, no. 3/4, 1988.

Wills, G., 'Action learning pan setting' in *Training & Management Development Methods*, vol. 5, 1991. [see Chapter 17]

Wills, G., 'Managing networking' in *European Journal of Marketing*, vol. 25, no. 4, 1991.

Wills, G., '1992 Revans Professorship Report', Enterprise School of Management, *Design & Process Newsletter*, International Management Centres, Buckingham, 1992.

Wills, G., *Your Enterprise School of Management*, MCB University Press, Bradford, 1993.

Wills, G. and Day, A., 'Marketing and selling at work: the IMCB/NatWest Management Development Programme' in *Business Education*, vol. 9, no. 3/4, 1988.

Zuber-Skeritt, O. and Howell, F., 'Evaluation of MBA and doctoral programs conducted in Pacific Region', report submitted to the International Management Centres, Pacific Region, 1993.

31 A Dialogue with Participants*

Krystyna Weinstein

The research described in this chapter was carried out in the summer of 1993. The idea for it arose out of my experiences – as a set adviser, and as secretary to the International Foundation for Action Learning (IFAL) – of people wanting to know more about Action Learning. Not the theory, or how to be a 'practitioner', but what happened in such programmes: what did participants 'do', what did they gain – and learn – and how did they do this. In particular:

- How is it possible to learn without teachers and experts?
- What did a 'project' consist of?
- Why does it take so long?
- Who are such programmes for?
- What purposes did companies using Action Learning specify as their reasons for using it?

There is a reasonable amount of literature now about Action Learning – and it is growing. In the past 18 months there has been the second edition of Mike Pedler's *Action Learning in Practice*,[1] and Ian McGill and Liz Beaty's *Action Learning, A Practitioner's Guide*.[2] There are to be two more books this year: a collection of articles by practitioners, and a book of case studies. I have found two articles also of extra significance.[3,4] But there is still nothing on the market that describes the 'experiences' of participants. Yet we practitioners make many claims for Action Learning and what it achieves. There are a few articles by past participants, but they are mostly published in journals safely hidden away on library shelves. The academic courses using Action Learning have a mass of data where participants describe and reflect on what they have learned – but not much of that sees the light of day.

I felt it was time that we went to those who have been on programmes and asked them what their experiences had been. Would their comments and insights back up ours – the practitioners' – or would they give us some food for thought? I hoped that this research would also give me material to produce a book for

*Originally published in *Management Bibliographies & Reviews*, vol. 20, nos 6/7, 1994.

those who ask questions about the processes and value of Action Learning, before committing themselves to such a programme.

THE BASES OF THE RESEARCH

I set out to look at the experiences of current and recent participants, and also those who had been on programmes up to five years previously, and to see how the learning had stuck. I soon realized that this was too great an undertaking, and decided to concentrate on current participants. I had not in fact anticipated such a willingness to share these current experiences with me. I felt this would have the advantage of being 'hot off the press' insights as opposed to things dredged up from memory.

I decided to use a 'rough' questionnaire, more for my own purposes as an aide-mémoire. I approached people, and gave them the option of writing something (using the questions as a prompt), or of meeting me. With four or five exceptions, people chose the latter! I met some participants individually; others I met as 'sets'. Virtually all those I spoke to were either still on or nearing the end of Action Learning programmes. I also spoke, where feasible, to those who had sent them or organized the Action Learning programmes – to gain an insight into why organizations used Action Learning.

I interviewed – face to face or by telephone – 69 people, on 16 different programmes. Of these, nine were in-company programmes, seven were mixed-company, and five had academic links. Of the individuals I spoke to, 18 (in five sets) were involved in working on group projects, and the rest on their own individual ones. To give a further breakdown: I met with five sets (20 individuals) in the sets in which they had been working. The interviews lasted anything from half an hour with individuals, to three hours with some of the sets. I also spoke informally to a few individuals who are currently on programmes which include an Action Learning element. I was given access to written documentation, largely from the academic programmes, but also some reflective documents from one of the other programmes. This reflects the same insights of which participants spoke.

The range of companies and organizations from which participants came included: WH Smith, TSB, Motorola, Lever Brothers, BUPA, Seagrams (these last two on IMC academic programmes), Surrey and Hampshire County Councils and Brighton Borough Council. Many other participants were on mixed-company programmes, run by independent consultants. The organizations they came from included finance institutions (pensions, insurance and merchant bank), the Civil Service, small business (building, bakery and computer software). A third category were again mixed-company programmes linked to study for further degrees – MSc and MBA in management, using Action Learning – run at Brighton University and Manchester Metropolitan University. Participants again came from a variety of organizations: universities, the NHS, telecommunications, and other businesses.

The functions and positions represented varied across the spectrum: from managing directors and chief executives to senior functional managers in personnel and finance to engineers, IT specialists, marketing and sales personnel, retail and banking, surveying, police administration, training and personnel, and lecturers and teachers.

ANALYSING THE RESULTS

Faced with a mound of interviews, some of which became stories in themselves – participants' journeys – and others which consisted more of thoughts, comments and insights on various aspects of Action Learning programmes, I decided to adopt a straightforward structure and look first at the learning and what was instantly useful back at work. I have then tried to analyse what aspects of the Action Learning experience participants said had given the various opportunities to gain and learn.

I have listed a selection of the 'words of wonder' that some participants had when I asked them for their lasting impressions. But to balance that I have listed also their quandaries, dilemmas and criticisms. A few also proffered their thoughts on why or whether their organizations would take up Action Learning on a larger scale.

Next, I pulled together some of my own thoughts and impressions, the main issues that I think we should be considering if Action Learning is to take greater hold. I end with some insights into my own learning – Alan Mumford suggested this as a useful corollary to an Action Learning research project!

Before presenting the detail, it is important to describe the highlights for me:

- The excitement of the participants in describing their learning. That, for me, was one of the advantages of meeting them as opposed to reading 'scripts'. Hearing how they talked gave me further insights into their experiences, and to the recognition of different targets for learning.
- 'Anticipated' learning – what they had planned or hoped to learn – because they had, in most but not all instances, relatively clear ideas of why they were on the programmes. (Some had merely been told that they were going on a management development programme, and no more!)
- 'Unanticipated' learning – what they gained as a result of this programme, and its elements – many of which were not what participants had been expecting.
- Action Learning is primarily about 'development'. We talk of it as being applicable for all sorts of 'actions' – managing change, teamworking, creating and putting into place new strategies, consulting on corporate issues, tackling

quality, relating it to Investors in People, and so on (see Mike Pedler's book for many examples). But the development and learning are what participants talk of. Doing something differently is important, but begins to take second place to the learning and the insights. So, it is the order: learning how to be a more effective person becomes more important than the end result. This does not diminish 'action', but puts it in perspective.

- Action Learning moves many action-based managers to being more reflective and pragmatic; and reflectors and theorists to be more active. It makes everyone reflect more on what they do – but that may not necessarily make them more 'aware' of themselves.

- It legitimizes, and shows up the value of, giving people space and time to stand back, think, reflect, see things in perspective; and of sharing their doubts, successes, questions and mistakes with others. Two participants' insights show this: 'I know I need to sit back and reflect – but unfortunately our time sheets don't allocate space for this'; 'Reflecting, stopping to think, has saved me from plunging in, and making mistakes as I go along'.

- The longer the programme, the more the participants felt they had benefited, for this allowed their development to take place, and their confidence to grow.

- It is attitude change that results in what I call the depth, breadth and complexity of Action Learning being achieved. Where behaviour was the focus of learning, that depth and breadth were not achieved to the same degree. It is the time factor, and the set and its processes, that are crucial elements in changing attitudes and building awareness (as opposed to, or in addition to, reflecting).

- The depth and breadth of learning was also greater where individuals worked on their own projects; where the set adviser was 'qualified'; and where there was some Action Learning-related P as part of the programme (in addition to a one-day introduction to Action Learning at the beginning of a programme), or where some other development programme had preceded it.

- But, most outstanding of all, everyone mentioned that it had given them increased self-confidence ... to do many things which they went on to specify.

Part of the problem, I have discovered, when trying to describe participants' learning and experiences, and making some sort of logical sense of it all, is – it does not work that way. If I view it as an unravelling process, the image that comes to mind is deciding how to take apart a piece of woven cloth – by pulling out first the weft or the warp. If, however, I try to picture a building process, I have an image of lace-making: crossing over the numerous strands and threads in the right sequence to create a piece that is both intricate and elegant. On a more prosaic level I often saw what I was doing as digging into a bowl of spaghetti and pulling out lengths of spaghetti, only to find they kept breaking!

THE ANTICIPATED LEARNING

The 'anticipated' learning is so called because it was part of the stated (though at times less clearly than at others) objectives and goals of the in-company programmes in particular, and the individuals attending. Participants on other, mixed-company programmes by and large had more vaguely stated learning objectives.

The organizations to whose programmes I was given access had the following objectives in mind:

- *Organization A*: 'to change the management culture, to create a more energetic, proactive responsive environment'. The candidates chosen for this were the 'blue-eyed boys and girls'. The means was a set project, chosen by senior managers, with recommendations as the end product.
- *Organization B*: 'to develop management skills, encourage participants to take responsibility, take decisions, to question, and to coach their own staff'. Those chosen were a cross-section of young managers, not only high-flyers. The means were individual projects selected for participants, with both recommendations and implementation built in.
- *Organization C*: 'to develop teamworking, consulting skills, and coaching and counselling skills'. For these programmes bright young managers were selected. They were given a choice of individual or group projects, chose the latter, and the end product was a recommendation.
- *Organization D*: 'to encourage teamworking and leadership'. Participants were middle/senior departmental managers. The means of learning was a group project chosen by the set, with implementation.
- *Organization E*: 'to engage senior managers in senior management problems, the aim of increasing managerial effectiveness and change the culture, creating a sense of ownership'. Those on this programme were senior departmental managers. The means were group projects, and the end product some recommendations.
- *Organization F*: 'to build a management culture which encourages initiative, enthusiasm and leadership'. The means were individual projects, with implementation.

So, participants were sent:

- to learn about teamworking (group projects)
- to increase their performance through teamworking (group projects)
- to develop themselves as managers, with a view to career prospects (individual projects)
- to manage their own personal development (individual projects).

Individuals on these in-company programmes – as well as participants on non-company-based programmes, whose purposes in virtually all cases were to develop their managerial and personal effectiveness – mentioned such aims as 'challenging myself intellectually', 'comparing and trying out new methods of working and managing', 'learning how to motivate my staff', 'learning about leadership', 'becoming a team member', 'growing as an individual'. In some instances they mentioned increased specific skills associated with communicating, implementing quality programmes, creating human resource development programmes, liaising with clients, implementing IT programmes, and so on.

So, there were also certain anticipated learnings linked to these objectives, which participants said they had achieved, or were in the process of gaining.

HOW TO ACHIEVE BETTER TEAMWORKING

The model to which everyone referred was Belbin's. Most had completed the questionnaire, and had been 'labelled'. The other widely alluded to 'categorization' was the Honey and Mumford 'learning styles'. Participants found these useful as reference points, and when they talked of changing many mentioned moving along a continuum, or learning how to use those with complementary skills, or – in the case of the Honey and Mumford characterization – of becoming more reflective or more active.

But they also gained a host of other insights, and learned in the process: thus they talked of listening more, being aware that some team members' skills were more useful at the end of a project than at the beginning, and not judging them for non-participation early on in the work, for fear of losing a valuable resource later on. They learned generally that early judgement was often based on false impressions and assumptions. They thus changed many of their attitudes and subsequent behaviours:

- 'I listen far more, and am more than ever now committed to teamwork. I'm a "shaper" (Belbin), so naturally I have a clear view of what I want, and am often tempted to impose it on others. Now I appreciate more where others are coming from, and can read their reactions better.'
- 'I've learned that my first impressions are often very wrong. That's the advantage of working in a set for a long time on lots of issues. You see people from many different angles, and you realize how wrong you can be, and how, if you act these out at work, you are likely to lose someone valuable.'
- 'During our joint project activities I developed set ideas on who had worked hard, who had contributed most – because they'd talked most! But then at some stage everyone pulled their weight. I remember one member who had said virtually nothing, and I was ready to condemn him, when he suddenly

offered some really useful insights on what we, as a team, were doing which wasn't leading us anywhere.'

- 'I'm normally frustrated when I'm not in control in a group. I've learned that I don't have to "own" and "control" everything. I'm more tolerant of others and they are then better able to work with me. I'm also more aware, more able to stop and see myself. Being a perfectionist is a problem!'

There is evidence here of people becoming more pragmatic, moving away from being activists (to use the Honey and Mumford definition of learning styles[5]).

HOW TO BE A MORE EFFECTIVE MANAGER . . . AND INDIVIDUAL

Included here were the 'normal' managerial needs: to create better relations with my staff, to motivate staff, to communicate more effectively, to learn to delegate. Company objectives in this category included also creating more responsive and energetic managers.

I had something of a problem deciding what was anticipated or unanticipated when it came to individual development. Few participants were very specific about their anticipations. But some aspects were clear because people stated what they had wanted to learn: 'I was very quiet and my manager wanted me to open out. That's what the programme helped me to do' was one such typical comment.

When it came to other aspects of individual learning, I listened to their phrasing. When, for instance, they said 'I never realized . . .' or 'it came as a surprise . . .', I judged those to be unanticipated learning. Participants' comments showed that they had achieved in no small measure what they had set out to learn:

- 'I wanted to learn how to manage, and I've achieved it, or at least begun to understand. Before I'd "mother" my staff and tell them what to do. Now I give them more rope. I ask them what they've done, how they think something should be done . . . if they're puzzled we work it out together.'
- 'I've learned that there are good ideas "out there". Even someone you've mentally dismissed has them. All you need to do is give people the opportunity to "give". I'm now delegating more to my staff and they're enjoying it.'
- 'I've realized the difference between managing and leadership. In the latter you set standards, and lead from the front, you take on board conflicts with others and don't retreat. They are a challenge, and when you resolve them you get a sense of achievement.'
- 'I've realized that I don't feel threatened by having my staff ask me questions and give me their opinions. Before, I feared I'd find that threatening, so resorted to being autocratic, and not being my natural self which wants others to share and be motivated. So, I've learned to motivate others, while simultaneously having to take tough decisions about resources or people.'

346

- 'People – your staff – respond more to what you do and how you do it than what you say. By changing your behaviour you begin to change the culture.'
- '... to be organized, write lists, structure what I'm doing. Before I was pretty chaotic.'
- 'Confidence is a movable feast. People's confidence at work varies – it jumps up and down. Sometimes you take on the world, other times you can't. I now recognize this, which of course helps me when I'm dealing with my staff or colleagues.'
- 'How to manage and organize my time. It's been vastly more useful than the time management course I recently went on!'

These examples and others show signs of managers becoming more reflective – and pragmatic.

HOW TO CONSULT AND FACILITATE

This category arose in one or two instances where projects did not include implementation. Participants talked of:

- 'How to look at issues in a more strategic way; how to gain people's confidence when you're suggesting change.'
- 'Learning to cope with a manager's non-availability – when we're consulting him but also needing to get information from him in order to help him ... we learned to keep him involved and updated on what we were finding, we scheduled regular meetings with specific agendas and questions. Our client even told us that he was learning from the project and the process!'
- 'I've just been coaching a sales team back at work and I got them to consider more options, look at what might stop them achieve what they set out to, and think about how best to approach the issue – by having a contract with one another, and working as a team with individual responsibilities...'

The evidence is of the pragmatists applying their thinking and behaving more effectively.

MODIFIED ACHIEVEMENT ON ANTICIPATED LEARNING

There were five group projects in this research and, although in each instance there was a great deal of learning, participants often lost sight of the stated objective, e.g. teamworking. They gained enormously from undertaking the projects, learned a great deal (often unanticipated – see below); but in two instances they agreed that they had not reviewed how they had worked as a team. 'Maybe we'll do so at the end' one set commented. The other set – with whom I met some months after their programme had ended – made the comment that, although their reason for coming on the programme was to learn to work as a senior management team, they had not stopped to look at this, nor had they met as such a team since the end of the programme.

Managers on one of the other group project-focused programmes told me that, although it had greatly increased the awareness of some participants who were making considerable changes in their departmental teams, there was no evidence of a senior management team emerging as a coherent group, although this had been one of the prime objectives. Blame for this was put down to 'no support from the chief executive'.

Organization A – which had sought to develop energy among its young managers – opted for 'imposed' group projects, which in effect 'hijacked' the programme, for they were chosen with no reference to the learning objectives, there was no management involvement or support for any inspirational ideas these young people might have had, and no interest was shown in their learning. In addition, their set advisers were replaced in midstream because they lacked process skills.

This last programme was judged by its participants to have been unsuccessful.

UNANTICIPATED GAINS . . . AND LEARNING

In the course of talking to participants, I became aware of two things: that they had come on the Action Learning programmes with certain preconceived notions, expecting to learn from the projects, because there was some action in them, and from the group with which they would be working. Group learning they saw as normal: you meet and discuss with a group, you get their advice and suggestions, you ask them what they have done, they tell you where you are going wrong, and thus you gain from working with them.

What they had not anticipated was that they would be working in a totally different way on such programmes:

- the group processes would be different
- the time factor would add a dimension
- there would be a host of learning 'triggers', in some ways unconnected to projects and yet emerging from working on them with the set.

Every set adviser is aware of some of the initial concerns, questions and assumptions in the early sessions of Action Learning:

- No lectures?
- How can a bunch of non-experts help me?
- So you are not allowed to give advice?
- What is the set adviser doing, then?
- The emotional turbulence that can arise at the beginning of any programme.

But these are mostly concerned with methodology. The learning, it is assumed, is drawn from action on the project.

What participants began to gain was 'situational' learning, affecting both attitudes and behaviours, much of it unanticipated. It was also interesting that many mentioned that, as time went by, the project and the specified outcomes became less important, and learning became the main focus. As many of them talked, I became aware of Alan Mumford and Peter Honey's 'opportunistic learners' multiplying before my eyes![6]

GREATER SELF-CONFIDENCE

Almost everyone I spoke to mentioned this:

- 'It gave me the confidence to say I don't feel confident.'
- 'I know I don't have to accept blindly what I'm told to do. I can and do go back and redefine issues . . .'
- 'I don't feel I always have to be good at something, or even everything. I can say I don't know, and that's OK. I know I'm good at certain things.'
- 'I can now admit to having made a mistake, to be honest in fact. That's what's required in the set. From that I also learned the confidence not to be overly diplomatic, conciliatory or accepting.'

HOW TO COMMUNICATE MORE EFFECTIVELY

Action Learning's main tenet is that by asking questions we not only learn ourselves, but also help others to learn. To do so, we also need to listen to, not just hear, what is being said.

What participants experienced, however, went beyond that:

- 'As you're asked questions and begin to explain, you realize that what you thought was the problem isn't.'
- 'I learned the power of asking questions, but very different ones from those I'd asked before. But that also added to my frustration because I gradually realized that managers didn't always have the answers, but also that they wouldn't listen to me.'
- 'I've realized we're not all singing from the same hymn sheet. It's useful for a manager to know that!'
- 'I've learned to listen to others, and through listening to ask myself why I don't think of doing something, or ask myself certain questions which can give me insights into myself.'
- 'I always had good ideas, and would mention them to others, or at meetings but they were never noticed. Now I repeat or say things more forcibly. I also didn't know how to react when people said "no" to me, or disagreed. I now have a wider repertoire of responses . . . the set helped me with that.'

HOW TO NETWORK

We talk a great deal about the networking that Action Learning promotes. Except in one or two instances this was not an objective specified by the programme or the individuals. Where participants did mention it, they talked of 'learning more about the company', meaning gaining more information. Just how valuable it is to have a network, not simply for information, became clear to many participants:

- 'I lost my fear of approaching people. I may still be apprehensive but I know that if I'm clear about what I want it'll be fine. I had to go to talk to senior managers as part of my project. It forced me to network, particularly with those senior people, as well as with the marketing department which I'd always been a bit scared of (I'm only a scientific researcher)! But I realized I had as much knowledge as them, and as much ability as others, and it gave me a great sense of my own power.'
- 'I've realized how much help others can, and are willing, to give you. I'd always feared people would be dismissive or would find excuses.'
- 'In our set we've had people from different departments, and you see them grappling with different problems, and you begin to have much more understanding of them and their problems. Also, communication is bad in our company so the set is making up for it. We can now pick up the phone to so many people in different parts of the company – and they can give us contacts beyond – so its tentacles can spread out further.'

HOW TO EMPOWER MY STAFF

I put this in under unanticipated learning, because the two people who mentioned it were really surprised at this turn of events! However, it is a thought for other hard-pressed managers who say they do not have the time to come on an Action Learning programme:

- 'This was not one of my learning objectives. I was learning how to work in a team. But I simply didn't have time to do everything at work once we started to work on the project. I didn't know how to delegate. So we – my staff and I – learned together, an offshoot, so to speak, of what I was doing on the programme! I didn't initially give my staff enough background or guidance on what they were to do. And they didn't at first ask me either – they were afraid of my reaction. So I'd phone and give them detailed instructions on what to do, and then phone to check how they'd managed. But then, as they began to cope better, I created a tape of tasks they need to carry out, but not how. And they managed. Soon I found that all I was doing was phoning to reassure them, praise them and tell them what a great job they were doing. They are so pleased, since it's given them much more responsibility – and they've proved they can do it.'

- 'I've delegated so much – successfully – I've told my manager that I'll have two free days a month now, once the programme is finished. My lack of time has empowered my staff.'

A MORE DISCIPLINED WAY OF WORKING

All participants had been introduced to the Kolb 'learning cycle' in terms of working around it on their projects with the help of the set. What was interesting, however, was the way that so many participants said they had adapted this concept of working around a cycle and had created their own derivations, to use on any task they tackled. They had in many instances built in various extra 'steps'. They talked of now always considering various options (i.e. reflecting on several possibilities) before taking a decision; they built in evaluation – i.e. reflection and analysis – at frequent stages of any task they undertook, and were prepared to change direction if the evaluation pointed to this:

- 'It invites a certain caution in what you do. I'm less inclined to give an instant decision or answer. I prepare my ground more, think, go away, come back.'
- 'I now feel much more confident about turning an idea into an action, and accomplishing it. It's given me some basic methods and systems – reminded me to look for help and ideas – to use the resources available.'

GAINED AN INCREASED AWARENESS ABOUT MYSELF

Those individuals, or sets, that had gained this awareness were the sets that had an academic or *P* element attached to them; and/or those that were well facilitated (I return to the latter point later on). Other sets and individuals by and large either did not talk to the same degree about these elements, or hardly touched on them at all:

- 'I've learned that I learn best when I'm challenged by others. I have a tendency to dismiss things quickly.'
- 'I've learned to be my natural self, to be direct, friendly, blunt when necessary . . . and to know what I'm talking about.'
- 'It's taught me to be honest with myself, and see my emotions as part – a valid part – of the picture. So, if I'm genuinely feeling frightened, threatened, hassled or uneasy . . . that's part of the equation and needs to be looked at, as well as what's causing the feelings.'
- 'This may sound melodramatic, but I went in a naive boy and came out a maturer adult.'

- 'You can learn from others if you're prepared to share – the more you share, the more you get back.'
- 'That only when you admit you're stuck can others help you.'

OTHER KINDS OF RESULTS

In addition to the learning and development there were also some real success stories with tangible, and visible, results: departments restructured to take account of client liaison, participative communication introduced, new marketing strategies put into place, cost-cutting exercises implemented, consultative projects about to be accepted and implemented, a workshop reorganized, a personnel department given a new lease of life, greater staff involvement and motivation in many departments, etc.

Of those I interviewed five individuals said they had learned nothing. They were unhappy, disillusioned, and felt the entire exercise had been a waste of time. Three others were slightly non-committal. Two of these admitted they had come on the programme to investigate whether Action Learning had any use back in their companies. Although both had gained, they were unsure about its value for their companies.

Those who were unhappy identified the reasons as being:

- no confidentiality in the set
- lack of interest and empathy with the Action Learning process, in particular with the set
- incompetent and unhelpful set advising
- irrelevance of the group project to that individual's work
- unhelpful set members
- 'my own emotional state'.

Comments from the non-committed people included: that the programme was too vague; that it might be more useful with everyone from the same function: the project chosen by one participant had also focused on an issue on which she alone could not influence the company in the direction she wanted. (Both these latter individuals were in mixed-company sets. Perhaps their views would have been different if they had been on in-company sets.)

In addition to the few instances just mentioned, there were also other aspects, or experiences, in their programmes that a few other participants did not like or were not happy about. I will highlight these later when I discuss the various elements of an Action Learning programme, and how each contributes to learning.

VERY SENIOR MANAGERS' EXPERIENCES

One group of participants, the more senior managers and managing directors, focused less on projects and more on themselves and their responsibilities for the organizations they managed. Although they had no specific projects as such on which to work, nevertheless they each came with the anticipation of discussing worries and questions, as well as giving themselves space and time to sit back, see things in perspective, and test out their assumptions, ideas and strategies in a safe yet challenging environment. These senior managers were all in mixed-company sets. They all commented that it was the only feasible, and safe, way they could come with their problems and, as one put it, 'gain from their cumulative wisdom'.

Asked what they had gained and learned, and what they were now doing back at work, they talked of benefiting from working openly with a forum of peers, valuing time to take stock – a time for themselves, a place to admit to doubts, a place to be challenged, and a place to share and to hear others:

- 'I'm a one-company man, I've had no experience of other businesses, and now I'm MD of my own company. It's been a great comfort to know that in other companies there are the same threads and themes, and to have the other set members ask me searching questions that my colleagues at work would never dare ask me because of my seniority. This is my time for myself to step back from everyday things to take stock, compare notes, and think where I'm going and how I can get there.'
- 'I now consciously watch people more carefully and listen to what's being said, and don't assume people agree with me. This is a trap you can fall into when you're the boss, and you think your staff are all nodding like dogs – but no more! I look for the signals as well as the words. I'm more aware of my effect on people, and others' effects on me. I'm very task-oriented and it's sometimes easy to forget the people.'
- 'I'm thinking more – thinking things through, away from action. I now plan, consider alternatives, evaluate them all, take a decision, and only then launch into the doing. I'm making decisions differently, and reaching different conclusions.'
- 'I got some of my most creative insights when it was someone else's slot and I found there was time to reflect during the eddies and back currents surrounding the work on someone else's problem. When you are the focus you are too busy giving and receiving information, responding to questions and defending your position.'
- 'I'm more committed to teamworking. I listen more. I try and appreciate where others are coming from. What I've learned is that I need this what I call "luxury" of half a day to think and reflect, and be able to rehearse some of my problems with others. Not having to appear crystal-clear and quite sure with all the answers gives me energy. I feel refreshed and invigorated.'

WHAT ARE PARTICIPANTS DOING DIFFERENTLY BACK AT WORK?

Participants' responses were rich and highly practical. But they did not talk only of increased skills. They talked more of understanding, being aware, empowering staff, giving feedback and modelling the type of behaviour they valued and wanted. There was talk of more listening and using the skills of their staff.

A number of managers talked of the learning cycle – which some termed a 'discipline' – as having wider application in their everyday tasks and work. Others talked of trying to introduce an 'Action Learning way of working' with their staff, or teams of which they were members. Many talked of their increased confidence, or being more forthright, of challenging their own managers, of having less fear of (but also less respect for) senior managers. They also commented on the response that such 'new' behaviour elicited from their managers and other colleagues.

Their responses show a general aliveness, awareness and energy to do things, rather than a withdrawing or shying away from responsibilities. They indicate both attitude and behaviour changes of four kinds:

1. Better teamworking/more open relationships with staff and colleagues.
2. Being more organized and effective.
3. Behaving with greater confidence and awareness.
4. Introducing an 'Action Learning way of working'.

PARTICIPANTS' DILEMMAS OVER ACTION LEARNING

Some participants, who were either trying out Action Learning approaches at work, or who were not, posed the problems they faced:

- 'It's too time-consuming [i.e. project work].'
- 'It's too nice and cosy, not challenging enough. This company is largely run by macho managers. Our department seems to be different, but we're not typical.'
- 'It's too vague for money-minded managers. Its benefits are not concrete enough – too hit and miss, not specific enough.'
- 'It needs some *P* to really catch on.'
- 'It claims to change culture, which it would do. But you'd have to involve everyone, and in particular senior managers . . . and they back away.'
- 'It doesn't seem to help with the politics that infest most organizations.'
- 'It advocates sharing, but doesn't address the other individualistic and competitive aspects in most organizations: the reward system, primarily.'

PARTICIPANTS' EXPERIENCES OF ACTION LEARNING, AND WHAT CONTRIBUTED TO LEARNING

What is it about Action Learning, and the experiences that enabled participants to gain and learn so much? How does it differ from other experiential programmes? For instance, what is there here that could not be learned elsewhere, on other team-building programmes? There are evidently specific elements of Action Learning programmes that offer this breadth and depth of learning that so many participants mention, especially in unanticipated learning.

There are five elements that constitute an Action Learning programme:

1. Work-focused projects.
2. Sets.
3. The processes in the sets.
4. The set adviser.
5. 'Time' factor (in the sense that Action Learning programmes are spread over a longer time-period than most other courses and programmes).

There was a great deal of interweaving of the experiences and learning as participants talked of what each element gave them, and how their learning occurred. Nevertheless some kinds of learning were clearly attributable to some experiences more than others. I have therefore tried to categorize them under the five elements.

But few things follow the logical paths I, or the participants as we talked about it, might have wished. Tom Bourner at Brighton University (who is both a member of two sets and a set adviser), likened Action Learning to a Möbius strip. It is 'an analogy of the "inside-outside" nature of Action Learning. You start learning about practical aspects of projects, and end up learning about yourself. Where the join, or separation, comes is unclear.' Maybe there is none.

PROJECTS

The undertaking of projects seemed, to most participants, one of the most familiar aspects of the programme. Most had already, in some capacity, worked on project or action groups. A project within an Action Learning programme differs from any other project in that it has to be seen as part of learning, rather than simply an action-directed undertaking. As one participant put it: 'It's like putting together your own programme. You find that in addition to the project, the ostensible learning vehicle, you're simultaneously working on time management, empowerment, presentation skills, assertiveness . . .'.

There were a variety of projects. They might be group, individual or hybrid (where a set tackled the project of one member). The origin of the projects also differed – some chosen by the individual or group, some chosen for them, some projects had 'implementation' built in, but others focused only on producing reports and recommendations, i.e. a consulting rather than a managing focus:

- Group projects were chosen to meet certain specific objectives, normally to do with teamworking. As such they gave set members many insights. One participant commented: 'If the company's intention is to help managers work better together, then group projects rather than individual projects are better'.
- However, where the set was able to exercise some choice – over whether to do an individual or group project, and on which of a number of projects to work – they showed greater commitment, and appeared to have learned more than where there was no choice.

The group project where the most learning appeared to have taken place, judged on participants' own statements, was also distinguished by having a more 'qualified' set adviser, i.e. where he commented on process, and made the set aware of their learning.

In the hybrid projects, the same applied. In one of the two such projects, the set – the only one I came across – worked without a set adviser, and their learning occurred through their own awareness of what they were experiencing. They learned a great deal, particularly from the actual project (on communication) on which they worked, but less on the stated objective.

Projects contributed to learning by:

- hearing, and beginning to understand, others' perspectives
- being 'pushed' to take a disciplined approach to tackling a project
- opening up networks
- having to implement or manage other elements.

One of the basic tenets of Action Learning for many practitioners is that projects have to have an 'implementing' stage to them, and not end with a report and recommendations. The latter is regarded as consulting, not managing.

Implementation was an integral part of two set projects: one, where the set was entirely made up of one department, with the specific task of reorganizing their workshop area. In the other, one of the hybrid projects, implementation of the communication strategies worked out by the set was ongoing in the one participants' department. This implementation definitely gave an impetus and sense of commitment and energy to these two set projects.

However, even where implementation was not built into the projects, as was the case with one set project (whose objectives had been to learn about team-working and consulting), the participants still found their project utterly absorbing.

This particular set had extremely good relations with their client for whom they were acting as consultants, and they were aware that their recommendations were being considered seriously. Their learning was centred on working with him as a client, acting as consultants to him, meeting with him, finding out what he wanted, investigating, reporting back, as well as learning about the company, and working together as a team. They learned, as did others with set projects, a great deal about how to manage a project. They also learned how to interact with a great number of people outside their own domain – often senior people with whom they had not had, and in other circumstances were unlikely ever to have, contact. It gave them insights into how such senior people work and think, and what concerns they have.

In another set project one member had the unplanned opportunity to implement a small part of the set's recommendations while the set was still meeting. Her comments make for interesting reading: she explained that it was only as she worked with the head of the section for which they had created some recommendations and in talking through the actual implementation that she became aware that, in any project where you recommend, you have to be aware of: 'What is practical, what is acceptable, and what is bearable':

- 'If you don't implement you have pie in the sky ideas of what you want to do. But you change these if you are responsible for implementing. And it makes you more aware the next time you suggest something be done in a different way.'

It seems that the distinction between 'consulting on' and 'managing' a project has blurred boundaries when it comes to assessing the learning. Where the project was consultative, participants learned a great deal about managing a consulting project, handling relationships with clients, gaining access to information, presenting their ideas, and gaining the client's acceptance of them. These are also skills that any manager needs, even when working with staff and colleagues. It begs the questions of how far implementation is vital for the learning.

Those involved with implementing were in a sense simply involved in another stage of managing – as one of them put it, were bound to learn 'more':

- 'the doing triggers off different experiences, thoughts and feelings ... and so new learning'.

HOW THE EXPERIENCE OF A SET CONTRIBUTED TO LEARNING

It is interesting to consider how the set contributed to learning, for, at the outset, most participants saw the set as 'just another group'. They therefore did not consider what they would learn from the group. A few mentioned they had reservations about whether non-experts, and mere managers, would be able to help them to learn anything.

Some of the findings so far have indicated a great deal of learning about valuing others, changing the way they worked (e.g. from being active to being more reflective), about the value of being supportive, growing in confidence. Most of these unanticipated learnings, for such they were, participants in fact ascribed to the set and its processes by:

- mixing with different functions in in-company sets
- seeing how different companies work (in mixed company sets); and by being able to 'step out of role'
- seeing the value of the non-expert
- seeing the value of sharing time, space and projects with others similarly engaged
- experiencing being in a support group
- having to take responsibility for myself
- realizing the value of being honest, with self and others
- experiencing a group at work.

LEARNING IS AN EMOTIONAL PROCESS

For many it was difficult and traumatic; some felt like quitting after the first session. The lack of structure upset them; the expectation of being open and honest frightened others; the prospect of having to complete a project worried, even scared, others:

- 'It felt like hell on the first day. A total culture shock, both in relation to work, and any other form of learning or education I'd experienced before.'

Others felt daunted and nervous. 'How will we know when we're working in an Action Learning way?' was a question several participants asked themselves at the beginning.

All programmes began with an introduction to Action Learning. Some lasted one day; others included a couple of days on some team-building exercise. Those who experienced the latter said it was most useful. It helped gel the set together. In a couple of other instances, a previous course, following which participants chose to continue learning together, also provided the same type of early bonding.

But several sets commented that they would have liked to be reminded of the 'Action Learning way of working' after that initial introduction. In some instances, again where the set adviser was not 'up to scratch', the sets either fell back into discussions, or forgot to stop and check what they were learning.

The advice of even those who had expressed ambivalence, fear or disappointment at the outset, though, was: 'Hang in, don't give up after the first one or two sessions'; 'The longer you're there, the greater the benefits'.

Sometimes the chemistry of the set did not work, and members found it a problem to tackle 'difficult' set members.

HOW THE EXPERIENCE OF SET PROCESSES CONTRIBUTED TO LEARNING

The processes of the set are a main feature of Action Learning programmes. Without them, the programme can easily become action-oriented, and set meetings merely talking-shop or discussion groups, little different from other gatherings. The processes include:

- having airspace, and giving it to everyone
- listening to others, and have others listen to me
- the discipline of asking, and being asked, questions; and not giving or getting advice
- by challenging, and being challenged
- helping others – a subtle feature of Action Learning. We normally talk of being helped by others. One of the insights that many participants gained was that by helping others you gain yourself. You gain insights into what are good questions to be asking yourself, you gain in confidence, and you gain others' willingness to reciprocate:

  'The more you share, the more you get back. You learn from others if you're prepared to share.'
  '. . . as you help others grapple and understand, you hear the questions you asked that were helpful, and realize they make sense . . . and that gives you confidence.'

- keeping a diary; very few participants kept diaries or wrote reflective documents. One programme required them to, but more for their own use than as a form of assessment. The academic programmes were slightly more insistent.

Those who kept diaries found them beneficial. They acted as a 'memory', part of the reflective element of Action Learning. It reminded them of what they had done and felt, and what they had thought, and what progress they were making. They found they moved on from initially simply registering events, to thinking about their reaction to them and what significance they had. 'Maybe the word diary is the wrong word to use', commented one participant. 'It's more of a daily portfolio of reflections, not so much of events and timing.'

ANY *P?*

A classic Action Learning programme does not have any taught inputs. These programmes varied: some followed on from workshops; others included some taught elements which had some relevance to the objectives of the programmes, e.g. the team-focused or the academic programmes; yet others included some *P* on issues related to Action Learning. Those who had had some 'inputs' – related to development, teamworking, Action Learning or simply other ideas to reflect on – appeared to have greater perspectives on issues they were working through . . . and had appeared to have 'pushed' themselves more.

HOW THE EXPERIENCE OF 'TIME' CONTRIBUTED TO LEARNING

Time is fundamental to Action Learning. It means that people get to know one another, grow to trust one another (usually), gain confidence to be themselves – and only then do they really 'work'. Time allowed participants to practise what they had been taught on other courses, and what they were learning through Action Learning. Gaining confidence, and feeling safe enough to be honest, and to be able to admit to emotions, or to not knowing – those all took time.

Time is also tied in with continuity – having the repetition of sets and set meetings and the same sort of questions, to give a sense of continuity to the discipline of thinking, planning and doing, reflecting and coming back to thinking again.

THE CONTRIBUTIONS OF THE SET ADVISER

Put another way: Reg Revans has said that a set adviser is not necessary. Others think differently. Did participants value and gain anything from such a presence?:

- 'Our set adviser "taught" me to listen and analyse, to question and encourage others to say more, to help them, and the others, understand . . . She did this by modelling that approach.'

A number of participants also commented on the role of the set adviser as being one model for managers to follow. 'Coaching and mentoring is part of every manager's job. By learning to work as an effective set member by using a good set adviser as a model, you're learning the processes you need for mentoring and coaching as a line manager.'

But most commented that the set adviser was able to stand back, be objective, challenge what was being said, help the set with processes and with learning. 'I can't imagine a set without a set adviser, particularly at the beginning'.

One participant observed that: 'If the set adviser isn't good, or present, then the temptation is to concentrate on the task (the project), and forget the Action Learning processes, forget the learning. That misses entirely the point of Action Learning.'

So, the set adviser helped the sets to learn, to become aware of how they were learning, and to start taking responsibility for this themselves . . . something that several participants said they were trying to adopt back at work with their staff. It was part of the empowering process.

One or two participants said they were using their set adviser as a model for managing: 'I see my role as being a "set adviser" to my staff – wanting them to achieve their full potential and not feel threatened by it.'

Several sets had two advisers in the lifetime of their programmes. This enabled them to make comparisons. 'One became quite involved with us. He knew a lot about our "task" (a set project) and our work environment and got us to ask questions we'd never thought of asking. He checked also how we felt we were doing as a "team". But he tackled individual issues outside the set in private.' The second adviser, by contrast, kept a distance – even sat outside the group – and commented only on processes. Neither was entirely satisfactory, they felt.

Several participants talked of set advisers who became too involved with them, almost part of the set, and thus less helpful because either 'he tended to agree too much with us' or 'he talked too much'. One participant said, 'I would have preferred a set adviser who understood more about processes . . . I'd have learned more'. Another said that 'subject expertise is the kiss of death for Action Learning. What you need, though, is a process expert.'

Others observed that the confidentiality, which set members agreed was one of their ground rules, had to apply also to the set adviser. But two participants found it had been breached by the set adviser talking to their managers. This destroyed their trust in the set and their ability to be open and honest. Another participant recalled one member who talked all the time, 'hogging the group'. 'The set adviser did nothing. We weren't sure how to tackle this man. Was it OK to tell him what he was doing? Eventually two of us did. I'm pleased I took the "risk". It helped us work better as a set, and learned that giving that sort of feedback isn't as terrifying as I'd thought.' Yet another had experienced a set adviser who was ' . . . critical, condescending and aggressive. We didn't trust him at all'.

EVALUATING THE ACTION . . . AND THE LEARNING

This issue cropped up in several programmes, and was discussed by the sets, who had both set and individual projects to work on. One set in particular was upset and angry that, at the end of the programme, their managers and client showed no interest in their learning, only in the practical recommendations associated with their projects.

One other group commented: 'Our projects were imposed ... and, when we didn't seem to be getting anywhere with them, we began to get negative vibes from managers ... but the problem for us was that we were learning, even though we weren't visibly achieving anything ...'

In many instances, sets and individuals were required to produce a written report. To ensure that individual and set learning was not lost, some programmes required participants to write short reflective documents, more for themselves than for a formal assessment. Even in one set which tackled a set project, and where their learning was considerable, when asked about how and when they evaluated their learning, they said they might put a few hours aside at the end of the programme to evaluate their learning. Others evaluated the learning as they went along, often at the end of set meetings.

For a number of sets, but only where the adviser instituted this, it became an ongoing process. One set referred to the adviser 'drip feeding' the question: 'So what have you learned from that?' until it became something they all muttered to themselves – and even, some of them commented, back at work to their staff!

As one participant said: 'I've realized that everything is data to learn from ... I now expect to learn from everything'. An opportunistic learner, as described by Honey and Mumford.

PARTICIPANTS' VIEWS ON THE ESSENCE OF ACTION LEARNING

Action Learning was seen as primarily about development. It is about participants changing their attitudes, and gaining a broader repertoire of behaviours. Activists became more reflective, reflectors saw the benefits of being more pragmatic, most became greater theorists, for questioning is something that most people learned to do and benefited from; most became better reflectors.

True, this development is achieved through undertaking a real work-focused project; true also that from any development spring new ways of doing things, new ways of working, new ways of managing – of managing staff better, managing change, undertaking new tasks and roles, etc. In this sense the ultimate result is new actions. But the main focus for most seemed to be developing and learning, above all. Many participants also commented that, as the programmes went on, the learning became a much stronger focus for them than the actions on which they were simultaneously engaged – paradoxically to achieve that learning. A watering-down of this focus could lead to the programmes differing little from other action or experiential programmes.

One example can be seen from comments on teamworking. The outcomes helped those objectives, and helped the participants learn about working as a group of people in a team, taking back with them ideas and insights on how to work with teams back at work.

But the programmes missed the deeper 'inner' developmental aspects. I wondered what they had therefore achieved that might not have been achieved on a teamworking programme. It left me pondering what is necessary for 'the real McCoy'. We need, I think, to be clear about this; otherwise we risk Action Learning being used to describe programmes which bear little resemblance to the reality and its potential.

A key element which gives participants the opportunity to reach the depth, breadth and complexity of Action Learning is, if only in the early stages, a qualified and competent set adviser to set the participants along a process road that will uncover the potential. Time alone, and projects alone, do not achieve this.

ACTION LEARNING AND LEARNING ORGANIZATIONS

Does Action Learning move us closer to, or give us insights into how to achieve, a learning organization? Many of the so-called communication skills together with the ability to network, to reflect, and the increased awareness that most participants said they had acquired, are also learning skills or behaviours. Learning to ask questions, explore options, to share, to listen, to gather information, to take risks, to convert mistakes into learning, and so on, are within the repertoire of learning skills and behaviours. Those who say they use them all the time in turn become 'opportunistic learners', a high accolade.

But a learning organization needs more than an understanding of what learning skills or behaviours are. It also needs the will to use them, has to create the environment in which they will be valued, and organize the means to work them. Many participants doubted their organizations could or would do this.

Can small beginnings lead to greater things?

MY OWN EXPERIENCES – AND LEARNING

Alan Mumford suggested, at the beginning of this research, that I should do it in 'an Action Learning way'. I adopted a deductive approach, i.e. with a broad picture in my mind which I adjusted as the data I collected shifted my view. I also kept a diary, which was lucky. Without it, many ideas, thoughts, insights, reflections and questions would have disappeared. I found the diary was more than a 'memory'. It became my partner for dialogue, my surrogate set. As I wrote I found that I was putting ideas and thoughts down on paper, or rather screen, that I had not known I had until I 'voiced' them in writing. This mirrored what several participants said to me about the advantage of the set: that as you talk, out loud, you hear yourself, and you answer your own questions, or realize what you are not doing that would be helpful.

My diary is also a stream of comments on my findings. What recurs is the feeling that so many programmes are not reaching what I increasingly called 'the breadth, depth and complexity of Action Learning'. They were in so many cases pale imitations of the potential.

My other main observation was that my research was a project, just as participants had their projects. I became more pragmatic when organizing it in the early days, and complained of the need to do this! I needed to talk to others to find in myself the energy to carry on – just as set members talked of the energy they gained from talking to others. In this sense I had a 'telephone set' of people to whom I regularly talked. I confirmed my belief that I am a reflector but reflect better following some 'action'. I learn through a combination of hearing myself talk, writing, drawing (visualizing) and listening. I also suspect I am an opportunistic learner. My diary confirms the ideas that emerged from a sermon in St Paul's Cathedral, a World Service programme, a tennis match commentary, a Polish novel, and an Australian film!

I gained confidence by talking through some of my thoughts with others. Two or three of the most helpful ideas, and the ones I particularly remember, emerged as a couple of friends – non-experts – asked me some simple questions about Action Learning! But the insights of 'experts' were helpful at the beginning stages of the research as I tried to formulate questions and construct structures and, latterly, as I tried to make some sense of the material I had gathered.

I moved away, in the course of the research, from a questioning approach, to more of a dialogue with the participants, though based on some initial questions, and with others loosely in mind. I found this more productive, and was reminded of one or two participants who talked of being 'in the firing line' of questions. But as I gained more insights from people through a dialogue with them (i.e. where I followed a train of thought they had begun and added some thoughts of my own) I began to wonder how useful it was to keep rigidly to a questioning approach in Action Learning.

Yet I feel ambivalent about this, for simultaneously some people with whom I was working, being newly introduced to Action Learning, found the questioning approach immensely helpful – a discovery and eye-opener in fact. Is there a time for questions, and a time for dialogue?

I also wondered about questions in a set: it concerned whether the most helpful questions were those which had a target in the questioner's mind – some picture. If this were the case, how do you accommodate a set in this process, where any member may interrupt such a train of thought?

My acceptance of what is Action Learning is now broader than it was, while simultaneously I am critical of much that goes under the name of Action Learning. I am not sure quite where I draw the boundaries.

As for my own processes: I gained more depth from individual interviews; I gained more sense of energy from set interviews. I found written responses to my questions stiff and in many cases only of limited value. What people say, and what they write are often poles apart. The latter is in some cases so intellectualized as to lose all sense of person. Others convey themselves well on paper. Yet others (particularly those associated with higher degrees) are helpfully analytical.

While undertaking this research I was asked by someone whether the entire process of an Action Learning programme cannot be undertaken by an individual on their own, without needing a set. The more I look at what people say about the set and its processes, the more I think it is a rare person who can gain as much on their own as from working with others productively. Or maybe some stages in an Action-Learning cycle can be done alone. Certainly I began the research with a hunch (a hypothesis?) that the set, with its processes and set adviser, would emerge as the vital element. I think for me it has.

This research, and my experiencing of it, has in many ways paralleled or mirrored what happens in an Action Learning programme. I had not anticipated that. I have become aware though, that I am not good at seeing my own journey around a learning cycle, although I follow one. But it still has to be pointed out to me!

This issue – of being reminded – was brought back to me on several occasions when I interviewed individuals or sets. They commented how good it was to be reviewing, or remembering what they had done and learned, 'Wouldn't it be good', they would comment, 'to meet up again, to start something similar?'. Is there a 'learning' here for us? Do we need to remind participants of what they did by 'revisiting' the experiences in some way at a later date?

I began the research with images, and they are still with me, and more have emerged. But the one I still like the most, to describe this breadth, depth and complexity of Action Learning, is the many-layered chocolate cake (I have no idea why culinary images abound. Maybe it has something to do with Action Learning feeding the body, mind and spirit!).

NOTE

Krystyna Weinstein's book, *'Action Learning': A Journey in Discovery and Development*, was published by HarperCollins in 1995.

REFERENCES

1 M. Pedler, *Action Learning in Practice*, 2nd ed., Gower, Aldershot, 1991.
2 I. McGill and L. Beaty, *Action Learning: A Practitioner's Guide*, Kogan Page, London, 1992.
3 L. Beaty, T. Bourner and P. Frost, 'Action Learning: Reflections on Becoming a Set Member' in *Management Education and Development*, vol. 24, part 4, 1993.

4 R. Vince and L. Martin, 'Inside Action Learning: An Exploration of the Psychology and Politics of the Action Learning Model' in *Management Education and Development*, vol. 24, no. 3, 1993.
5 P. Honey and A. Mumford, *The Manual of Learning Styles*, 3rd ed., Honey, Maidenhead, 1992.
6 P. Honey and A. Mumford, *The Opportunist Learner*, Honey, Maidenhead, 1990.

32 Intrapreneurship and Entrepreneurship amongst MBA Graduates*

Carol Oliver, Sandra Pass, Jayne Taylor and Pam Taylor

This chapter sets out to examine intrapreneurship and entrepreneurship as it manifested itself in the spread of the International Management Centre's (IMC) MBA dissertations, both in writing and subsequently in action.

We took Gifford Pinchot III's[1] definitions of intrapreneur and entrepreneur:

Intrapreneur. Any of the 'dreamers who do'. Those who take hands-on responsibility for creating innovation of any kind within an organization. The intrapreneur may be the creator or inventor but is always the dreamer who figures out how to turn an idea into a profitable reality.

Entrepreneur. Someone who fills the role of an intrapreneur outside the organization.

Within the contexts of our research, it was thought highly probable that although intrapreneurs pursuing the IMC MBA would be encountered, there would be few, if any, entrepreneurs. This is partly due to the fact that managers undertaking the programme are required to have company sponsorship; also the programmes are, by and large, targeted at individuals who have competence in one or two functional areas but who wish to broaden their managerial base.

We therefore needed to determine what exactly intrapreneurship was, and if any of IMC's associates identified with the concept. For the purposes of our research we selected 32 MBA graduates who had made specific recommendations within their project. To these 32 we then addressed our questionnaire, to find out whether or not they had succeeded in doing what they set out to do, what problems they encountered and what support they had received. We defined intrapreneur and entrepreneur at the beginning of the questionnaire and used a multiple-choice box system for answering the questions.

We achieved a 50 per cent reponse rate to our questionnaire, then analysed the data and made a further selection of eight associates whom we would

*Originally published in *Management Decision*, vol. 29, no. 5, 1991.

interview in-depth to ascertain how they had fared with the implementation of their project.

WHAT IS INTRAPRENEURSHIP?

Gifford Pinchot III coined the term intrapreneur, derived from '*inter*nal entre*preneur*', and defined practitioners as 'dreamers who do'. In Europe, the more commonly used term is 'corporate entrepreneurship'. In addition to Gifford Pinchot's definition we also looked at others, including:

> An intrapreneur is an employee of a large organisation who has the entrepreneurial qualities of drive, creativity, vision and ambition, but who prefers, if possible, to remain within an established company.[2]

> An entrepreneur is therefore someone who perceives an opportunity and acts on it to create a new venture for which he or she will assume the risk and the management. The three key words are 'perceives', 'opportunity' and 'acts'.[3]

It would appear, therefore, that intrapreneurs are goal oriented and self-motivated whilst also responding to corporate rewards and recognition. That said, they may also be cynical about the 'corporate system' but optimistic that they have the ability to outwit and manipulate it. To do this they need a 'mentor' or 'protector' from within their company who will support them whilst they are taking risks. The existence of sponsors is perhaps the most important aspect of the intrapreneurial culture.

THE ROLE OF THE MENTOR

Mentors may have the ability to solve most of the basic barriers to intrapreneuring: lack of resources, threat of withdrawal or lack of funding at every setback, and political attacks. Mentors also help the intrapreneur think and execute their projects.

For the mentor to fulfil his or her role successfully s/he needs special skills and characteristics to manage intrapreneurs. From discussions with our test group these include:

- being a colleague not a boss
- judging intrapreneurs on results not methods
- giving clear and frequent feedback
- expecting mistakes – no recriminations
- strategic vision as to where the company is going.

Mentors appeared to have a fairly common quality – the desire to see innovation happen. The mentor, therefore, should preferably not solely be money-motivated, but should possess the desire to advance the company through the intrapreneur's development. Mentors should be in a position of authority within the company so that they are able to 'protect' their intrapreneur; however, they may not necessarily be the chief executive officer (CEO). Indeed, to fill the innovation needs of the company, it would be necessary for large organizations to have several mentors. The research reported here revealed that, where this does happen, the CEO/MD is more likely to fill the role of a facilitator whilst delegating others to the role of mentor.

Interestingly, the managing director of one of the associates questioned was so fully supportive of the merits of innovation and intrapreneurship that, despite the current economic uncertainty, he had agreed to put money into a new product development project which would be led by that associate.

In addition to having the support of a sponsor/mentor, one associate also pointed out that, especially in those organizations whose cultures lack entrepreneurial vision, it is most important for the intrapreneur to enlist the support, at an early stage, of the people who will be involved in the implementation of the project. This would help ensure the project's success by instilling a feeling of ownership in those people.

DEVELOPING INTRAPRENEURS

One hypothesis we considered was that Action Learning could provide a useful learning vehicle for the intrapreneur. Students of the IMC's Action Learning MBA programme are encouraged to base their dissertations on a project that could be implemented within their organization. One of the main selling points of IMC's MBA is that, for the cost of participating on the programme to provide a return on investment, the project to be undertaken must be agreed between the associate and the appropriate decision-making body of his company. This agreement, or congruence of objectives, should help ensure the successful implementation of the project. A further requirement is that the associate should have a sponsor who will guide him through the project. Both these points draw us back to the description of intrapreneurial behaviour.

We therefore wanted to look at what had happened to associates who had taken the Action Learning MBA programme with IMC. Did they see themselves as intrapreneurs? Was their project implemented? Who aided them? What barriers, if any, did they have to overcome? Figures 32.1 and 32.2 give some basic details of our findings.

One discovery was that intrapreneurial activities require an organizational structure which promotes an innovative climate, and essential to this is top management support. Those associates we questioned cited the following characteristics of mentors and top management, necessary to promote intrapreneurship:

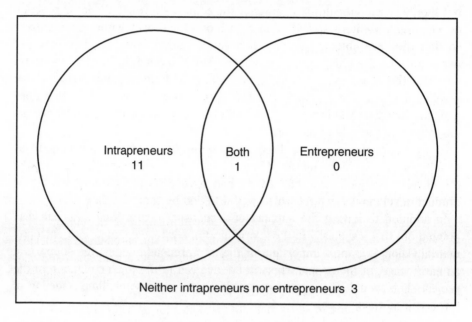

Figure 32.1 How associates described themselves

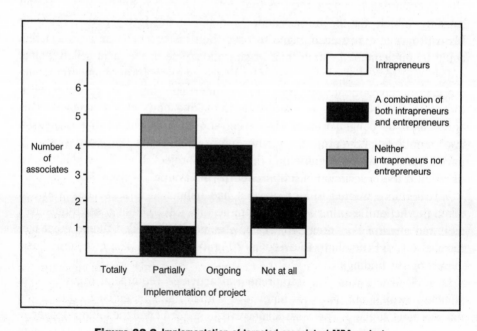

Figure 32.2 Implementation of targeted associates' MBA project

- high level of commitment to staff and projects
- generation of trust and co-operation
- delegation of responsibility
- rapid feedback on performance
- involving staff in the decision-making process
- open-minded and supportive
- strategic vision
- responsive to change
- tolerant of risk, failure or mistakes
- allowing autonomous behaviour.

The comments reflect both the structure and the culture of organizations that were supportive of the MBA projects and their ultimate implementation.

One interesting point to emerge was that one of the 'intrapreneurial' associates said that there were times when he had to go outside his organization and take on the role of an entrepreneur to start off a project before bringing it back into his company for acceptance and further development.

It was also intriguing to learn that all those questioned, who described themselves as intrapreneurs, gave the same reasons for undertaking the MBA programme. They all saw it as a way of gaining promotion and a higher visibility within their organization. This appears contrary to the traditional view that rewards sought by intrapreneurs are more to do with being able to continue to innovate, take more risks and launch new products. By seeking promotion, these self-styled intrapreneurs could place themselves in positions unsuited to their interest. As Pinchot suggests:

> Let us avoid promoting intrapreneurs to their level of incompetence, let them go on starting business for the corporation, and let us reward them with substantial stock options and bonuses for each start-up.[1]

Of the associates who claimed they worked for organizations that rewarded innovative ability it was generally agreed that this meant promotion and promotion equalled a higher salary.

Few of those questioned had followed up their MBA project with another intrapreneurial activity, despite the fact that they appeared to be 'natural' intrapreneurs who had been instrumental in introducing innovative projects. Indeed, some had a history of intrapreneurial behaviour. Perhaps, as the majority had gained the sought-after higher visibility and promotion, they were no longer in a position to innovate: if so, maybe their company is now missing the opportunity to continue a successful programme of innovation. By only partly rewarding and exploiting this valuable resource a company's future success may be threatened. New and flexible companies may overtake it by offering these talented intrapreneurial people enough space and comprehensive challenges. It is an historical fact that organizations continually lose their most innovative and enterprising people – they either become new competitors (entrepreneurs) or they improve the competitiveness of existing competitors. One of the conditions for future success is to ensure the recruitment, motivation and retention of intrapreneurs within the company.

As observed by the former chairman of ICI, Sir John Harvey-Jones,[4] 'organisations will have to adapt to the needs of the individual rather than expecting the individual to adapt to the needs of the organisation'. Otherwise, companies will lose their most promising intrapreneurial talent.

Such future success requires intrapreneurial thinking within the organization. It does not come solely from the expressed will of top management but from making the entire system support innovation. One way to achieve this is by giving managers the necessary autonomy to encourage them to take ownership of projects and, ultimately, secure their implementation.

SUCCESS IN IMPLEMENTING PROJECTS

Our discussions with graduates highlighted many reasons for success in implementing their projects. These included the necessity to:

- have a champion or mentor
- have support and encouragement
- secure approval and interest in the project from top management
- have freedom
- involve people who will be responsible for the early stages of production
- know when to 'pick up the project again' after delegation
- be empowered by choosing a project that will be good for the company, good for the market, and good for the individual
- take ownership of the project but relinquish or delegate when necessary
- brainstorm other people, build on their ideas, learn from their mistakes (it may be possible to forestall future problems with implementation)
- have sufficient funding
- have sufficient time and resources
- match the project to the company plan.

BARRIERS TO SUCCESS

Even those graduates who had totally implemented their project had been obliged to overcome some barriers at one stage or another. Some problems they solved themselves: to solve others, graduates had to depend upon the support of their mentor. Problems encountered, anticipated or overcome included:

- lack of a champion or mentor

- lack of support and encouragement
- insufficient funding
- lack of empowerment
- project not related to company plan
- non-ownership of project
- lack of resources
- unfavourable economic climate (external)
- lack of technical skills
- fear of change.

The two who failed to have their project implemented both cited an unfavourable economic climate as being the reason for non-implementation. It is interesting to note that this is an external factor that is often beyond an individual's control or ability to predict or overcome. A further observation was that one of the individuals who failed to implement their project did not describe himself as an intrapreneur.

THE NEXT STEP . . .?

Business schools traditionally teach their MBA students about finance, marketing, organizational structures, and team-building skills. The subjects ignored are leadership, determination, vision and innovation. These are the qualities of both the intrapreneur and the entrepreneur. We wondered if such individuals are born, not made.

From discussions with intrapreneurs we concluded that most people have the necessary skills to become an intrapreneur, but that these skills usually remain hidden until the right opportunity comes along. Leavitt wrote: 'it has become rather obvious that there is much more to modern management than what we are teaching in our business schools. Some significant and painful changes seem in order'.[5] Companies are recognizing the importance of intrapreneurship and entrepreneurship, innovation, vision and leadership. Business schools should adjust their training to catch up and keep pace with them.

To develop the talents mentioned above Leavitt further suggests that business schools should increase the diversity of their student body and recruit new faculty members from previously unconsidered disciplines (historians, philosophers, psychologists and humanists, for example).

CONCLUSIONS

- Companies must innovate or they will stagnate.
- Intrapreneurs are difficult people; they may be unpopular within an organization but are essential to the success/failure of an organization.

- Intrapreneurs act as catalysts.
- We felt that associates may be confusing intrapreneurs with creator/innovators. Although they had indeed implemented their projects and felt that they were intrapreneurial, only two had actually identified further projects they had been directly involved with.
- We concluded as a result of our research that, for successful implementation of a project, associates needed:
  - a favourable corporate environment/climate
  - a champion or mentor
  - approval and interest at a high level
  - freedom
  - empowerment
  - someone to take ownership of the project
  - a project relevant to the corporate plan
  - sufficient funding
  - sufficient time and resources
  - effective communication network.
- Further research should be undertaken to discover how long MBA graduates stay with their organizations after they have completed their MBA programme. Why did they leave? Where did they go to? Did they go on to more intrapreneuring? Did they become entrepreneurs?

REFERENCES

1 G. Pinchot, *Intrapreneuring*, Harper and Row, New York, 1985.
2 A. Gibb, 'The Enterprise Culture: Threat or Opportunity?' in *Management Decision*, vol. 26, no. 4, 1988, p. 10.
3 I. McDonald Wood, 'Corporate Entrepreneurship – A Blueprint for Action' in *Management Decision*, vol. 26, no. 4, 1988, p. 14.
4 J. Harvey-Jones, *Making It Happen. Reflections on Leadership*, Collins, 1988.
5 H. Leavitt, *California Management Review*, Spring 1988.

FURTHER READING

Atkinson, S. and Wills, G., 'Entrepreneurs: A Blueprint for Action' in *Management Decision*, vol. 26, no. 4, 1990.
Howard, K. and Peters, J., 'Managing Management Research' in *Management Decision*, vol. 28, no. 5, 1990.
Howard, K. and Sharp, J.A., *The Management of a Student Research Project*, Gower, Aldershot, 1983.
Peters, J. (ed.), *Action for Implementation*, 2nd ed., IMC Putting Learning into Action Research, MCB University Press, Bradford, 1990.

33 Action Learning and Action Research in Management Education and Development*

Faith Howell

The relationship between theory and practice in management education and development through Action Learning is explored in this chapter.

The conclusions from this research illustrate that managers can successfully operationalize Action Learning and action research methodologies to bring about organizational, professional and personal development, and they provide further confirmation and justification for the use of Action Learning and action research in senior management development and organization development in the private and public sectors.

This chapter is drawn from a published report[1] commissioned by the International Management Centres (IMC), an independent Action Learning-based business school, and based on interviews with its graduates, clients and faculty over the period 1987–92. One of the main findings of this report was that all parties participating in the research highly valued Action Learning and action research as an appropriate and effective approach to management education and organizational development.

Zuber-Skerritt[2] has cited recent Australian research[3–6] to argue that management development for the future needs to be process-oriented, rather than merely content-oriented, and that Action Learning is an appropriate method for developing process managers for the year 2000. This research has found that much of our current management development technology is obsolete and inadequate for today's organizations, and that managers of today and the future need to develop skills and competences which will enable them to solve new problems, to anticipate change, to adjust rapidly to change, and to manage the process of their employees' learning.

Numerous definitions have been provided for Action Learning and action

*Originally published in *The Learning Organization*, vol. 1, no. 2, 1994. © MCP University Press 0969-6474.

research in an extensive literature both in Australia and overseas (e.g.[7-13]). There are also many documented case studies showing the successful application of these theories (e.g.[14-16]). Such is the adaptability of these methodologies across professional disciplines that individuals tend to create their own definitions grounded in their own professional practice.

Morgan[17] provides the following general definition of Action Learning as an approach to organizational change and development (p. 9):

> Action learning is both a concept and a form of action which aims to enhance the capacities of people in everyday situations to investigate, understand and, if they wish, to change those situations in an ongoing fashion, with a minimum of external help. Action learning is concerned with empowering people in the sense that they become critically conscious of their values, assumptions, actions, interdependences, rights, and prerogatives so that they can act in a substantially rational way as *active* partners in producing their reality.

McTaggart,[18] offers a concise definition for the action research process as follows (p. 54):

> Action research involves participants in planning action (on the basis of reflection); in implementing these plans in their own action; in observing systematically this process; and in evaluating their actions in the light of evidence as a basis for further planning and action and so on through a self-reflective spiral.

The present chapter uses the IMC Action Learning MBA programme as a case study to illuminate Action Learning and action research as they relate to management by presenting images and impressions from senior managers and academics who have been directly involved in these programmes. It relates the findings to the literature on Adult Learning, self-directed learning, experiential learning and critical thinking and concludes with a discussion of the implications for traditional management education and development programmes.

BACKGROUND

The IMC was established in England in 1982 as a multinational business school conducting Action Learning MBA (Master of Business Administration) and other qualification programmes in several countries. This case study focuses only on the IMC Brisbane MBA programmes.

According to the IMC *Conspectus*,[19] the entry requirements for the Action Learning MBA include the provision that the candidate must have at least four years' experience in a professional position and must normally be working in a managerial position. The IMC MBA is achieved by acquiring 100 credit points and it is undertaken in two parts, each of nine months' duration. The programme begins with a start-up residential session of four days when associates (the participants in the programme) meet fellow Action Learning set (group) members and get to know the precise structure of the programme. During the following nine months, the five core concept modules of part one are undertaken, each module requiring three full days (or six evenings) of tutor-led activity (a total of 15 days or 30 evenings). The core concept modules include: human resource management, marketing, operations, finance, and information management. At the end of each module associates are required to write a paper, the written action case (WAC). The purpose of this paper is to test out the theory on a real case of importance to the associate and his/her organization.

Three residential skill-building weekend sessions are interspersed throughout the nine months that concentrate on reading, presentation skills, time management, team management and communication, project writing and action research methods. A further two assignments must be submitted during this first nine-month period and these are: the written analysis of business intelligence and information systems (WABIIS) and the written analysis of interface relationships (WAIR) between departments. The WABIIS assignment requires associates to assess and make recommendations on the business intelligence and information systems used within their organizations. The WAIR project draws on the associate's role as a manager, analysing the way in which other functions or systems within the organization interface with the associate's own responsibilities.

During part two (the second nine months) of the programme associates strategically apply the concepts presented in part one to their own organizations undertaking a strategic review of policy and interrelationships, the written analysis of all corporate integration relationships (WACIR) of all functions assignment. They complete a literature review and research for their master's projects, and write up their master's dissertation. An evaluation of personal learning, the evaluative assessment of managerial learning (EAML) project, is the last submission before graduation. During these nine months, three residential weekend sessions are convened to discuss strategic policy and the ongoing preparation and progress of the dissertations.

Associates in the IMC Action Learning MBA programme come with a range of experiences and it is the process, not the content, of the programme which is the greater determinant of their subsequent learning experiences and changed behaviours. Associates become involved in the critical questioning of their own beliefs, values, assumptions and professional practice as well as the critical questioning of others. Consequently they are challenged into moving from the status quo to looking at new and improved ways of doing things.

Associates form an Action Learning set which is assisted by facilitators, and tutorial input is provided as needed. All associates have a real organizational problem to solve, usually of high priority to their organization. IMC programmes require that each associate has a sponsor from their own organization who supports their project and who can provide access to the resources, the contacts and whatever else is needed to see the project to its successful completion. The sponsor agrees to make a commitment to helping the associate complete his or her project by offering advice and support and by 'opening doors' within the organization for data gathering.

All learning in sets for the MBA is facilitated by the set adviser, the tutors and the sponsors. The primary focus for learning, however, is shared set experiences, discussion and action by the associates themselves. All internal assessment is monitored externally by external moderators (senior academics).

The action research component of the programme emerges as the associates take the first step towards a solution to their business problems. On the basis of collaborative discussion with all the project stakeholders, and after sharing ideas with the Action Learning set, an action plan is prepared and the first action research cycle begins. The cycle provides the framework for monitoring, reflecting on, discussing, evaluating and revising the plan as preparation for the next action step, and so on. This systematic and rigorous approach to problem solving using continuous short-term improvement cycles leads to improved professional practice and ensures that plans are always flexible and responsive to change. Futhermore, the process of reflecting on the action research cycles, applied to a particular problem, gives the basis for creating new management theories to explain complex problems for the benefit of future management practice.

RESEARCH OBJECTIVES AND METHODOLOGY

This case study is based on data gathered over a period of nine months from IMC stakeholders associated with the IMC Brisbane Action Learning MBA programmes and from the external researcher observing and participating in numerous IMC activities.

In keeping with the philosophies underpinning the IMC programmes, participatory action research has been used as the methodological framework for this evaluative study (e.g.[13,20-22]). The findings are based on a series of semi-structured, open-ended interviews conducted with the clients, graduates and faculty who were associated with the first three Action Learning MBA programmes conducted by the IMC in Brisbane during the period 1987–92.

Graduates were provided with a broad interview framework which consisted of a series of headings relating to their own academic and professional experience, the positives and negatives of the IMC MBA, the set, project implementation and any other points they may have wished to discuss in the interview. Clients were contacted by letter requesting a brief interview to discuss the following questions:

1. To what extent has your organization been involved in the IMC MBA or other IMC degree programmes?
2. How effective have these IMC programmes been for:

- the professional development of the managers who participated; and
- facilitating improvements in the management of your organization? (Please give examples.)

External moderators, tutors and set advisers were also contacted by letter asking for an interview to discuss two questions:

1. What has been your involvement as an external moderator/tutor/set adviser for the IMC?
2. What are your thoughts on the standard of IMC academic programmes and the standard reached by associates? How do they compare with university programmes and outcomes?

Participants in this research were assured of the complete confidentiality of all information provided and they each received a summary of the interview for their confirmation or amendment.

In this study, a total of 32 people were involved in interviews and questionnaire surveys, i.e. 17 graduates, seven clients, four external moderators, three tutors and one set adviser associated with Brisbane MBA sets nos 1, 2 and 3. Table 33.1 gives the response rates for the graduates involved in this in-depth case study. The response rates for both the seven clients and the eight faculty who were contacted for interviews was 100 per cent in each case.

Programme	Commencement	Number of graduates	Number of responses	Percentage rate
Brisbane MBA no. 1	March 1988	6	4	67
Brisbane MBA no. 2	July 1989	7	7	100
Brisbane MBA no. 3	July 1990	7	7	100

Table 33.1 Graduates of the IMC Brisbane MBA programmes 1987–92

FINDINGS

One conclusion from this survey is that Action Learning programmes appeal to experienced senior managers because these programmes are work-related, they demand accountability and they provide tangible organizational benefits. The projects encourage associates to go beyond recommendations to action and, in doing so, to extend themselves out of their 'comfort zone'. In taking action on a problem the associate consults, collaborates and networks with key stakeholders. Those stakeholders who might have previously been perceived as obstacles (e.g. the difficult bosses, the unreceptive colleagues, the sceptical subordinates, the critical clients) suddenly hold the keys to successful project completion.

One graduate summed up this view with the following comment:

- 'The discipline of having to do written action cases on a live topic was very fruitful for my organization because I was able to pick out the things that I worked on in consultation with my client who also happened to be my boss. We were able to pick up some quite worthwhile topics. One in particular realised A$100,000 worth of savings for the organization. I may have done this anyway, but the discipline, the rigour of having to go through the process in a structured way forced me to have a look at something that had been bugging me for a while. So the least that happened was that it was brought forward on the agenda.'

Implicit in this manager's success in generating a return on investment from his participation in the Action Learning programme is the support of his sponsor. This study has revealed that this support is critical to project success. Five of the 17 graduates interviewed had minimal impact on their sponsoring organization because of inadequate support. Most of these graduates have subsequently been successful in other organizations. One high-ranking sponsor made the following statement:

- 'My view, generally, is that a lot of education, especially management education is just wasted money. In particular, educating bodies have got a lot to answer for. There is not enough linkage between requiring people to improve their work performance as a result of spending A$X,000 on training . . . 99 times out of 100 there is no change in performance. Action Learning at least gives employers some confidence that they are getting something in return. Action Learning is a good idea if there is a clear commitment from the three parties involved [i.e. education provider, client and associate] as to what is going to be delivered.'

Another conclusion from this case study is that participants in the IMC MBA have been receptive to Action Learning as a preferred learning style. These managers were brought together from various business and academic backgrounds for the Action Learning programmes. In one of the sets evaluated in this study, managers with master's, and even doctoral, degrees were combined with managers with no tertiary qualifications but with many years of experience at senior managerial levels. These set members found that each had something to contribute, in supportive and constructively critical rather than competitive group meetings and tutorials. The emphasis was on using one another's experiences as a resource rather than relying chiefly on tutors to provide the expert input.

One graduate with prior degrees from more than one traditional university expressed his surprise to find that fellow associates in his set reached the same end point in completing this course, given that some had prior qualifications at junior high school level only. However, being hands-on-managers with many years of experience, these associates were qualified in a practical sense to talk about work-related problems and they shared an enthusiasm to research and discuss the relevant theories to improve their own practice and to implement organizational change.

As adult learners, these managers appreciated the flexible learning environment and the opportunities for self-directing their learning which Action Learning allows. Many of these managers had rejected traditional learning approaches at this stage in their career, based on their past experiences with undergraduate and postgraduate university programmes. There was a strong dissatisfaction with attending lectures and studying prescribed subjects. This reasoning is illustrated by the following comment:

- 'I never liked group work during my tertiary study. The group work we have here is really a meeting of sharing. Talking about work-related projects is interesting rather than group work talking "academic jargon". The by-product is meeting the academic requirements of the course. The course is structured so that associates have control over what they are doing.'

The literature on adult learning (e.g.[23-27]), self-directed learning (e.g.[28, 29]), experiential learning (e.g.[30-34]) and critical thinking (e.g.[35]) can be related to Action Learning and can provide some theoretical explanations and support for the popularity of Action Learning among these managers. For instance, there are parallels between the andragogical model for adult learning described by Knowles et al.[25] and Action Learning. The assumptions underpinning the andragogical model are, among other things, that the learner is self-directing, can make a valuable contribution from prior experience, and is motivated to learn in order to improve performance, self-esteem, recognition, quality of life, self-confidence, and self-actualization. Many of the comments from graduates of the IMC Action Learning programme support this view; for instance:

- 'I don't study to get a piece of paper – I study to get smarter.'
- 'I now feel reasonably qualified [in comparison] with people in other organizations. It has been a big confidence booster.'
- 'For me personally it has been a very useful programme. It meant a lot to me at 40 years of age and was appropriate to my position within the organization. A programme like that, regardless of its content, is also a very personal challenge.'
- 'Action Learning becomes a part of your individual habit and way of thinking. It affects your everyday behaviour at work and at home.'

The parallels between Action Learning and experiential learning provide another reason for the appeal of these programmes to these experienced managers. As suggested by the earlier quotes about the work-related nature of the programme, learning from experience is an easily accepted philosophy for these managers. The experiential learning cycle, associated with the work of Lewin[31] and Kolb,[33] involves observing and reflecting on concrete experience, formulating abstract concepts and generalizations, and testing the implications of these concepts in new situations. Similarly, the action research cycle of planning, acting, observing and reflecting places the emphasis on generating theories from action and experience, not vice-versa.

Furthermore, Brookfield[35] makes the link between learning from experience and critical thinking with the following statement:

> As a process, critical thinking is not purely passive. It involves alternating phases of analysis and action. This process of active inquiry combines reflective analysis with informed action. We perceive a discrepancy, question a given, or become aware of an assumption – and then we *act* on these intuitions. As our intuitions become confirmed, refuted, or (most likely) modified through action, we hone and refine our perceptions so that they become further refined, and so on. Critical thinking is a praxis of alternating analysis and action.

Critical enquiry and reflection are necessary skills for managing complex environments. Brookfield acknowledges that, given the uncertain environments in which managers work, learning should consist of critical enquiry and reflection rather than the acquisition of previously specified performance behaviours.

It is also true that the graduates have appreciated the opportunities for reflection and critical enquiry provided by the programme as shown by the following typical comments:

- [Using a medical analogy] 'a good diagnosis is often made by good history and good history is made by asking the right questions. The philosophy of Action Learning focuses on the need to ask the right questions to solve new problems.'
- 'The power of the programme is the focus on reflecting on what you do and what others do and enabling that interaction to influence the next set of actions that you do.'

Critical thinking occurs within the set as associates, facilitated by the set adviser, question one another's assumptions and viewpoints. Brookfield,[35] explains the strengths of this type of critical questioning as follows (p. 29):

> We hold up our behaviour for scrutiny by others, and in their interpretation of our actions we are given a reflection, a mirroring of our own actions from an unfamiliar psychological vantage point. This is how critical helpers function; they are mirrors who help us interpret and question our ideas and actions from a new viewpoint.

One IMC graduate explained his first reaction to this process:

- 'I can recall numerous discussions, not so much heated discussions, but criticisms; the early experience was that I didn't take the criticisms very well ... but after that they became the real learning.'

This reflective component of Action Learning programmes encourages the operationalization or transfer of learning to the work environment. Again, the literature (e.g.[36–38]) supports reflection as a method of improving professional practice. Keeping log books of conversations, events, new ideas and learning points builds up a discipline in following the learning cycle through to implementation. Transferring learnings to the work environment creates a multiplier effect. In many cases the graduates have been able to model Action Learning at their workplace. Typically this has been done with groups of staff or managers as part of a training and development programme. The emphasis has been on team building and collaborative problem solving.

Some graduates have used the Action Learning philosophy to improve client relationships. For instance, one manager set up a training programme to teach field officers to be 'facilitators' rather than 'experts' when dealing with clients. The clients had always perceived these field officers as being out of touch with their real problems. By developing groups of clients, as Action Learning communities, field officers were able to facilitate the sharing of expertise among these clients, thus empowering them to find the best solutions to their own problems.

Other graduates regarded the main multiplier effect of the course in monetary terms, both personally and for their organization. At the personal level, demonstrated positive results from Action Learning projects completed during the programme led to promotions or were catalysts in winning positions with new employers. One graduate claimed that he saved his current employer A$6 million in capital outlay and a previous employer A$1.6 million by establishing different approaches to managing these organizations. The shift in approach which contributed to these savings was a shift from subjective decision making to objectivity and a systems approach to problem solving.

CONCLUSIONS

On the basis of this study, I am convinced that the philosophies of Action Learning and action research hold the keys to the future for management education and development. Since managerial practices are work-based and grounded in day-to-day issues, management theories must reflect and be informed by practice. Action Learning and action research methodologies provide a framework for approaching complex business problems collaboratively, supportively and with an open mind so that fresh questions about these problems are encouraged to emerge. This approach to problem solving is of high value to organizations today and in the future because of the constant need to cope with rapid changes.

As illustrated by this case study, Action Learning and action research have become popular among managers and their sponsors from a variety of academic and business backgrounds because these programmes are work-related, results-based, group-focused and appropriate to the preferred learning styles of the managers. These managers and sponsors are valuable sources of information and resources for academics in that they are the links for collaboration between higher education and industry in the management field. The external moderators and tutors interviewed for this case study commented positively about the synergies between traditional MBA programmes and the IMC's innovative approach to management education and development. Overall, they have commented that the standard reached by the IMC Action Learning MBA graduates is at least equal to, and in some cases, superior to that reached by traditional MBA graduates.

My own conclusion is that the managers interviewed as part of this case study are keen to learn in order to stay ahead of the competition, both organizationally and personally, and are prepared to learn mainly what is relevant to achieving these goals. They are highly motivated and committed to focusing on priority business problems and they seek to optimize a return on investment from project implementation. They are pragmatic managers who, while recognizing the limits of their academic knowledge, are not convinced that studying prescribed management subjects under traditional methods of instruction is appropriate to their needs. Action Learning and action research methodologies provide the potential for traditional academic institutions to integrate theory and practice better in their management programmes, thus improving their relevance to industry in a wider marketplace.

REFERENCES

1 O. Zuber-Skerritt and F. Howell, *Evaluation of MBA and Doctoral Programs Conducted by the International Management Centre, Pacific Region: A Report*, The Tertiary Education Institute, The University of Queensland, Brisbane, 1993.

2 O. Zuber-Skerritt, 'Management Development and Academic Staff Development through Action Learning and Action Research' in *Educational and Training Technology International*, vol. 27, no. 4, 1990, pp. 437–47.

3 D. Limerick, B. Cunnington and B. Trevor-Roberts, *Frontiers of Excellence*, Australian Institute of Management, Brisbane, 1984.

4 B. Cunnington, 'The Process of Educating and Developing Managers for the Year 2000' in *Journal of Management Development*, vol. 4, no. 5, 1985, pp. 566–79.

5 B. Cunnington and B. Trevor-Roberts, 'Developing Leaders for the Organisations of Tomorrow' in *Business Education*, vol. 7, no. 4, 1986, pp. 37–47.

6 D. Limerick and B. Cunnington, 'Management Development: The Fourth Blueprint' in *Journal of Management Development*, vol. 6, no. 1, 1987, pp. 54–67.

7 R.W. Revans, *The Origins and Growth of Action Learning*, Chartwell-Bratt, Bromley, 1982.

8 S. Kemmis (ed.), *The Action Research Reader*, 3rd substantially revised ed., Deakin University Press, Victoria, 1988.

9 S. Kemmis and R. McTaggart, *The Action Research Planner*, 3rd substantially revised ed., Deakin University Press, Victoria, 1988.

10 S.N. Oja and L. Smulyan, *Collaborative Action Research: A Developmental Approach*, Falmer Press, London, 1989.

11 O. Zuber-Skerritt (ed.), *Action Learning for Improved Performance*, Action Learning, Action Research and Process Management Association, ÆBIS Publishing, Brisbane, Queensland, 1991.

12 O. Zuber-Skerritt, *Action Research for Change and Development*, Avebury, Aldershot, 1991.

13 O. Zuber-Skerritt, *Professional Development in Higher Education: A Theoretical Framework for Action Research*, Kogan Page, London, 1992.

14 C.S. Bruce and A.L. Russell (eds), *Transforming Tomorrow Today: Proceedings of the Second*

World Congress on Action Learning, Action Learning, Action Research and Process Management Association Incorporated, Brisbane, 1992.

15 O. Zuber-Skerritt, *Action Research in Higher Education – Examples and Reflections*, Kogan Page, London, 1992.

16 T. Carr and O. Zuber-Skerritt (eds), *Working Together for Quality Management: Action Research in Management and Education*, The Tertiary Education Institute, The University of Queensland, Brisbane, 1993.

17 G. Morgan, 'Action Learning: A Holographic Metaphor for Guiding Social Change' in *Human Relations*, vol. 37, no. 1, 1983, pp. 1–28.

18 R. McTaggart, 'Reductionism and Action Research: Technology versus Convivial Forms of Life' in C.S. Bruce and A.L. Russell (eds), *Transforming Tomorrow Today: Proceedings of the Second World Congress on Action Learning*, Action Learning, Action Research and Process Management Association Incorporated, Brisbane, 1992, pp. 47–61.

19 International Management Centres (IMC), *Conspectus 1991–1993*, IMC, Buckingham, 1991.

20 M. Elden, 'Sharing the Research Work: Participative Research and Its Role Demands' in P. Reason and J. Rowan (eds), *Human Inquiry: A Sourcebook of New Paradigm Research*, John Wiley, Chichester, 1981.

21 P. Reason and J. Rowan (eds), *Human Inquiry: A Sourcebook of New Paradigm Research*, John Wiley, Chichester, 1981.

22 W.F. Whyte, D.J. Greenwood and P. Lazes, 'Participatory Action Research' in *American Behavioral Scientist*, vol. 32, no. 5, 1989, pp. 513–51.

23 P. Jarvis *Adult and Continuing Education: Theory and Practice*, Croom Helm, London, 1983.

24 P. Jarvis, *The Sociology of Adult and Continuing Education in the Workplace*, Croom Helm, London, 1985.

25 M. Knowles and associates, *Andragogy in Action: Applying Modern Principles of Adult Learning*, Jossey-Bass, San Francisco, CA, 1984.

26 S.D. Brookfield (ed.), *Training Educators of Adults: The Theory and Practice of Graduate Adult Education*, Routledge, London, 1988.

27 V.J. Marsick and K.E. Watkins, *Informal and Incidental Learning in the Workplace*, Routledge, London, 1990.

28 S.D. Brookfield (ed.), *Self-directed Learning: From Theory to Practice*, Jossey-Bass, San Francisco, CA, 1985.

29 P.C. Candy, *Self-direction for Lifelong Learning*, Jossey-Bass, San Francisco, CA, 1991.

30 J. Dewey, *Experience & Education*, Collier-Macmillan, New York, NY, 1938.

31 K. Lewin, 'Group Decision and Social Change' in G.E. Swanson, T.M. Newcomb and E.L. Hartley (eds), *Readings in Social Psychology*, Henry Holt, New York, NY, 1952, pp. 458–73.

32 J. Piaget, 'The Role of Action in the Development of Thinking' in W.F. Overton and J. McCarthy Gallagher (eds), *Knowledge and Development, Volume 1: Advances in Research and Theory*, Plenum Press, New York, NY, 1977, pp. 17–42.

33 D.A. Kolb, *Experiential Learning: Experience as a Source of Learning and Development*, Prentice Hall, Englewood Cliffs, NJ, 1984.

34 F. Marton, D. Hounsell and N. Entwistle (eds), *The Experience of Learning*, Scottish Academic Press, Edinburgh, 1984.

35 S.D. Brookfield, *Developing Critical Thinkers: Challenging Adults to Explore Alternative Ways of Thinking and Acting*, Jossey-Bass, San Francisco, CA, 1988.

36 D. Boud, R. Keogh and D. Walker (eds), *Reflection: Turning Experience into Learning*, Kogan Page, London, 1985.

37 D.A. Schon, *Educating the Reflective Practitioner*, Jossey-Bass, San Francisco, CA, 1987.

38 C. Bunning, 'The Reflective Practitioner: A Case Study' in *Journal of Management Development*, vol. 11, no. 1, 1992, pp. 25–38.

34 Rogue Learning on the Company Reservation

Tom Reeves

Action learning is subversive
- it values everyone
- it's democratic
- it stresses questioning
- it stresses listening
- it insists on actions
- it gives courage
- it encourages responsibility
- it examines everything.
Krystyna Weinstein[1]

Action Learning is unpredictable. People undertake a challenging problem or task in their work, and learn from the experience. But it cannot be known in advance quite what they will gain from their experience, nor exactly how, if at all, the organization will benefit from the project.

While undertaking their learning project, Action Learners are normally members of a small group of other Action Learners who support and encourage each other through the vicissitudes of their enquiries, action and learning. The discussions and reflection in these groups, or 'sets', can cause participants to question current ways of doing things. They can develop fundamentally new, perhaps highly critical, understandings of their organization and their place within it. As they grow in confidence – as tends to happen on Action Learning programmes – they seek outlets for their new-found capabilities and ideas.

Both from the point of view of an employer wanting to develop staff to perform a particular job and from that of an individual seeking to make him or herself more effective, Action Learning clearly has 'rogue' propensities. This has not, however, deterred many employers who regularly send their managers and other staff on Action Learning programmes, nor staff from going on them.

Indeed, within limits, the 'rogue' elements of Action Learning are usually seen as something to be welcomed. It is valuable to have middle and junior managers seeking greater responsibility or autonomy, who are not afraid to challenge the status quo, and who are willing to initiate change from their level in the organization. In fact, these are all ingredients of what is coming to be known as the 'learning organization'.

CORPORATE DEVELOPMENT

Action Learning combines profound and lasting individual learning with the organizational benefit of a useful project. But can it do more than this? Can Action Learning be made to yield corporate benefits that go beyond developing the capabilities of individuals with projects undertaken as a spin-off? Can Action Learning programmes be used to develop an organization as a whole, using the individual learning as a platform for developing a way of operating or a culture that promotes wider 'corporate learning'? These are the kinds of questions that led to the present research.

Using the metaphor of the title of this chapter can Action Learning's rogue propensities be tamed and harnessed to corporate goals? Can the corporate good be served by allowing Action Learners freely to roam the 'company reservation'?

Before addressing these questions, however, it is first necessary to give some background to this research and the companies in which it was conducted.

MCB UP AND IMC

MCB University Press is in the business of publishing academic journals and has grown from small beginnings to being possibly the largest management journal publisher in the world. It is nevertheless only a smallish company employing about 190 staff.

MCB University Press has invested considerable sums over many years in 'Action Learning' programmes offered by its sister company, International Management Centres. Managerial, professional and administrative staff have all taken these programmes, obtaining qualifications such as an MBA, Diploma or Bachelor's degree. MCB UP has also regularly mounted non-qualificatory management development programmes based on Action Learning. Both types of programme have had the intention of developing the company's business as well as its staff.[2]

Professor Gordon Wills, Principal of IMC and Chief Executive of MCB University Press, in a book about these and other IMC programmes, has suggested that using Action Learning to develop in-house experts who can then develop others can turn a company into a form of school.[3] He has also reviewed the possibility that MCB University Press might have developed into a 'learning organization'.[4] MCB UP has repeatedly adopted the recommendations of individuals and groups who have undertaken Action Learning projects, with numerous resulting changes in MCB UP's policies and operating procedures.

But whether or not MCB UP measures up to some ideal type of 'learning organization' is primarily of academic interest. The more practical issue is whether MCB UP could be harnessing individual or group Action Learning to corporate ends more effectively. What kinds of corporate contribution are feasible and how can they best be achieved?

These are questions of concern to any company investing heavily in staff education and development. Developing people's capability may have only marginal effects on corporate performance. Are there more effective ways in which individual development can be made to contribute to corporate development?

It was these kinds of concerns that prompted Gordon Wills to ask the author, who had been invited to be IMC's 1995 Revans Professor, to undertake a comparative analysis of MCB University Press and another company that had also made extensive use of IMC's Action Learning programmes. The task of the Revans Professor is to carry out a piece of research that will advance the practice of Action Learning. It is intended that the conclusions drawn from this comparative analysis should do this.

SEAGRAM

The company chosen for the purposes of comparison was the international drinks company, Seagram, which over the years has put many of its staff through the IMC MBA programme, and had recently put a cohort of staff through IMC's BA Administration programme.

In the event, Seagram proved of less value as a basis for comparison with MCB UP than expected. Nevertheless, it afforded some useful parallels and contrasts, particularly in relation to the fulfilment and disappointment of the expectations of staff undertaking an Action Learning programme.

OBJECTIVES

The agreed purpose of the project was to explore how far it has proved possible in these two companies to enhance 'organizational learning' through the use of individual Action Learning. Three aims were specified:

- provide IMC and its client organizations with an understanding of the process of moving from individual learning to corporate development and how this might be extended
- identify good practice in arrangements for in-house learning that could be used by IMC and elsewhere
- explore how managerial attitudes and thinking might be conditioned by working in a learning culture.

388

METHOD OF RESEARCH

Individual interviews were carried out during the summer of 1995 with senior managers in each company and group discussions were held with managers and others who had undertaken, or were currently undertaking, an Action Learning programme.

These interviews and discussions were relatively unstructured, in order to allow relevant topics that emerged to be discussed. They did, however, focus broadly on the following:

- the outcome of the Action Learning for the individual and for the company
- whether Action Learning by others was affecting them
- views on the organization, its culture and effectiveness
- opportunities for taking initiative, contributing ideas, feeding back experience, sharing learning and getting one's recommendations heeded.

Within MCB UP, four of the directors were interviewed and five group discussions held with representatives from a current MBA set, a SEMAP (senior management programme) set, a bachelor's degree set, and those who had earlier completed an MBA or bachelor degree. Altogether just over 30 people were interviewed or participated in a group discussion.

Within Seagram, the president of the division that had used IMC's Action Learning programmes and its human resources manager were interviewed, and a group discussion held with five administrative staff who had recently completed a bachelor degree. It had been hoped also to interview some managers who had earlier completed an MBA. However, many of these have since left the company, while others are posted abroad. The few it might have been feasible to interview declined.

KEY FINDINGS

A recurrent theme of the research was the apparent tension within MCB UP between Action Learning's encouragement to expand the scope of people's thinking and activities and what was believed to be impermissible behaviour within the company. Informants – at all levels – talked about, on the one hand, the autonomy provided by the 'Action Learning culture', and, on the other, perceived 'bounds' to enquiry and action. There were of course other issues raised and these will be discussed, but the reconciliation of these conflicting messages was dominant. It is this tension that the title of this chapter attempts to encapsulate in its metaphors of rogue learning and a company reservation – a space within which people had a licence to apply Action Learning principles.

It needs at once to be stressed that virtually everyone interviewed seemed to be quite adept at handling the tension. Despite new aspirations and new capabilities, they had accommodated their evolving selves to the constraints, which were largely accepted as an inescapable aspect of working in an organization. They were far from being 'rogue learners'. They well understood that to survive and be successful, their new-found capabilities and aspirations had to be contained within the company reservation. 'Rogue learning' was thus domesticated.

ACTION LEARNING CULTURE

A second key finding was that within MCB a climate or culture had evolved in which many of the key aspects of Action Learning – its emphasis on questioning and enquiry, on projects and change, on openness of discussion and debating decisions on the basis of evidence – could be safely manifested, indeed were encouraged. Within its bounds – and even in the most liberal of organizations there inevitably are bounds – the company reservation was a place where one could overtly practise an 'Action Learning style'. One could be open, ask potentially awkward questions, expect collaboration, criticize present ways of doing things, put forward ideas for change, be allowed to make mistakes, and indeed exercise a considerable degree of autonomy. Action Learning principles and practices pervaded MCB UP and had shaped the corporate way of doing things. The following quotations give a flavour of the nature of this culture.

MCB UP'S Action Learning Culture

- 'Action Learning culture is represented all the way through the company – in meetings, relationships, etc. It's actively encouraged. In one's day-to-day job Action Learning happens. You're left to discover the answers, look at alternative ways of tackling problems. It slows the process but you get a richer outcome.'
- 'There's a language, jargon, acronyms. It (the learning culture) nibbles away. Not leaps and bounds. The company's financial stability, the certainty of profit, gives confidence to experiment. We're cash rich – at least richer than most. Action Learning prevents complacency. It's helping us to stay ahead of the field. There's also the academic influence – papers are thorough, nothing is overlooked.'
- 'Board members involve people at bottom level in the thinking process behind projects. It's not unusual to get faxes from a director. But several people can be involved without co-ordination. However it seems to work. There are different agendas which are not always pulled together. But if something was felt to be going off the rails it would be pulled together by academic debate. Eventually we would reach consensus.'
- 'If you have a problem you go and seek a solution – every day.'
- 'You get such learning in the company – you have to find out. You move

around. You survive by finding out. There are few hostile barriers. People are not threatened by you asking.'

- 'The owners will back you if they feel you are right. We pull together in a logical way. And there's always an eye on the bottom line.'
- 'Projects wouldn't be done without SEMAP (compulsory Action Learning programme for managers). It takes you into other areas. You wouldn't go into other departments otherwise and ask them why or how they do things . . . You can't do anything on your own in this company.'
- 'The Action Learning culture is "Ask the right questions and act on the results". The majority of people feel they can ask questions and have a go.'
- 'The founders believed in Action Learning and involved every one in discussions.'
- 'In MCB you're not given the answers – you're encouraged to address the issues.'
- 'You ask "How do you think it should be done?"'
- 'Management is not usually prescriptive.'
- 'You're given rope – but you're caught before you drop.'
- 'You agree outputs and the budget. Action Learning helps people to be comfortable with this.'
- 'The Action Learning culture is so strong, you sink or swim. There's little allowance for people just getting on with their job and not going on any of the programmes. There's no stigma if you don't, but you're ignored. Squeezed out. At a certain level it's expected that you'll do an Action Learning programme. Someone who is now senior avoided the MBA for several years. Could he have continued to refuse?'

MOTIVES FOR INTRODUCING ACTION LEARNING

The degree of corporate impact of Action Learning in the two companies was largely determined by each company's motives for using it, and the extent to which top management encouraged its manifestations. There was little evidence of Action Learners acting as a force for corporate change other than within parameters set by top management.

In Seagram, it had never been intended that Action Learning should be a vehicle for corporate, as opposed to individual, development. The divisional president, a PhD holder, has had a lifelong interest in continuing education. IMC's route to educational qualifications for employed staff via Action Learning filled, as he saw it, an individual development need. In an article describing an earlier programme he had sponsored in the International Distillers and Vintners Company, the Action Learners were said to have had a catalytic effect on others in the company.[5] But then, as now, the benefits to the company were seen primarily in traditional terms: having more competent, knowledgeable and effective staff, plus of course having actionable recommendations. Thus, while the

Action Learning projects could be expected to result in operational improvements, the rationale for using Action Learning was essentially one of promoting individual rather than corporate development. This intention was reflected in the benefits cited by Seagram informants reported below. The focus of discussion was exclusively on the benefits to themselves as individuals, and the difficulties encountered in capitalizing adequately on these benefits within the Seagram structure.

A further factor inhibiting a wider corporate impact in the case of Seagram may have been the dispersal of the Action Learners throughout the company; there appeared never to have been a significant number of them in any one place at any one time.

Cited Benefits of Action Learning in Seagram

- 'The BA (Bachelor's Administration degree) has given me a much broader outlook. It has changed me as a person.'
- 'The degree gives you a better, more effective attitude. But not a lot more specific benefit.'
- 'The projects built our skills. They were relevant at the time, but we've since moved on – you need to know when to leave something. Although the project wasn't personally relevant, it enabled me to use skills I learned doing it – assemble facts, market research. I'm still putting them into practice ...'
- 'I spent hours! I did something one wouldn't otherwise have done. I wouldn't have had the time without being made to do it. I chose my project out of interest, and it became even more relevant.'
- 'A traditional degree feeds you with knowledge. This degree was not so much about the quantity of knowledge, but attitudinal – how you worked, and how to make things work in your favour.'
- 'The benefit for me was learning how to learn. How to glean information.'
- 'You can go away and apply Action Learning. It's "common sense", an attitude. This degree gave me a good attitude. I'm not frightened to ask questions. I'm able to show ambition, commitment, prove myself, able to fight – a big spin off.'
- 'The course was great for my credibility in the company.'

FORCE FOR CHANGE

MCB UP, on the other hand, did intend its use of Action Learning to have a corporate as well as an individual impact. This has undoubtedly been achieved: Action Learning has been used in a way that has been profound and far-reaching. Virtually all managers and administrative staff have been through an Action Learning programme of some kind, if not one leading to an IMC qualification, e.g. an MBA, then almost certainly one of MCB UP's regular management development programmes which are compulsory for certain managerial grades.

This extensive exposure to Action Learning processes and principles creates the possibility that the Action Learners themselves might have become an independent force for corporate change. There was, however, little evidence of this having happened. The corporate impact of Action Learning would appear to have resulted almost entirely from top management's intentions for it.

The motives for making use of Action Learning in MCB UP were complex. In large part its use originated in the fact that the company's founders were academic management specialists who were already convinced of the advantages of Action Learning as a means of developing managers. Founding a company offered an opportunity to put theories in which they believed into practice, and indeed it was said they felt a moral commitment to do so.

However, the rationale for the use of Action Learning in MCB UP is far broader than this. As stated by one of the directors, the aims of Action Learning for MCB UP were, and are:

- to build a business – with more capable people
- to grow from within, promoting internal people wherever possible
- to increase turnover
- to control costs
- to avoid the use of external consultants – through the Action Learning projects MCB UP's own people make the recommendations for change
- last, but far from least, to promote collaborative networking within the company.

There were several indications that these objectives have been realized. The company has grown and been financially successful. The number of projects which have had their recommendations adopted demonstrate the company's commitment to innovation in marketing and operations, and generally to sustaining continuous improvement. The Action Learning projects provide the occasion for these changes, while the repeated Action Learning programmes sustain the impetus. It is difficult to see how so much innovation could be achieved by other means.

MCB UP's owners have had sufficient confidence in staff capabilities to have pursued a policy of promotion from within. Several staff have risen through the ranks to director level – all of them had been through at least one Action Learning programme, most through several; and they were willing to attribute their advancement at least in part to the way their Action Learning experiences had enhanced their capabilities. Other staff who had been through the Action Learning process similarly testified to their enhanced capability, as can be seen from the following quotations. Recurrent themes were growth in confidence, greater knowledge about the company and its business, an ability to tackle problems, the acquisition of a new outlook and new ways of going about work tasks. Unlike Seagram, there was a strong emphasis in the discussions on how new capabilities could be put to use within MCB UP.

Cited Benefits of Action Learning in MCB UP

- 'Action Learning gives you an approach to problems – a methodology that will stand you in good stead . . . It opened my mind to new possibilities, e.g. using ANBAR. We take this access for granted. We have all the learning resources we need, e.g. Bradford Management Centre. It sets you up for working life.'
- 'I'm more confident. Better able to cope when negotiating outside the company.'
- 'Action Learning builds a psychological contract with MCB – you want to do this.'
- 'It exposes you to different people in the company; bonds you to people you wouldn't normally be exposed to.'
- 'It's good from a personal point of view. It develops you. Brings you out. It's a massive undertaking. It was a great sense of satisfaction to graduate – I never imagined. The social side – the weekends – were very good. We learned to work together.'

Improves knowledge of company and other departments

There were numerous comments on this theme:

- 'I've made more sense of links about the place.'
- 'You get to know what problems are being tackled.'
- 'I know what are the issues of importance.'
- 'When I started I didn't know anything outside my department. I wouldn't have approached people outside my department.'

Specifically gained from project

- different ways of working
- different ways of research
- knowledge about different subjects
- sense of achievement

Other comments

- 'I gained from the group discussions.'
- 'It's nice to have responsibility.'
- 'It prevents complacency.'
- 'We're staying ahead of the field.'
- 'There's all-level involvement.'
- 'You can implement things.'
- 'The company gets "free" consultancy on top of your normal work.'
- 'The learning from course assignments enabled me to do my job better.'
- 'I am seen in a different light.'

BOUNDARIES

A corporate culture has developed in MCB UP which was repeatedly referred to as the company's 'Action Learning culture'. The nature of this culture has already been indicated (see p. 390); it included problem-solving based on enquiry, collaboration across company networks, openness in sharing information, and debating decisions around evidence. The Action Learning culture is both an ethos and a way of doing things. It straddles all levels, and is actively supported by top management, who appear conscientiously to strive, in accordance with the spirit of Action Learning, to be receptive to ideas for change. Using the metaphors of the title again, they have created a relatively safe reservation on which Action Learners can roam and apply their Action Learning principles.

But, as noted earlier, the reservation has its boundaries. Some of these related to the owners' sense of prerogative regarding key business decisions. Several informants, in this context, said there was a power culture, reflecting the domination of the owners. But some boundaries, according to certain informants sensitive to the human factor, were believed to derive from owners' and top managers' natural resistance to criticism and challenge – which several felt good Action Learners should know how to cope with. The boundaries of the 'reservation' were not always clear, indeed were sometimes only surmised, as the following comments show.

The correctness of the informants' perceptions could no doubt be questioned. The point, however, is that within the context of an 'Action Learning culture' some people felt it was inappropriate, indeed risky, to speak their mind too openly or attempt to do certain things.

The Sense of Barriers and Boundaries in MCB UP

- 'There *are* barriers. They need to be removed ... But you can speak out here. I wouldn't want to work elsewhere. The scale of the problem compared with other firms is miniscule.'
- 'I'm more comfortable myself knowing the bounds. We're told there are no bounds. But they are there – invisible. Sometimes you make a decision, but you're uncertain whether you're transgressing a senior manager's view.'
- 'It's not OK to step on toes, to uncover things that are not OK. It's difficult to challenge established practice ...'

This group then debated the political consequences of making 'untoward' criticisms, concluding:

- 'It can damage your career if you step on too many toes.'
- 'The resistances to change (of senior managers) are not dissipated by going through Action Learning processes. They're not sitting there with a belief

that because it's Action Learning it's OK. It affects them personally. It questions their judgement.'

- 'They tell you to be open, but you've got to recognize that you're dealing with people.'

- 'There are few restrictions for most people. There is a band of what might be called "senior" managers. That's an ambiguous term. It includes some junior managers who are verging on being middle managers. It's not clear where the line of influence is drawn.'

- 'In areas where change is not encouraged, not accepted, it's frustrating.'

- 'I certainly feel I have questioned too much . . . I want to do different things and get frustrated because I can't. I want to question things. If you don't get satisfaction then there's frustration. It can build up to such an extent you ask is it worth doing?'

- '(In carrying out our projects) we did stir up some hornets' nests. You had to be careful what you asked. We got some cagey replies. But it was the only way to do it – not to mind if you trod on toes . . . If you're doing a project it implies that someone is not doing what they ought to be doing.'

Certain projects were said to be out of bounds

- 'The major processes of production and publishing tend to stay the same, with the structure changing around them. You can experiment in marketing as long as you don't touch the core. We don't tamper with the core of the business. The business formula we've got works.'

- 'You can try to take a project too far. It's easy to get involved in the politics and then out the door! No one was actually directly sacked from the course. But it added to someone's downfall.'

RECOMMENDATIONS SUBJECT TO APPROVAL

One boundary that is well-defined on the MCB UP reservation is the clear division within projects between recommendation and implementation. Reports and dissertations submitted for IMC qualifications require the 'student manager' to undertake and write up only the problem definition and investigation phase of the project, together with recommendations for action. Of course in very many cases recommendations are approved and implementation follows. But an account of the implementation phase does not have to form part of the dissertation, though IMC does encourage its graduates to submit such an account (the A+Enhancement) as a follow-up to its Action Learning project. This practice contrasts with many Action Learning programmes where the learning project cycle is expected to encompass implementation as well as problem investigation.

IMC's practice, aligned as it is with the academic research tradition, undoubtedly makes for sound MBA dissertations. But it also means, intended or otherwise, that senior management in MCB UP have a very direct control over whether or not an Action Learning project proceeds beyond the recommendation stage. A considerable number of projects within MCB UP have indeed proceeded to implementation and an impressive list of such projects has been published.[4] On the other hand some project recommendations have not gained acceptance and progenitors reported their frustration at this. Sometimes they did not even know, so they claimed, what had happened to their recommendation and why it had been rejected, if indeed it had been.

A possible consequence of stopping an Action Learning project at the point of making recommendations is that the political skills of advocating a cause or promoting as yet formally unauthorized changes are not adequately developed. Certainly there was no mention by MCB UP informants of this aspect of the project process. Indeed, submitting recommendations seemed in many cases to be somewhat of a passive process. Persons whose recommendations had not been accepted, or who did not know the outcome, did not seem to think that they should, or could, 'champion' their cause beyond the point of submitting their report and recommendation. They perceived, correctly or otherwise, this boundary of the reservation and were disinclined to transgress it. Possibly their recommendations were, from a corporate point of view, unacceptable; certainly they seemed to assume so, but without them pushing their cause they could not actually know this.

CULTIVATING A MANAGERIAL APPROACH

Action Learning was originally conceived as a means of *management* development, and in both Seagram and MCB UP it had that objective.

Terms such as 'greater confidence', 'new outlook', 'new ways of tackling problems', 'improved networking' were repeatedly used to describe the benefits of Action Learning. These are all valuable ingredients of managing. Some further ingredients that were being developed can be inferred from what people did not say.

There were no references to fashionable or simplistic solutions to managerial problems, for example to 're-engineer', or 'introduce total quality'. Problems were, so it appeared, all examined and dealt with in their own terms rather than approached with preconceived solutions. Technological innovations were being closely evaluated rather than advocated just for their newness. The inference to be drawn is that MCB UP managers had developed an open-minded, enquiring, problem-solving style, which can presumably be attributed to the Action Learning approach.

Also marked by their absence in the MCB UP discussions were 'barriers' or 'blockages' to authorized action. Once a recommendation had been approved, people seemed to be able to find wide support for its implementation. Talk was more of autonomy than of constraints. If there were barriers, they were seen as something for the project-holder to overcome rather than externalized and blamed on others, again presumably an outcome of the Action Learning approach.

DIFFICULTIES WITH ACTION LEARNING

Learning from the experience of undertaking a project is often far from easy. It can seriously add to pressures at work and interfere with home life. The process of learning by finding out can be frustrating as well as challenging.

It was not to be expected therefore that the Action Learners interviewed would universally endorse this method of learning. In fact the group discussions, both in Seagram and MCB UP, spontaneously took the form of debates about the value of the process and how worthwhile it was for them as individuals. It was often difficult to steer the discussion onto the wider corporate development issues with which the research was primarily concerned – perhaps not unnaturally since the approach of the programmes is based on the individual. The benefits to the company are in a wider, longer-term perspective. Individual sacrifices of time with family and the like are immediate and influence evaluation.

Not having an opportunity to use their new capabilities was an important issue for a number of people in both MCB UP and Seagram. The problems surrounding the acquisition of a suitable outlet were much debated, and considerable frustration was expressed when there was not one. In Seagram, programme participants said they had been clearly warned at the outset not to expect new responsibilities, though this had not lessened consequent disappointments. In MCB UP, expectations had been higher but the situation was also less clearcut. While hoped-for promotion might not always have materialized, the Action Learning culture often enabled new capabilities to be put into practice anyhow.

The mix of satisfactions and dissatisfactions with the Action Learning programmes are captured in four *vignettes* of individual responses (see appendix to this chapter). They have been compiled in each case by extracting the same person's comments throughout the course of a group discussion. While what was said at a particular point may have been triggered by someone else's previous comment, it can be seen that each of these persons was following a thread of their own while contributing to the group discussion. The common themes were the balance of benefit to the person's career compared with the sacrifice needed to gain the qualification, with perceived benefits to the company as secondary considerations.

DISCUSSION

One purpose of this research was to explore whether the use of Action Learning could lead to some kind of corporate development that was more than the personal development of the individual Action Learners.

Before conducting this research, the author had thought it possible, if a sufficient number of people in an organization were exposed to the questioning and challenging ethos of Action Learning, for these Action Learners to act as an independent force for corporate development and change. However, in the test case of MCB University Press, where all managers and many administrative staff have been through at least one programme, Action Learning did not appear to be having this kind of autonomous impact.

Action Learning had, however, had a profound impact on MCB UP's culture and style of operating. But, as far as could be ascertained, this was only in ways that reflected top management's intentions and objectives. There was no licence for Action Learners in MCB UP, nor in Seagram, to take unauthorized initiatives, and these tacit bounds appeared to be understood and accepted.

MCB UP, unlike Seagram, had deliberately sought to use Action Learning as a basis for establishing a particular corporate culture and style of operating. The kind of corporate development that might be expected to result from doing this would be for business and operational developments to be shaped continuingly by new projects, and for the company's management style to take on characteristics that reflected the ethos of Action Learning. A positive outcome would be for management style to become more open and collaborative, for new ideas and proposals for change to gain a more ready hearing from senior management, for them to be widely shared and discussed constructively, and for there to be a high degree of 'decision-making by debate' rather than by command. A less sanguine scenario, of course, could be a growth of dysfunctional activity, for example, defensiveness and secrecy in the face of questioning and enquiry, or the pursuit of divergent priorities and directions with consequent dissipation of effort.

MCB UP seems by and large to have achieved the positive benefits. It has established a companywide collaborative network, it has benefited from a considerable number of projects and, critically, it has created a corporate atmosphere in which experimentation and learning can flourish.

It would be fanciful to suggest, as most such suggestions probably are, that a 'learning organization' had been established. Organizations only learn in a metaphorical sense. The invariable reality is that it is individuals within an organization who learn. They may, in the course of their everyday work, have a catalytic effect or pass on their learning to others; or, when project recommendations are adopted, have their learning permanently incorporated in new ventures, practices or procedures. The point is that for individual learning to have a corporate benefit specific steps have to be taken to make it happen.

STEPS TO CORPORATE BENEFIT

Some steps are well known; for example, ensuring that the learning is relevant, that senior management supports its application, and providing suitable outlets for people's new capabilities.

On the basis of this research, a number of other steps to enable individual learning to lead to a corporate benefit are as follows:

- Create a companywide climate in which learning and its application is encouraged, expected and supported.

In MCB UP, this was manifested in the so-called 'Action Learning culture'. This culture had resulted in part from repeatedly running Action Learning programmes over many years, but also from, initially, the owners, and then others, manifestly practising the principles of Action Learning themselves. The success of this culture was evidenced by the complete absence of people saying they had to fight to get a hearing for their ideas or recommendations.

- Make induction into this culture a standard part of everyone's learning.

In Seagram, it was clearly understood that the Action Learning was essentially a personal benefit, preparing employees for relevant opportunities should they arise (which they did for some). But, otherwise, they were warned they would have to find ways of applying their learning within their original jobs.

In MCB UP, by contrast, in addition to the personal benefit, Action Learning participants were also inducted into a corporate culture. They were expected to operate in future on a wider front. This might mean doing one's own original job differently, though several stressed that this was not possible, but did mean one could participate in the general problem-tackling life of the company.

- Establish well-defined circumstances in which the outcomes of learning can be put into practice.

Action Learning enables this to happen through projects. The IMC brand of Action Learning, however, tends to separate the problem investigation from the implementation stage. This means that the presentation of their recommendations assumes considerable significance for the learners. It would be desirable, therefore, to have *all* project-holders present their findings and recommendations to relevant senior managers. This was something that was spontaneously commented upon in Seagram as having been done *comme il faut*, but appears to have suffered occasional lapses in MCB UP.

It is perhaps worth noting that the frequent recurrence of Action Learning programmes in MCB UP was leading to difficulties in finding suitable projects for everyone. There was talk of some projects being cosmetic.

- Strike an appropriate balance between compulsion and voluntarism in getting people to participate in learning programmes.

Middle managers always have to resolve the conflicting pressures of the routine aspects of their job and initiating improvements and change. This conflict was heightened in MCB UP by the pressures to engage in demanding Action Learning programmes. In MCB UP, some of these programmes were compulsory; for others participation was strongly expected. There was much debate in the group discussions about these pressures and their appropriateness. On the one hand, it seemed that an obsession with having been compelled to participate was getting in the way of learning for some people, and there may well have been some cosmetic demonstrations of learning; on the other hand, some people, looking back, said they would never have found the time to do the learning they now valued had they not been made to do so.

- Back-up action programmes with relevant formal teaching and open learning materials.

Back-up action happens routinely on programmes that lead to IMC qualifications, and IMC provides succinct, well produced Open Learning materials. Some comments were made, however, in both MCB UP and Seagram about the seeming superficiality of the formal teaching, both lectures and materials, compared with the project learning.

Does there in fact need to be such a clearcut division between project learning and 'content' learning? Might there not be scope for treating the development of 'content' for teaching as a project for Action Learning and involve a wide range of staff in this? (The author in fact volunteered to enquire whether the MCB BA group could visit another publisher to view their systems and practices. The request was in fact turned down, but could not the group be encouraged to do this kind of thing for itself?) The venture would add variety to the present diet of Action Learning projects, and might also enhance the credibility of IMC qualifications, questioned by some participants.

- Define the reservation.

A theme that has run through this report has been the idea that individual learners can most effectively turn their learning into a corporate benefit if they are operating on a 'reservation'. While the precepts delineated above are all relevant to the creation of such a reservation, there are a number of other ingredients that this research has shown go to make up an effective one:

– granting a clear licence for initiative and action (in the case of MCB UP, the repeated Action Learning programmes do this);

- acceptance of investigation, i.e. a lack of defensiveness towards enquiry and questioning;
- giving scope for taking on more responsibility without promotion or transfer (something that was difficult for the group interviewed in Seagram where there was no intent for Action Learning to drive corporate development);
- acceptance, indeed expectation, of innovation from all;
- allocating specific time for problem-solving and initiating action – not only allowing time for this, but not unduly diverting people with directives to attend to other matters;
- cultivation of an ethos that people can roam free (within bounds), that they are not 'tethered' to their job description;
- setting some bounds to the reservation – this was done implicitly in MCB UP and possibly this is the most appropriate way of doing it, despite the *angst* it caused in some. These boundaries need to go wider than the limits of a person's everyday duties, but not be so wide as to allow autonomous action where there should be a collective responsibility or where top management wishes to retain a prerogative.

BRIDGING THE INDIVIDUAL–CORPORATE GAP

MCB UP has successfully harnessed individual learning to corporate ends. It has cultivated a culture of co-operation, enquiry and innovation, which contributes to business performance; while at the same time benefiting from the projects that have driven the development of this culture. The lessons that can be drawn from its experience for the design of in-house learning elsewhere relate to, respectively: the individual, the bridge between the individual and the organization, and the support given by the organization to the application of learning.

The Individual: Motivation to Learn

When staff development has overt corporate purposes (e.g. providing 'free consultancy'), motivation to make the necessary sacrifices of time and leisure may be eroded. In these circumstances how can people be induced to learn? Is obtaining a qualification at the end an adequate inducement?

Staff in both MCB UP and Seagram had evaluated the reward they had gained from their heavy personal investment in learning. There clearly has to be a happy balance of corporate and personal benefit, and in this context the value of the IMC qualification *vis-à-vis* a traditional qualification was intensely debated. Similar considerations of credibility would of course apply to any use of 'academic credit' to reward in-company learning.

The 'deal' in most in-house training and education is normally weighted in favour of the employee who benefits directly from the learning and a possible qualification. One can envisage counter-productive consequences, however, if the deal was felt to be too one-sided in favour of the company. 'Company reservations' have no fences; staff can leave their employment. In Seagram someone did wryly comment that IMC's Action Learning programmes were a very expensive way of losing the company's staff.

The Bridge to Corporate Benefit

Are Action Learning and its associated projects essential ingredients for linking individual learning to corporate benefit? Action Learning was so instrumental in generating corporate benefits for MCB UP that it is not easy to imagine an alternative scenario to the use of 'learning sets' and, more especially, projects. Indeed, for MCB UP's particular objectives there may well be no alternative to Action Learning.

Broadly, there seem to be three possible approaches. One is simply to leave individual training and development to have such effects on corporate development as may spontaneously result from subsequent individual initiatives. This is the traditional approach, widely reputed to be of limited effectiveness.

A second approach is for top management, by its pronouncements and actions, to demonstrate that staff have a clear 'licence' to initiate and experiment, and overtly to support the exercise of this licence. This approach complemented the use of Action Learning in MCB UP.

A third approach would be actively to support individual learning with a further programme designed to amplify its effects. Such an 'amplification programme' would need two thrusts:

- The first would be to develop in individual learners the organizational management and personal effectiveness skills they need in order to apply their learning to practical corporate purposes. In MCB UP this was done through the Action Learning programmes, but other means such as personal development workshops or outdoor courses could also be used. An approach to developing these kinds of effectiveness skills, which links Action Learning projects to self-management, is delineated in Reeves.[6]
- A second thrust would be to review, in a similar way to the present research, the organization's responsiveness to new ideas and initiatives. This diagnosis could then be followed up with appropriate steps to enhance the corporation's ability to harness individual learning, including perhaps running developmental workshops for managers who are in a position to determine the outcome of learners' initiatives.

Organizational Support: Reservations and Rogues

The effective use of individual learning will almost certainly demand the existence of some kind of company reservation, whether explicitly or implicitly defined. One cannot rely on simply harnessing the obviously useful outcomes of individuals' learning, in MCB UP's case the project recommendations. Learners must also be provided with opportunities to use their learning to contribute to corporate purposes in their own way. This, of course, is restating the well-worn admonition that if staff who have been exposed to development are to apply their new ideas in their work, they will need a conducive organizational environment. This research has shown how a conducive environment can be constructed.

It so happens that MCB UP and Seagram have made use of a type of learning that has a reputation for encouraging subversiveness. But this is a feature of many other forms of learning too; indeed, without it important sources of creativity and innovation would dry up. The issue is how far actively to encourage 'roguery'.

The term 'rogue' has many connotations, some favourable, some not so favourable, all of which depend upon the perceiver. Here, 'rogue' is taken to mean someone who pursues a personal agenda for action based on his or her alternative view of the organization's best interests, the directions it should take and how it should be run, and who does this with disregard for the formally agreed or authorized corporate agenda. Such persons, although perhaps appearing subversive to the organization's power-holders, may well not see themselves as subversive since they believe that they have the organization's best interests at heart. Rogues may appear particularly dangerous if they stray beyond the company's bounds of acceptable or prohibited behaviour. But, within the boundaries of the metaphorical reservation, rogues, although disruptive, may be seen as a creative, constructive force.

Discovering where the bounds are, when to challenge them and when not to, is an important part of any middle manager's development, and to have middle managers who can do this is desirable for any organization's well-being. Exposure to 'rogue learning', whether Action Learning or other forms of learning that encourage independent thought, will almost certainly develop this necessary capability. The paradox is that a willingness to expose staff to 'rogue learning' and to risk any consequent 'roguery' is a necessary support for any learning from which corporate benefits are sought.

REFERENCES

1 K. Weinstein, *Action Learning: A Journey in Discovery and Development*, HarperCollins, 1995.

2 G. Gore, K. Toledano and G. Wills, 'Leading Courageous Managers On' in *Empowerment in Organizations*, vol. 2, no. 3, 1994, pp. 7–24. [see Chapter 26]

3 G. Wills, *Your Enterprise School of Management: A Proposition and Action Lines*, MCB University Press, 1993.

4 G. Wills, 'Enabling Managerial Growth and Succession' in *Management Decision*, vol. 30, no. 1, 1992, pp. 10–26.

5 J. Espey and P. Batchelor, 'Management by Degrees: A Case Study in Management Development' in *Journal of Management Development*, vol. 6, no. 5, 1987, pp. 61–8. [see Chapter 21]

6 T. Reeves, *Managing Effectively: Developing Yourself Through Experience*, Butterworth–Heinemann/ Institute of Management, 1994.

Note This is a revised version of an article with the same title published in *The Learning Organization*, vol. 3, no. 2, 1996.

ACKNOWLEDGEMENTS

The author wishes to thank senior management at MCB University Press and at Seagram for agreeing to allow their companies to be exposed to scrutiny and the individual members of staff within those companies who spoke freely about their experience of Action Learning. Thanks go also to International Management Centres who sponsored the research through the award to the author of the Revans Professorship for 1995.

APPENDIX

FOUR INDIVIDUAL PERSPECTIVES ON ACTION LEARNING IN MCB UNIVERSITY PRESS

Informant A

- I learned that there is always a lesson to be learned from experience. So if I do something wrong I look at it positively . . .
- One of my first marks (on bachelor's course) was a distinction. That was a shock! It taught me to value myself . . . I've learned never be afraid to ask. I push myself to ask now . . . You can get people to help you . . .
- We made good use of set meetings. Our set adviser was not much use. So we ran our own set. We ignored him. He seemed not to know his role . . . We met weekends as well. That added to our learning. Because you know everyone personally you are not afraid to say anything. I lost my fear of getting things wrong – 'What will they all think of me?'
- I learned that management is a process, not managing people – a stupid thought! I hadn't seen beyond people management. Management encompasses every function – it's a process. The penny just dropped! . . . I learned that everyone manages differently. By working with your opposite you get best results.
- There was quite a bit of recommended reading. But it only scratched the surface. Reading a book and having a tutorial gets the most out of a book.
- How can you convince another employer of the value of this course? I know I got more from my IMC course than I did from my Diploma in Direct Marketing. The case studies were fantasy land. Here we have £1m waiting to be spent – it could be on your recommendation. This is real life. I had more enthusiasm.
- I was promoted afterwards . . . They had implied if you didn't do the course your prospects of promotion would be drastically reduced. But also they didn't say you will be promoted . . . I don't know whether my promotion was a result of my doing the course . . . We recognize that not everyone can be promoted . . .
- My project was of immediate benefit – saved the company money. It was of a cost-cutting nature. It was on a production operation and there was a big saving. But even projects on processes can save money or time . . . The way you think from there on is 'How can I do better?'
- Recognition (for your achievements) depends on who you work for. I've worked for someone who didn't appreciate work I've done.
- What will happen to all these IMC graduates? Bit of a joke really, running all these

programmes ... I've done the bachelor's in management and that was useful. But if I was asked to do another course I would say no. I have now learned the Action Learning skills. Would the MBA really be different? So I wouldn't do another one.

- MCB has a culture which gives an image of empowerment, being innovative, etc. But often they don't want to know. They're going down the road now of being a large hierarchical company. But they're not recognizing (the implications of) this.

Informant B

- (The bachelor's course) got you speaking to each other. We shared information in the groups ...
- I also learned that you can learn from experience. I've also gained more self-confidence in the job I do. I now know I can do it even if I think I can't ... I'm accepting the strengths of others and letting them do tasks.
- I was surprised there was nothing on the course that was about managing people or psychology ... Not having staff of your own actually makes you be a manager ...
- The course taught us to look at what we're not and build on that. I had to push myself. I used to only get enough information to get by ... I had thought I did my best (on the Action Learning course). But I discovered I only did just enough. I looked at what others could do. I was watching another girl doing more, sticking at it longer than me. I realized I *could* do it. It goes back to lack of self-esteem ...
- I found not being promoted afterwards demotivating ... When I applied internally for a job, I was told an IMC degree wasn't adequate – a proper degree was wanted. Why bother? I spent all that time and effort. I found it hard work. I had to organize baby-sitters. There was stress on my family. The prospect of promotion was the carrot for me doing it.
- We all became mini-consultants. The company has more people to choose from. Everyone has moved up a peg (in their competence) ...
- With everything I do now I ask 'How can I do better?'. You get into the mode of finding a better way of doing it.
- I would like recognition through *money*, not just job satisfaction ...
- An IMC degree should be recognized. So someone without one shouldn't get promoted. I wouldn't do another course now ...
- MCB is unique. They do it their way. You learn the 'right' way on outside courses, but MCB don't want to know. For example, they spend more money on a duff journal. Because you have to spend the budget. You can see that you could spend the money better on another journal. But your judgement is over-ruled. You get no explanation of the rationale for the other choice ...
- I wanted a degree. I always did something – night school and so on. I've done enough now. I've got my qualifications.

Informant C

- I agree with the others (i.e. has learned to learn from experience and has gained in self-confidence). I look at things now from a different perspective. My communication skills have improved. I'm improving various aspects of my communication and realizing its importance ... Everyone contributes to the team now ...
- Till you've done one of these courses, you're intimidated by the directors at the top ...
- I've thought about *administration* (i.e. the title of the course). I don't think I'm a better administrator as a result of the course. In fact I'm not sure how administration

ties up with the course. We were just scratching the surface, for example on finance and then you do an assignment. We were not going into depth across the board. I wouldn't be very good in practice. I felt I didn't know what I was doing a lot of the time. I got good marks by accident. I didn't understand why.

- We didn't make best use of the set meetings. We said what we had to say and got out . . .
- I only understood what Action Learning was about at the end of the course. I couldn't see how it was working in our set. I saw lost opportunities. It was quite difficult to arrange set meetings. It took us six months to arrange a meal together!
- For some people the project can be the kiss of death. Some have left before finishing it. There's a lot of stress. It's too much.
- If you want, you can just do enough to get by (on an Action Learning course). But you can put more in. It's up to you. Learning comes from application – more than from reading and tutorials . . .
- We were told that an IMC degree was recognized in MCB. If not here, then where? . . . The degree shows the company what you're worth, how you manage your time, your abilities. The company can see how you react under pressure. Have you got staying power?
- If you're going to be considered for a management position you now have a wealth of information that you couldn't otherwise have. Another side is that you're not promoted to your level of incompetence on the basis of your technical expertise, and then end up having to leave. So, the more you understand about management the more likely you are to be successful in a higher level job.
- We're all now looking at the job and seeing how you can improve it . . . You can't just judge the success in the immediate wake of the programme . . . The company gets value (for money spent on the programmes) just from the information they receive. For example, better questionnaire design and the better information thus obtained . . .
- The programme impacts on one's whole life . . . For the future, I would like to specialize in something, rather than another course scratching the surface.

Informant D

- Action Learning wouldn't work in a lot of companies. It does work here. Everyone at all levels gets together. Action Learning is a levelling out at work and in communicating. It teaches you not to be afraid to seek out whoever you need. It teaches assertiveness too. For some this means increasing their confidence; for others lessening their arrogance. Some people are confused as to its meaning. It's not about driving a steamroller, teaching you not to be a Napoleon, appreciate that you stand on the backs of others. Being nice to people has worked for me. Get a win–win situation in mind. You get the best out of everyone this way . . .
- I didn't get very good marks on the programme, I think because I'm too academic. I had to learn a more simplistic approach. It didn't matter how you got it down on paper. I have a science degree. I enjoyed the different approach. It was interesting. I liked being in a group where you could talk. You could speak to people – unlike a lecture . . .
- I didn't learn a lot about administration. But we were dealing with issues that might arise – I learnt a hell of a lot. There were eight of us on the course. We divided up into two groups of four. Each group had to do four projects over eight months – with Christmas in that time! It was really hard work. I learnt so much about other departments in the company. Had to cram each topic into four weeks. It's amazing how you do get on with it and how much you learn – a lot about different departments.

- Some of our recommendations were actually implemented! So it was worthwhile ... We did a project on the induction programme. Our recommendations were put into action immediately afterwards ...
- There was very little emphasis on the management of people and delegation. They recommended a book on empowerment ...
- I found I changed in style over the programme ... I had no increase in status afterwards, but I am at the top level already in my department ...
- You tell the company how you see yourself in five years time. That helps them to help you ... But there is not always promotion from within ...
- Action Learning doesn't help you to do your own job as such – you do that anyhow. But Action Learning comes into the way you regard your department and your relationships with other people, and with outside people – editors and authors.
- I need some recognition, not necessarily promotion. The company's actually not too bad on that – through appraisal. But they are not altering the structure to accommodate all the IMC graduates ...
- I don't know everyone now. The company's bigger, more impersonal. That's inevitable with expansion ...
- During the course I found myself cutting myself off from my family – working weekends and so on ... I've been involved in Action Learning programmes of one kind or another for three years. Enough!